OFFICIAL (ISC)²
GUIDE TO THE
CISSP®-ISSMP®CBK®

SECOND EDITION

OTHER BOOKS IN THE (ISC)²® PRESS SERIES

Official (ISC)²® Guide to the ISSMP® CBK®, Second Edition
Joseph Steinberg, Editor
ISBN: 978-1-4665-7895-1

Official (ISC)²® Guide to the CISSP® CBK®, Fourth Edition
Adam Gordon, Editor
ISBN: 978-1-4822-6275-9

Official (ISC)²® Guide to the HCISPP℠ CBK®
Steven Hernandez, Editor
ISBN: 978-1-4822-6277-3

Official (ISC)²® Guide to the CCFP℠ CBK®
Peter Stephenson, Editor
ISBN: 978-1-4822-6247-6

Official (ISC)²® Guide to the ISSAP® CBK®, Second Edition
Adam Gordon, Editor
ISBN: 978-1-4665-7900-2

Official (ISC)²® Guide to the CAP® CBK®, Second Edition
Patrick D. Howard
ISBN: 978-1-4398-2075-9

Official (ISC)²® Guide to the SSCP® CBK®, Second Edition
Harold F. Tipton, Editor
ISBN: 978-1-4398-0483-4

Official (ISC)²® Guide to the ISSAP® CBK®
Harold F. Tipton, Editor
ISBN: 978-1-4398-0093-5

CISO Leadership: Essential Principles for Success
Todd Fitzgerald and Micki Krause, Editors
ISBN: 978-0-8493-7943-X

Official (ISC)²® Guide to the CISSP®-ISSEP® CBK®
Susan Hansche
ISBN: 978-0-8493-2341-X

OFFICIAL (ISC)²
GUIDE TO THE
CISSP®-ISSMP®CBK®

SECOND EDITION

Edited by
Joseph Steinberg, CISSP-ISSAP, ISSMP, CSSLP

CRC Press
Taylor & Francis Group
Boca Raton London New York

CRC Press is an imprint of the
Taylor & Francis Group, an **informa** business
AN AUERBACH BOOK

CRC Press
Taylor & Francis Group
6000 Broken Sound Parkway NW, Suite 300
Boca Raton, FL 33487-2742

© 2015 by Taylor & Francis Group, LLC
CRC Press is an imprint of Taylor & Francis Group, an Informa business

No claim to original U.S. Government works

Printed on acid-free paper
Version Date: 20150414

International Standard Book Number-13: 978-1-4665-7895-1 (Hardback)

Visit the Taylor & Francis Web site at
http://www.taylorandfrancis.com

and the CRC Press Web site at
http://www.crcpress.com

ISSMP

CISSP®

Contents

Domain 2 — *Security Lifecycle Management*

Domain 3 — *Security Compliance Management*

Domain 4 — *Contingency Management*

Domain 5 — *Law, Ethics, and Incident Management*

Foreword

Foreword to the Official (ISC)² Guide to the CISSP-ISSMP CBK, Second Edition

Today, information security is revered as an imperative business function to global corporations and governments alike. When security breaches cost CEOs and other C-level executives their jobs, it elevates the level of importance placed on the industry and specifically, the professionals working within it.

The Certified Information Systems Security Professional (CISSP®) is globally recognized as the industry benchmark for information security credentials. But for many professionals, it shouldn't be the final step in their career path. For those aspiring to further their career or specialize in certain areas such as Architecture, Engineering, or Management, (ISC)²® offers CISSPs the opportunity to expand their area of expertise with concentration credentials. I liken our CISSP concentration credentials to specialized areas of practice in the medical field: Doctors are required to earn their medical degree, however, many go on to specialize in a specific area of the medical field such as Oncology or Dermatology.

The CISSP concentration, Information Systems Security Management Professional (CISSP-ISSMP®), was developed for professionals seeking to specialize in the managerial concepts of information security as they relate to business principles. The content of the CISSP-ISSMP credential has a managerial focus on areas such as project management, incident response, risk management, developing a security awareness program, and implementing a business continuity plan. They must understand and explain business functions such as Return on Investment (ROI) and comprehend all business lines of the company or government ministry.

A CISSP-ISSMP is the best of both worlds – the master of technical and managerial IT, with the added bonus of business acumen that resonates with the C-suite. Typically, these credential holders establish, present, and govern information security programs demonstrating management and leadership skills, and construct the framework of the information security department. They may hold a job title such as Chief Information Security Officer, Chief Information Officer, Information Security Director, Chief Technology Officer, Senior Security Executive or Enterprise Security Manager. In a short time, we will see these individuals moving directly into executive business positions across the board.

The *Official Guide to the CISSP-ISSMP CBK®* textbook provides practical insight into creating and implementing effective information security management programs that meet the security needs of today's businesses. As you review the information in this book and study for the CISSP-ISSMP certification exam, remember that venturing beyond the solid foundation of the CISSP certification should ultimately help to enhance your career path as well as your ability to mentor up-and-coming information security professionals.

We wish you success in your journey toward earning the CISSP-ISSMP certification.

[signature]

— W. Hord Tipton, Former Executive Director, (ISC)²

Introduction

Technology and information have become the lifeblood of twenty-first century society. The proliferation of information systems ranging from devices in our pockets to server farms connecting over a billion people on a social media network, coupled with the simultaneous surge in capabilities among those seeking to exploit such systems for nefarious purposes at the expense of their legitimate owners and users, mandates that security be approached in a formal, organized, and well-managed fashion. Ad-hoc approaches that may have sufficed in earlier decades are simply inadequate; formal security programs are critical for success.

(ISC)²'s information security management certification — the CISSP-ISSMP — is a concentration built upon the solid foundation of the CISSP certification, and focuses on the comprehensive management aspects of enterprise information security programs. While the CISSP certification is broad, and addresses major aspects of information security, including management issues, at a relatively high level, the CISSP-ISSMP certification is far more focused, and delves far deeper into specifically the management aspects of information security. The ISSMP is an ideal certification to be pursued by senior information security executives such as CTOs, CISOs, and CIOs, or those with significant relevant experience seeking to attain such positions.

Security management can be defined as the development, documentation, and implementation of policies and procedures for protecting an entity's assets. At a more detailed level this entails ensuring that the creation and maintenance of the information security structure of an enterprise protects the confidentiality, integrity, and availability of critical and/ or sensitive business systems and the information that flows through them, while also being in compliance with external and internal policies, legislation, and regulations.

The ISSMP certification is intended to serve as a benchmark for individuals seeking to be accredited as professionals in this demanding field.

The second edition of the Official Guide to the CISSP-ISSMP® CBK® features a substantial amount of new material addressing new areas of the (ISC)² ISSMP exam DCO (Detailed

Content Outline); these improvements are found throughout the book and impact each of the five domains covered by the ISSMP exam.

The CISSP-ISSMP covers five domains: Security Leadership and Management, Security Lifecycle Management, Security Compliance Management, Contingency Management, and Law, Ethics and Incident Management.

Topics covered are listed below:

1	**SECURITY LEADERSHIP AND MANAGEMENT**
1.A	Understand Security's Role in the Organization's Culture, Vision, and Mission
1.A.1	Define information security program vision and mission
1.A.2	Align security with organization's goals and objectives
1.A.3	Understand business processes and their relationships
1.A.4	Describe the relationship between organization culture and security
1.B	Align Security Program with Organizational Governance
1.B.1	Understand the organizational governance structure
1.B.2	Understand the roles of key stakeholders
1.B.3	Recognize sources and boundaries of authorization
1.B.4	Define the security governance structure
1.C	Define and Implement Information Security Strategies
1.C.1	Identify security requirements from business initiative
1.C.2	Evaluate the capacity and capability to implement security strategies
1.C.3	Manage implementation of security strategies
1.C.4	Review and maintain security strategies
1.D	Manage Data Classification
1.D.1	Sensitivity
1.D.2	Criticality
1.E	Define and Maintain Security Policy Framework
1.E.1	Determine applicable external standards
1.E.2	Establish internal policies
1.E.3	Garner/build organizational support for policies
1.E.4	Direct development and approval of procedures, standards, guidelines and baselines
1.E.5	Ensure periodic review of security policy framework
1.F	Manage Security Requirements in Contracts and Agreements
1.F.1	Evaluation of service management agreements (e.g., risk, financial)
1.F.2	Governance of managed services (e.g., "infrastructure, software, platform" as a service)
1.F.3	Understand impact of organizational change (e.g., mergers and acquisitions, outsourcing, divestitures)
1.F.4	Monitor and enforce compliance with contractual agreements
1.G	Develop and Maintain a Risk Management Program
1.G.1	Understand enterprise risk management objectives
1.G.2	Evaluate risk assessment results
1.G.3	Communicate security business risk to management

3.A	Validate Compliance with Organizational Security Policies and Procedures
3.A.1	Define a compliance framework
3.A.2	Implement validation procedures outlined in framework
3.A.3	Utilize and report on security compliance metrics
3.B	Manage and Document Exceptions to the Compliance Framework
3.C	Coordinate with Auditors and Assist with the Internal and External Audit Process
3.C.1	Preparation
3.C.2	Scheduling (e.g., availability, mitigation timeline)
3.C.3	Evaluation (e.g., validate findings, assess impact, provide comments, and resolution)
3.C.4	Formulate response

4	**CONTINGENCY MANAGEMENT**
4.A	Oversee Development of Contingency Plans
4.A.1	Address challenges related to the business continuity process (e.g., time, resources, verification)
4.A.2	Address challenges related to the disaster recovery process (time, resources, verification)
4.A.3	Coordinate with key stakeholders
4.A.4	Understand organizational drivers & policies
4.A.5	Oversee Business Impact Analysis (BIA) process
4.B	Guide Development of Recovery Strategies
4.B.1	Identify and analyze alternatives
4.B.2	Recommend and coordinate strategies
4.B.3	Assign security roles and responsibilities
4.C	Manage Maintenance of the BCP and DRP plans (e.g., lessons learned, architecture changes)
4.C.1	Plan testing, evaluation, and modification
4.C.2	Determine survivability and resiliency capabilities
4.C.3	Manage recovery process

5	**LAW, ETHICS AND INCIDENT MANAGEMENT**
5.A	Understand the Impact of Laws that Relate to Information Security
5.A.1	Understand global privacy laws (e.g. customer, employee)
5.A.2	Understand legal footprint of the organization (e.g., trans border data flow)
5.A.3	Understand export laws
5.A.4	Understand intellectual property laws (e.g., trademark, copyright, patent, licensing)
5.A.5	Manage liability (e.g., downstream and upstream/direct and indirect)
5.B	Develop and Manage the Incident Handling and Investigation Processes
5.B.1	Establish and maintain incident handling process
5.B.2	Establish and maintain investigation process
5.B.3	Quantify and report the financial impact of incidents and investigations to senior management
5.C	Understand Management Issues as They Relate to the (ISC)2 Code of Ethics

A candidate for the CISSP-ISSMP certification should demonstrate a thorough understanding of the topics listed above, while applying her or his expertise to successfully manage the information security program for an enterprise.

I would like to thank $(ISC)^2$ for giving me the opportunity to contribute to, and, edit this book. Also, I would like to convey a big thank you to my family for the sacrifices that they made so that I could work on this project.

— Joseph Steinberg, CISSP-ISSMP, ISSAP, CSSLP

ISSMP

CISSP®

Editors

Joseph Steinberg – *Lead Editor*

Joseph Steinberg (CISSP-ISSMP, ISSAP, CSSLP) served as an author, and the editor, of this book.

Joseph is a respected cybersecurity expert, executive, consultant, and author, who has spent nearly twenty years in the information security industry. He advises firms and the government on high-level matters related to cybersecurity, serves as an expert witness on information-security related matters, has written books and many articles on information security topics, and is a frequent media commentator on related matters. He currently writes a column covering both cybersecurity and business for Forbes.

Joseph is the founder and CEO of SecureMySocial (a provider of technology that helps businesses protect themselves from the risks of employee personal social media usage by warning people if they attempt to make problematic posts). Earlier, he served for nine years as CEO of authentication provider, Green Armor Solutions, before becoming its Chairman. Joseph also held several senior positions at Whale Communications (acquired by Microsoft) for the five years beforehand.

Joseph is the inventor of several information-security technologies in use today; his work is cited in over 100 published patents.

Joseph earned an M.S. from the Courant Institute at New York University (NYU). In 2007 he was named one of New Jersey's top businesspeople under the age of forty by NJBiz. He has also chaired the Financial Advisory Board for a New Jersey municipality with combined municipal and education budgets of ~$150Million.

Joseph can be reached at: www.JosephSteinberg.com or on Twitter at @JosephSteinberg

Barbara Johnson – *Technical Editor*

Barbara Johnson (BSIE, MBA, CISSP, ISSMP, CISA, CBCP and MBCI) is a senior security management consultant, the Chairman of (ISC)² Common Body of Knowledge (CBK) Committee and an Authorized (ISC)² Senior and Lead Instructor. For over 20 years, Ms. Johnson has provided information security and business continuity management consulting services to U.S. government agencies, defense contractors, entertainment, finance, healthcare, technology, travel information services, along with (ISC)² and The Business Continuity Institute (BCI). Her expertise includes developing governance and designing risk-based controls to protect corporate proprietary, personal privacy, and government classified information from fraud, misuse, intrusion and interruption. She strategizes enterprise-wide security architectures, establishes information protection and business continuity programs, devises information security policies, standardizes technologies and processes, and creates relevant education, training and awareness workshops and collateral.

As Chairman of the (ISC)² Common Body of Knowledge (CBK) Committee, Ms. Johnson identifies key subject areas in the security industry and edits (ISC)² Course Seminar and (ISC)² Book offerings. Furthermore, she develops curriculum for and teaches information security and business continuity courses. As a Senior and Lead Instructor for (ISC)², she prepares hundreds of security professionals each year to earn Certified Information Systems Security Professional (CISSP) and Information Systems Security Management Professional (ISSMP) certifications. She provides training in a classroom and the Live Online virtual platform. In addition, she is a Certified Information Systems Auditor (CISA) and teaches the CISA preparation course. Earlier, Ms. Johnson advanced the Business Continuity Institute (BCI) Course and readied business continuity professionals for The BCI Certificate Exam.

ISSMP

CISSP®

Contributors

Thank you to the following people for contributing to this work:

***Harold F. (Hal) Tipton**, **CISSP-ISSAP, ISSMP** –* Mr. Tipton, a pioneer of the information-security industry and a co-founder of (ISC)², edited the first edition of this book. He passed away in 2012 at the age of 83. Hal had a tremendous impact on thousands of information-security professionals around the world, and served (ISC)² selflessly, and with dedication, for 25 years.

James Litchko**, **CISSP-ISSEP, CAP, MBCI, CMAS, is Senior Security Expert at Litchko & Associates. Mr. Litchko has worked as a security and management expert for over 30 years. He has been an executive with five organizations and supervised and supported the securing of over 200 military, government, and commercial IT systems. Since 2008, he has supported the securing of IT systems at DHS, DOE, VHA, NASA, EPA, USAF, DOJ, and FEMA. Jim created and taught the first graduate IT security course at Johns Hopkins University (JHU) and was a manager at NSA. Jim holds a master's degree from JHU and has authored five books on security and management topics. Jim contributed to Domain 1 of this book.

Craig S. Wright**, **CISSP-ISSAP, ISSMP, is a director with Information Defence in Australia. He holds both the GSE-Malware and GSE-Compliance certifications from GIAC. He is a perpetual student with numerous postgraduate degrees including an LLM specializing in international commercial law and ecommerce law, a master's degree in mathematical statistics from Newcastle, and is working on his fourth IT-focused master's degree (in system development) at Charles Stuart University, Australia, where he lectures on subjects in digital forensics. He is writing his second doctorate on the quantification of information system risk at CSU. Craig contributed to Domain 5 of this book.

Cheryl Hennell**, **EdD, MSc, CISSP, SBCI, has worked in the IT industry for 40 years. Her employment includes systems development for the Ministry of Defence, systems analysis for the Civil Service, European consultancy for a blue chip organization, and 20 years as a senior university lecturer. She is currently head of IT and information assurance for Openreach, BT.

She earned her master's in information systems design from Kingston University, London, and her doctorate from the University of Southampton, UK, and is a specialist in the Business Continuity Institute, UK. She is also an ambassador for Childnet.

Cheryl was the course director for the first digital forensics degree in the UK, which she created and delivered for the University of Portsmouth. She has been an invited speaker at international conferences in Europe, the Middle East, and Africa. Her subjects include information assurance, audit, risk and governance, physical security, and business continuity and disaster recovery. Cheryl contributed to Domain 4 of this book.

Maura van der Linden spent over a decade in software testing at Microsoft Corporation with a specialization in security testing, including working in the Security Technology Unit on the Malware Response Team. After serving as a technical reviewer for *MSDN Magazine*, she wrote her first article on SQL injection testing for *MSDN Magazine*. She then wrote her first book, *Testing Code Security*, Auerbach, Boca Raton, Florida, in order to teach other testers the need for and intricacy of security testing. Though now working as a programming writer, she maintains her close ties to the test and security communities. Maura contributed to Domain 2 of this book.

Keith Willett, **CISSP-ISSAP,** has over 25 years' experience in information technology spanning academia and commercial, local, and national governments. Mr. Willett has a BS in computer science from Towson University, Maryland, an MS in business from the University of Baltimore, Maryland, and an MSIA from Norwich University, Vermont, and he holds the CISSP and ISSAP designations from (ISC)². Willett is the author of *Information Assurance Architecture* and coauthor of *How to Achieve 27001 Certification*, both published by Auerbach. When not working, Mr. Willet enjoys world travel, cuisine, and wine, and has enjoyed all in over 125 cities across 30 countries. Keith contributed to Domain 3 of this book.

Additional tables, graphics, and edits were made by **Andrew Schneiter, CISSP**

Domain 1
Security Leadership & Management

The Security Leadership and Management domain addresses the fundamental requirements for a security program. It embraces the concepts of security from an enterprise wide perspective, defines the role of policy, and supports the establishment of an effective security department. An expert in this domain understands the relationship between security policy and the business requirements of the organization as reflected through mission statements, goals, and objectives. In addition, an expert will be cognizant of the individual and sometimes conflicting objectives of different business units and will be familiar with the requirement of due care and diligence when conducting operations across political, regulatory, or market boundaries.

This domain requires an understanding of risk management through risk, threat, and impact assessment, risk mitigation, and controls. It also highlights the value of data classification, the certification and accreditation process, and change control.

TOPICS

The Security Leadership and Management domain assesses the candidate's fundamental skills and knowledge in managing an organization's information security program. It is built upon the concepts of information security from an organizational perspective and emphasizes information security's role in supporting the overall goal of the organization. In this domain, emphasis is placed on application and management of appropriate processes and technologies to achieve organizational goals and objectives for information security.

The CISSP-ISSMP candidate should have an understanding of:

- Collaborating with organizational leaders to develop, document, and enforce information security strategies and governance.

- Developing information security goals and objectives in support of organizational missions, goals, and objectives.

- Developing and maintaining policies and procedures for achieving goals and objectives.

- Working successfully across organizational, political, regulatory, or market boundaries.

- Utilizing risk management principles in problem solving and goal prioritization, including threat and impact assessment, and risk mitigation.

- Developing key performance indicators and meaningful metrics to monitor and assess the effectiveness of the security program.

- Assisting organizational leaders in determining data classification and establishing efficient, effective controls.

- Participating in the change control process to manage the security implications of proposed changes.

- Managing the security aspects of contracts and procurement of managed services.

- Determining information security training and awareness goals and overseeing implementation of an organizational information security training and awareness program that includes: information security policy, roles and responsibilities, acceptable use of system resources, regulatory compliance, incident detection and response, and information security processes and procedures.

- Using sound management practices to administer the security program, its staff, and its budget.

OBJECTIVES

The management tasks that an enterprise security manager will face are diverse and extensive. While individual responsibilities will vary according to organizational priorities, the following key areas of knowledge encompass many of the duties of an enterprise security manager:

- Understand the goals, mission, and the objectives of the organization from an enterprise perspective.

- Apply the concepts of availability, integrity, and confidentiality to the enterprise.

- Develop an enterprise wide security policy.

- Develop and implement security processes.

- Develop an enterprise wide security plan.

- Delineate roles and responsibilities of employees, managers, data owners, and security personnel from a security perspective.

- Develop and implement security related service level agreements.

- Develop risk measurement and management programs.

- Integrate personnel security with business operations.

- Oversee enterprise wide security awareness and training programs.

- Develop and implement a data classification program throughout the organization.

- Develop certification and accreditation strategies.

- Address privacy issues and requirements.

- Oversee security assessment practices.

- Market security programs to management and stakeholders.

- Measure and leverage protection of enterprise resources.

Mission Statements

Senior management is responsible for establishing the organization's mission and goals. Additionally, it is responsible for the achievement of those goals, which includes assuring that due care and due diligence are applied as appropriate. This is achieved through its awareness and understanding of financial and operational risks and subsequent management of that risk by either providing the necessary resources to remediate critical deficiencies or knowingly accepting the risk. This is what enterprise governance is all about (i.e., ensuring that an adequate level of security is applied to the organization's information systems so as to protect the organization's personnel, operations, information, and assets, as well as meeting all applicable legal, regulatory, and ethical standards).

The job of the Information System Security Management Professional (ISSMP) is to establish, implement, and manage an effective information system security program and ensure that senior management is provided with an accurate status of all the risks and alternatives to reducing unacceptable risks. To establish an effective security program, the ISSMP will need to identify the program's requirements, which requires a very interactive process with senior management or the managers of the specific system being secured. This process is necessary in order to understand the true security requirements of the system, potential security solutions, and risks. The initial and critical step is for the ISSMP to know the organization's mission.

Senior management provides mission statements to give overall direction and focus for all of the organization's activities. These mission statements take weeks if not months to develop because senior management bases these statements on business analysis, market trends, organizational capabilities, and, most importantly, its understanding that it will have to find the resources to support the agreed upon mission. Every individual, group, and information system within the organization must in some way support the organization's mission, which is why the ISSMP must understand the organization's mission statement. Mission statements are simple and straightforward. Following are a few examples:

- **Merck's Mission Statement -** "To discover, develop and provide innovative products and services that save and improve lives around the world."

  (Source – http://www.merck.com/about/mission.html)

- **Google's Mission Statement –** "Google's mission is to organize the world's information and make it universally accessible and useful."

  (Source – http://www. google.com/corporate/)

- **Saint Vincent Hospital's Mission Statement –** "Saint Vincent Hospital is a medical institution dedicated to providing quality patient care with unrelenting attention to clinical excellence, patient safety and an unparalleled passion and commitment to assure the very best healthcare for those we serve."

  (Source – http:// www.stvincenthospital.com/aboutUs/missionStatement)

- **Department of Homeland Security's (DHS's) Mission Statement –** "There are five homeland security missions: Prevent terrorism and enhancing security; Secure and manage our borders; Enforce and administer our immigration laws; Safeguard and secure cyberspace; Ensure resilience to disasters;"

  (Source – https://www.dhs.gov/our-mission)

Federal Trade Commission's (FTC's) Mission Statements:

- **Competition Mission –** "The Commission is dedicated to that task, and uses a variety of tools to promote competition and protect consumers from anti-competitive mergers and business conduct. Through enforcement, study, advocacy, and education, the FTC's competition mission is to remove private or public impediments that prevent consumers from receiving the benefits of such competition."

- **Consumer Protection Mission –** "The FTC protects the public from unfair, deceptive, and fraudulent practices in the marketplace and addresses consumer protection issues that touch all Americans."

  (Source – 2008 Chairman's Report, The FTC in 2008 – A Force for Consumers and Competition, March 2008, http://www.ftc.gov/os/2008/03/ChairmansReport2008.pdf)

Where does the ISSMP find the organization's mission statement? Depending on the organization, it may be found in one or more of several places:

- Organization's website – All of the above examples were found on websites.
- Senior Management Reports – Annual reports to Congress (FTC 2008 Chairman's Report identified above), stockholders, the Securities and Exchange Commission (SEC), and so forth.
- Capabilities statements developed for potential clients.
- Organizational introduction presentations for employees or internal groups.
- Organization's strategic plan, like the DHS example above.

Notice from the above examples that an organization's mission is broad; this is to allow for the next step – the ISSMP and the system's manager to determine the specific mission, goals, and objectives that apply to the system or systems being secured. During this step, it is important that the ISSMP focuses on critical systems first because rarely is it effective to provide the same level of security to all information systems within an organization's entire IT enterprise. Generic policies and security solutions for all corporate systems are rarely cost or operationally effective because each system's operational and security needs are different. Goals and objectives provide more specificity on the requirements for that system. The DHS has used the following as an example of this:

- **Awareness –** Identify and understand threats, assess vulnerabilities, determine potential impacts, and disseminate timely information to our homeland security partners and the American public.
- **Prevention –** Detect, deter, and mitigate threats to our homeland.
- **Protection –** Safeguard our people and their freedoms, critical infrastructure, property, and the economy of our Nation from acts of terrorism, natural disasters, or other emergencies.
- **Response –** Lead, manage, and coordinate the national response to acts of terrorism, natural disasters, or other emergencies.
- **Recovery –** Lead national, state, local, and private sector efforts to restore services and rebuild communities after acts of terrorism, natural disasters, or other emergencies.
- **Service –** Serve the public effectively by facilitating lawful trade, travel, and immigration.

- ***Organizational Excellence*** – Value our most important resource, our people. Create a culture that promotes a common identity, innovation, mutual respect, accountability, and teamwork to achieve efficiencies, effectiveness, and operational synergies. (Source – Securing Our Homeland, U.S. Department of Homeland Security Strategic Plan, 2004.)

The DHS consists of multiple organizations (i.e., U.S. Coast Guard [USCG], Federal Emergency Management Agency [FEMA], Transportation Security Administration [TSA], etc.), each with a responsibility for supporting one or several of the above goals.

- ***USCG*** – Prevention, Protection, and Response related to maritime
- ***FEMA*** – Response and Recovery
- ***TSA*** – Prevention, Protection, and Response related to transportation

Within the same organization, DHS, internal groups with different goals and objectives exist; thus their systems will have different security requirements.

Organizational goals are very specific to each internal element of an organization. Goals are statements that tell what the system is intended to accomplish. Goals can define the system's purpose and include timelines and metrics. Examples of goals are the following:

- Provide information to a specific group or everyone.
- Share research information with other researchers.
- Pass sensitive or classified information only to authorized systems.
- Sell a product to the healthcare organizations or everyone.
- Allow gamblers to gamble over the Internet from their PCs.
- Connect people who need organs to newly harvested organs.
- Command the release of a nuclear weapon onto a specific target.

Because the types of security needed for a specific system vary depending on the organization's mission, goals, and objectives, it is critical for the ISSMP to identify these from the very beginning of the efforts in building the system' information system security plan.

Business Functions

In commercial businesses, both for profit and not for profit, there are internal groups that support different business functions, i.e., accounting, sales, production, marketing, research and development (R&D), human resources (HR), legal, and so forth. Each function's requirements have different security requirements because each has different goals and objectives. *Table 1.1* provides an example of how a functional group's system security requirements change just by the group's need to access the Internet.

Functional Group	Internet Access Requirement	Security Requirements	Security Requirement Justification
Accounting	Customers/banks	Strong	Payroll/privacy/financial
Sales	Everyone	Little	Sensitive client lists
Production	Suppliers	None	Ordering parts
Marketing	Everyone	None	Promotional activities
R&D	Everyone	Moderate	Intellectual property
HR	Recruiters, recruits, insurance companies	Moderate	Privacy information
Legal	Other lawyers	Moderate	Corporate sensitive information

Table 1.1 – **Business Function Impact on Security Requirements**

Group Business Processes

Also, within each of these functions, the ISSMP must be aware of the specific business processes and types of information that support and are produced by the system. The things that the ISSMP needs to understand about business processes are as follows:

- Who is in charge and manages the business?
- Who is responsible overall for controlling the system's operations and resources?
- How does the business work?
- What is the determination of success – input, output, profit, number of customers, and so forth?
- How is the information entered?
- Who receives or reviews it?
- Who does what with it (change, consolidate, delete, store, transmit, etc.)?
- To whom is information transmitted and from where and why?
- Are there any product or service providers?
- Are there any external or internal customers or buyers?
- Are there any management reviews and approvals required in the processes?
- Who does any required reviews and approvals and what is approved?
- How fast do these actions need to happen?
- What is the impact if they do not happen?
- Who provides oversight and how often?

The above list is not a complete list, but it is an appropriate start. As the review is conducted, more questions will become obvious as the ISSMP tries to gain solid insight into the business the system supports or will be supporting. With a full understanding of the business process, the ISSMP can determine things such as:

- What is the flow of the information?
- Who communicates what and with whom?
- What privileges will each person require?
- Who drafts requests and who approves them?
- How critical are the individual system components and their capabilities to supporting the success of the organization?
- What information types and sensitivities are being processed in the system?
- Who are the providers and what agreements are in place or are needed?
- Who are the customers and what are their capabilities and expectations?
- Who is the owner of the system?
- Who will be the ultimate person to accept any residual risk and authorize the system to become operational or continue to operate?

The above are all key pieces of information required for the ISSMP to ensure that the most effective security is applied to the system. Some people may say that this is the job of a systems analyst and they would be right, but it is recommended that the ISSMP work closely with the systems analysts and designers to ensure that security is considered during the entire development process.

Identity Management

The information collected has a major impact on the security needs of the system, specifically in the area of identity management, by identifying where the concepts of "least privileges" and "role based security" can be applied. Both of these concepts are demonstrated in the following example:

> There are three individuals who work in the payments section of a major corporation. Mary is the supervisor, who oversees the efforts of Sally and John. Sally and John draft fund transfers from banks to pay corporate bills. Mary is the only one who can authorize and make the transfers online. Each bank has a unique method of authenticating Mary prior to her making a money transfer, i.e., one-time passwords and challenge-and-response tokens.
>
> To make the transfers, Sally and John review the vendor invoices using a word processing program, and using that data they use a standard Funds Transfer Form to create a Draft Funds Transfer, which they submit to Mary. Mary reviews the Draft Funds Transfer and creates a Final Funds Transfer using the word processing program. Mary then connects to the bank via the Internet using an Internet browser program. With the connection to the bank, she authenticates to the bank using the book or token authentication processes, which are secured in a safe that only Mary has access to, and she uploads the Final Funds Transfer to the bank. Upon acceptance of the funds transfer, the bank forwards a Transfer Confirmation Notice to the system. At any time during this process, any individual can print a copy of any file. To ensure that proper oversight is conducted, the corporate auditors must have access to all of the files that are created during this process.

Knowing all of this, the ISSMP can now recommend the "role based" security solutions that can be used to implement the concept of "least privilege." *Table 1.2* provides a summary of the privileges that each role ("Drafter" [Sally and John], "Approver" [Mary], and Auditor [senior management, auditing staff, or third-party auditors]) will be granted in the system to support this scenario.

Note that in this example, Mary, although she is in the role of supervisor, does not have full privileges in the system. Specifically, she cannot change the Submitted Draft Funds Transfer or the Transfer Confirmation Notice. This is to ensure that she cannot modify key documents required by the auditors to ensure that the process and the actions of the employees are in full compliance with standard accounting procedures.

Privileges	Approver	Drafter	Auditor
Word processing program	Execute	Execute	Execute
Vendor invoices	Read	Read	Read
Funds transfer forms	Read	Read/Write	Read
Draft funds transfers	Read	Read/Write	Read
Submitted draft funds transfers	Read	Read	Read
Final funds transfers	Read/Write	Read	Read
Submitted draft funds transfers	Read	Read	Read
Internet browser program	Execute	No Access	No Access
Authentication books/tokens	Access	No Access	No Access
Transfer confirmation notice	Read	Read	Read
Printer	Write	Write	Write

Table 1.2 – **Roles and Privileges**

Compliance

In addition to the mission, business, and operating requirements, the ISSMP must understand the legal and regulatory restrictions and demands that are imposed on each group in the organization. These are critical because deploying security that fails to make the system compliant with one of these can result in major fines or negatively impact the reputation of the organization. The following are some of the more common legal and regulatory compliance needs:

- **Privacy Act of 1974 –** The purpose of this act is to protect the rights of individuals by placing restrictions on government agencies as to what they can do with personal information (e.g., transferring, matching, etc.), and it mandates security requirements to prevent the unauthorized release of the information.

■ ***Computer Security Act of 1987*** – The U.S. Congress declared that improving the security and privacy of sensitive information in federal computer systems was in the public interest and established the means to create minimum acceptable security practices for such systems.

■ ***European Union (EU) Directive of 1995 (95/46/EC)*** – The EU issued this directive to protect individuals with regard to the processing and free movement of their personal data.

■ ***Health Insurance Portability and Accountability Act of 1996 (HIPAA)*** – The purpose of HIPAA is to protect an individual's healthcare information from being used in an unethical and fraudulent manner. The act mandates that the officers and employees of organizations related to healthcare (e.g., hospitals, healthcare providers, insurance companies, etc.) deploy safeguards to ensure the integrity and confidentiality of all individual healthcare information, and violations are punishable by fines and jail time.

■ ***The Health Information Technology for Economic and Clinical Health (HITECH) Act*** -- Subtitle D of the HITECH Act addresses information relevant to an ISSMP. It mandates privacy and security related to electronic transmission of health information and strengthens rules (both civil and criminal) beyond HIPAA.

■ ***Personal Information Protection and Electronic Document Act of 2000 (PIPEDA)*** – PIPEDA is a Canadian law supporting and promoting electronic commerce by protecting personal information that is collected, used, or disclosed in certain circumstances by providing for the use of electronic means to communicate or record information or transactions.

■ ***Sarbanes-Oxley Act of 2002 (SOX)*** – The purpose of SOX is to protect investors by improving the accuracy and reliability of corporate disclosures made pursuant to the securities laws, and for other purposes.

■ ***Federal Information Security Management Act of 2002 (FISMA)*** – The purposes of Title III of this act are to provide a comprehensive framework for ensuring the effectiveness of information security controls over information resources that support federal operations and assets, effective government wide management and oversight of the related information security risks, and a mechanism for improved oversight of federal agency information security programs (e.g., FISMA compliance reporting to the Office of Management and Budget [OMB], Congressional Federal Computer Security Grades identifying Agency security status, linking deficiencies with budget process, etc.).

Take note that under FISMA, Congress linked the reporting of IT security deficiencies to the government budget process. This connection is one of the keys to gaining and maintaining IT security in the government and commercial sectors. This will be further discussed later in this chapter.

There are also guidances related to security that are issued by various regulatory bodies. The Federal Financial Institutions Examination Council (FFIEC), for example, has issued several security-related guidances to financial institutions.

Cultural Expectations
The "Soft" Nature of Culture

Culture can be defined as "the attitudes and behavior characteristic of a particular social group." [1] It consists of a group of people's shared behaviors, languages, attitudes, systems, values, practices, goals, etc.

The culture of an organization, or of particular units or divisions within an organization, can dramatically impact security in many ways, and it is important for the ISSMP to understand, and be able to address, various cultural factors and their respective relationships to security.

Unlike technical aspects of security, cultural factors cannot be assembled into a well-defined and detailed checklist for a professional to review. While more relaxed environments often pose more security challenges than disciplined ones, the unique nature of both individual and organizational personalities, people's interpersonal communication dynamics and styles, corporate values, the specifics of how an enterprise manages its physical locations and its technological architecture, and numerous other "soft" elements that combine to form organizational culture make each environment and scenario sport unique challenges, with significant variations between organizations.

Likewise, corrections or controls that may be technically and culturally appropriate to address risks identified as resulting from an organization's culture in one environment may be culturally incompatible with another's.

The ISSMP, therefore, must be able to "get a feel for" an organization's culture and, based on such a familiarity as well as based on his or her experience in managing security, make educated decisions as to what risks exist and what culturally appropriate countermeasures can help address those risks.

Examples of How Culture Can Impact Security

While it is obvious that employee behavior and mannerisms – an important element of corporate culture – are going to have a significant impact on organizational cybersecurity, the security impact of culture emanates not just from people working for an organization but also from the organization itself.

For example, some organizations – such as government intelligence agencies – are naturally security-conscious, while other groups may all but ignore security. Different cultural attitudes towards security impact not only what types of policies an organization is likely to have in place and how well they are implemented but also how well people accept and follow rules in order to maintain security, how likely people are to "innocently" attempt to circumvent policies, etc. Furthermore, if controls to address risks are needed in an environment in which people are averse to making any accommodations for security, resistance may be an issue, and significant interpersonal and communication skills may be necessary if security is to be successfully implemented, something that may be taken for granted in a security-aware group.

Cultural shifts – especially among organizations employing younger workers – create additional challenges. The cultural shift toward "open" work environments – in which everyone sits at tables in a large room rather than at individual desks in private offices or

---

1   http://www.oxforddictionaries.com/us/definition/american_english/culture

cubicles – means that physical computers and communication devices are often accessible to anyone in the room, be they a co-worker or visitor. Anyone who can physically access a computer can potentially hack it or cause it to be exposed to hacking, for example, by inserting a USB drive with malware-infested plug-and-play drivers into a target computer. Hence, "open" work environments – in which people regularly have physical access to other peoples' computers – create significant security challenges. Storage space may also be at a premium in shared environments; people may be apt to leave sensitive documents and electronic media in insecure locations. Likewise, the trend toward "sharing" creates many new challenges. Shared office space – in which multiple businesses share one workspace – exacerbates the risks inherent in open environments. It is important to understand, however, that groups that choose to operate with open work environments, or that have elected to utilize shared space for economic or social reasons, are unlikely to be willing to change their practices due to security concerns, and, as such, controls that accommodate the culture of the organization must be employed, or, if reasonable countermeasures are rejected for cultural or business reasons, a clear explanation of the resulting risk must be conveyed to management.

The mass adoption of social media has led to a rapid and dramatic increase in the sharing of information that just a few years ago would have been considered private or personal. Some organizations encourage employees to utilize social media while others do not. The proliferation of such data can impact security in many way, for example, by weakening the security of challenge questions or knowledge-based authentication schemes. How difficult is it for a criminal to guess someone's mother's maiden name when that person has posted pictures of family gatherings on social media with the names of his uncles and aunts tagged?

People using social media may also inadvertently post proprietary or confidential information and photographs, violate regulations by publicizing insider information or disclosing financials information prior to its official time of release, jeopardize corporate secrets by sharing information from which they can be extrapolated, etc. Controls against these types of risks must account for the cultural shift toward sharing of information, with the exception of their application in certain highly sensitive industries in which employers yield significant power over employees' "outside of the office" non-work related activities (for example, Department of Defense projects that require Security Clearances). Policies that prohibit people from using social media, for example, are unlikely to be successful and may be viewed unfavorably by parties performing a security audit if they feel that the organization implementing such policies knew that the policies were not going to be followed.

Similarly, organizations that allow people to work from home rather than from offices, or that allow people to use their own smartphones, tablets, or laptops for work-related matters, create a whole slew of security concerns. Organizational strategies for addressing such scenarios range from organizations that prohibit any work to be done outside of official work facilities and do not allow personal electronic devices into such locations, to those that supply workers with electronic devices that they may use for personal tasks but which remain under organizational control (this is called a Corporate Owned and Personally Operated (COPE) approach) and those that fully allow employees to utilize their own devices even within the office (Bring Your Own Device or BYOD).

Compiling a list of all cultural factors that can impact security is impossible because the concerns are too numerous and too varied between environments.

As such, the ISSMP must be able to adequately leverage her or his knowledge, experience, and understanding and extrapolate from an environment what risks may exist and what controls or countermeasures can be utilized to successfully address those risks without jeopardizing corporate culture or business aims. As part of this process, he or she should be able to gain a good understanding of the cultural factors and drivers within the organization and understand which aspects of culture are negotiable. Based on that information, he or she can appropriately target the resulting risks in a maximally effective manner.

The ISSMP needs to be aware of each group's cultural differences regarding security, including its perceptions and expectations. Here are some examples of the cultural differences and the basis for the differences:

- **Accounting** – It will be expecting and accepting of the need for security because the function is frequently audited, has very detail oriented tasks, is subject to many regulatory requirements, and so forth.
- **Research &Development (R&D)** – If researchers are from or in an academic community, they will want very little security because they desire an environment that is open, sharing, and allows the ability to seek inputs or reviews from their colleagues. On the other hand, if they work for a product, defense, or intelligence research group, they will be expecting a lot of security because they are used to handling intellectual property or classified information.
- **Production** – It will understand physical and personnel security very well and may be less confident in the use of computers, so the use of physical access controls and strict screen scripts may be seen as more acceptable methods of securing its systems.

With this understanding of the groups' perceptions and expectations, the ISSMP can determine the best solutions and strategies for promoting security to each business function. An example of how this works is as follows:

CASE STUDY

The ISSMP for an R&D company with the majority of personnel being from academic research groups needed to solve two problems – one security and one operational. The security problem was to provide controlled access to the building to replace the existing physical keys and alarm codes solution. The operational problem was to direct phone calls to individuals wherever they were in the building. Because researchers are typically in discussions in the offices of other researchers, the front desk would inform the individual over the public address system. When the company had 30 employees this was acceptable, but when the company grew to 100 employees the frequency of pages became disruptive.

> The ISSMP researched several solutions and found a solution that was perfect for both problems: a system with infrared (IR) badges that would track the location of individuals and direct phone calls to the phone nearest to them. After the solution was presented to the researchers, they clearly identified that they did not like the idea of having to wear an external badge and having a record of their movements maintained. The acceptable solution deployed was to issue each person a proximity badge they could keep in their wallet, implement a voicemail system, and only page the individual if it was an emergency.

External Influences

In addition to understanding the internal factors that influence a system's security program, and in addition to any laws, regulations, industry standards, or guidance that may impact the program, there are two external influences: customers (i.e., clients) and competitors. Each of these has a very profound influence on the level and type of security to be deployed. With customers, the ISSMP needs to be aware of their capabilities (computer and technical) and, like the functional groups' employees, their expectations. The ISSMP should know the following about the customers who are buying the organization's products or services over the Internet:

- Computer type and capabilities
- Connection bandwidth
- Technical knowledge and abilities
- Span of attention
- Security expectations

All of this information can be obtained through market surveys and interviews with the organization's reseller sales force personnel.

What the ISSMP needs to know about the competitors is:

- Reputation for ethical behavior
- Industrial espionage capabilities
- Technical capabilities
- Competitive desire
- Success obtaining the organization's clients
- Type of security they use with their clients

Information related to the first three items can be gained from doing searches on the Internet and talking with other security professionals. Knowledge of the latter three can come from the marketing research conducted by the organization's competitive analysis.

Why is the above information on the customers and the competitors important? The ethical reputation, espionage capabilities, technical capabilities, and desire will support the ISSMP's risk analysis, which will be discussed later in the chapter under the risk management sections. The rest of the information is critical in order to select the right security solution. The following example will help explain this:

- **Situation** – An organization decides to deploy a smartcard solution to verify online clients before allowing them to purchase products or services. This smartcard solution is selected because it will achieve close to a 100% security solution.
- **Result** – Even though the organization's advertising is drawing more potential buyers to its site than to any of its competitors, very few people buy at its site.
- **Why?** – Because the potential buyers are "impulse buyers" – they want to buy now and do not want to wait for a smartcard to come in the mail, and the competitors are using SSL and static passwords, allowing for immediate online transactions. Additionally, if the buyers did get the smartcard, where and how would it be integrated into the environment? Is it realistic to expect people to carry it with them at all times so that they will have it when they need to use it to make a purchase?

Of course, shareholders (i.e., investors) can also influence a security program as well.

Influence Summary

There are many things that influence the deployment of the most efficient and effective security solutions for an individual system or an enterprise system. The influences discussed above and summarized in *Figure 1.1* are mostly related to the type of business supported and the individuals who interact with the system, both internal and external to the organization. The ISSMP needs to be aware of these and include them when recommending the most effective solutions for an information system.

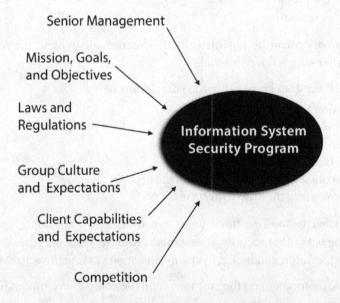

What Influences a System's Security Program?

Senior Management

Mission, Goals, and Objectives

Laws and Regulations

Group Culture and Expectations

Client Capabilities and Expectations

Competition

Information System Security Program

Figure 1.1 – **Business Influences**

Additionally, this awareness of the business and the cultures will help to promote security recommendations to all levels of the organization during senior management presentations, resource requests, employee awareness efforts, and so forth.

Recognize Sources and Boundaries of Authorization

Authorization is the process of granting or denying access rights to resources, including subcomponents of resources. After a party (a human user or a computer system) has its identity confirmed via authentication (or potentially not confirmed individually but rather confirmed to be a member of a group or determined to be unknown), a set of access rights are afforded to that party based on pre-determined access policies. The party is then said to be authorized to access those resources to which it has access rights, in the manners prescribed by those rights.

The source of authorization should be policies previously established by parties authorized to set them (usually the "owners" of the information). That is the people ultimately responsible for the business function of the data. Their specifications are normally set in conjunction with input from technical team members regarding their need for authorization in order to properly manage the system, from compliance and audit departments regarding their authorization needs, and all pertinent business units regarding their needs. The authorization should also be based on careful thinking and planning, not based on technical limitations of systems being accessed or of technologically inadequate authentication, authorization, or identity management engines. That said, practically speaking, while authorization is ultimately the responsibility of the party accountable for establishing and enforcing access control policies (usually an executive or department manager), the actual process is typically de facto delegated to technical personnel such as system administrators or security managers.

Authorization has boundaries in several regards. While it is normally better to proactively address as many potential scenarios explicitly in security policies, planning is never perfect, and unforeseen situations can arise in which adhering to existing policies can cause disturbances to business operations or other significant problems. For that reason, policies should include authorization for certain people or groups of people (depending on the nature of what is being approved) under certain situations to make certain types of exceptions, with all approvals of exceptions recorded for audit purposes. A formal process for waiver and exceptions should be created to avoid ad-hoc authorized waivers or exceptions causing problems. Executives acting under authority granted to them in policies are, therefore, another source of authorization. Of course, there must be separation of duties; a person should never be able to authorize an exception for himself or herself.

It is important for the ISSMP to understand, however, that not all authorization requests from executives should be immediately honored. When people wishing to gain access to resources to which they do not normally have access make requests that circumvent standard operating procedures, for example, unless the ISSMP is explicitly authorized to make such decisions herself or himself, it is essential that the ISSMP escalates any such requests up the chain of command to someone who is explicitly authorized in existing policies to approve them, thus ensuring that the organization continues to consistently adhere to its policies.

Likewise, court orders or other government actions may require that an organization authorize parties to access resources that they normally do not have access to or prohibit access to parties that otherwise would be authorized to have such access, and, as such, government bodies are also effectively potential sources of authorization. As was the case with "special requests," ISSMPs should – unless ordered by the law to act otherwise – consult with appropriate parties authorized by their organization to address such scenarios before granting/removing/modifying any access based on government action. Of course, the request (demand) and any actions taken should be extremely well documented, and the legal department should be consulted. Typically, the party to be consulted for any particular incident will be the "owner" of the information requested or of a particular system demanded by the authorities.

Authorization databases are also accurate only as of a certain time, and maintaining authorization information is often more difficult that it may seem. While every effort should be made to update access control lists and/or any authorization systems that may exist as quickly as possible after an event occurs, there is often some lag. If a person quits his job via email sent at 2 AM, for example, it may, practically speaking, take some time for administrators to actually update authorization records.

Define the Security Governance Structure

What Is Security Governance?

At a high level, security governance refers to the collection of everything involved in ensuring security for an organization; security governance includes the sum total of all the people, technology, policies, procedures, environments, and processes involved in information security.

Often, however, the term "security governance" is used to refer to a subset of governance that deals with board-level and executive management's roles vis-à-vis security. As such, security governance can be thought of as the security-related subset of "general governance," defined by the International Federation of Accountants (IFAC) and the Information Systems Audit and Control Association (ISACA) as "the set of responsibilities and practices exercised by the board and executive management with the goal of providing strategic direction, ensuring that objectives are achieved, ascertaining that risks are managed appropriately and verifying that the organization's resources are used responsibly."

Why Is Security Governance Necessary?

The goal of elevating security to an executive level is to ensure that security is a consideration throughout an organization, its efforts, and its operations. Additionally, such a scheme seeks to ensure leaders are security-conscious and, therefore, adequately prepared to lead the organization in defending its data, operations, reputation, valuation, and legal standing against hazards and risks.

Information security used to be a technical specialty found within, and managed by, IT departments. As technology improved and proliferated, however, such a model became insufficient. Today, we live in a world of perpetually connected computers and devices, of sensitive information being collected, analyzed, and transmitted by systems around the world every second, and of increasing dependence on information technology. As a result, the security of systems, communications, and data must be addressed in totality at an organizational level by people of sufficient rank as to be empowered to guide the entire organization in terms of establishing, communicating, enforcing, monitoring, and auditing security compliance.

Simply creating security policies and encouraging or demanding that people follow them or letting the IT department select and purchase security technologies to be deployed without executive planning is a recipe for failure. It is necessary for management to clearly communicate that security is a non-negotiable, essential ingredient in organizational success.

The responsibility of executives, and of boards of directors, to ensure the security of data and information technology may be more than simply a fiduciary responsibility. Various federal and state laws governing the privacy of data or related to security may mandate such involvement. Executives at financial firms, for example, may have requirements placed upon them by the United States Securities and Exchange Commission (SEC), Financial Industry Regulatory Authority (FINRA), or the Federal Financial Institutions Examination Council (FFIEC) .Healthcare related firms may be subject to Health Insurance Portability and Accountability Act (HIPAA) privacy laws, pharmaceutical companies may be subject to the United States Food and Drug Administration (FDA) rules, non-profits may be subject to various the Internal Revenue Service (IRS) rules, and, of course, organizations interacting with parties outside the United States may be subject to a whole slew of regulations from countries or regions in which they do business. People working in management in regions of the world outside the United States may likewise be subject to various legal obligations vis-à-vis maintaining the security and privacy of data and information systems.

Security Governance Roles

While roles and responsibilities may vary somewhat between organizations, some general structure exists:

Board of Directors

- Establish security is non-negotiable and pervasive throughout the organization.
- Direct executives to establish security and a security-conscious culture.
- Ensure that executives have the resources they need to ensure security.
- Ensure that executives are carrying out security as required.
- Ensure that management is meeting any pertinent legal and regulatory requirements.
- Ensure proper auditing by independent third parties occurs as necessary.

Executives

- Define the specific strategic security objectives of the organization.
- Design and implement plans that establish security and align it with business objectives.
- Report to the board confirming that security-related objectives are being addressed.
- Larger firms may establish a security steering committee to represent executives.

Chief Information Security Officer - CISO (or similar role)

- Develop the security strategy at a much more granular level.
- Advise executives on information-security-related matters.
- Manage the corporate information security program and its implementation.
- Interface with business managers to ensure information security in all units.
- May report directly to the board, to the executives, or a CSO.

Chief Security Officer - CSO (or similar role)

- Develop the overall security strategy (physical, informational, human, etc.) at a much more granular level.
- Advise executives on security-related matters.
- Manage the corporate security program and its implementation.
- Interface with business managers to ensure security in all units.
- May report directly to the board, to executives, or to both.

Chief Risk Management Officer – CRMO
(Sometimes known as Chief Risk Officer) (or similar role)

- Develop the overall risk management strategy for all types of major risks (reputational, operational, financial, strategic, legal/regulatory/compliance related) at a much more granular level.
- Advise executives on risk and risk management-related matters.
- Ensure that at all times the organization is in compliance with all applicable laws, regulations, and guidance.
- May have chief compliance officer reporting to him/her.
- Interface with business managers to ensure security in all units.
- May report directly to the board, to the executives, or to both.

Chief Compliance Officer (or similar role)

- Develop the overall compliance strategy.
- Advise executives on compliance-related matters.
- Ensure that at all times the organization is in compliance with all applicable laws, regulations, and guidance.

Information Security Concepts

Before determining what type of security is necessary for securing a specific system, an ISSMP needs to identify what assets need to be protected and to what degree. To do this, the ISSMP needs to understand some basic security concepts. These concepts include the following:

- System Security Requirements – Availability, Integrity, and Confidentiality
- Business Impact Analysis
- Information Classifications
- Security Categorization
- Security Boundaries

This section provides a thorough review of these security concepts.

System Security Requirements

The three key security requirements required by most information systems are availability, integrity, and confidentiality. They are objectives of an information system security program and properties that should be included and deployed to most, if not all, information systems. The following are definitions for these three attributes. The parts within quotes are from SP 80053; FIPS 200; FIPS 199; or 44 U.S.C., Sec. 3542.

- **Availability –** "Ensuring timely and reliable access to and use of information." Availability is impacted by human error, cabling problems, software bugs, hardware failures, staff absences, malicious code, and the many other threats that can render a system unusable or unreliable. The requirement for high availability is a critical requirement for online transactions, flight control, monitoring, and command and control (C2) systems.

- **Integrity** – "Guarding against improper information modification or destruction, and includes ensuring information nonrepudiation and authenticity." This is the requirement to ensure that the accuracy of the information is maintained when residing on the system, being correctly processed, or being transmitted from or to the system. The goal is to ensure that the information is not intentionally or accidentally corrupted. Integrity is critical to commercial and military tracking, safety, production, and financial systems.

- **Confidentiality** – "Preserving authorized restrictions on information access and disclosure, including means for protecting personal privacy and proprietary information." This requirement prevents the unauthorized disclosure of information while on the system, during transmission to other systems, and during the physical transfer of information from one location to another. This property is a key objective in systems with intellectual property, trade secrets, individual healthcare and personally identifiable information, and classified documents.

It would be totally cost prohibitive for organizations to provide all systems with a maximum level of protection. Fortunately, different systems require different levels of these properties depending on levied legal and regulatory requirements and, most importantly, on the impact that could result if one of these capabilities was lacking. It is the ISSMP's responsibility to determine how much protection related to these three properties is needed to meet legal, regulatory, and business security requirements. Then the ISSMP must gain senior management's approval to implement recommended safeguards or accept the risk.

Modern technology projects normally begin with the definition of business requirements. Businesspeople responsible for defining these requirements, however, may be unfamiliar with cybersecurity and, in many cases, tend to overlook necessary security requirement. It is imperative, therefore, that the ISSMP contribute to technology projects in this regard. The ISSMP should have detailed conversations with organizational management and other project stakeholders during which business goals are discussed in detail so that the ISSMP can apply his or her expertise in evaluating what risks the project creates and how those risks are best addressed.

As the project proceeds and business requirements are translated into functional requirements, and the ISSMP has a clearer and more detailed understanding as to what the project will and will not include, he or she should perform similar assessments to ensure that any risks that have been created are properly addressed. The same is necessary when functional specifications are created, and also at every subsequent stage of the development lifecycle.

Identifying security requirements is not always simple, and even an experienced ISSMP may overlook some risks. Therefore, it is ideal for multiple experienced professionals to participate in this process when possible. It should be noted that many projects today involve the use of third-party components, sometimes utilized locally, sometimes utilized across the Internet in a "cloud" like model. Assessing security requirements, therefore, must address such scenarios and the risks that they create. The ISSMP should also remember to identify the human risks to cybersecurity that any project creates, as well as consider any security-related regulations, guidance, best practices, or standards that may apply to the project.

At a high level, the steps involved with identifying security requirements are essentially:

1. Gather information from business stakeholders.

2. Review the functional requirements provided by the business stakeholders. These requirements will specify the goals of the project as well as contain information about the business logic that the project will implement.

3. By examining the aforementioned information, perform an assessment to ascertain what security requirements are created by the project and need to be addressed as part of the project.

When proposing security requirements for a project, the ISSMP should keep in mind that requirements cannot be vague, but, rather, they must be specific and measurable. Also, they must not interfere with any of the business goals of the system; it is simple, for example, to dramatically reduce the risks of Internet-based hackers breaching an online sales system by disconnecting the system from the Internet, but doing so would obviously undermine the business goal of the system. While that may be an extreme example, much smaller interferences with business goals are often proposed, and, if not managed carefully, they can lead not only to security risks remaining unaddressed but also to hostility between business stakeholders and the information-security team including the ISSMP himself or herself. Hence, if certain business requirements cannot be met in a secure fashion, or if doing so would come at an extremely high cost that the business stakeholders are unwilling to endure, or if human issues (such as internal organizational politics) preclude implementing necessary controls, the ISSMP must clearly communicate to the business stakeholders what risks exist, what options exist for addressing them, and what he or she recommends. The businesspeople, if so authorized, are then free to choose to acknowledge the risks, accept them, and proceed without addressing them, but armed with the appropriate knowledge of the risks for which they are assuming responsibility.

After risks are identified and security requirements are defined, the ISSMP must evaluate the capability of the organization to address those risks with various strategies and formulate a clear list of deltas, that is, what is lacking from the organization's capabilities now that needs to be there. The ISSMP should then assemble a list of what the organization needs (in terms of people, technologies, funding, etc.) in order to properly meet the security requirements.

The ISSMP should ensure that such improvements are included as requirements for the project; the project budget, for example, must account for any costs related to ensuring security.

As the project proceeds, the ISSMP, or his or her counterparts, must manage the security elements of the project to ensure that they are properly implemented. This includes both identifying the exact steps to be taken to implement the strategies decided upon previously, as well as confirming that what needs to be done was actually done and done correctly. This step, which may seem obvious, is critically important because often there are deviations from expectations, and corrections must be made. Proper testing (and testing for exception handling) is also a must.

After technologies are implemented, it is often within the ISSMP's role to ensure that any security related systems are properly maintained. This includes not only keeping the actual systems up to date but ensuring that any datasets that they use are kept current as well. This includes identity management, authorization tables, configuration information, etc.

Furthermore, the ISSMP must keep vigilant to identify new threats that may emerge and pose risks to the existing system, and to address them as needed.

Sometimes, business requirements to "make sure everything is secure" or "make sure the existing system is secure" are passed from businesses to security teams. In such cases, in which security is the project rather than a component of a business-system project, an assessment of the organization and all of its systems should take place. In this kind of a scenario, the project is essentially to perform a full security assessment, which is a topic unto itself.

Security Impact Analysis

The need for these properties on diverse systems will vary. Some systems will require very strong confidentiality (High), such as national intelligence systems. Others may require no confidentiality, such as the public information systems in the Library of Congress. Other systems will require varying degrees of confidentiality. Similarly, the levels of availability and integrity for a system used for purchasing shoes online and a system presenting airplane tracks to an air controller will be very different. Identifying the difference is critical to identifying the level of protection that a system requires. Doing so requires a subjective look at all of the business or mission specifics to determine which of the three are required and at what level (for example, Low, Moderate, or High).

In an attempt to provide some guidance to both commercial and government sectors, the National Institute of Standards and Technology (NIST) published guidance in their 800 series of Special Publications by linking levels to the magnitude of potential impact. While not all organizations will utilize such a scheme, it does serve as an example upon which the ISSMP may build his or her own model or from which lessons about how to develop a model may be deduced. The example levels are defined as shown in *Table 1.3*.

Potential Impact	Overall	Organizational Operations	Organizational Assets	Individuals
High	Catastrophic or severe	Severe degradation or loss of capability	Major damage	Loss of life or life-threatening injuries
Moderate	Serious	Significant degradation	Significant damage	Significant harm
Low	Limited	Some degradation	Minor damage	Minor or no harm

Source – This table was created from various descriptions provided in NIST SP 800-30, 800-64, 800-53, and FIPS-199.

*Table 1.3 – **Magnitude of Impact***

Each system has a different mission, business model, and potential impact level. Therefore, *Table 1.3* and NIST guidance are general, but they give the organization a reference for conducting its analysis. This analysis must include an honest review of the system to determine the potential impact on operations, assets (tangible and intangible, e.g., reputation), and individuals (employees, surrounding public, clients, etc.) so that management can begin to identify the impact and determine what levels of availability, integrity, and confidentiality are appropriate. Again, it is the ISSMP's responsibility to help the system owner determine this and senior management's responsibility to approve remediation or risk acceptance.

How does the ISSMP do this analysis? One way is to do an impact analysis. During the discussion of missions, goals, and objectives, systems with different goals are identified, each requiring different levels of availability, integrity, and assurance. Using some of those systems, the following provides a general look at how a manager would analyze different systems and approximate what the requirements could be:

Providing Information to the Public

- **Availability** – Depends on how time critical the information is to the operations or decision making needs of the receiver. Airplane tracking information to traffic controllers is High because people could die from plane crashes; local shoe sale in the next week is Low because the information could hold for several days.
- **Integrity** – Depends on the need for accuracy of the information. Airplane tracking information is High because inaccurate tracking data can result in providing inaccurate advice to pilots and potential plane crashes; weather reports to the public is Moderate because of the minimal accuracy of the reports and impact.
- **Confidentiality** – Depends on the type of information. Shoe sale is not applicable because vendors selling shoes want people – even unknown people – to see it; a person's private information is Moderate or High because it is sensitive information and there is the potential for lawsuits and fines; weapon capabilities documents for Top Secret weapons is High for obvious reasons.

Sharing Research Information

- **Availability** – Low because research is normally a methodical, long term effort.
- **Integrity** – Moderate because results are used for the development of solutions that have to be tested.
- **Confidentiality** – Not applicable if it is publicly available research. Moderate or High if R&D supports future products development; and up to High if R&D supports weapons systems.

Matching Harvested Human Organs to Patients in Need

- **Availability** – High because harvested organs only last hours.
- **Integrity** – High because of the need to get the right information for organ matches and shipping.
- **Confidentiality** – Moderate if the patient's private protected information and health information are identified, but it could be Low if patients are identified by codes. Of course, federal and various state laws may apply, or their foreign equivalents may apply, which may make this a High as well.

Allowing Gamblers to Gamble Online

- **Availability** – High because gamblers want to gamble now.
- **Integrity** – High because the money and reputation of the casino can be impacted.

- **Confidentiality** – High because of the reputation of the casino for protecting client confidentiality.

NIST has identified another way to conduct an impact analysis: Security Categorization.

Security Categorization Process

In an attempt to provide a checklist process to help organizations identify what level of protection a system requires, NIST produced the Security Categorization process and supporting tables to do an initial assessment based on the system information types and the mission supported. This process is called Security Categorization (SECCAT). The process is documented in FIPS 199, Standards for Security Categorization of Federal Information and Information Systems. The process is mandatory for U.S. government systems, and has been adopted by other parties as well.

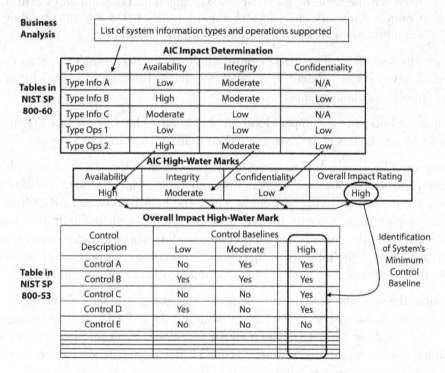

Figure 1.2 – **Security Categorization Process**

SECCAT uses basic tables located in NIST SP 80060, "Guide for Mapping Types of Information and Information Systems to Security Categories," and NIST SP 80053, "Recommended Security Controls for Federal Information Systems." These documents are used to equate the system's types of information and operations supported, both internally and externally, to the three security properties – availability, integrity, and confidentiality (the AIC triad) – to provide an overall system impact rating of High, Moderate, or Low for each property for each information type and operation supported. With this impact rating, NIST 80053 tables are used to provide recommendations on the types of controls to be used to secure the system. *Figure 1.2* provides a visual presentation of the process. Following are the basic steps:

- **System Information and Supported Operations –** Identify the types of information and operations supported by the system. This data was collected during the review of the business processes supported by the system, discussed in the section on Group Business Processes.
- **Recommended AIC Impacts –** Using the tables in the NIST SP 80060 series, determine the impact levels (Low, Moderate, or High) for each type of information and operation supported.
- **Overall System AIC Impact –** Consolidate all the AIC impacts determined in the last step by identifying the "high water mark" for each AIC property, and, by finding the "high water mark" with those three impacts, identify the overall system SECCAT as Low Impact, Moderate Impact, or High Impact. *Figure 1.2* provides a simplistic view of this consolidation process.
- **Recommended Baseline Security Controls –** Using the system SECCAT, reference the table in NIST SP 80053, Appendix D, Minimum Security Control– Summary, and select the column related to the category providing the minimum security controls required for the system.

The security controls are from the 17 control families in the management, operational, and technical classes of controls described in NIST SP 80053. *Table 1.4* provides a list of these security control classes and families.

Minimal controls for each impact level are 100 controls for Low Impact Systems, 212 controls for Moderate Impact Systems, and 277 controls for High Impact Systems.

Caution must be exercised when using this process because the "minimal controls" may not all apply. Remember, the overall system impact is a "high water measurement of impact." For example, take a High Impact System in which the individual overall AIC ratings were Availability impact High, Integrity impact Moderate, and Confidentiality impact was Not Applicable. Many of the controls that support only confidentiality requirements may not be required, and some of the integrity controls may be overkill for the system. These must be reviewed, the risks assessed, and justifications documented to support security reviews.

Of course, the opposite is also true; the organization may add additional controls because management wants the system to have fewer security risks or for business or management reasons. An example of the latter is when all the systems in the organization are using two factor authentication devices and it is more economical to deploy the devices on all systems, even those that only require passwords.

Information Classification

Information classification establishes a formal process for identifying what information needs to be protected and labeling the information in a uniform manner so individuals and systems can provide the level of protection they require. An accurate and clear information classification system is critical for identifying what information needs to be protected, the level of protection required, and setting resource priorities. Appropriate and adequate controls need to be established based on the information in question.

There are several concepts related to information classification that need to be understood: level of impact, "need to know," classification, and compartmentation. Basically, the first two are the basis for establishing the latter two concepts.

- **Level of Impact** – The level of impact is the negative result on the success of the mission or business if the information is not available, is modified without authorization, or is disclosed to unauthorized people. As discussed in the last section, the impact can be on operations, assets, or individuals.
- **Need to Know** – The concept of "need to know" is based on what individuals or processes need the information to support their actions. Least privilege ensures that only those people or processes with access to the information have that access in order to do their work.

The ISSMP needs to determine which individuals and processes require what information. This is derived from the business processes review mentioned in the last section. From that review, the ISSMP will be able to identify what information is "required" and what information is "desired." Good security is about minimal access, so the ISSMP needs to reduce the availability to what is required, what the individual or role truly "needs to know."

Classification is a label used to identify the sensitivity level of the information based on impact. There can be several classifications, but keeping them to a minimum makes it easier to document and manage and for the employees to understand. Organizations use a lot of different labels for identifying the various levels of sensitivity. Below are some examples:

Sensitive	Corporate Confidential
Private	Proprietary Information
Public	Product Sensitive
Restricted	For Company Use Only
Trade Secret	Personnel Information

Each organization uses labels that are meant to be understandable by its employees and relate to the sensitivity level of the information. One of the most well-known information classification systems is the one used by the U.S. government, which defines three levels of security classification as follows:

- **Top Secret** – "shall be applied to information, the unauthorized disclosure of which reasonably could be expected to cause exceptionally grave damage to the national security that the original classification authority is able to identify or describe."
- **Secret** – "shall be applied to information, the unauthorized disclosure of which reasonably could be expected to cause serious damage to the national security that the original classification authority is able to identify or describe."
- **Confidential** – "shall be applied to information, the unauthorized disclosure of which reasonably could be expected to cause damage to the national security that the original classification authority is able to identify or describe."
  (Source – Executive Order 12958, as Amended, Classified National Security Information, http://www.archives.gov/isoo/policy-documents/eo-12958-amendment.html)

Notice that each level is based on the expected damage (impact) if the information is disclosed. Restricting information to only those trusted individuals who have authorized access reduces the potential for disclosure of that information and the risk of the damage occurring. Using the concept of compartmentation, one can further lower this risk. Compartmentation is defined as the establishment and management of information about personnel, internal organization, or activities of one component that is made available to any other component only to the extent required for the performance of assigned duties.

Compartmentation further limits access to the information by strictly adhering to the "need to know" security concept and creating sub compartments for a classification level. A commercial example of this is as follows:

A corporation has classified its product designs and capabilities as Product Sensitive and allows only the executives and R&D and Production Department heads and personnel to see the information with this label. It also has special proprietary information that is being created for future products in a select group in the R&D Department that is working on a future product project called "Quintus." This information is labeled "Product Sensitive–Quintus" and is restricted to only nine personnel: the executives, the R&D Department head, and the individuals in the special R&D section.

From *Figure 1.3*, you can see how the risk to the information is reduced, due to the decreased number of personnel who can see the information.

The government also uses compartmentation to support the concept of "need to know." Below are examples of some existing government compartments and labels:

- **SCI** – Special Compartmented Intelligence
- **PCII** – Protected Critical Infrastructure Information
- **SSI** – Sensitive Security Information
- **CVI** – Chemical Vulnerability Information
- **SGI** – Safeguards Information

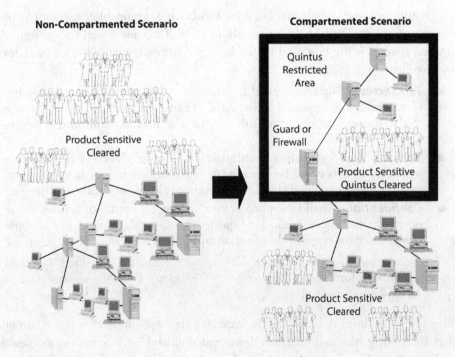

Figure 1.3 – **Compartmentation**

In May 2008, the President created the new "Controlled Unclassified Information" (CUI) categorization, which establishes three CUI categories. Under those categories, agencies that are part of the federal information sharing environment or the information sharing council should label unclassified data that is considered sensitive.

The framework sets out the three categories for the data to further identify how CUI information will be protected and released:

1. ***Controlled with Standard Dissemination*** – This information requires standard safeguarding measures, and dissemination is allowed to the extent that it is believed to further a lawful or official purpose.

2. ***Controlled with Specified Dissemination*** – This information requires safeguarding to reduce the risks of inadvertent disclosure and when allowed contains additional dissemination instructions.

3. ***Controlled Enhanced with Specified Dissemination*** – This information requires more stringent safeguards because unauthorized disclosure could produce significant harm, and when allowed contains additional dissemination instructions. (Source – White House Memorandum for the Heads of Executive Departments and Agencies, SUBJECT – Designation and Sharing of Controlled Unclassified Information [CUI], May 9, 2008, http://www.whitehouse.gov/news/releases/2008/05/200805096.html)

The increase in identity threat incidences has driven the U.S. government to create another label for individuals' private information, Personally Identifiable Information (PII). Regulations like the Privacy Act, FISMA, and HIPA A have mandated that increased attention be applied to securing PII information by the government and commercial sectors. Examples of PII data are:

- Name
- Date of birth
- National identification number (like the U.S. Social Security Number)
- Telephone number
- Home address
- Email address
- Driver's license number
- License plate number
- Healthcare information (like prescriptions, operations, diagnosis, lab results, etc.)
- Credit card numbers

Due to increased government awareness of the need to protect PII information, many reporting requirements have been mandated by the U.S. Office of Management and Budget (OMB). Some of these mandated actions for government organizations are as follows:

- ***Privacy Impact Assessment (PIA)*** – A PIA is conducted on each information system to determine the extent of PII in that system.

- ***Public Notification*** – A system of records notice (SORN) is publicly posted identifying each system processing or storing PII.

- ***PII Protection*** – PII that is transmitted or physically transported will be encrypted only using NIST certified cryptographic modules.

  (Source – OMB M0716, SUBJECT – Safeguarding Against and Responding to the Breach of Personally Identifiable Information, May 22, 2007, http://www.whitehouse. gov/omb/memoranda/fy2007/m0716.pdf)

Securing Classified Information

After determining the levels of classification that will be necessary to support the organization, the ISSMP may be called upon to to identify what controls, procedures, and access criteria will be required for each classification and compartmentation level. Obviously, the greater the impact for the classification of information, the stronger the criteria, controls, and procedures will need to be applied. At a minimum, the organization will have to document and ensure the implementation of the following mandatory requirements for the information:

- Storing
- Auditing
- Shipping and transmitting
- Recording who has had access
- Destroying
- Reporting secure destruction or loss
- Downgrading

Additionally, the level of trust of the individuals will have to be determined and documented to ensure that people granted access to a classification are capable and reliable enough to protect the information. This is accomplished through background, credit, reference, and police checks and verifying their identity. These processes and procedures will have to be documented, and the clearance levels for the individuals will have to be managed and monitored.

Controls

Controls may be grouped into families based on their roles. An example table appears below:

Control Class	Control Family	Identifier
Management	Certification, Accreditation, and Security Assessments	CA
	Planning	PL
	Risk Assessment	RA
	System and Services Acquisition	SA
Operational	Awareness and Training	AT
	Configuration Management	CM
	Contingency Planning	CP
	Incident Response	IR
	Maintenance	MA
	Media Protection	MP
	Physical and Environmental Protection	PE
	Personnel Security	PS
	System and Information Integrity	SI
Technical	Access Control	AC
	Audit and Accountability	AU
	Identification and Authentication	IA
	System and Communications Protection	SC

Table 1.4 – Controls

1

Security Boundary

Early in the process, the ISSMP must determine and document exactly what the security boundary for the system is. This is very critical because the effort can quickly grow to building an information system security plan for the entire corporate enterprise, if not the Internet. To help identify the true security boundaries, the ISSMP must do six things:

1.   Understand and focus on the system's mission, goals, objectives, and business processes as discussed above.
2.   Closely coordinate the review with the person who manages the business group, e.g., in NIST terminology, the system owner.
3.   Identify the groups of system components that support each of the business functions.
4.   Establish the security requirements for each group.
5.   Determine what is under the control of the organization and the business group and what is not, control meaning both operationally and fiscally.
6.   Thoroughly document the security boundaries and gain the system owner's concurrence.

Following is an example of how to set the boundary for a system:

Green, Inc. sells products from several manufactures to buyers all over the world via the Green website. When Green receives an order, it sends the information to the product manufacturer, and the manufacturer ships the product to the buyer. The buyer pays Green via credit card for the product and shipping, and Green pays the manufacturer a wholesale price for the product and shipping. Green's profit is the price to the buyer minus the wholesale price. Green has two internal business functions, accounting and website graphic developers, with an IT staff maintaining the systems. Green's systems consist of a connection to the Internet, a website server, transaction server, three accounting workstations and a server, five graphic developer workstations and a server, and three workstations for the chief executive officer (CEO), chief operating officer (COO), and office manager. What are the system's security boundaries?

WHAT IS NOT IN THE BOUNDARY?

The buyers and manufacturers are not in the boundary because they are outside of Green's control, but security controls will have to be identified to protect any sensitive information that is transmitted over a public network between the manufacturers and buyers. Additionally, security agreements will have to be formalized between the manufacturers and Green in the form of terms in a contract or an interconnection service agreement, which will be discussed later in this chapter.

WHAT ARE THE DIFFERENT PROCESSES IN THE ORGANIZATION?

- Management controlling and managing operations
- Sales allowing transactions over the website
- Accounting maintaining the books and billing the manufacturers
- Graphics developing new website pages

WHAT ARE THE PRIORITY PROCESSES AND SUPPORTING SYSTEMS SECURITY IMPACTS?

Process	Availability	Integrity	Confidentiality	Priority
Management	Low	Moderate	High	3
Sales	High	High	High	1
Accounting	Low	High	High	2
Graphics	Low	Moderate	Not applicable	4

*Table 1.5 – **Impacts***
(Source – http://bit.ly/1pRhjio)

JUSTIFICATION OF RESULTS

- ***Availability is Rated Low*** for all but Sales because the website is bringing in all the revenue. The other elements are not time-critical processes. A small delay in shipping and billing will have less of an impact on profits. Management and Graphics can work in a manual mode with minimal impact.
- ***Integrity is Rated High*** on Sales and Accounting because of the need for accuracy in ordering, billing, shipping, and so forth. Management and Graphics is rated Moderate because most of their outputs are reviewed prior to sending or posting.
- ***Confidentiality is Rated High*** for three processes because Management has personnel and strategic planning information, Sales has buyer information, and Accounting has sensitive buyer, manufacturer, profit, and payroll information. Graphics has nothing that is sensitive.

SO WHERE ARE THE SECURITY BOUNDARIES FOR THIS ORGANIZATION?

One answer could be that everything from the firewall inward is the security boundary; because the organization is small and everyone can be trusted, rate the system at the high-water mark and deploy strong security controls.

Another answer could be to set four different security boundaries and secure each system with security controls related to their risk-based security needs. This could require firewalls between systems or creating isolated systems and physically transferring information between the systems.

Other solutions can be in between both of the above solutions, like connecting Accounting, Sales, and Management, because of their High security requirements, and just isolating the Graphics system. Or isolate the Management and Graphics systems because Sales and Accounting are both financial systems and have common High security requirements.

All of these options are valid security boundaries; the organization just needs to decide which one is most appropriate and document the details of the agreed upon security boundaries.

System Security Program Influences Summary

There are many things that impact information system security programs. Many of these are identified in *Figure 1.4*. On the left side of the figure are the business influences and on the right are the operational influences. All of these must be thoroughly understood by an ISSMP prior to developing an information system security program because with these the ISSMP will understand the "true problem" that needs to be solved.

Using this knowledge of the organization's systems, the ISSMP can take the next step of developing the Enterprise System Security Framework for the systems.

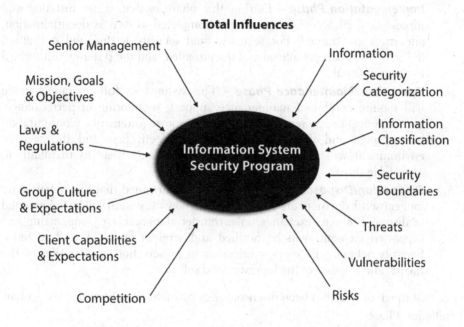

Figure 1.4 – **Total Information System Security Program Influences**

System Development Life Cycle (SDLC)

An enterprise system security program must support the systems continuously from "cradle to grave" because systems' environments, missions, threats, and vulnerabilities are constantly changing throughout the life of the systems. Security reviews and actions must be taken to ensure that each system remains secure, so before moving on to the next topic, the concept of system development life cycle (SDLC) must be understood to provide the ISSMP with a point of reference for future topics.

The SDLC title can sometimes be misleading because of the word "development." When one reads the title, the initial perception is that it only supports development of the system and stops at the acceptance of the system. Actually, SDLC covers the system from conception to disposition.

There are many SDLC models used for information systems, but most of the models consist of five basic phases:

1. ***Initiation Phase –*** This phase identifies what the real and perceived needs are for the system and a determination of how they link to the business mission being supported by the system. Security actions during this phase include conducting a security categorization and preliminary risk assessment.

2. **Development/Acquisition Phase** – Here the statement of functional requirements is drafted, various analysis activities are conducted (e.g., requirements, alternatives, cost benefit, etc.), and a risk management plan is drafted. Security activities include conducting a risk assessment, a security functional and assurance requirements analysis, security planning, and security test and evaluation activities.

3. **Implementation Phase** – During this phase, system(s) are installed and inspected, final acceptance testing is completed as well as documentation, and users are trained. For security, final security testing and evaluation (ST&E) efforts are completed and documented, and the system is authorized to go operational.

4. **Operations/Maintenance Phase** – The systems in full operation mode will require continued maintenance support, monitoring of performance, and modifications as required to meet mission requirements. Configuration management and monitoring of security effectiveness and the security environment will be conducted on a continuous basis to maintain an acceptable security posture.

5. **Disposition/Disposal Phase** – When it is determined that the system is no longer useful, decisions are made regarding how the system will be transitioned or disposed of (e.g., exchange, sale, transfer, donation, etc.), supporting and supported elements will be notified and services finalized, and so forth. Security actions will support information preservation, sanitization of the media, and disposal of the hardware and software.

Notice that much of what has been discussed thus far includes actions that were identified in the Initiation Phase.

As mentioned, many versions of the SDLC are being used by organizations. The versions can range from five to many phases. It is imperative that the ISSMP understand the SDLC model used within the organization to ensure that appropriate security support is provided to the process in a timely manner and security is implemented from the beginning of the cycle to the end. So one of the first actions an ISSMP should take is to verify what the specific SDLC model for the organization is. Typically, it can be found in the corporate or CIO policies and procedures; if not, ask the system program manager.

Enterprise System Security Framework

An Enterprise System Security Framework is created to ensure that IT security is designed, implemented, authorized, and maintained to provide an acceptable level of risk and is cost-effective. An Enterprise System Security Framework is a structure developed by the organization and must have the following components identified, developed, and documented:

- Policies
- Standards
- Guidelines–Best Practices
- Roles and Responsibilities
- Procedures and Processes
- Baselines
- Enterprise Wide Security Consistency

Twenty-first century ISSMPs are fortunate because there are many tools and materials available to them for helping them build this framework in the form of standards, guidelines, control baselines, examples, and so forth. Because these were created by the IT security experts who preceded them in various types of organizations (governmental and commercial), they are like the materials (wood, brick, glass, nails, etc.) available to make a house (i.e., they all need to be modified and reshaped to build the specific framework for the individual organization's enterprise system security architecture).

Enterprise Security Policy

An enterprise security policy establishes the framework for how security will be implemented, maintained, and modified as the security and business environment changes. A successful enterprise security policy provides answers to the following:

- What are the controls, processes, and procedures related to maintaining an adequate security posture as the environment changes, new systems are deployed, and existing systems are modified or decommissioned?
- How are these reviewed for compliance and enforced?
- Who is responsible for all the above and the associated resources?
- How are these responsibilities communicated and monitored?
- To whom does one report issues, and from whom does one gain further clarification?

Overall, it is critical that the enterprise security policy be accurate, robust, and complete. It must accurately reflect the needs of all of the information systems in the organization. Robustness is necessary to ensure the security policy is flexible enough to support the differences in the systems and changes in the organization's mission, operation, and environment. Finally, the enterprise security policy must cover all the security requirements necessary to provide the best security for the systems.

To ensure that the enterprise security policy meets all of these requirements, ISSMPs must have a thorough understanding of the organization's systems. This is why this chapter began with a focus on identifying the organization's missions/business goals and objectives, functional groups, and individual systems boundaries, cultures, and security functions. Without these, the ISSMP will be ineffective in building the enterprise security policy or any other component within the enterprise security framework. Many have tried using "standard" or "generic" security policies and failed because they lacked an understanding of the problem.

To achieve the above objectives and create their organization's enterprise security policy in an efficient and effective manner, ISSMPs must incorporate the most basic of all management principles and methodologies. The following are considered absolute "musts":

- **Understand the Current Environment** – Ensure that the policies are robust enough to support the current operating environment and the true reality of the organization, including the business, culture, expectations, local laws, regulations, and operational needs.
- **Use Standard Project Management Practices** – Organizations must build their programs using proven management concepts and processes. Developing unique, creative management processes frequently results in a costly and unsuccessful experience. It is highly recommended to leverage the

information provided by the Project Management Institute (PMI) to reduce risks related to managing projects and programs.

- **Be Based on Risk and Cost** – Policies must be based on the results of risk assessments and cost benefit analyses to ensure that they are in the best interests of the organization.

- **Be Enforceable** – Policies must be enforceable to be effective and should address what the consequences will be for those who violate the policies. Not enforcing one policy can degrade all of the organization's policies.

- **Be Supported by Executives** – Policies that do not have the support of senior management, HR, and the legal department will not be effective. Therefore, all concerns from these groups must be addressed and resolved prior to the release of any policies.

- **Include Representatives** – To increase the effectiveness of the policy in any organization, one must ensure that the development of the policy has the participation of those who will be using (and bound by) the policy. User representatives from all elements (functional, business, and support units) will ensure that the policies are practical and applicable to all of the elements. Additionally, these representatives can become great promoters to other users during the implementation of the policies. This will also prevent the perception of senior management creating policies "in a vacuum" without an understanding of reality.

- **Communicate Policy** – Organizations must ensure that all of their employees, clients, and partners are fully aware of their policies to ensure effective and efficient operations and compliance with regulations. It is recommended that there be a proactive and consistent awareness program that extends beyond the initial employee indoctrination efforts. Promotion of policies via memos, emails, newsletters, banners, senior management presentations, town hall meetings, and so forth can be used.

- **Be Reviewed Regularly** – As the organization changes, the policy will need to change and grow to support those changes. All policy changes must be documented to include who approved the change, when, and what caused the change. Reasons for changing policies include changes in threats and vulnerabilities, mergers, acquisitions, testing and exercise results, and so forth. Routine reviews should be scheduled at least annually.

- **Track Exceptions** – Although the entire organization is supposed to comply with the organization's policies, there are situations where exceptions must be made. Whenever exceptions are made, the following must be documented: the exemption, justification and time period for the exemption, who authorized the exemption, and when. This documentation needs to be centrally located with the enterprise's policy documents.

- **Create One Central Location** – The organization should have one central location where all policies are maintained so everyone can access them. This supports the requirement that all employees should be aware of an organization's policies.

- **Leverage Technology and Expertise** – Enterprise security policies should always leverage two things – technology and the experience of other experts, e.g., the previously mentioned use of PMI for project management.

Leveraging technology to automate manual processes and procedures can be either very cost-effective or not. Having technology that replaces the manual updating of each computer by pushing down patches and anti-virus updates for a very large, dispersed system should be considered when building a security policy. But not all technology can be leveraged without the additional implementation of more controls, like using an automated tool for system personnel to document and report their security control status, when the system personnel do not understand security. Another example is stating a policy that everyone will use smartcards for system access, and when smartcards are deployed the systems are not configured with smartcard readers. Do leverage technology, but ensure that it is practical and not vulnerable. Also be aware of what will have to be done when established enterprise security policies are confronted with technology inherited from acquisitions and mergers. Integration of old and new technologies can be very expensive, and planning the transition of the two security policies can be very complicated.

Leveraging the expertise of others does not necessarily mean hiring an expert. Remember that the policy for a specific enterprise system must be tailored to each organization, but the ISSMP should take advantage of the examples that have already been proven successful by others. As previously mentioned, other security experts have contributed their experiences, so ISSMPs do not have to make the same costly mistakes made previously. They have provided their knowledge, recommendations, and processes in the form of lectures, whitepapers, standards, and guidelines. ISSMPs would be irresponsible not to leverage this experience. In fact, the previously documented standards and guidelines provide great resources that ISSMPs can use to begin to tailor their security programs. Additionally, where conformance to laws and regulations is required, it is mandatory for ISSMPs to use them as a foundation for their programs but modify them for their specific organization's environment and requirements.

So, what are these standards and guidelines, and how does the ISSMP use them to build the policies and other components of the enterprise system security framework?

Standards and Guidelines

As discussed in the CISSP study guide, it is important to understand the difference between standards and guidelines:

- Standards are mandatory (i.e., they must be followed).
- Guidelines are provided as discretionary recommendations.

In many cases, organizations publish standards to state an overall mandatory requirement and then publish more flexible guidelines on how the requirement can be satisfied. This allows for more flexibility in how the standard will be complied with at the organization or system level.

There are two sets of standards and guidelines: external and internal. The external ones are created by organizations such as government and nonprofit groups, e.g., the National Institute of Standards and Technology (NIST) and the International Organization for Standardization and International Electrotechnical Commission (ISO/IEC). External standards and guidelines are usually driven by regulatory, professional, or business demands.

NIST was directed by the U.S. Congress to develop and issue standards and guidelines for government organizations and those working with the government. NIST is well known for its 800 series of Special Publications (SPs) and its mandatory Federal Information Processing Standards (FIPS) related to all aspects of IT security, which can be found at http://csrc.nist.gov/publications. For the U.S. government and associated organizations, NIST FIPS are standards (mandatory) and NIST SPs are guidelines.

ISO standards and guidelines are driven by the needs of the international communities to develop something they could use to guide them in securing their systems. Two of these are well known in the IT security community:

- One is a standard, ISO/IEC 154081:2009, Evaluation Criteria for IT Security – Part 1 Introduction and General Model, which provides the standard framework for the evaluation of individual information technology products for conformance to the International Common Criteria for Information Technology Security Evaluation.
- The other is a guideline, ISO/IEC 27002:2013, Code of Practice for Information Security Controls, which "establishes guidelines and general principles for initiating, implementing, maintaining, and improving information security management in an organization."

  (Source – http://www.iso.org/iso/iso_ catalogue/catalogue_ics/catalogue_detail_ics.htm?csnumber=50297)

Currently, NIST is working with public and private sector entities to establish specific mappings and relationships between the security standards and guidelines developed by NIST and ISO/IEC.

Some very large organizations have published their own standards and guidelines, like the U.S. Department of Defense in its 8500 series of directives and instructions for the U.S. military and the Information Systems Audit and Control Association (ISACA) IS Standards, Guidelines, and Procedures for Auditing and Control Professionals (Source – https://www.isaca.org/).

Internal standards and guidelines are created by an organization, based on "best practices," to provide direction to its employees and partners on how to develop, operate, interconnect, and maintain the organization's security. These are typically recommended by the ISSMP, but they are always approved and promulgated by senior management. They are typically referenced or stated in enterprise security policy, system security plans, operations manuals, and so forth.

Examples of internal standards include the following:

- ***Passwords*** – Employees will use 12 character passwords, using random combinations of alphanumeric characters, special characters, and upper and lowercases.
- ***Awareness*** – All employees will complete IT security indoctrination prior to logging on to any system and annual awareness training to maintain access privileges. Compliance will be reviewed by the chief information security officer (CISO) and formally reported on a quarterly basis to the chief executive officer.
- ***Contingency Plan testing*** – Contingency plans will be exercised annually for each IT system.

Examples of guidelines include the following:

- **Passwords** – Systems can use multi-factor authentication to meet the requirements of the standard.
- **Awareness** – Employees will have 30 days to complete their annual IT awareness requirement after notification of noncompliance. Awareness compliance can be reinstated after taking the computer based training or attending the monthly IT awareness event.
- **Contingency Plan testing** – To be compliant with the annual contingency plan exercise requirement, refer to the following, which are acceptable for the applicable systems:
  - ¤ **Low Impact Systems** – Tabletop exercise
  - ¤ **Moderate Impact Systems** – Walkthrough exercise
  - ¤ **High Impact Systems** – Full deployment exercise

Leveraging Externals to Produce Internals

When developing internal standards, guidelines, and procedures, ISSMPs should freely use external sources of standards, guidelines, procedures, and best practices to locate the various options for identifying the best security solution for their systems. A good example is when looking at creating an outline for their enterprise system security framework, ISSMPs can start with the NIST SP 80018, Guide for Developing Security Plans for Federal Information Systems, which provides a short outline for building a generic security plan. Having conducted the work identified in the first section of this chapter, the ISSMP can easily complete the first half of the plan describing the mission, business functions, goals and objectives, interconnectivity with internal groups and externally with partners, and so forth.

The next item in the plan is the development of the roles and responsibilities, policies, standards, and guidelines. Identifying roles and responsibilities will be discussed later in this chapter. The following references are good sources for information relative to developing baseline controls:

- **NIST SP 800-53** – Guide for Assessing the Security Controls in Federal Information System
- **ISO/IEC JTC 1/SC 27** – Code of Practice for Information Security Management
- **Department of Defense Instruction (DoDI) 8500.2** – Information Assurance (IA) Implementation

Each of these three documents provides a comprehensive list of controls that should be taken into consideration when securing an IT system. Although the numbers of families are different, the total list of controls within each document is very similar to the others

Since each document was developed for a different audience, ISSMPs should find which of these documents they are comfortable with and use that control listing to build an outline of the standards, guidelines, and procedures they will need to develop for their systems.

> ***Note** – When developing something others will have to implement and live with, involve them in the development of the solution or options. Why? Participation provides education and understanding of the need and ownership for the end solutions.*

Other sources for best practices include the following:

- **Commonly Accepted Security Practices and Regulations (CASPR)** – Developed by the CASPR Project (http://infosec101.org/), this effort aims to provide a set of best practices that can be universally applied to any organization "regardless of industry, size or mission." CASPR delves into specific technologies, recommending fundamental principles and practices for creating a stable and secure IT environment.
- **Control Objectives for Information (and Related) Technology (COBIT)** – Developed by IT auditors and made available through the Information Systems Audit and Control Association (http://www.isaca.org/Knowledge-Center/COBIT/Pages/Overview.aspx), COBIT provides a framework for assessing a security program, developing a performance baseline, and measuring performance over time.
- **Operationally Critical Threat, Asset, and Vulnerability Evaluation (OCTAVE)** – Created by Carnegie Mellon's CERT Coordination Center (www.cert.org/octave), OCTAVE provides measures based on accepted best practices for evaluating security programs.
- **NIST Special Publications** (http://csrc.nist.gov/publications/PubsSPs.html):
  - ¤ Generally Accepted Principles and Practices for Securing Information Technology Systems
  - ¤ Contingency Planning Guide for Information Technology System
  - ¤ Guide for Assessing the Security Controls in Federal Information Systems
  - ¤ Computer Security Incident Handling Guide

The above steps provide the ISSMP with an understanding of the enterprise's systems and the key areas that need to be reviewed. To make the Enterprise System Security Program successful and cost effective, the ISSMP must ensure that the program is risk based.

Service Management Agreements

Service management agreements are typically contracts established between two parties that state with detailed terms how one party will provide services to the other in exchange for financial compensation. The service to be provided is spelled out in the contract in what is known as the service level agreement (SLA); The SLA includes details to ensure that there is a mutually agreed upon understanding regarding all sorts of aspects of the relationship, for example, the exact nature of the services to be provided, who is responsible for what, what guarantees are being made, what response times to issues will be offered by the provider, what warranties the parties make to one other, what compensation will be required should either party violate the aforementioned terms, which jurisdiction's laws and venues for arbitration and/or court actions will be utilized in the event of unresolvable conflicts, etc.

It is ideal for security professionals to be involved in the process of establishing service management agreements prior to their actual execution because adequately addressing any security concerns is obviously an integral element of any properly written technology-related service agreement. Sometimes, however, business people may ask security professionals to review existing agreements that were established with less-than-adequate attention to security in order for security recommendations to be made that will either be requested from the third-party provider immediately or that will be included in negotiations upon the agreement's renewal.

Obviously, service agreements differ dramatically in their content based on the type of service provided, and the metrics used in SLAs will, therefore, vary as well. A telecommunications line provider, for example, may guarantee certain bandwidths as a measure of its primary metric of properly delivering service, while the provider of physical security tokens may promise that each token will work for x number of years without issue. It is important for the ISSMP, therefore, to understand what the business considers essential from a business standpoint in terms of service delivery so that when he or she reviews agreements, he or she can ensure that (a) the metrics used for measuring satisfactory performance are the right metrics and (b) that the values associated with those metrics are acceptable as well.

How are key performance indicators and metrics determined? Some may be set by business owners based on their understanding of their business, some may be based on prior experiences, some may be based on industry standards, some may be based on comparisons with competitors, and various other information may be incorporated into such decisions. The ISSMP should be aware of the source of the input into such decisions because not all sources of input may weight security equally or give it sufficient weight as necessary for the organization for which the ISSMP works.

The risks that the ISSMP may need to identify are not necessarily all technological. Financial risk to the organization may exist if the third-party provider fails to deliver service as promised, and, depending on the specifics of the scenario, controls may need to be taken either proactively, reactively, or both. For example, if the failure of the service provider to deliver could cause catastrophic risk to the organization, perhaps insurance and/or a backup provider for the service are warranted and should be arranged before commencement of the services with the original provider.

Understanding and managing service management agreements is becoming increasingly important as organizations outsource an increasing number of technical functions to "cloud" based providers offering software, servers, or development platforms as a service across the Internet. What was unthinkable not so many years ago – reputable organizations utilizing business applications, virtual servers, and other software packages hosted at another company – is now becoming commonplace. As managed services become increasingly prevalent, properly governing them is become increasingly essential.

While the business function owners are normally responsible to ensure that third-party providers are delivering services as promised, the ISSMP may be responsible for various aspects of the relationship with the third party. Several key techniques for governing managed services relevant to the ISSMP include:

1. Ensure that the environments and technologies being utilized by the third-party provider are compatible with those used internally. Confirm that any communications between them can – and will – be handled securely.
2. Ensure that all contracts are properly written to address business and security needs as described above.
3. Ensure that no surprise charges will occur – sometimes managed service providers have huge fees for unanticipated needs – and that security needs to not generate additional charges beyond what has already been agreed upon.
4. Ensure that clear resolution processes are in place in case of issues or conflicts.

Inadequate service levels pose another risk to an organization; arguments could be made that the company paying for services has not practiced "Due Care." If a mission-critical system suffers a breach on a Friday night, for example, and a company's SLA with the pertinent vendor specifies that the vendor does not need to respond until Monday morning, the consequences can be severe, and parties impacted by the breach may attempt to sue the company for negligence.

When you are negotiating an SLA, it is often possible to obtain the standard agreements of multiple vendors bidding on a contract; while a vendor may be selected based on the terms of the SLA, it is sometimes possible to convince a vendor to modify its SLA to match the terms of another bidder.

Furthermore, it is imperative that the ISSMP also understand the impact that organizational changes at the service provider can have on service and on service agreements, and that he or she address those risks. For example, a service level agreement should include language to ensure that service levels are maintained even if the provider is acquired or merged with another firm and to guarantee that arrangements provide for the event in which the provider is impacted by a natural disaster or war or otherwise fails or declares bankruptcy. Even smaller changes at the service provider, however, can impact service levels; a reorganization, a decision to focus on other aspects of its business, etc. can all adversely impact service.

Furthermore, a scenario in which a provider is acquired by a firm with which the organization does not want to do business can make matters complicated, to say the least. Would a firm outsourcing its CRM system to a third-party software as a service provider, for example, really be comfortable with the system and data being housed at the site of a competitor if that competitor acquired the service provider?

Service agreements should, therefore, include language to address such scenarios. As with other aspects of agreement negotiation, the ISSMP will likely need to coordinate with business function owners as well as with the legal department or outside counsel when working on the agreements.

Likewise, human issues must be addressed. Multiple points of contact within the service provider organization should be identified, and the relationships with those folks must be kept current. This helps to ensure that if a reorganization (or layoffs, etc.) occur, the relationship will not be jeopardized.

When appropriate, testing should be done to ensure that service providers are delivering their service at levels that meet or exceed the metrics guaranteed in SLAs.

Once a service level agreement has been put into place and services are being delivered, the ISSMP might be asked to help monitor compliance. While business function owners will likely monitor compliance with business requirements, the ISSMP may be called upon to confirm that all security requirements to which the third-party provider agreed are actually being delivered upon as agreed. The ISSMP will need to discuss internally as well as with the outside provider any deficiencies that he or she finds. If the provider cannot – or is unwilling to – correct such problems, the ISSMP will need to escalate the matter internally.

Other Forms of Agreements

Two other forms of agreements that are important to understand are operational level agreements and underpinning contract agreements.

Operational level agreements (OLAs): An organization might have OLAs, which are contracts that define how the various operational teams within the organization work together in order to deliver a promised product or service. Sometimes the terms SLA and OLA are used interchangeably; technically speaking an internal contract is an OLA, not a SLA. A provider signing SLAs must ensure that it can deliver certain performance and should set internal OLAs to provide at least that level of performance if not higher.

Underpinning contract agreements (UCAs or UCs): UCs are agreements between a service provider – for example the one with whom the organization has signed an SLA – and a third party that agrees to provide some product or service that is part of what the service provider will be providing under the SLA. Any level of performance in a UC should be at least as high as the level in the SLA being serviced by the UC.

Risk Management Program

The concept of risk management programs is nothing new to organizations. These programs are in place at most organizations from the National Sports Organization for Badminton to the National Aeronautics and Space Administration (NASA). Organizations find that having programs that are proactive in preventing failures, unnecessary costs, or losses are necessary for successfully accomplishing the organization's mission by knowing potential risks prior to making decisions. Risks related to the following should be assessed in order to support optimum management decision making: producing a new product, reviewing new marketing strategies, deciding between older proven technical and innovative solutions, determining the need for changes in operational processes, identifying potential problems in project schedules, and projecting the impact of security solutions.

With this in mind, the overall objective of a security risk management program is to identify potential security incidents before they occur, so that:

- Controls can be put into place to prevent or reduce the potential of the incident from occurring, to identify when an incident is occurring, and reduce impact if the incident occurs.
- Risk handling activities, like incident response and contingency plans, can be in place for activation to respond to or recover from an incident.
- Security controls remain effective across the life of the system.

When one is implementing an enterprise risk management program for information systems security, the risks related to the enterprise systems will be known, so management can make "risk based, cost-effective" decisions on security issues. Knowing the security risks for each or all of the enterprise systems allows management to:

- Be more proactive in protecting the systems.
- Make more educated decisions.
- Manage security as a routine business.
- View security incidents as operational anomalies.

By conducting risk assessments for the enterprise systems using the same processes used in the organization's risk management program, security becomes viewed as more of a service supporting the organization's business functions, thereby making security's relationship more understandable and acceptable to management. Additionally, the ISSMP and management begin to speak the same language and support the same goals. Subsequently, users gain increased acceptance of the need for security.

There are many models for risk management that have been published and provided as automated tools. Following are some examples:

- **NIST SP 800-30, Guide for Conducting Risk Assessments**, and **NIST SP 800-37, Revision 1, Guide for Applying the Risk Management Framework to Federal Information Systems: A Security Life Cycle Approach -** Both of these provide a risk management framework and guidelines for conducting a risk assessment and how to apply the results to securing an information system.

- **ISO 13335, Information technology -- Security techniques -- Management of information and communications technology security –** This guideline defines a variety of security controls and outlines the framework for risk management.

- **AS/NZ ISO 31000:2009, Standard: Risk Management - Principles and Guidelines –** This is the matrix used in the Australian/New Zealand Standard (AS/NZ) 4360 to determine risk management priorities through placing risk assessments in a table (matrix) and using this to highlight areas of most critical importance as compared to less critical risks.

- **OCTAVE (Operationally Critical Threat, Asset, and Vulnerability Evaluation) –** This is an automated, self-directed, risk based strategic assessment and planning tool for security. The tool allows a small team from operational, business, and IT units to work together to define the organization's current state of security, identify risks to critical assets, and set a security strategy. More on this tool can be found at http://www.cert.org/octave/.

Risk Management Components

There are three components to risk management: risk assessment, risk mitigation, and evaluation and assurance.

Risk assessment is a process that has been broken into nine steps by some, including NIST publications. The nine steps discussed in NIST SP 80030 are as follows:

- **Step 1 – System Characterization –** Here the ISSMP gains a full understanding of the system (e.g., mission, key players, interconnections, boundaries, etc.), as discussed in the first section of this chapter. The information can be collected using questionnaires, interviews, automated analysis tools, and by conducting document reviews.

  Output from Step 1 – Detailed System Description

- **Step 2 – Threat Identification –** The goal here is to identify all the threats that can potentially attack the system.

  Output from Step 2 – List of Threats

- **Step 3 – *Vulnerability Identification* –** Just like the previous step, the goal is to identify all the vulnerabilities related to the system. These can be obtained from audit and incident reports, testing results, CERT and vendor advisor notices, NIST ICAT vulnerability database (http://icat.nist.gov), etc.

Output from Step 3 – *List of Vulnerabilities*

- **Step 4 – *Control Analysis* –** In this step, the ISSMP identifies all of the system's current and planned Management, Operational, and Technical security controls.

Output from Step 4 – *List of Controls*

- **Step 5 – *Likelihood Determination* –** Using the results of the last three steps, determine the likelihood that a threat would exercise a system vulnerability considering the effectiveness of the current controls. Try to identify these either quantitatively or qualitatively (more will be discussed later in the chapter on why one should be used over another in specific circumstances). Any quantitative method can be used (there are various tools that can be used for calculating risk that also will be discussed later in this chapter). Create a likelihood rating of High, Medium, or Low using the following guidance:
  - ¤ **High** – The threat source is highly motivated and sufficiently capable, and current controls to prevent the vulnerability from being exercised are ineffective.
  - ¤ **Medium** – The threat source is motivated and capable, but controls are in place that may impede successful exercise of the vulnerability.
  - ¤ **Low** – The threat source lacks motivation or capability, or controls are in place to prevent, or at least significantly impede, the vulnerability from being exercised.

Output from Step 5 – *List of Likelihood Ratings*

- **Step 6 – *Impact Analysis* –** In this step, the ISSMP determines the adverse impact resulting from a threat exercising a specific vulnerability. What would be the effect if the system lost integrity, availability, or confidentiality functional capabilities? Several sources will help the ISSMP determine the impact, such as the system's description from Step 1, the organization's business impact analysis (BIA) documents, and the system's business owner. Remember to take into consideration other factors, such as frequency of the attack, cost of an attack, and so forth. Also try to identify these in a quantitative or qualitative manner. Remember that whatever method you used in the previous step should be used in this step because the next step will need uniform results. A method of determining a quantitative impact is again by using High, Medium, and Low ratings, as follows:
  - ¤ **High -** when exercising the vulnerability (1) may result in the very costly loss of major tangible assets or resources; (2) may significantly violate, harm, or impede an organization's mission, reputation, or interest; or (3) may result in human death or serious injury.
  - ¤ **Medium -** when exercising the vulnerability (1) may result in the costly loss of tangible assets or resources; (2) may violate, harm, or impede an organization's mission, reputation, or interest; or (3) may result in human injury.
  - ¤ **Low -** when exercising the vulnerability (1) may result in the loss of some tangible assets or resources or (2) may noticeably affect an organization's mission, reputation, or interest.

Output from Step 6 – *List of Impacts*

- ***Step 7 – Risk Determination –*** The ISSMP identifies the level of risks to the organization for each viable threat/vulnerability pair by taking the results of the last two steps and creating a risk matrix with likelihood on the vertical and impact on the horizontal. As shown in *Table 1.6*, this analysis can be done quantitatively (shown as Likelihood [0.1–1.0] and Impact Rating [1–100]) and qualitatively (High, Medium, and Low). Examples are provided in *Figure 1.6*. It is highly recommended that a group consisting of the ISSMP, key system personnel (business owner, information system security officer [ISSO], etc.), and a corporate risk analyst decide on the overall scheme. The group in a collaborative effort should also identify individual values for the impacts and likelihoods. It is also highly recommended that the ISSMP ensure that a short justification is identified and documented for each agreed upon value. This will help in providing verbal and written explanations and justifications during future reviews and budget proposals.

No.	Action	Description	Why?
0	Purpose/Contact	Identify if the presentation or paper is to provide information or get a decision	So audience knows what is expected from them from the beginning
1	Problem/Issue	Present one problem or issue to focus on so they can absorb the information or make a quick decision	Presenting multiple items frequently confuses the audience
2	To the Audience	Know your audience and create the presentation or paper to the audience's level of knowledge and needs	You always sell someone on THEIR needs or goals, NOT yours
3	Options	In presentations to senior management, always give three options – one can be "to do nothing" – and a recommendation	The job is to make decisions, so they need options to make decisions
4	Slides/Actions	Only use four slides in a presentation and four actions on one page – Purpose – Problem – Options – Recommendation	Keeps a presentation simple, clear, and quick Easy to read one page
5	Minutes	Give the four-slide presentation or write the one-page paper, so they can process the situation in five minutes	Senior management has very busy schedules, so be quick and respectful

Table 1.6 – 0–5 Approach description

An example of how these would be used is if the quantitative likelihood and impact ratings were determined to be 0.4 and 15, the end result would be 6, so the resulting risk would be rated "Low." But if the quantitative likelihood and impact rating were determined to be 0.5 and 40, then the risk would be rated as "Moderate." As can be seen, a lot depends on the impact. If the qualitative impact and likelihood rating were both considered Moderate, the resulting risk would be "Moderate."

Quantitative

Impact / Likelihood	1–10	11–50	51–100
0.6–1.0	0.6–10	6.6–50	31–100
0.2–0.5	0.2–5	2.2–25	10.2–50
0.0–0.1	0–1	0–5	0–10

Low = 0–10
Medium = >10–50
High = >50–100

Qualitative

Impact / Likelihood	Low	Medium	High
High	Low	Medium	High
Medium	Low	Medium	Medium
Low	Low	Low	Low

These are general results. With sound justifications and group consensus, results can be changed.

Figure 1.5 – **Examples of Quantitative and Qualitative Risk Matrixes**

This is one way to do this analysis. There are other ways, like the method discussed in AS/NZ 4360, which provides a similar but different matrix to determine risk management priorities by weighing both the impact (consequence) with a rating of 1-5 and likelihood with a rating from almost certain to rare (see *Figure 1.6*). In this scheme, the first risks that should be mitigated are the ones that fall into the extreme risk category.

Output from Step 7 – Prioritized List of System Security Risks

	Consequence				
	Insignificant	**Minor**	**Moderate**	**Major**	**Catastrophic**
Likelihood	**1**	**2**	**3**	**4**	**5**
A (Almost Certain)	H	H	E	E	E
B (Likely)	M	H	H	E	E
C (Possible)	L	M	H	E	E
D (Unlikely)	L	L	M	H	E
E (Rare)	L	L	M	H	H

E	**Extreme Risk:** Immediate action required to mitigate the risk or decide to not proceed
H	**High Risk:** Action should be taken to compensate for the risk
M	**Moderate Risk:** Action should be taken to monitor the risk
L	**Low Risk:** Routine acceptance of the risk

*Figure 1.6 – **AS/NZ 4360 Risk Matrix***

- **Step 8 – Control Recommendations –** With the output of the previous step, the group will review potential controls to reduce the risks to an acceptable level. A cost benefit analysis should be conducted on all recommended controls to demonstrate that the cost of implementing the control is justified by the reduction in the level of risk.

  Output from Step 8 – Recommended Risk Mitigating Controls

- **Step 9 – Results Documentation –** Finally, the ISSMP must document the result of the risk assessment by creating a management report and a presentation for management with a list of risks and recommendations.

  Output from Step 9 – Risk Assessment Report or Report on Risk and Presentation

> **Key Question –** Which is the best to use – qualitative or quantitative?
>
> **Answer –** The one most understood by the organization's management.

Risk mitigation is the second part of risk management. This is where senior management uses the results of the above reports to prioritize, evaluate, and approve which recommendations will be implemented from the risk assessment report. Because the elimination of all risks is often impractical or close to impossible, it is the responsibility of senior management and functional and business managers to use the most cost effective approach based on reducing risk to an acceptable level.

What level of risk will be acceptable is how the organization responds to the risk assessment recommendations, e.g., are there any acceptable options open to management? Their decision depends on management's "risk appetite" or willingness to accept risk. The general mitigation options that are open to management are as follows:

- **Risk Assumption** – To assume the risk identified and not implement any additional controls.
- **Risk Avoidance** – To stop doing the action that is causing the risk, like allowing employees to take sensitive information home to work on over the weekend.
- **Risk Limitation** – To implement controls that would limit the exposure to the threat, like deploying encryption to ensure files are encrypted when not being accessed by employees.
- **Risk Planning** – To be prepared so that when an incident occurs there is an incident response and contingency plan to respond and recover from the incident.
- **Risk Transference** – To have another organization accept some or all of the risk. The most common way to do this is to take out an insurance policy. In some cases, organizations have transferred risk by outsourcing the control. By outsourcing the control, the organization can hold someone else liable for failures.
- **Research and Acknowledgment** – To accept the risk due to the fact that there are no acceptable solutions available at the time and continue to conduct research for an appropriate, cost effective control.

Sometimes these steps are instead broken into a four step process:

1. **Assume, Accept, and Acknowledge** – Acknowledging that a particular risk exists and is real, accepting responsibility to address it.
2. **Transfer** – Transferring responsibility to the appropriate parties within the organization to address the risk.
3. **Reduce Exposure via Controls** – Take action to reduce the likelihood of the risk becoming a real problem and reducing the exposure if it does.
4. **Avoidance for the Future** – Make changes to the security program to prevent the risk from recurring in the future, or to reduce the likelihood that it will recur.

Whatever the response is, the risks will have to be continuously reviewed and monitored to maintain the security of the system to an acceptable level, which leads to part three of the Risk Management components.

Evaluation and Assurance

Risk assessments are not just done at the beginning of the information system's lifecycle; they must be done throughout the lifecycle of the system to ensure that the level of risk is monitored and corrective actions are taken. Conducting a risk assessment should be done on an event basis and a time basis:

- **Event Basis** – The risk assessment is conducted when significant changes occur to the system, environment (e.g., physical, threat, vulnerabilities, personnel, etc.), business, mission, competition, and so forth. The significant change does not have to be something that requires more security; it could be something that downsizes the need for security. Remember, security is supposed to be cost effective. Retaining a costly security measure that is no longer required is not in the best interest of the organization. Also, the risk assessment could be a full assessment as described above or a subset, depending on the extent of the change.

■ **Time Basis –** It is good to do a periodic risk assessment just to ensure that changes have not been overlooked. Many compliance regulations also require that risk assessments be conducted and documented for this reason. Most require one to be conducted once a year.

The Risk Management Framework (RMF) provided in the initial release of NIST 80037 is represented in *Figure 1.7*, which puts the RMF in perspective with respect to the SDLC and the nine steps discussed previously.

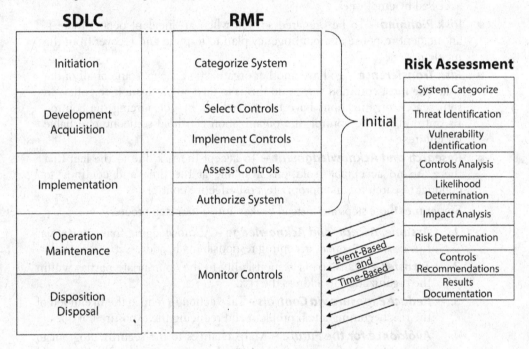

Figure 1.7 – **Risk Management Framework**

The key to conducting continuous risk assessments is how to report the results to senior management. It is recommended that this also be conducted as events occur on the system and in the media and conducted on a periodic basis, preferably timed with an important action, like a budget submission, regulatory report, senior management review, and so forth. More on how to provide reports will be discussed later.

Assurances are those activities that provide management with the confidence that something is providing or will provide the security that is expected. Assurances can be gained by review, audit, evaluation, certification and contract, and other methods. This activity provides due diligence.

The perfect examples of the first two, review and audit, are conducting periodic risk assessments (the time-based risk assessments mentioned above) or having audits conducted on the system and organization.

Evaluation and certification can provide assurance for solutions and services. To gain assurance that security products will be working in accordance with marketing literature, the government created the Common Criteria Evaluations. Product vendors pay Common Criteria Testing Laboratories (CCTLs), which are approved and licensed by NIST, to evaluate their security products against Product Protection Profiles in order to gain a Common Criteria certificate. The certificate, with the associated validation report, confirms that an IT product or protection profile has been evaluated at an accredited laboratory using the Common Evaluation Methodology for conformance to the Common Criteria. The National Information Assurance Partnership Common Criteria Evaluation and Validation Scheme (CCEVS), which is managed and staffed by the National Security Agency (NSA), issues the certificate in the United States. More can be found on Common Criteria at http://www.niapccevs.org/ccscheme/.

To gain some assurance that a company can provide developing products and services to its clients, Carnegie Mellon's Software Engineering Institute (SEI) created a process improvement approach, CMMI (Capability Maturity Model Integration, *Figure 1.8*). Similar to the Common Criteria concept, CMMI provides organizations with the essential elements of effective processes and provides customers with an understanding of the maturity of an organization's ability to provide quality of services and products. As organizations grow, they should be improving and formalizing the processes in the company by learning from past efforts and instituting changes that increase the quality of their output and the effectiveness of their processes. As time moves on, these review and change processes become institutionalized and the reviews become less qualitative and more quantitative (measurable metrics) based, thus improving on the fine-tuning and timely analysis of the metrics in support of the improvement processes.

0	1	2	3	4	5
Not Performed	Performed Internally	Planned and Tracked	Well Defined	Quantitatively Controlled	Continuously Improving
	Base Practices Performed	• Committed to Perform • Planning	Defining a Standard Process	Establishing Measurable Goals	Establishing Quantitative Process Effectiveness
		• Performance • Tracking Performance • Verifying Performance	• Tailoring the Standard • Using Data • Performing the Defined Process	• Determining Process Capabilities to Achieve Goals • Objectively Managing Performance	Improve Process Effectiveness

*Figure 1.8 – **SEI-CMMI Scale***

Appraisals are conducted to evaluate an organization's processes to determine how they conform to the CMMI requirements, which are defined in the Appraisal Requirements for CMMI (ARC) document. The appraisals focus on identifying improvement opportunities and comparing the organization's processes to CMMI best practices. Appraisal teams use a CMMI model and ARCconformant appraisal method to guide their evaluation of the organization and their reporting of conclusions. The appraisal results are used (e.g., by a process group) to plan improvements for the organization and provide their clients with a level of assurance.

(Source – Software Engineering Institute, A Systems Engineering Capability Maturity Model [SECMM] Version 1.1, SECMM9501, SEI, Carnegie Mellon University, Pittsburgh, 1995. Also see CMMI® for Development, Version 1.3, for further info).

Procedures and Processes

CMMI evaluates an organization on the maturity of its procedures and processes because no matter how great the company's technology and environment are, limited or ineffective procedures and processes impact how successful an organization will be. The same applies to the success of an IT security program. The best encryption, anti-virus, access control, and firewalls will soon become vulnerabilities unless the proper product updates and patches are applied, operators are trained, physical security controls protect them, audits are conducted, and deficiencies are corrected.

In all of the documents identified above that provide lists of controls that should be applied to systems, almost all of the controls are or require specific procedures and processes to ensure security is maintained. Some examples are:

- Visitors are required to go through a check-in process, there are procedures for visitor control in the facility, and visitor logs are maintained in highvalue environments.
- Access controls require that the Access Control Lists (ACLs) be reviewed periodically against the list of employees and that the specific permission per individual be validated.
- Contingency plans and emergency response plans must be exercised on a quarterly or annual basis, and employees must be trained on the procedures and their responsibilities.
- Background and drug checks are conducted on new hires, and new hires must be trained, tested, and read and sign a Rules of Behavior document prior to being given a new IT responsibility or account.
- Maintenance must be conducted on the system components and supporting systems (e.g., UPS, emergency power generator, air conditioning, fire suppression, monitoring systems, etc.).

The process for conducting annual risk assessments evaluates whether the current threats, vulnerabilities, and controls status still represents an acceptable risk to management. Procedures and processes are critical to ensuring the systems remain secure.

Outsourcing provides another example of how the concept of assurance can be applied. Frequently, organizations find that money can be saved by outsourcing functions to professional organizations, like security monitoring, maintenance, auditing, personnel augmentation, off-site backup or storage, and so forth. Prior to procuring and implementing these services, the organization must take actions that will provide it with an assurance that the provider's integrity and operations do not add additional risk to the organization. In other words, the organization must exercise due diligence. These actions should include the following:

- **Approval** – Senior officials determine whether outsourcing is consistent with the organization's goals and objectives and is an acceptable risk.
- **Background Checks** – Contact all references provided by the provider, business, and client. Conduct a review of publicly available information on any criminal, financial, and legal actions related to the provider. This review should include a review of the provider's Dun and Bradstreet reports.

- **Financial Reviews** – Review the provider's financial statements to determine the provider's fiscal strength. For public companies, be sure to include the provider's reports to the Securities and Exchange Commission (SEC).
- **Site Reviews** – Conduct an initial and periodic review of the provider's operations to ensure that the personnel are knowledgeable and the capabilities are operational.
- **Business or Liability Insurance** – Check if the provider has business or liability insurance to cover matters like errors and omissions, property and casualty losses, and fraud and dishonesty. Also, check if the organization will have to take on similar insurance due to the potential of taking on additional liability when outsourcing.
- **Contract** – Contractually require that providers implement specific security protection measures, report violations to the organization on a timely basis, and allow for periodic audits of the protection measures. Additionally, consideration should be given to the outsourcer's business partners should they process, handle, or transmit any or all of the organization's data.
- **Legal Reviews** – The organization's attorneys should review all contracts and ensure that the rights and responsibilities of both parties are clear and in the best interest of the organization.

All of the above provide increased assurance that outsourcing with a specific provider will have a high potential to be a successful, low risk alternative for the system.

Service Level Agreement Key Performance Indicators

As was alluded to in several prior sections, metrics must be established against which to check various aspects of security performance; without clearly defined metrics against which to measure, there simply is no way to determine how successful a security program actually is. There is no way to answer the fundamental question: Has the security program reduced risk exposure over time, and, if so, by how much?

Because each and every organization has its unique set of information-related risks and tolerance for those risks, Key Performance Indicators (KPIs) for measuring the success of security programs and their components vary across organizations.

Key Performance Indicators are essentially a form of performance measurement used to evaluate the success (or lack of success) of a particular activity. In business, they are often industry-standard measures of performance; for example, in the retail sector, a common KPI is year-over-year same-store-sales. In the case of information security, multiple types of indicators are often used to evaluate the performance of the security program: Some are qualitative (that is something that can be measured with a number), and some are qualitative (meaning that it is not simple to describe them using a number and that they must be converted to a measureable metric if one wants to measure them).

Of course, not every metric used in an organization is as important as others. KPIs measure the most important elements, using measurements that truly underscore whether something is working or not.

It is fair to say, therefore, all Key Performance Indicators are metrics, but not all metrics are Key Performance Indicators.

Some examples of Key Performance Indicators might include: Number of known major security incidents (where such a term is defined), ratio of the cost of the security program to the value of the assets the program is designed to protect, number of security-related downtimes per year, the total cumulative duration of downtimes over the past 3 months caused by security incidents, number of security vulnerabilities and other deficiencies identified during testing, etc.

Although executives must be involved in the process and provide ultimate "sign off," the ISSMP is a likely candidate for the team that will establish what the security KPIs are for a particular organization or unit within an organization. KPIs should be established based on the organization's business goals and acceptable levels of risk; sometimes they may require perfect performance for an effort to be considered successful, while in other cases various imperfect levels may be deemed adequate. For example, an organization may want to have zero cases of unauthorized access into its internal network but may be willing to have 1% of its transactions reversed as fraudulent. An organization may be unwilling to have a single virus on a mission-critical network but may consider it a success if its employees make two or fewer inappropriate social media posts during a 12 month period provided that the posts were also removed within 5 minutes of their having been made.

The point of measuring is not simply to generate numbers but to manage security more effectively. Measurements can tell the ISSMP if security or various components of the security program are adequate or insufficient, if security is remaining the same, improving, or worsening.

Periodically, consistently, and at scheduled intervals, therefore, measurements should be taken for the Key Performance Indicators. As was the case with training as described earlier, adjustments to the security program should be made based on the information garnered from the collection of this data. If particular areas of the security program are determined to be weak, for example, adequate and appropriate resources should be dedicated to improving them. Measuring can also help establish priorities for future actions.

Furthermore, if the metrics used are industry standard, comparisons can sometimes be made with other organizations' performance (when such information is available) to help determine how well the organization is doing vis-à-vis security as it exists in the real world. It makes a big difference, for example, if company X has suffered two successful Denial of Service attacks in the course of a year if all of its competitors suffered twenty such attacks versus if they suffered none. Likewise, if all firms in an industry group seem to be achieving proper security, but one firm is achieving that goal at a much lower Security-to-Value ratio, that information is highly pertinent in establishing proper goals going forward.

When one is outsourcing security or support (i.e., component maintenance or replacement, offsite alternative processing capability, offsite storage facility), the best practice is to document all the system's needs in a legally binding document called a service level agreement (SLA).

SLAs will be required for an offsite processing or storage facility, vendor maintenance, emergency transporting of people, components, and data, staff augmentation, and communications. At a minimum, SLAs should contain the following information:

- Cost/fee structure (e.g., usage, administration, maintenance, transportation, storage, utilities, preparation, payment schedules) and cost of additional services
- Reservation process and site availability expectations
- IT system requirements, including data and telecommunication requirements, for hardware, software, and any special system needs (hardware and software)
- Security, e.g., sensors, alarms, guards, vaults
- Facility environmental capabilities, e.g., parking, lighting, temperature, humidity, fire suppression, power, water, bathrooms
- IT system service, e.g., maintenance, replacement, response time, point of contact information
- Workspace, e.g., chairs, desks, telephone, PCs
- Supplies provided/not provided, e.g., maintenance tools, paper, pens, folders
- SLA modification, termination, and extension process

SLAs are developed and put into place prior to the deployment of an IT system. During an incident, there is no time to think about negotiating an SLA. More about metrics can be found in NIST SP 800-55.

Interconnections

The majority of IT systems are not standalone systems; they support or require the support of other systems for communications paths, processing, or data. When connecting two systems together, one must consider several things, and they all relate to the security objectives – availability, integrity, and confidentially. Interoperability of communications, protocols, authentication methods, data schema, crypto algorithms and key management, labeling standards, and outages and incident response notification procedures are just a few technical items that will have to be resolved, agreed upon, and documented.

Like outsourcing and developing SLAs, interconnecting to other internal or external systems must be formally agreed upon and documented in a document similar to the SLA – the interconnect service agreement (ISA). The ISA must be in place prior to the systems being connected.

The ISA will contain all the information related to both systems and answer the what, why, how, and who of the connection. Specifically, items like the following:

- Statement of the requirements for interconnecting the two systems
- Description of the systems and their points of contact
- Services offered by the systems (passing of the information to other systems, storage, processing the information, distribution)
- General information description and sensitivity
- Criteria for allowing access to the information
- Security specifics, e.g., who can see information, security requirements, what type of crypto will be used, protection requirements for paper and stored media, loss or compromised data reporting
- Procedures for emergency disconnecting and reconnecting the systems

Most times, they share sensitive data with each other, in which case the owner of the sensitive data will want the receiving systems to protect the data appropriately. Operations can require that the information or the capabilities of another system have a high degree of availability to ensure operations can successfully accomplish their functions. Recently, a commercial system was being provided patient information from a hospital so they could distribute medical supplies to the patients. The hospital required that the commercial system protect the information with NIST approved cryptography and have their system certified by a third-party certifier prior to closing the services contract and shipping them any patient information. All of these requirements were clearly spelled out in the contract for services.

It is critical that both parties have a thorough and legal understanding of each other's expectations and requirements prior to connecting.

Budgeting for Security

Information-security services and products are not free, and organizational funds are not unlimited, so the ISSMP needs to understand various financial aspects and responsibilities associated with managing security.

There is a finite amount of money available from which to establish and maintain security. Hence, the ISSMP needs to take dollars and cents into account. Security budgets must be established, "sold" to management (often to the CFO), and authorized/approved by, or obtained from, management. Such budgets should be initially created containing enough funds to appropriately implement security as the ISSMP believes is necessary based on the KPIs discussed above. Often, management will "push back" and request that the ISSMP make do with less. It is important that before accepting such cuts, the ISSMP perform a thorough check to determine if the proposed cuts will impact his or her ability to implement adequate security. Any area that will suffer due to the cuts must be clearly explained in revised budget documents and communicated to management. Ultimately, both managing financial resources and ensuring security are management's responsibility, so if sacrifices must be made it must be management that decides what they will be; the role of the ISSMP is to ensure that management has all of the pertinent information to make an educated decision. In most cases, in which firms are not under terrible financial pressure, management will want the ISSMP to determine and then demonstrate to management that sufficient security (as determined by the KPIs discussed above) can be achieved on the reduced budget that they are willing to approve. The ISSMP must then perform various adjustments and analyze if that is the case. He or she must then communicate with management on this matter. If, however, the ISSMP determines that with the reduced budget, security will be at unacceptable levels of risk, he or she must alert management of the potential impact of the cuts.

In nearly every organization, there will be gaps between the "most perfect" plan for security and the plan that the business is willing to implement; not every "wish and want" that the ISSMP may have will actually be able to be paid for and implemented. The ISSMP must evaluate not only which particular items or services can be purchased but which projects are worthwhile to undertake; it is silly to pursue a security project that will cost valuable money, for example, if the compromises that must be made in order to keep that project under budget will undermine the effectiveness of the project to a point that it will no longer improve security or even create the perception of security.

It should be noted that certain risks may simply be too costly for a particular organization to address properly, and a "let's do what we can and hope for the best" approach may be taken by management – to the ISSMP's chagrin. Such scenarios must also be dealt with by the ISSMP: He or she must communicate what risks persist if the security budget is constrained as such by management, and he or she should, therefore, also communicate and justify any requests for increases in financial backing for IT security over what management has in mind.

Because there is more awareness today of the importance of cybersecurity, "selling" IT security budgets to management is easier than it was a decade ago. At the same time, however, security is not a profit center for businesses (it does not generate revenue) and, as such, there is often pushback when it comes to spending. Ultimately, CEOs and Boards are focused on the bottom line and net income, not on security, which often leads to pressure to cut costs, especially in areas in which greater spending does not lead to enhanced revenue or improved profit margins. Security budgets are often set by the CFO of an organization (or by someone in an equivalent role) based on input from the CIO, CSO, and CISO (or their equivalents), but all of these people ultimately report to the CEO and need to justify their budgets.

It is imperative, therefore, that any presentations or documents created to request funds for a security budget must present a clear explanation as to the benefits to the organization that the spending will produce. Quantifying risk may be difficult, but doing so can greatly enhance the chances that a budget (or budget item) will be approved. Backing up any figures with sound arguments is important so as not to discredit the numbers utilized in the request.

For example, if a particular technology that the ISSMP wishes to utilize to improve the organization's defenses against malware will cost $100,000 on an annual basis, and it is estimated that the damage that the new technology would protect against would otherwise cost the organization $250,000 in damage per year (in terms of the calculated value of man hours lost, in addition to any frustration, morale issues, and reputational damage) including that information in the budget proposal can help convince management to approve the entire spending amount.

In cases in which no damage has yet occurred to the organization from a particular threat, and a purely proactive approach has been taken (as is obviously preferred from a security standpoint, but, in which case, getting budget approval is not always as easy), information garnered from industry analysts, media articles (from reputable media outlets), etc. can be of great assistance. For example, if a competitor suffered a public-relations nightmare and a 1% stock price drop as a result of one of its employees compromising a future product campaign by leaking confidential information via social media, including pertinent information from media and analysts about the incident, and showing as much quantitative information as is publicly available about the cost of the resulting damage, it may help convince those responsible for establishing and approving budgets to allocate funds for a social media security system. Simply requesting such a system without the supporting information may not be as effective.

The ISSMP must also understand the true total cost of initiatives and budget accordingly. Implementing a technology may involve not only license fees but integration fees, consulting fees, maintenance fees, annual license fees, and all sorts of other financial outlays. Some costs may be overt (a few that must be paid to a vendor, for example, while others may be less simple to identify such as the need for a person to dedicate more time). Various systems may require additional spending for infrastructure needed to support technical countermeasures (e.g., upgraded networking equipment), and the need to add staff may also arise. Hence, the Total Cost of Ownership should be taken into account in all budget-related discussions, proposals, and approvals.

In the end, in many cases, as part of the budgeting process, the ISSMP will need to prioritize, ensuring that the most important security initiatives are pursued, and that others are delayed or cancelled.

It is important to understand that organizational budgets are impacted – sometimes dramatically – by both the prevailing macroeconomic climate as well as by industry-specific situations. During the recession of 2008 and 2009, for example, there was significant pressure on many information security managers to reduce spending, regardless of whether threat levels were increasing or not. Likewise, firms whose primary target industry for customers was the hard-hit financial sector exerted tremendous pressure on their technology departments to cut spending due to expected drops in sales revenue.

Likewise, the ISSMP should realize that not all expenses are equal under the tax code, and, as such, CFOs may prefer certain types of expenditures over others. Some technologies and products, for example, may need to be depreciated over time – meaning that if they are purchased in a particular year, their cost must be gradually recognized over a period of years, not deducted entirely in the year of the purchase.

As such, the ISSMP must be able to create a budget, prioritize spending, and manage finances accordingly. It is a good idea to maintain a good working relationship with the parties ultimately responsible for the security budget and to keep them apprised of major milestones as well as, at a high level, industry trends. Informal conversations in a less pressured environment than budget meetings can prove helpful. Remember, budgets are set by human beings, and people work better with people whom they like and trust than with others.

Part of budgeting is understanding how many people are necessary to perform certain tasks and to implement the security program in general. Budgets often reference the number of Full Time Equivalents (FTE), which is a measurement of how many people are necessary for a particular task or unit, measured in the number of full-time workloads that the task will take. A project that requires 4 FTEs, for example, could theoretically be staffed by 4 workers working full time or 8 workers working half time. Reality states, however, that there are significant deviations due to human shortcomings: Learning curves, communication needs, etc. render FTEs only approximations; on a small project that requires 4 FTEs for a week, for example, 400 workers working 1/100 the time are unlikely to deliver the same result as 4 workers working full time. So, while FTEs are useful for budgeting, they serve only as a guide for actual hiring. The ISSMP must leverage his or her expertise to determine the nature of the positions that must be filled in order to achieve a specific task and figure out how many workers he or she needs as a result.

By the time someone has earned an ISSMP credential, he or she should have enough years of experience in the real world to have a good "feeling" (based on experience) about how much time is necessary for various information security related tasks. It is important to keep in mind that human beings are not productive 100% of the time; in fact, studies show that even the most productive of people often perform at less than maximum productivity for the majority of the day. Pushing people (to work too many hours, to work without breaks, not to take vacations, etc.) can reduce productivity and morale. In some cases, doing so may even violate contracts or laws. Hence, when calculating the number of people needed for a task, "real life" must be accounted for.

Budgeting is a complicated process, and it is beyond the scope of this book to discuss it in full detail. It is suggested that an ISSMP read at least one of the many books on the subject.

After any information system's security assessment, the ISSMP must identify options as to how to reduce the residual risk by identifying, evaluating, and recommending security controls. Depending on the level of individual residual risk, the ISSMP should identify several options for each risk. To save the ISSMP some time in researching options for all the residual risks, it is recommended that the ISSMP request guidance from senior management on what will be funded. In some organizations, senior management has established policy that states security issues with low risk levels are acceptable and will not be corrected. In others, the policy is that any issues related to "software updates" and "configuration management" will be a high priority and corrected as soon as possible because without these fundamental controls, existing safeguards may become ineffective or vulnerable.

Several other things need to be kept in mind when attempting to identify potential controls:

- Not all solutions are technical. Not all solutions cost money. Question the basic cause of the risk.
- Multiple risk areas may be reduced using one security solution. Some security solutions can cause more vulnerabilities.
- One option is to do nothing (i.e., accept the risk).

All of the above are obvious, except for "Question the basic cause of the risk." Sometimes the system retains a capability that is not required to support the current mission but is the cause of a residual risk to the system. A perfect example of this is when a network is connected to the Internet and there is no business requirement supporting the connection. Why would an organization spend $50,000 to $200,000 procuring and supporting a firewall and connection, and accepting the increased vulnerability to Internet threats and potential legal liabilities when there is no requirement for an Internet connection? Some organizations may see an Internet connection as being in the best interest of maintaining employee morale because it allows the employees to use the Internet for personal searches and email. In that case, the organization may find it to be less expensive and risky if the organization paid for the employees' Internet connections at their homes. This would remove the high cost of the security controls, connections, and risks related to the Internet connection and potential legal liabilities.

Cost benefit analysis or return on investment (ROI) is usually required for each option identified for management's review. There are many methods for calculating and conducting a cost benefit analysis to determine the ROI for a solution. One of the best methods is the annual loss expectancy (ALE) method. The ALE provides an estimated amount of damage (in monetary terms) that the organization can be expected to lose per year due to a risk. Using the ALE, the organization can calculate the ROI and justify spending funds for countermeasures to reduce the likelihood or impact of an incident. The following are examples of how this can be calculated:

■ **Virus ALE and ROI –** An organization with 100 employees produces $10,000 a day. Each employee has a computer connected to the network; the network is connected to the Internet. There are no anti-virus controls in place. The organization operates 200 days a year. The potential of having a virus incident on the network infecting all the computers is once a day. Recovery time for an incident is one day. What is the basic ALE and ROI for this risk?

ALE = Number of Potential Incidents/Year × Potential Loss/Incident × % Exposure

ALE = 200 Days/Year × 1 Incident/Day × $10,000/Day × 100% Vulnerable

ALE = $2,000,000/year

Cost of providing an anti-virus solution for the system is $40,000/year.

ROI = ALE/Cost of Countermeasure × 100%

ROI = $2,000,000/$40,000 × 100%

ROI = 5000%

■ **Spam ALE and ROI –** The same organization has no protection from email spam. The team identifies that on average each employee will receive 10 email spams each day, and it will take at least one minute to identify each as spam and delete the spam message. This results in 10 minutes per day of lower productivity for each employee. What is the basic ALE and ROI for this risk?

ALE = Number of Potential Incidents/Year × Potential Loss/Incident × % Exposure

ALE = 200 Days/Year × 10 Incidents/Day/Employee × (1 Working Minute/ Incident/480 Working Minutes/Day/Employee × $10,000/Day) × 100%Vulnerable

ALE = $42,000/year

Cost of providing a spam filter solution for the system is $25,000/year.

ROI = ALE/Cost of Countermeasure × 100%

ROI = $42,000/Year/$25,000 × 100%

ROI =170%

With this ROI data, the ISSMP has conducted a very effective cost benefit analysis for justifying the risk based security countermeasures. Remember, just like calculating risks, there are many ways to determine the ALE and ROIs using anywhere from two to many variables. Choosing which one to use is based on which one will be the most appealing to the organization's senior management.

Information System Security Cycles

Before moving on to discussing the organization's roles and responsibilities, the ISSMP must understand the overall concept of establishing, testing, approving, and monitoring the information system's security, so the roles and responsibilities can be put into perspective.

Once again, in the publications and practice, there are various methods, but basically all have the same components. The following is a generic approach to system certification and accreditation (C&A). See the accompanying graphic for a visual representation of the phases.

- **Initiation Phase** – Basically, all the actions described thus far in this chapter are done during this phase. These actions include identifying the organization's mission, goals, and objectives; describing the system components, boundaries, functions, and connections; determining and implementing the security controls that are necessary; and conducting an initial risk assessment. Then, identify the responsible individuals, and document all of these findings in a security plan.

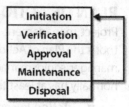

- **Verification Phase** – A comprehensive assessment of the management, operational, and technical security controls in an information system in support of system accreditation. This includes verifying that the controls identified in the security plan are implemented correctly, operating as intended, and producing the desired outcomes, and documenting the results in a formal document, i.e., a Security Assessment Report.

- **Approval Phase** – The actions taken to review the System Security Plan, Security Assessment Report, and Corrective Action Plan or Plan of Actions and Milestones (POA&M, see sidebar) are completed prior to a senior management official's approval of an information system for operation or for continued operation. This official is responsible for the information system's business function and supporting resources and is knowledgeable of the security status, including the security controls and risks, and for formally accepting the risk to the individuals and organization (including mission, assets, functions, image, and reputation).

- **Maintenance Phase** – Taking actions to ensure that the authorized configuration, security controls, and level of risk are maintained. The actions will include an active configuration management program, ensuring that all updates are implemented, risk assessments are continuously conducted, senior management is kept up to date on all changes to the security status, contingency and incident response plans are exercised, personnel are trained, and security awareness is maintained.

- **Disposal Phase** – This phase occurs when a determination is made that an information system is no longer required. Actions must be taken to ensure that the security of any residual information is protected and the permanent disruption of services is not a surprise to anyone. Information that must be retained for legal or regulatory purposes must be transported and archived in a secure location. In disposing of software, media, and hardware, one must take steps to ensure that inappropriate reuse of licenses does not occur and that storage media are sanitized. Discontinuing services to other elements and interconnections must be thoroughly coordinated in advance and during the disconnecting process.

Other system security cycles are suggested in various publications. They have similar phases, but in fact they are also similar in the actions that must be conducted to ensure that the security for an information system is correctly implemented, maintained, and disassembled. *Figure 1.9* provides several examples of these other cycles and how they relate to the one described above.

PLAN OF ACTION AND MILESTONES

Project management processes provide many tools that are useful to ISSMPs. One such tool is the Plan of Action and Milestones (POA&M). This is a spreadsheet used by the project manager, senior management, and financial personnel to track project actions. The POA&M normally has at least the following items in the columns:

- **Action** to correct a weakness or to support a mission or business need
- **Priority** of the action relative to the other actions in the POA&M
- **Point of Contact** for the individual who is responsible for completing the action
- **Resources Required** to pay for the activities and material to complete the action
- **Complete by Date** for the action
- **Milestones and Completion Dates** for major activities to complete the action
- **Source of Action**, e.g., exercise report, audit, testing, and so forth
- **Status** as of the date of the POA&M

The POA&M provides management with a list of prioritized actions that need to be accomplished and the status of each for planning and funding purposes. Also, the POA&M provides financial personnel and senior management with a prioritized list of actions that need to be funded to reduce the mission or business risks.

Information System Security Cycles

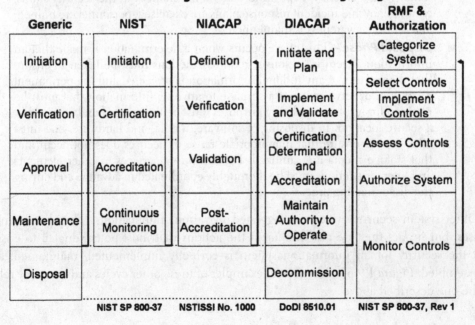

Generic	NIST	NIACAP	DIACAP	RMF & Authorization
Initiation	Initiation	Definition	Initiate and Plan	Categorize System
				Select Controls
Verification	Certification	Verification	Implement and Validate	Implement Controls
Approval	Accreditation	Validation	Certification Determination and Accreditation	Assess Controls
				Authorize System
Maintenance	Continuous Monitoring	Post-Accreditation	Maintain Authority to Operate	Monitor Controls
Disposal			Decommission	
	NIST SP 800-37	NSTISSI No. 1000	DoDI 8510.01	NIST SP 800-37, Rev 1

Figure 1.9 – Information System Security Cycles

Tofurther understand how the information system security cycles relate to the other cycles that have a heavy impact on the development, implementation, operations, and security of an information system, see *Figure 1.10*.

Of the many project management tools, POA&M is one that can be very important to an ISSMP because this tool provides a living record of the priority actions for improving the security of an information system. The POA&M is also a document recognized by project managers, management, and financial personnel as a list of actions that need to be funded to reduce the mission or business risks. In fact, under the Federal Information Security Management Act (FISMA), the Office of Management and Budget (OMB) is responsible for overseeing the management of all government IT systems and related security. In support of this responsibility, on a quarterly basis, all organizations submit their list of IT system security deficiencies and plans to correct them to the OMB in the form of a POA&M. The OMB uses these POA&Ms to track the deficiencies and the funding for correcting them. The OMB can track the funds because it is responsible for reviewing the government organizations' requests for funding prior to the president submitting the annual budget request to Congress for the allocation of funds for the next fiscal year.

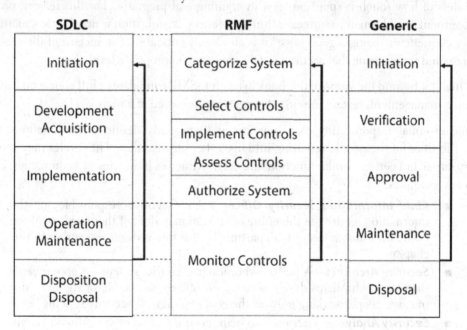

Figure 1.10 – **Development and Security Cycles**

Cycles, processes, and reports are all very effective tools, but as can be seen in the OMB/POA&M example, tools are only effective if individual roles and responsibilities are identified and monitored.

Managing the Security Organization

Sometimes people confuse management of the security organization with security management, but, in reality, management of the security organization encompasses far more than just security management.

Security management refers to the process of identifying all of an entity's assets and establishing and implementing security policies and procedures to protect those assets. Management of the security organization, on the other hand, refers to the management of the organization responsible for carrying out the mission of security management. This includes not only overseeing the creation of, and implementation of, the aforementioned security policies and procedures, but it also includes management of all of the resources necessary to achieve those aims.

The most important resource of any security organization is its people. The success of people, more than anything else, determines how successful the organization is going to be at implementing security. Efficient, smart, careful people can produce amazing results, while inadequately skilled personnel, or people who are sloppy or careless, can undermine security regardless of how much is spent on security training and programs. For this reason, proper management of all human resources within the security organization is not simply a matter of proper etiquette or "being a good boss;" it is absolutely critical for the success of the security program and for ensuring that security is delivered at an appropriate level.

While it is beyond the scope of this book to teach ISSMP candidates a full course on human resource management, several important aspects are discussed at a high level.

One essential responsibility of a manager is to properly define roles, functions, and responsibilities for the people reporting into his or her organization. These roles may vary by organization, but certain similar functions are pervasive across industries and companies. Here are a few examples:

- *Chief Information Security Officer* – An executive responsible for the information security of the entire organization and all of the people working in the information security department. This role is discussed earlier in this chapter.
- *Security Architect* – A person who designs security systems or components thereof, or who helps design security for other systems. He or she may also manage people working towards the goal of designing security systems.
- *Security Analyst* – A person who helps ensure that an organization is secure by analyzing systems, networks, equipment, etc. for possible weaknesses from a security standpoint and, if he/she finds issues, helps identify solutions to those problems. This person might be responsible for researching various security technologies to address vulnerabilities. Security analysts also assess the impact of breaches and other security incidents, and they play other analysis-type roles within the security process as needed by management.
- *Security Engineer* – A person who performs the technical aspects of security. This includes implementing technical solutions, monitoring, etc.

By establishing clear definitions as to what is expected from whom within an enterprise, staff members feel empowered and authorized to make decisions and take action, something that not only motivates them but also contributes to the effectiveness of the organization.

Clarity of roles also helps people understand where they fit within the larger organization, and it facilitates an understanding of how their actions contribute to the success of the overall enterprise. Furthermore, properly clarifying roles helps avoid disputes and misunderstandings, and it reduces the risk of inefficiencies caused by multiple people performing the same tasks or of "ball dropped" situations in which some important action is not taken because everyone thought that someone else was going to do it. It should be obvious that when it comes to security, preventing such an error is essential.

While there are different approaches taught in management classes as to the best method for defining roles and responsibilities, one simple method for the ISSMP running a security organization to do so is to start by writing down a list of all members of his or her team (the security organization) and in a second document compile a list of all of the roles and tasks for which the organization is responsible. After these two lists are complete, the ISSMP matches up people with roles. The information on the resulting chart is then translated into prose, which becomes the formal job descriptions, from which formal reporting structure charts and organization charts can be (and should be) created and disseminated to team members.

During this exercise, an ISSMP might notice that there are insufficient resources to carry out all of the responsibilities of the security organization, in which case he or she may need to request budget for more staff. He or she may also notice that there are too many people in which case cutbacks may be necessary (this seems to happen quite infrequently; cutbacks seem to happen far more often as a result of financial pressures than an oversupply of security resources as determined by the security managers).

Of course, management is also responsible for making sure the personnel within the department are properly trained, and that plans are in place for succession in case someone quits, is disabled, or dies. It is often wise to cross-train – that is, to make sure people within the department are trained to handle more than one role – in case of such scenarios.

Another essential part of management is performing performance appraisals, which are periodic, formal assessments of an employee's job performance and productivity as compared to certain pre-established criteria, which typically include not only tasks but also various other aspects of professionalism.

Entire books have been dedicated to the subject of performance appraisals, and the ISSMP who will manage people is highly encouraged to read some.

One critical concept that the ISSMP must consider is that the primary goal of performance appraisal is not to review employees but to improve their performance with constructive feedback, goal setting, and determination of what resources (e.g., training) could help an employee perform better.

At a high level, here are some important tips to know about performance appraisals:

1. Appraisals typically include information of two types:
   a. **Objective Measurements** – e.g., if a person has a quota of calls to make, did he or she make that number, did he or she deliver things on time, how many times was he or she late to work without calling in, etc.
   b. **Subjective Analysis** – Is the person showing dedication, how good a job did he or she do on unmeasurable tasks (how well written was a report), etc.

2. Some organizations formally solicit input from people's peers and reports for their appraisals, while others do not. It is important to avoid any possibility of people retaliating against someone by providing unfounded negative input to an appraisal.

3. At a performance appraisal, clear, measurable goals for the upcoming appraisal period should be established against which both objective measurements and subjective reviews can be done at the next performance appraisal.

4. While formal appraisals should be done at least annually, there should not be any negative "surprises" to an employee being appraised. If the employee is having issues, guidance should be provided at the time the issues arise.

5. Because performance appraisals are a sensitive subject, it is imperative that any new manager learn more about these before engaging in them.

As with all aspects of human resource management, it is important for the ISSMP to always keep in mind that he or she is dealing with people – people who may be dealing with personal successes or challenges, medical improvements or problems, wonderful new relationships or relationships falling apart, joyous occasions or devastating circumstances, or complex mixes of all of the above. Understanding and grace are always appropriate. The ISSMP should always treat others with at least the same level of respect as he or she would want to be given.

Roles and Responsibilities

Organizations have management structures to ensure that all elements work together to meet the organization's mission, goals, and objectives in the most effective and efficient manner possible. Management at all levels provides the leadership, planning, programming, oversight, and direction to ensure that activities are on time and on schedule. To maintain a successful organization, one must clearly communicate individual roles and responsibilities to the specific individuals in the roles and the rest of the individuals in and working with the organization (e.g., vendors, partners, clients, etc.).

As in so many other processes discussed in this chapter, there is no one best organizational structure for information system security. The correct organization should be derived from the inputs discussed during the initial reviews of the systems in the organization (e.g.., mission, culture, environment, professional, and so forth). ISSMPs may have little control over how the organization is structured, but they must have a firm grasp of the structure and which individuals and groups are responsible for resourcing, operating, managing, monitoring, and approving the information systems and providing all the other security controls, such as physical, environmental, personnel, and technical; even so, the ISSMP may influence decisions by making various recommendations to management.

Various documents identify potential positions with roles and responsibilities that are necessary to support the security for information systems. The tables for three of these are identified in *Figure 1.11*. The specifics for each can be found in the reference documents identified in the titles of each column.

NIST – SP 800-53	ISO – ISO/IEC 27002:2005	DoD – DODI-8500.2
Authorization Advocate	Board of Directors	Designated Approving Authority (DAA)
Authorizing Official/DAA	General Management – CEO/COO	Certifier and Certifying Team
Designated Representative	Chief Security Officer (CSO)	Program Manager
Chief Information Officer (CIO)	Chief Information Security Officer (CISO)	User Representative
Senior Agency Information Security Officer	Risk Management Officer	Intelligence Systems Support Office (ISSO)
Information Owner	Business Unit Security Officer	Developer, Integrator, or Maintainer
Information System Owner	Cybercrime Incident Response Team (CIRT)	
Program Manager		
Information System Security Officer (ISSO)		
User Representative		
Certification Agent		
Risk Analyst		

Figure 1.11 – **Various Security Organizational Models**

Analysis of the various roles in these models and others discloses a key set of five generic security roles that are necessary to ensure success in any information system security program. These are senior management, approving authority, verification entity, system owner, and user representative, who may correspond to one or more of the roles in the aforementioned table.

1. **Senior Management** – Senior management refers to the individual or individuals who have the vision, responsibility, and authority for setting and leading the organization toward meeting its mission, goals, and objectives. These people have the legal responsibility for ensuring that the organization is successful, the safety of employees and products, and that all actions are ethical and compliant with the appropriate laws and regulations.

2. **Approving Authority** – The Approving Authority conducts the business security risk assessment of the system and formally approves the operational use of the system. This individual must be a senior employee of the organization, formally assigned the responsibility and authority for reviewing and approving information systems with all of their associated risks for operations. To have the appropriate authority, the Approving Authority must have adequate influence over both the business operations and resources to make balanced cost benefit, mission analysis–risk determination on the acceptability of the residual system's security risks.

3. **Verification Entity –** This is a person or group that takes actions to verify that what is documented in the approved system security plan is what is being done in the operations of the system. This is done by:

   a. Conducting reviews of documents, such as compliance regulation and directives, security plans, operations manuals, audit logs, and journals

   b. Interviewing personnel

   c. Testing (system mappings, vulnerability scans, penetration and social engineering tests, etc.)

   d. Onsite inspections

Separation of duties is important to ensure that the parties doing the verifying are not the same parties who implemented the system because a clear conflict of interest might exist in such a scenario, and there is also the risk that someone with nefarious intentions might be able to hide his or her actions if he or she can both carry out damaging actions and also "verify" that they were not done.

Throughout, the Verification Entity reports to the Approving Authority and system owner, identifying vulnerabilities and noncompliance issues in the system and potential options for correcting the same. A document detailing these matters is typically called the security assessment report.

1. **System Owner –** Of all the individuals in an organization responsible for security, the system owner is responsible for a great majority of the actions. This person is responsible for everything from developing, implementing, managing, manning, training, educating, resourcing, operating, maintaining, monitoring, exercising, assessing, and reporting, to correcting the information system's security on a daily basis. This individual is responsible for developing and maintaining all of the key security documents, including the system's security, contingency, incident response, patch management, configuration management, POA&M, and budget plans. Additionally, the system owner must report the security status, issues, and risk to senior management.

2. **User Representative –** The users are one of the main keys to the success of any security program. The user representative ensures that concerns including mission, cultural, frontline operational, environmental, and user acceptability are included in any system security solution. Additionally, they become the conduit for communications between management and the user com munity to facilitate security promotion to the users and provide alternative solutions back to management.

All of these vary in title and description of duties from one organization to another. Examples of these are:

- **Senior Management –** Can serve as a member of the Board of Directors, who are ultimately responsible for the overall health of the enterprise, or the General Managers in officer level positions (like CEO and COO), who are responsible for daily decision making and the infusion of values and culture throughout the organization. Senior management must establish that security is a non-negotiable, essential component of business activity

- **Approving Authority –** In some financial organizations this is the Chief Financial Officer (CFO); in other organizations it is the newly designated CSO; but in the majority of cases it is the CIO.

■ **Verification Entity -** Has been one or a combination of internal and external audit and information system security professional functions, sometimes called the Inspector General, Auditing, Compliance, Certifier, or Certification Agent/ Group.

■ **System Owner –** Is the person who is in charge overall of directly managing the information system's operations and is called by a variety of titles in different organizations or during different phases of the SDLC. Some of these are Business Functional Manager or Director, or Project or Program Manager.

■ **User's Representative –** Can be anyone from a representative appointed by the users to the systems administrator.

Understanding the roles of each of the above, the ISSMP can now see why the level of security education and awareness with each of these individuals is very important to the success of any system security program. This will be discussed more at the end of this chapter.

Some organizations have additional professional personnel who support the above individuals in establishing and maintaining the security for a system. The following are examples of some of these:

■ **Risk Analyst –** The Risk Analyst is responsible for overall risk management activities that can include fiduciary, legal, regulatory, investment, health and safety, and security. Additionally, this person knows the standard methods for calculating risk and how to determine the various values for risk equations.

■ **Chief Information Security Officer (CISO) –** The CISO is responsible for developing, implementing, and overseeing the information security program, policies, standards, and guidelines, and conducting risk assessments, identifying practical security solutions, and promoting security awareness to all levels of an organization.

■ **Information System Security Officer (ISSO) –** The ISSO is responsible for direct oversight of the system's security by conducting routine reviews of system security logs and operations, and he or she provides security advice to the system owner. Sometimes the ISSO is called the Business Unit (Information) Security Officer (BSO/BISO) because he or she reports to a business unit manager. The ISSO or BISO sometimes has an additional reporting structure to the CSO or CISO for receiving additional guidance, tasking, and reporting.

With the exception of the ISSO, who typically works with the System Owner, the others can work for any number of senior managers. In some organizations the Risk Analyst is a general staff person who works for single or multiple business units, providing risk assessment support to a broad variety of reviews and decision making processes, while in others, this individual is the Chief Risk Officer (CRO), providing risk analysis to the General Managers and the Board of Directors on compliance and business issues. The CISO can work for one or more General Managers or the CIO, CFO, or CSO, depending on the internal structure, his tory, cultures, business focus, personalities, and politics within an organization. In the majority of cases, the CISO works for the CIO because system security is viewed as an information technology function. In some cases, the CISO works for the CFO because the organization is viewed as being a financial business, and information systems are viewed as only a support element. In others, the CISO works for the CSO where there is one because information security is viewed as an organizational requirement that requires the integration of all security disciplines (personnel, computer, and physical). Sometimes the CISO does not work for the CIO because there is a concern for conflict of interest, e.g., the CIO could be more concerned with availability, whereas the CISO is concerned with all security functions (availability, integrity, and confidentiality). Another reason could be a senior management concern that the CIO does not fully respect the priority of business requirements over technology.

Each of the above roles holds a key responsibility for ensuring that an information system maintains an adequate level of security, but the most key roles are the system owner and ISSO because they are the ones who are supposed to be monitoring the system's security status on a daily basis and have the most security knowledge. They are also responsible for making sure that the system's needs are reflected in the organization's budget and the approving authority is aware of any security concerns related to its systems. The latter is accomplished by providing reports and presentations to senior management, so they can take actions to resolve any security issues.

An ISSMP has the potential to support or be in the position of any of the above roles because the ISSMP's professional expertise is needed for ensuring the success of each role. To become qualified for any of these roles does require experience and additional qualifications and knowledge. To be successful in an organization, all of the above need to understand how to successfully gain resources and present them to management.

Resourcing Security

To understand how to gain additional resources requires an understanding of several additional concepts and processes.

- Maslow's Hierarchy of Needs
- Project Management
- Planning, Programming, Budget, and Execution
- Needs Justification

Hierarchy of needs is the result of Maslow's theory of what motivates individuals to take the actions that they do. Maslow identified five levels of needs – physiological, safety, love, esteem, and self-actualization. *Figure 1.12* provides a visual representation of the five levels and some of the actual needs at each level.

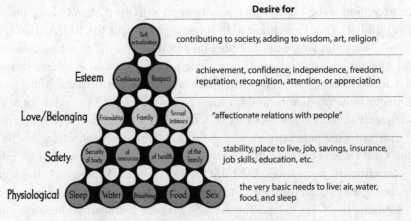

Figure 1.12 – Maslow's Hierarchy of Needs

Maslow's theory is that one must achieve, maintain, and satisfy the lowest levels before one can take on the next level of needs. This theory is not as rigid as it seems because an individual's priorities can fluctuate from minute to minute (for example, if one cannot breathe, one quickly refocuses on the physiological level, or if one's home is lost, one refocuses on the safety level until shelter is obtained), but for the most part individuals are subconsciously at one or two levels. Knowing which need levels individuals are at is very important to the ISSMP because understanding what motivates individuals is one of the keys to developing strategies for influencing, managing, leading, selling, and convincing other individuals. For example:

CASE STUDY

Situation – A manager of a profit center supported by an information system is in fear of losing his job. Which level is he at and how do you convince him to buy a firewall?

Strategy – He is focused on the safety level, so explain how the lack of a firewall can adversely impact the success of the profit center and that a security incident can be highly embarrassing to the organization, which will result in the loss of clients.

Situation – A project team of professionals is working on a project in a very high growth industry with a lot of competitors paying higher salaries. Which level are they at, and what do we do to motivate them to stay working on this important project?

Strategy – In general, the team is financially stable and educated, so they can be at the love level or the esteem level. If the members are at the love level, the ISSMP will need to take actions to improve the group dynamic to increase the individuals' sense of belonging. Increasing group interaction by holding meetings with interactive exercises would be one solution; another action could be to generate a name for the team, create a logo, and produce a banner, caps, buttons, or shirts. If some or all of the members are at the esteem level, an appropriate action would be to compliment individuals on providing good ideas or compliment the group for successes.

All too often, when a manager is asked, "How do you motivate someone?" the manager's immediate answer is, "More money!" Usually the best answer is to determine what level the person is at and take an action appropriate for supporting the need at that level. (Source – Maslow, A. H. A Theory of Human Motivation. *Psychological Review 50* (1943) – 370–96)

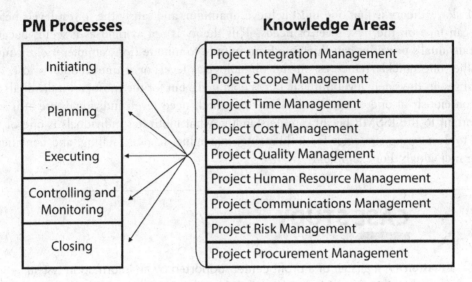

Figure 1.13 – **PMI Body of Knowledge**

Project management principles need to be understood if an ISSMP is going to be successful in managing or assisting in any medium or major effort. One good source of knowledge about how to manage a project is the Project Management Institute (PMI), which has chapters and learning facilities around the world. According to the PMI model, project management consists of understanding dozens of processes that are required for successfully managing projects. These processes consist of five basic process groups and nine knowledge areas (see *Figure 1.13*).

The basic process groups are defined by PMI as follows:

- *Initiating Process group –* Defines and authorizes the project or a project phase

- *Planning Process group –* Defines and refines objectives and plans the course of action required to attain the objectives and scope that the project was undertaken to address

- *Executing Process group –* Integrates people and other resources to carry out the project management plan for the project

- *Monitoring and Controlling Process group –* Regularly measures and monitors progress to identify variances from the project management plan so that corrective actions can be taken when necessary to meet project objectives

- *Closing Process group –* Formalizes acceptance of the product, service, or result and brings the project or a project phase to an orderly end

(For more information please see: A Guide to the Project Management Body of Knowledge (PMBOK® Guide; 5th edition)

Note that the above groups are similar to the other security cycles using different names but very similar functions (see *Figure 1.14*).

As can be seen from *Figure 1.14*, the nine knowledge areas have processes that are about managing specific key functional elements, some of which were identified in previous security cycles. Scope, quality, and risk management are areas that are very similar. Others related to managing costs, time, personnel, procurement, and communications between groups are areas in which successful management skills could very much support the various actions that need to be managed in any of the development and security cycles previously discussed.

The success of ISSMPs can depend on how well they understand the above 45 processes because this knowledge will allow them to manage projects and work with project managers more effectively.

> ## Security Professional's Goals are to
> - Provide risk based system security.
> - Recommend cost-effective security.
> - Deploy practical and acceptable security.

> ## Security Professional's Goals are NOT to
> - Assume risk.
> - Build a 100% secure system.
> - Have the largest budget or staff possible.
> - Deploy the most technical solutions.

PM, Development, and Security Cycles

PM Processes	SDLC	RMF	Generic
Initiating	Initiation	Categorize System	Initiation
Planning	Development Acquisition	Select Controls	Verification
		Implement Controls	
Executing	Implementation	Assess Controls	Approval
		Authorize System	
Controlling and Monitoring	Operation Maintenance	Monitor Controls	Maintenance
Closing	Disposition		Disposal
	Disposal		

*Figure 1.14 – **Cycle Comparison***

Influencing resources is a required skill for every ISSMP because all security programs must have funding to operate. Understanding the process for obtaining the necessary funding to support existing security needs (e.g., personnel, infrastructure, services, specialists, supplies, training and education, etc.), initiatives, and emergencies is very important. Seeming very complex at first, the processes are easy to learn, and this learning process can provide an advantage for the ISSMP if handled correctly. Of all the individuals in an organization, the people who control or contribute to the organization's budget process are most important to the ISSMP because they have a large say as to what is funded and what is not.

It is recommended that the ISSMP contact the budget personnel and request a tutorial on how the budgeting and execution of funds are accomplished in the organization. This initiative serves two purposes: It provides an understanding of the process and schedule and establishes a cooperative relationship with these influential individuals. This is very important because these individuals will provide formats and information that will make the ISSMP successful.

The need for the ISSMP to actively participate in the budgeting process, and to understand FTEs and the true cost of controls, was discussed earlier in this book. It is important to understand that the funding process has essentially four phases – planning, programming, budgeting, and execution. The following provides an overview of each of these phases:

- **Planning Phase** – During this phase, senior management identifies the organization's strategies, goals, and objectives for the future. Depending on the organization, this projection can be anywhere from 2 to 10 years out. These projections are the results of changes in laws and regulations, business trends, market analysis, growth and financial projections, and so forth. Using these, senior management issues guidance (including future goals, objectives, priorities, strategies, etc.) to the organization's managers, so they can identify what they need to do in the future to support the successful accomplishment of the future goals and objectives.

- **Programming Phase** – In the programming phase, functional managers review alternatives to expand or reduce existing projects and programs or develop new initiatives to support senior management's guidance. Senior management will review these alternatives and determine which have the best potential of success and which are the most cost effective. The outcome of this phase is some type of a program decision from senior management.

- **Budgeting Phase** – The budgeting phase is where the functional managers develop detailed budget estimates for the changes approved in the decision memorandum. The budget personnel will review these budget estimates for accuracy, completeness, and compliance with the decision memorandum. Senior management resolves any issues and promulgates a budget decision.

- **Execution Phase** – With the budget decision, senior management allocates funding to the functional managers to fund the approved programs. Typically, the funding allocations support one year's efforts, but sometimes the funding supports a specific phase of a project. The budget includes funding for personnel, utilities, facilities, services, materials, advertising, infrastructure, and so forth, for both direct and indirect costs.

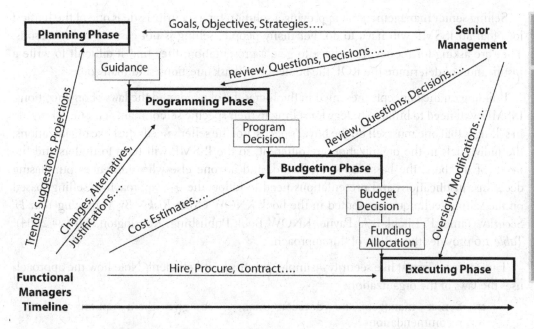

Figure 1.15 – **Planning, Programming, Budget, and Execution Cycle**

Figure 1.15 illustrates the timing, organization's interactions, and outcomes of each phase. The specific time required to accomplish each phase is totally dependent on the organization. In some organizations, a phase may take a year and, in others, weeks or days. The size of the organization, geographic diversity of management, complexity of the business environment, level of competitive demands, fluidity of the marketplace, and so forth can have major impacts on how long and how fast the process moves. This is why ISSMPs must gain awareness of their specific organization's funding process from the individuals who control the budget process.

Once the process is understood, the ISSMP can anticipate budget requests in support of the process and become very responsive to related management actions. It is recommended that the ISSMP request the budget individual review and comment on inputs prior to the inputs being requested to ensure that the inputs are correct and demonstrate awareness of the process. Additionally, determine when funding reviews occur during the execution phase because this is an opportunity to identify the need for additional funding or highlight savings initiated by the ISSMP. An example of this is in the government, whose goal is to spend all allocated funding within the fiscal year (1 October to 30 September), so government organizations conduct a midyear review in the spring and expedited contract funding at the end of the summer. ISSMPs should take advantage of these times to gain resources for unfunded improvements. In the commercial sector, ISSMPs should look for times of large cash inputs to the company, for example, at the end of every quarter when a large contract renewal check is received from clients. Each organization is different. However, the information can be gained from the budget or financial personnel.

One final comment on gaining resources: Funding is almost always available for proposals that have a major impact on reducing risk or increasing profits, but the ISSMP must be credible and have a strong justification to gain them.

Selling senior management on approving a solution for a security issue is one of the hardest jobs that an ISSMP will have to do. For many people, selling is not easy for many reasons: They are asking for money; they have to give a presentation; they find it difficult to write a justification or determine the ROI; the audience will ask questions; and many others.

Building on the concepts presented in the hierarchy of needs and the laws of organizations, ISSMPs will need to build a strategy for selling to their specific senior management. A key rule in selling is that one must sell on the buyer's needs, not the seller's needs. Just like organizations, the individuals in the organization are different, so the ISSMP will have to understand the needs of the boss, the boss's boss, the board, and anyone else who influences purchasing decisions. Justifications and presentations need to follow the 0–5 approach to selling, based on the selling techniques presented in the book *KNOW Cyber Risk – By Managing Your IT Security* (James P. Litchko, Al Payne. KNOW Book Publishing; Kensington, MD © 2004). *Table 1.6* provides the details of this approach.

The approach is just like security – simple, practical, and efficient. Note how the approach uses the laws of the organization:

- Senior managers are decision makers, so give them options and recommendations.
- Senior managers have limited time, so give them one page and five-minute presentations.
- The higher up in the organization, the more resources; therefore, also know the boss's boss.

Typically, new ISSMPs have difficulties with implementing the 0–5 approach because of the following concerns:

- How can I present everything in five minutes? The majority of senior managers are not technical, and they are all about making decisions. They will appreciate the fact that you understand and respect the time that they have given you. Give them the basics, and if they have questions they will ask. The presenter wants them to ask questions because it gets them involved with the problem and the solution, giving them the feeling of owning the solution.
- How can I present everything on one page? Justifications for additional resources should be no longer than one page, again, because senior managers do not have lots of time. Whenever possible, base the justification on mission or business needs.
- Where do I get the format for the one-pager? Get the format from the financial or budget personnel. Remember, they are the ones who will be getting the approval for changing the allocation of the funds, so why not use their format and save everyone time?
- How do I know what the audience's needs and goals are? The best way is to talk to the executive assistant to know who will be in the meeting and what their backgrounds and roles are. Do a Web search and read articles about them, presentations and papers from them, and so forth. Also, ask the finance or budget personnel and your mentor for advice. Many people think that the way to sell to senior management is to present a solid return on investment (ROI), but remember Maslow's hierarchy of needs. Some people are more driven by needs other than ROI; sometimes being successful and being recognized by their peers at a conference or in an article is what drives them – esteem. Or knowing that they will not get into trouble with their evaluators,

the board, or their boss is their goal – safety. Remember, everyone is different, present to the whole audience, and not all problems need to have an ROI component.

■ How do I find a mentor? It is recommended that when you are picking a mentor, always pick someone who is positive and successful in the organization and does not always agree with you because you want someone who will challenge you and give an honest opinion.

The ISSMP has the responsibility to ensure that management is aware of the risks that impact the organization in accomplishing the mission or being successful in business ventures, as well as providing them with options and recommendations for reducing the risks. The actions taken by the ISSMP related to both gaining information security resources and proactively educating and maintaining a constant level of awareness for information security for every employee in the organization can be mutually beneficial.

Security Awareness, Education, and Training

Before talking about awareness, education, and training, the ISSMP needs to understand the differences between each because they are often confused. NIST SP 80050 provides the following definitions:

■ **Awareness** – A learning process that sets the stage for training by changing individual and organizational attitudes to realize the importance of security and the adverse consequences of its failure.

■ **Training** – Teaching people the knowledge and skills that will enable them to perform their jobs more effectively.

(Source – NIST SP 80016, Information Technology Security Training Requirements – A Role and Performance Based Model, Appendix C, Glossary, Mark Wilson, Dorothea E. de Zafra, Sadie I. Pitcher, John D. Tressler, and John B. Ippolito, April 1998.)

■ **Education** – IT security education focuses on developing the ability and vision to perform complex, multidisciplinary activities and the skills needed to further the IT security profession. Education activities include research and development to keep pace with changing technologies and threats.

So, by these definitions, awareness is for all employees, training is for people using information systems, and education is for information security professionals. This is important to recognize because it impacts the objective and the specificity of each, so the ISSMP can tailor the programs for each group. For example, related to viruses:

■ **Awareness** – All employees do not need to understand how viruses work, only how they can help to prevent bringing viruses into the system and what the symptoms are, so they can recognize when they have one and to whom to report it.

■ **Training** – Information system personnel need security awareness as well as training on how to install, update, and maintain anti-virus controls and how to respond to virus attacks.

■ **Education** – Information security professionals need both the awareness and training and the knowledge of how various viruses work, the trends, countermeasures, recovery options, resources, and so forth.

Each employee has a different depth of knowledge so the employee can do his or her job based on his or her roles in the organization. Providing an individual with more than what's needed would be ineffective, costly, and counterproductive (e.g., too much information can result in the individual becoming bored and missing the instruction that is really needed to support information security needs). Additionally, the topics covered have to be relevant to the information system because providing security information on Internet and laptop security is unnecessary when an information system is not connected to the Internet or does not utilize laptops. So the ISSMP must very carefully identify exactly what level of awareness, training, and education is required for all levels of employees.

The awareness program must include everyone from the facilities worker to the chairman of the board. In fact, the program should highlight visible support from the senior executive to demonstrate senior management emphasis and encouragement for all employees to support the organization's security efforts.

The ISSMP needs to use every tool available to leverage the effectiveness of the organization's awareness, training, and education program. One approach is to use the outcomes of the information security cycle phases discussed previously (see *Figure 1.11*). As discussed earlier, the following is how they can be used to tailor and provide inputs to the program:

- **Initiation Phase** – Basically all the actions described thus far in this chapter are done during this phase. These actions include identifying the organization's mission, goals, and objectives; describing the system components, boundaries, functions, and connections; determining and implementing the security controls that are necessary; and conducting an initial risk assessment. Then, identify the responsible individuals and document all of these findings in a security plan.
- **Verification Phase** – A comprehensive assessment of the management, operational, and technical security controls in an information system in support of system accreditation. This includes verifying that the controls identified in the security plan are implemented correctly, operating as intended, and producing the desired outcomes, and documenting the results in a formal document, i.e., a Security Assessment Report.
- **Approval Phase** – The actions taken to review the System Security Plan, Security Assessment Report, and Corrective Action Plan or Plan of Actions and Milestones (POA&M, see sidebar) are completed prior to a senior management official's approval of an information system for operation or for continued operation. This official is responsible for the information system's business function and supporting resources and is knowledgeable of the security status, including the security controls and risks, and for formally accepting the risk to the individuals and organization (including mission, assets, functions, image, and reputation).
- **Maintenance Phase** – Taking actions to ensure that the authorized configuration, security controls, and level of risk are maintained. The actions will include an active configuration management program, ensuring that all updates are implemented, risk assessments are continuously conducted, senior management is kept up to date on all changes to the security status, contingency and incident response plans are exercised, personnel are trained, and security awareness is maintained.

- **Disposal Phase –** This phase occurs when a determination is made that an information system is no longer required. Actions must be taken to ensure that the security of any residual information is protected and the permanent disruption of services is not a surprise to anyone. Information that must be retained for legal or regulatory purposes must be transported and archived in a secure location. In disposing of software, media, and hardware, one must take steps to ensure that inappropriate reuse of licenses does not occur and that storage media are sanitized. Discontinuing services to other elements and interconnections must be thoroughly coordinated in advance and during the disconnecting process.

Awareness, training, and education are required throughout the entire information security cycle to increase the assurance that all controls are working properly at all times. Also, many of the actions discussed previously can be used to ensure that the actions related to these three areas are accurately targeted to support the system's needs and threat environment as both evolve.

Security Awareness

Awareness is one of the most key of the three because awareness helps people conduct themselves in a manner that is conducive to security rather than in a fashion that is likely to undermine it. Awareness helps people notice potential security issues and report them. There are many methods of increasing employee awareness. The following have proven very successful:

Senior Management

Employees will follow the lead of senior management, so management must visibly demonstrate that they support and follow information security controls. This means increasing visibility to managers, clients, partners, vendors, supervisors, systems, operators, guards, and maintenance workers, not just the users. The following are methods that management can utilize to make security visible:

- Making information security an important element of any general meeting agendas
- Discussing security successes and changes at organizational "town meetings"
- Requiring security control clauses to be included in all contracts
- Displaying posters related to information security that include images of senior management personnel on them, and that contain quotes from senior management about the importance of information security
- Rewarding individuals for reporting security concerns or giving suggestions
- Requesting group inputs on options for security initiatives

Promotion

In marketing, frequency and diversity of advertising is the key to increasing product awareness. Information security responsibility and actions need to be presented frequently and in a variety of ways to ensure that employees maintain a level of awareness. The following are methods of maintaining that awareness, but the key is they have to change on a frequent basis; if not, they may represent the organization's lack of interest:

- Security awareness banners to users prior to logging on to the computers

- Giveaways – buttons, napkins, pens, stress toys, postcards, coupons, and so forth
- Posters or displays in common areas
- Free 30minute brown bag lunches with speakers presenting on topics that support the employees' personal needs and subliminally promote the organization's security policies
- Exercises related to security incidents
- Surveys, often conducted by senior management, asking for feedback on the status of security or soliciting security concerns or suggestions

At times, employees may attempt to, or successfully, circumvent security controls for the sake of convenience or other reasons. When an employee does so, if it is the first time the employee has done so, the security team should, in general, in a nice way, provide the employee guidance on appropriate security behavior. Such a notification should also include a polite warning that a repeat of such behavior might lead to disciplining or firing. In some especially sensitive environments, however, even a single violation may lead to termination.

Employee Onboarding

Prior to giving any employee access to any information system or facility, the employee must complete an organization security education course, which verifies that a level of understanding has been gained by the employee. Presentations can be provided in multiple ways, such as lectures from a security official and computer based training. Presentations can be made more effective by incorporating incidents that occurred in the organization.

Security Education

Education for security professionals is very important. The ISSMP must ensure that employees are both trained and aware of their responsibilities related to ensuring that information security is maintained in the organization. Leveraging the outputs of other security actions will increase the effectiveness and efficiency of these actions. Additionally, ISSMPs must not neglect the security education of the security team members and themselves. Many organizations are now requiring various professionals to become certified in their area of expertise and to maintain the certification as a requirement for employment. Other companies are also requiring their professionals to gain a new certification every year to retain employment or to be qualified for the next promotion, bonus, or raise.

Security Training

It is imperative to realize that information security training needs vary dramatically within an organization; while all people should have a basic awareness of the importance of information security and the adverse consequences of its failure, not all people need the same amount of knowledge and skills to actually ensure information security. A security engineer who is monitoring activity logs, for example, does not need to know about the budgeting process to the same extent that the Chief Security Officer does, and vice versa.

While there may be a temptation in some organizations to simplify information security training by standardizing on a small number of curricula, or even on just one curriculum, oversimplifying can lead to two problems:

1. Some people may receive inadequate training, yielding a situation that can lead to security problems. When we speak of inadequate training, we refer to either too little training or training in the wrong areas.

2. Other people may be over-trained, which, while at first glance may appear to be a positive situation, is actually highly problematic because overtraining can cause people to focus on material irrelevant to them rather than on knowledge that is pertinent to their responsibilities, effectively producing a situation in which they have inadequate training with regard to what they actually need to know, and eventually lead to security problems. Also, overtraining can lead to people erroneously believing that they have expertise in areas in which they do not, thereby causing them to make decisions and take actions that adversely impact security. Also, overtraining may cost more than adequate and appropriate training.

Hence, it is important to identify the appropriate security training needs for each group within an organization. The nature of each group's specific training depends heavily on roles and responsibilities, but other factors may weigh in as well. Technical team members will need training on different matters, for example, than receptionists, but if either group is not appropriately trained, security incidents may result.

Another aspect of information security training that is important for the ISSMP to understand is the need to monitor and report on the effectiveness of security awareness and training programs. After all, it is not the running of training programs that improves security: It is people's actual learning from the training that improves security. Hence, it is important to verify what people are and are not "picking up" from the training. Failing to do so often will result in an organization learning that parts of the training were unsuccessful "the hard way" when a preventable security incident occurs that would not have occurred if the training had been successful.

The goal of analyzing the effectiveness of training is not simply to know whether the training was effective but to fine tune it so as to improve its effectiveness in the future. Proper analysis may determine, for example, that modifications are necessary to the topics, the actual material being taught, the frequency of training, the scheduling of the training, and/or the methodology and tools used to teach. If any security incidents have occurred whose chances of recurring in the future would be reduced by including some new material in the training, or by modifying the training in some other way, and those adjustments would not have adverse side effects, that material should obviously be added and those changes made.

Some aspects of the monitoring are subjective; polls or surveys may be conducted, and a general assessment of the security culture of the organization by a skilled professional such as the ISSMP may be ordered. Other measurements are objective; for example, how many times were policies violated, or did various "test attacks" succeed or fail? Others are a combination of both; how many security incidents were there compared to before the training, and can any change in that ratio be reasonably ascribed to the training (or were other factors at play)?

Summary

Concepts, processes, cycles, frameworks, strategies, and terminologies for securing, developing, managing, budgeting, resourcing, and providing awareness have been provided in this chapter. Although called something different and originating from different professions, many of them follow the same logic and generic formats and processes. Although they were developed to support different professional objectives, because of their similarities, the ISSMP should see how conveniently they can be worked in parallel to support the ISSMP's goals and objectives. Even more, their actions can augment or replace actions and make cooperative efforts more efficient than if done separately. Additionally, ISSMPs with this knowledge will be able to relate to their counterparts' needs and executives' requests more effectively and responsively. This chapter has provided an introduction to many topics that will require additional research for ISSMPs to understand all the possible applications that will enhance their capabilities and skills.

Domain 1: Review Questions

1. Organization mission statements

    A. Are nontechnical in nature, so ISSMPs do not have to understand them

    B. Are quickly put together by senior management

    C. Provide everyone in the organization overall direction and focus for their activities

    D. Are very specific and provide specific goals and objectives

2. Which types of organizations need to have a formally documented mission statement?

    A. Commercial enterprises

    B. Nonprofit organizations

    C. Government agencies

    D. All the above

3. Deploying Internet security solutions that are acceptable by clients requires knowing the client's

    A. Expectations and location

    B. Location and technical knowledge

    C. System capabilities and expectations

    D. Expectation and technical knowledge

4. All organizations' security solutions are influenced by the following:

    A. Laws, employee culture, profit, and competition

    B. Goals, client expectations, regulations, and profit

    C. Group and client expectations and competition capabilities

    D. Profit, organization objectives, client capabilities, and senior management

5. A system's security solutions must be

    A. Cost effective, risk based, and acceptable

    B. Risk based and within division budget restraints

    C. Practical and 95% effective

    D. Acceptable by senior management and provide an ROI

6. A specific piece of information's level of classification is dependent on

    A.   Need to know

    B.   Cost of producing the information

    C.   Impact if compromised

    D.   Affordability of required security

7. System security boundary must be determined early based on all but the following.

    A.   Understanding the mission, goals, and objectives

    B.   Coordinating the review with the end users

    C.   Identify the system components that support each of the business functions

    D.   Determining who is operationally and fiscally responsible for the system

8. Security boundary is important to establishing

    A.   Who will be doing the certification effort

    B.   Scoping the security effort

    C.   Determining which regulations and laws apply

    D.   If the system will need an Internet connection or not

9. The implementation phase of the System Development Life Cycle includes

    A.   Conducting an initial security test

    B.   Identifying security solutions

    C.   Determining if the security is acceptable to operate

    D.   Defining the system security requirements

10. The ISSMP's job is to provide security support at the end of which phase in the System Development Life Cycle?

    A.   Disposition and Disposal

    B.   Operation and Maintenance

    C.   Implementation

    D.   Initiation

11. Risk assessments are done in which phases of the System Development Life Cycle?

    A.   Initiation

    B.   Initiation and Implementation

    C.   Implementation and Disposition and Disposal

    D.   Initiation, Implementation, and Operations and Maintenance

12. Who sets the information security standards for the public sector?

    A. National Security Agency (NSA)

    B. International Organization for Standardization (ISO)

    C. National Institute of Standards and Technology (NIST)

    D. International Electrotechnical Commission (IEC)

13. Families of controls are identified in which of the following documents?

    A. NIST Special Publication 80053

    B. ISO 27002

    C. DODI8500.2

    D. All the above

14. The ISSMP decides between using quantitative and qualitative risk assessment based on

    A. The budget process

    B. Threats

    C. Vulnerabilities

    D. Management decision processes

15. Assurances are those activities that provide management with what about security solutions?

    A. Due diligence

    B. Protection

    C. Cost effectiveness

    D. ROI

16. Which of the following provides a measurement of how well an organization's process includes the capability of continuously improving its processes?

    A. Common Criteria Evaluation and Validation Scheme

    B. OCTAVE

    C. Software Engineering Institute's Capability Maturity Model

    D. Commonly Accepted Security Practices and Regulations

17. Interconnections with other systems outside the system security boundary can have the following effects on a system:

    A.   Increased dependencies to support the other system's security requirements

    B.   Requirement to notify when a security event occurs on your system

    C.   Obligation to inform the other system when outages are going to occur

    D.   All the above

18. Annual Loss Expectancy and ROI are expressed in the following units:

    A.   Currency and percentage

    B.   Percentage and level of risk

    C.   Cost of security and percentage

    D.   Percentage and cost savings

19. Plan of Actions and Milestones (POA&M) is

    A.   A security plan

    B.   A management tool

    C.   A list of all the systems security solutions

    D.   A checklist of actions for monitoring security during the Implementation Phase

20. The ideal presentation to senior managers should follow which of the following rules?

    A.   20page justification

    B.   Five slides

    C.   Answer all the questions that the audience could ask

    D.   Be presented in 5 minutes

CISSP®

Domain 2
Security Lifecycle Management

People often fail to realize the potential value of an information system and its contents to criminals or other hackers. Internal systems may house proprietary data, information about customers and prospects, marketing plans, data regarded as "insider information" by the SEC, and all sorts of other sensitive materials that can be exploited by unauthorized parties for financial or other gain. Protecting the organizational information infrastructure is, therefore, extremely important.

The goal of the Enterprise-Wide Systems Development Security domain is to provide the ISSMP with knowledge pertaining to defining, designing, developing, testing, implementing, and maintaining the enterprise-wide infrastructure for the day-to-day business environment. The ISSMP should understand the importance of protecting the business operations, deployment of applications and operating platforms, and the threats and vulnerabilities associated with data, systems, personnel, and processes.

TOPICS

- Manage the Integration of Security into the System Development Life Cycle (SDLC)
  - Identify lifecycle processes within the organization
  - Integrate information security gates (decision points) and milestones into lifecycle
  - Monitor compliance with the lifecycle
  - Oversee the configuration management process

- Integrate New Business Initiatives into the Security Architecture
  - Participate in development of business case for new initiatives to integrate security
  - Address impact of new business initiatives on security (e.g., cloud, big data)

- Define and Oversee Comprehensive Vulnerability Management Programs (e.g., vulnerability scanning, penetration testing, threat analysis)
  - Classify assets, systems, and services based on criticality to business
  - Prioritize threats and vulnerabilities
  - Oversee security testing
  - Remediate vulnerabilities based on risk

OBJECTIVES

The CISSP-ISSMP candidate should be able to:

- Describe the process for integrating security into the System Development Life Cycle (SDLC).

- Define the process for integrating new business initiatives into the security architecture.

- Describe the vulnerability and threat management program.

- Identify process for implementing the vulnerability and threat management program.

This chapter focuses on the management of security efforts in the development of systems designed for enterprise-wide use rather than the implementation details of various security measures.

It should be noted that people interested in studying the security aspects of the software development lifecycle in detail should consider also reviewing (ISC)²'s official study guide for the CSSLP exam, which focuses specifically on those areas.

2

Security Lifecycle Management

Managing Security in Different Methods of Systems Development

There are two main types of system development methods: waterfall and iterative. It's important to understand these two methodologies and where security falls within them in order to best manage security efforts to achieve the greatest success. Typically, a development team is accustomed to using one method or the other; flipping between them is rare due to major inherent differences in approach between them.

There are many examples of each of these, but the two listed here are the most common. Keep in mind that every company and group puts its own spin on them and modifies them to meet its unique challenges or situations. None of them is cast in stone, so you should always get a rundown from the project manager or a knowledgeable person on the team you will be working with as to just what process is in use and what stage the system being developed is currently in.

The closer to the start of a development project that functionality or features are added, the less expensive they are. This is especially true for security measures. But in the case of security, the measures are not only less expensive but also more effective when planned into a system from the start of the design process.

Building security into a system as it is created has benefits not only in terms of how secure the completed system is but also in the reduction of any pain or retraining for the users and administrators of the system. This can be an important aspect of the overall effectiveness of security measures.

Attempting to graft security solutions or mitigations onto existing systems can be expensive, incomplete, or inadequate and is often painful to the system's users and administrators. In fact, the older the existing system is, the more extreme these issues can be—so the rule for any security is always "the sooner, the better."

User convenience and education are important considerations when implementing a security effort. Users are prone to finding ways to circumvent security that is inconvenient or confusing; sometimes these workarounds can jeopardize security, even without malicious intent.

It should be noted that there are other development models. The spiral model, for example, involves utilizing formal risk analysis and management at regular intervals during development; one might think of it as a combination of the waterfall model, some aspects of RAD (discussed later), and risk management. Because risk management happens during development, development personnel need to understand a bit more about security risks than developers utilizing other models, they must be trusted to address risks, and the organization utilizing it must be prepared to spend more on "development" because it may take longer and cost more as a result of the earlier, proactive risk management.

Systems Development Life Cycle

Systems development life cycle (SDLC) refers to the process and events that occur throughout the lifetime of a computer system from its initial conception until its disposal. Processes included in the SDLC include those for planning, creating, testing, deploying, supporting, managing, terminating, and disposing of an information system.

The rationale for having defining formal processes for each stage of the SDLC is to ensure that by properly planning and utilizing a structured execution at each point in the SDLC, both schedules and budgets are more likely to be successfully adhered to, fewer mistakes are likely to occur, and the organization using the system is likely to benefit from a higher quality product than they would with less structured development processes. Likewise, incorporating formal security procedures during the SDLC is likely going to improve the security of the finished product versus trying to address security "after the fact."

Over the last few decades, multiple methodologies for managing the SDLC have emerged. It is beyond the scope of this book to discuss them in detail, or even to cover all of the security aspects of the SDLC. (ISC)²'s CSSLP certification exam and study guide go into far more detail, and anyone interested in exploring these topics in further detail is encouraged to obtain CSSLP exam study materials. However, despite the CSSLP exam covering much of this area, the ISSMP is not exempt from understanding about it; in fact, there are several elements that are actually critical for the ISSMP to understand. It is those points that are addressed in this section.

The standard systems development life cycle (SDLC) is probably, to some extent, familiar to most readers of this book because it is the most common waterfall systems development method; the following is an overview specifically targeted to security's place in that process.

Despite the fact the traditional SDLC is typically shown as a purely waterfall method in which one stage is begun only as the prior stage is completed, in practice this is becoming less and less the case. Certainly when you are managing a security effort, you cannot wait for a stage to finish before you think about and begin planning for the next stage. Keeping in touch with all the details and deliverables of the project as it progresses through the SDLC is an ongoing and very necessary part of effectively managing the entire system's security needs (*Figure 2.1*).

The SDLC is often broken into seven primary phases:

- Defining Requirements
- Design
- Implementation – includes coding and integration
- Testing
- Deployment
- Maintenance
- Disposal

These stages however can be further refined, and various other models may utilize more stages by breaking down into more granular levels, or fewer stages by merging some together. All of this is a matter of semantics. What the ISSMP needs to understand is what the various lifecycle stages are (regardless of what they are called and whether they are each considered independent or not), and how they exist within the model in use in his or her work environment; he or she should also understand the role of security personnel as appropriate at each corresponding phase.

The following graphic – created by the United States Department of Justice and viewable in its context at http://www.justice.gov/jmd/irm/lifecycle/ch1.htm – shows one high-level explanation of the various phases within the SDLC that is broken down further than the standard phases described above. While other breakdowns of the stages exist, the various explanations of the SDLC are similar in concept, and this model is well designed for serving as a basis for the security professional to understand other models.

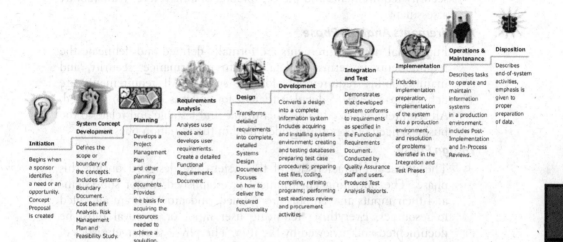

Figure 2.1 – Example of a Typical IT Systems Development Life Cycle (SDLC) Phases
(US Department of Justice (2003). Information Resources Management Chapter 1. Introduction)

In order to ensure that proper privacy and security are delivered by an information system, ensure that these factors are considered not only when utilizing the system but earlier in the process when preparing for and developing it, as well as when disposing of it after its useful life. In fact, security is one of the factors in determining how much planning is appropriate for a system; with all other factors being equal, a system handling extremely sensitive data may require more planning than one handling information of little sensitivity. In any case, information management and associated security must be considered throughout the SDLC.

The DOJ SDLC encompasses ten phases (quoted from the DOJ document):

1. ***Initiation Phase***
   - The initiation of a system (or project) begins when a business need or opportunity is identified. A project manager should be appointed to manage the project. This business need is documented in a concept proposal. After the concept proposal is approved, the system concept development phase begins.

2. ***System Concept Development Phase***
   - Once a business need is approved, the approaches for accomplishing the concept are reviewed for feasibility and appropriateness. The systems boundary document identifies the scope of the system and requires senior official approval and funding before beginning the planning phase.

3. ***Planning Phase***
   - The concept is further developed to describe how the business will operate once the approved system is implemented, and to assess how

the system will impact employee and customer privacy. To ensure the products and services provide the required capability on time and within budget, one should ensure the project resources, activities, schedules, tools, and reviews are defined. Additionally, security certification and accreditation activities begin with the identification of system security requirements and the completion of a high level vulnerability assessment.

4. Requirements Analysis Phase

   ¤ Functional user requirements are formally defined and delineate the requirements in terms of data, system performance, security, and maintainability requirements for the system. All requirements are defined to a level of detail sufficient for systems design to proceed. All requirements need to be measurable and testable and relate to the business need or opportunity identified in the initiation phase.

5. Design Phase

   ¤ The physical characteristics of the system are designed during this phase. The operating environment is established, major subsystems and their inputs and outputs are defined, and processes are allocated to resources. Everything requiring user input or approval must be documented and reviewed by the user. The physical characteristics of the system are specified, and a detailed design is prepared. Subsystems identified during design are used to create a detailed structure of the system. Each subsystem is partitioned into one or more design units or modules. Detailed logic specifications are prepared for each software module.

6. Development Phase

   ¤ The detailed specifications produced during the design phase are translated into hardware, communications, and executable software. Software shall be unit tested, integrated, and retested in a systematic manner. Hardware is assembled and tested.

7. Integration and Test Phase

   ¤ The various components of the system are integrated and systematically tested. The user tests the system to ensure that the functional requirements, as defined in the functional requirements document, are satisfied by the developed or modified system. Prior to installing and operating the system in a production environment, the system must undergo certification and accreditation activities.

8. Implementation Phase

   ¤ The system or system modifications are installed and made operational in a production environment. The phase is initiated after the system has been tested and accepted by the user. This phase continues until the system is operating in production in accordance with the defined user requirements.

9. Operations and Maintenance Phase

   ¤ The system operation is ongoing. The system is monitored for continued performance in accordance with user requirements, and needed system modifications are incorporated. The operational system is periodically assessed through in-process reviews to determine how the system can be made more efficient and effective. Operations continue as long as the system can be effectively adapted to respond to an organization's needs. When modifications or changes are identified as necessary, the system may reenter the planning phase.

10. **Disposition Phase**

  ¤ The disposition activities ensure the orderly termination of the system and preserve the vital information about the system so that some or all of the information may be reactivated in the future if necessary. Particular emphasis is given to proper preservation of the data processed by the system so that the data is effectively migrated to another system or archived in accordance with applicable records management regulations and policies, for potential future access.

While security must be considered throughout the SDLC, there are specific points during the SDLC at which security-related decisions must be made. Of course, as just discussed, the names of any particular stage or stages may vary among the models, but the basic concepts and structure will remain the same. Below are several examples of incorporating security into the various phases of the SDLC, using the DoJ model for the stages as described in the previous list:

■ During the planning phase, system security requirements must be identified. That process may include performing a high level risk and vulnerability assessment – determining what risks exist, what new risks the system being planned may create, etc.

■ During the requirements analysis phase, the requirements being analyzed must include security requirements. It is also wise to establish "gates" at this point, meaning that security personnel decide what must be completed vis-à-vis security at each stage in order to proceed to the following stage. Theoretically, such gates might also include determining what criteria might exist for terminating the project after any particular stage in the SDLC, but such a decision will likely be one made by business stakeholders, not the security team. (Security, of course, will not be the only gate created for many stages.)

■ Security needs must be accounted for during the design phase, not only in terms of addressing the security risks and requirements identified in earlier phases but also to ensure that secure design is utilized so as to ensure that no new security risks are introduced. Essentially, all design requirements from a security perspective need to be identified, considered, and compiled. The design of the system (including its architecture, technologies to be used, coding methodologies, who is doing the coding, etc.) must all be evaluated from a security perspective. It is also useful at this point to model threats. It is also important to consider third-party products and services that will be integrated into a system, as well as the network infrastructure that will be utilized along with the system; designs should address any security concerns that these elements might create.

■ When systems are being written and integrated during the development phase, security professionals should help ensure that coding is done properly, that any security requirements related to coders are obeyed, that any data used for testing during coding is not sensitive, that code is created according to best practices for security (e.g., bounds checking, etc.) to avoid creating vulnerabilities, etc.

2

Security Lifecycle Management

- The testing phase must include security-related testing. Tests should include checks to see that the system performs properly when fed appropriate data, as well as extensive fuzz testing (testing using improper data such as alpha characters in a field expecting numeric input). Security personnel should review testing plans to make sure that they are robust enough to catch any mistakes and vulnerabilities. Security tests should also include tests designed to ensure that the network infrastructure and server infrastructure supporting a system are secure, as well as ensuring that if any security issues occur on devices used for accessing a system, those problems (or problems that they may cause) cannot propagate to the system itself. Checks to ensure that denial-of-service attack situations can be addressed are also important.

- When systems are disposed of, the ISSMP will need to ensure that data is not put at risk through improper disposal methods, that necessary backups are maintained and adequately protected, that information that needs to be preserved for legal or regulatory reasons is properly protected, etc.

It is important to monitor compliance with the SDLC. One way to do so is to confirm that all SDLC-related deliverables from each stage are produced and conform to the standards expected by the organization. For example:

- At the planning phase, documents might include a flow diagram showing how the business operates, manuals for users and system managers of information systems being replaced with the new one, etc.

- At the requirements phase, a list of requirements, a list of problems to be solved, desired new flows to replace old flows (as shown in flow diagrams), etc. might be shown.

- At the design phase, there should be substantial documentation produced detailing the design and including lists of user roles and their associated access rights, documents detailing the user interface, database description documents, code description documents, etc.

- At the implementation stage, there should be a user manual for the new system.

If you overlay security concerns and fit them into the SDLC methodology, the process now looks as shown in *Figure 2.2*.

> ### *Maintain access control and permissions*
>
> ### *Carry out log and access monitoring*
>
> ### *Periodically review risk analysis and security*
>
> ### *Plan in light of new threats*
>
> ### *Security review all system changes or upgrades*

Figure 2.2 – **Security Integrated SDLC**

Rapid Application Development

Rapid application development (RAD) is a common iterative systems development method. It has some advantages over the more traditional waterfall or modified waterfall of SDLC, but it also has some disadvantages.

RAD, by its nature, has considerably less time between releases available for planning, fact-finding, and research. Issues and changes that are introduced late in a cycle often run into this method's signature hard-line message of never taking design changes after the initial pre-project or requirements stage. This means security issues and requirements must be brought up early and stressed frequently to prevent them from falling off the radar and being deferred to a later cycle or determined as an issue that will not be fixed.

RAD also places a strong emphasis on reusability. This can be of particular concern if the code or functionality being reused is not secure (or, even if thought to be secure, if it is not adequately tested to confirm that it truly is secure) because this can cause security vulnerabilities to permeate the end system.

The premise of iterative development methods is to build increasingly more functional systems using short, fast construction cycles with each one building on the working system presented at the end of the prior construction cycle. RAD also makes considerable use of prototyping and prototyping tools, and thus it has a tendency to fall victim to the issues of prototype code written via tools or wizards finding its way into the finished product without adequate security review or mitigation of security risks. All reused and prototype code must be reviewed for security before being included in the final system.

Figure 2.3 shows a basic illustration of the RAD process with an overlay of security concerns and tasks for each step.

Pre-Project	Requirements	User Design	Construction	Implementation/Transition	End Project
Step 1	**Step 2**	**Step 3**	**Step 4**	**Step 5**	**Step 6**
Include security as a project requirement. Identify risks inherent in tools, languages, prototyping, and methodology that need mitigation Add skeleton risk analysis to the project plan.	Security manager participation at requirements gathering meetings. Build security into project diagrams. Document security concerns not typically raised by users. Update risk analysis.	Review all new diagrams and design documents for security concerns and risks. Update risk analysis.	Monitor and enforce security. Ensure continual security testing. Review all documentation for security concerns. Update risk analysis.	Ensure deployment plans are followed and security mitigations implemented. Update risk analysis.	Maintain access control and permissions. Review and monitor logs. Periodically review the risk analysis and security documents in light of new threats.

Figure 2.3 – **The Rapid Application Development (RAD) process with an overlay of security concerns and tasks**

Pre-Project

This is the first stage in the RAD process and is usually completed before the start of each systems development project, though its documents and information may be further updated and modified as the project is under way.

During this stage, all of the details that affect the project as a whole are determined. This includes what the project schedule will be, what the approach to coding will be, the overall risks, etc. This is the stage in which security is included as a project requirement and a careful examination of the tools, languages, prototyping, etc. that are decided upon must be made to identify risks that must be mitigated and language or methodology concerns that require special handling. There are also security concerns around source control, defect tracking, and other bookkeeping issues used during the actual systems development efforts.

The overall project manager will develop a project plan during this stage, and a skeleton risk analysis is begun to list the various security risks and mitigations that affect the system. This will be built upon during each cycle of the RAD process until the project is complete and will sit beside the project plan and other project documentation or be referenced by them.

Requirements

In this second stage of the RAD process, initial customer requirements are gathered, usually by a group of designers who conduct multiple meetings with key customers and compile a draft list of requirements. These meetings are brainstorming sessions in which both the designers and the customers must participate fully to obtain the best results. If at all possible, the security manager for the project needs to be a part of these brainstorming sessions in order to bring security issues to light by asking relevant questions and raising potential concerns early.

A typical deliverable from this stage is a set of project diagrams that show the interaction between parts of the system along with the business entities that will use the system and how. Security must be built into these diagrams and plans as they are produced. This allows the RAD construction cycles to build these in as the system is developed rather than having to add it later.

Another security focus during this stage is to understand and document the requirements not usually considered by the business users. This includes things like access restrictions, server and database security, etc. Because these things are not typically considered by users, the security manager has to be sure to cover as many of them as possible as early as possible to avoid negative impacts on the project or late-requested security fixes being postponed to a later release. Optimally, this would take place in the brainstorming session but can be done later, if necessary. The risk analysis is expanded to include any new security risks, mitigations, and their priorities.

User Design

This third stage of the RAD process is focused on taking the rough requirements, diagrams, and documents for the project and refining them into more detailed design documents that are regularly reviewed with the key end-users for accuracy and any additional required information.

This is the stage that is most focused on setting a concrete schedule and development of system dialogues and the look and feel of the user interface, among other things.

The focus of security at this point is to review the new diagrams and design documents as well as the construction methodology for risks or security concerns that are not yet documented. An example of this is secure coding processes and known vulnerabilities that center around a particular language or software whose use is listed as a system requirement. When security concerns are found, they are added to the ongoing risk analysis document as well as documented in the ongoing RAD documents for the system.

Construction

This fourth stage of the RAD process is the part that truly makes the process iterative. In this stage, the software is actually coded and built with multiple cycles of coding, testing, and revising. Depending on the size of the system, this may be done by several small teams that are each assigned a portion of the system to work on. Typically, this is done under the constraints of a strict set of mini-schedules, often referred to as time-boxing, and under the close supervision of the main project manager.

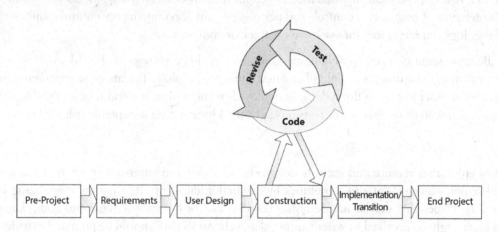

Figure 2.4 – **Representation of the fourth stage of the RAD process in which the software is actually coded and built with multiple cycles of coding, testing, and revising**

In addition to actual coding, testing, and revising, this phase includes other deliverables like user instructions, deployment instructions, and management instructions.

During this phase, security must be enforced and monitored as the construction and revisions occur. Security tests need to be performed continually to catch security issues as quickly as possible because it is easy for security to be overlooked or left until a later cycle with no guarantee it will happen then.

All documentation produced during this stage is reviewed and tested for security flaws, risks, or potential issues.

Any new security risk and mitigations of any kind are added to the risk assessment and security plan documents.

Security Lifecycle Management

Implementation/Transition

This is the fifth stage of RAD, and it is the stage where the system being developed is deployed or transitioned to being "live." Depending on the system, this may be a gradual transition or a more abrupt one. This stage also includes training users and migrating or somehow accommodating any existing data or information.

All steps of this stage need to be monitored with an eye toward security to ensure that the deployment plans are followed and any required security mitigations are implemented. It's especially important that security practices are followed when staging out a deployment over a period of time or when migrating or converting data to prevent mixing secure and insecure systems or importing insecure and possibly contaminated data.

All security documentation is kept up to date and alongside the other RAD documentation for this system.

End Project

This is the final stage of RAD where the system is turned over to the system owners. Unlike SDLC, RAD has no clear maintenance stage, but security is an ongoing process and requires maintenance of both access controls and permissions but also ongoing review and monitoring of user logs and server logs for evidence of attack or compromise.

Because security is an ever-changing landscape, periodic reviews of the risk analysis and security design documents in light of any new situations, exploits, threats, or requirements are needed in order to ensure the system, as deployed, is still within the realm of acceptable risk or, if it is not, to drive changes or revisions to bring it back within acceptable risk levels.

Approval of Security Design

Most enterprises require that security designs be reviewed and approved by internal auditors and senior management and sometimes by external auditors or other parties specializing in security. Depending on the nature of the business and of the system, legal and compliance auditors might be involved in system approval as well. An ISSMP should be prepared to review designs for general security soundness and to ensure that they adhere to policies, standards, plans, and best practices. Even if there is no strict requirement to review a risk analysis and resulting security plan, reviews by key players in a variety of roles both inside and outside of the actual systems development team typically benefit the system as a whole. The more potential risks or issues that can be discovered and addressed early on in the process, the better.

In some cases, the approval process will require documents and processes to be followed, and the security manager needs to start putting these in order as soon as possible to allow for a timely and accurate review of the security design. Even if the risk analysis is not a required document, it's often a great backup tool and should be kept updated and accurate.

Business Unit Priorities

Another key part of building security into the system is to understand the priorities and needs of the business unit or units that will use the system. It is very common for the perceived priorities of the security manager to not be the actual priority of the business units or customers when it comes to security.

It is also common for the business unit to place requirements on the system that create greater security risks but which, on closer examination, either prove to not be actual requirements but are "nice to have" or can be achieved a different way from the stated requirement and thus meet the business unit's needs while still reducing the security risks.

It can be helpful to drill down to the core functionality of the system and walk step by step out from there with the help of the overall project manager to ensure that the business unit's needs are met with the least risk possible.

Security Cost

The other side of security is the fact that it comes at a cost, both in terms of money needed to implement security plans and in terms of the effects it can have on the enterprise or users. The cost of security is a factor in the need to balance security against system functionality and usability. This issue is addressed in detail in this book in the discussion about budgeting in the previous chapter and with regard to other budgetary concerns. When it comes to software development, various aspects of security may cause costs to rise: Technological tools cost money to license and utilize; people's time is expensive and the more time people involved with development spend on security, the more development time costs, etc. Sometimes, waivers will even be requested due to cost.

For each security measure or mitigation in the risk analysis, there must be consideration for the various costs it may incur. These include the following.

Impact on Productivity

Security measures, at their best, don't interfere with the productivity or ability of users to do their job or of the system to perform the tasks it was designed to do. Unfortunately, this aim is not always achievable. Some technologies do adversely impact user productivity, convenience, or both.

Things as simple as having to request special access to a system and have it granted by a superior can mean the user will be unable to use the system for whatever length of time it takes to grant access. Having to enter a password can make access take longer and thus have a small impact on productivity. As an example, encryption can cause data to be inaccessible to users not utilizing specific equipment, or it can slow down performance of a system. Applications "locked" to run from only certain networks may also not be usable remotely.

Each security measure that might impact productivity needs to be documented on the risk analysis and its impact quantified so each measure can be justified and balanced against the benefits gained by taking that measure.

Constantly Changing Landscape

Security should not be an "implement and forget" part of a system, but, sometimes it becomes one, which can be a recipe for problems. Not only is the world of security a constantly changing and evolving one, but the world of the enterprise itself is in constant flux. Employees come and go. Regulations are created and retired, hardware is replaced, and data is modified. Sometimes, even the enterprise's business model and core competencies change.

2

Security Lifecycle Management

Unlike many aspects of a system, security requires initial mitigations and design decisions at the start of the project, as well as ongoing processes, procedures, and monitoring. This, of course, costs the enterprise money.

Hence, a balancing act can develop between having a lot of security and being able to afford it. If there is a way to obtain the same or very nearly the same security mitigation in a less expensive way, it should be investigated and called out in the risk analysis for consideration.

Additional Hardware and Software Expense

In order to provide security beyond that of simple username and password combinations to networks and systems, there may be expenses incurred for additional hardware like routers, hardware firewalls, biometric readers, security card systems, software-based authentication systems, etc.

Because physical equipment has both the initial cost of purchasing the hardware and the costs associated with ongoing maintenance, training, and enforcement, changes that involve a lot of new hardware should be carefully considered before becoming a requirement. Some factors that may impact the cost of hardware (and may force upgrades to a system later on) are increased needs in areas of capacity, storage, performance, etc.

User and administrator training may also be needed for specific hardware, manuals may need to be developed, helpdesk personnel and engineers might need to be taught how to troubleshoot, etc.

Consulting Expense

Another potential expense is for consulting or outsourcing fees. In some cases, there is a need to have an external security audit, often to fulfill a legal or regulatory requirement. Sometimes a decision is made to outsource security testing or the maintenance of some portions of the systems security measures, either because the necessary expertise or resources do not exist in house or because there is a requirement that prohibits that work from being done internally.

Although consulting expenses can be difficult to project with complete accuracy, the need for consulting services should be detailed as completely as possible in the risk analysis and the justification for this need documented so any necessary funding can be obtained and it's not a surprise.

Never hire a security consultant simply because he or she was the least expensive among a group of bidders. Remember the old adage: "You get what you pay for."

Security of Project Elements

The various elements of the project must each be analyzed to find and document their specific security risks. Up until now, security has been looked at with an eye to the system as a whole, but this is the point at which the design documents are analyzed and security concepts are applied to each of the individual pieces of the project.

Tracking each element of the project can become complex and chaotic, so it is important to be organized and methodical. One method that seems to work well is to start by recording the risks and mitigations for each project element, then translating that into a worksheet for each mitigation, cross-referenced with the element and risk it mitigates. This method results in a list where the mitigations can be judged by how many risks they mitigate, and then a cost to implement the mitigation can be determined to assess feasibility as the security plan is developed.

Because risk analysis is truly a balance and is very individual to each company and each project, the following sections give samples of questions that will help uncover important security considerations that may need mitigation. Not all questions will be applicable to all situations, and you may develop key questions of your own, so this is intended as a starting point.

This may seem daunting, but the first time you run through these questions and security assessments, you will do the bulk of the work for the company's software environments. After that, you merely need to update the list to cover any changes and can focus more closely on the project under development in its immediate dependencies.

Hardware

One of the most basic elements of any project is its hardware. The project, after all, has to run on something, and the more complex the project, the more common it is for it to run on multiple systems. This is often one of the more ignored aspects of security, but it is a legitimate source of security risks.

In some situations, new hardware can be purchased for the project that can help lessen the security impact of hardware, but in some cases the project must work on existing, sometimes quite disparate, hardware that is already in place. Either way, the physical hardware, the hardware drivers, and the policies around hardware all require security-conscious decisions.

Common Criteria

Common Criteria is an internal standard for computer security certification. It is sometimes known as ISO/IEC 15408.

Different bodies operate the Common Criteria in different participating countries, but their joint purpose is to test hardware, via independent labs, to be able to report back on how well each item being tested performs against various security-focused tests. This, in turn, allows some surety that security testing has occurred and what testing took place. It also allows side-by-side comparison of test results between different hardware being considered.

Common Criteria Recognition Arrangement (CCRA) is an international arrangement that provides for mutual recognition by member parties. Products certified in one country up to a certain level of security are considered to be certified at that level by other nations. For more details please consult https://www.commoncriteriaportal.org/ccra/. Besides the United States, signatories to this agreement include Australia, Canada, Finland, France, Germany, Greece, Israel, Italy, the Netherlands, New Zealand, Norway, Spain, and the United Kingdom.

Depending on the hardware requirements of your project, you may or may not be able to utilize hardware that has gone through the CCR process, and not having a CCRA certification may mean that you may have a harder time determining what, if any, security testing has been done by the manufacturer.

The most important question to ask about CC as it relates to each piece of hardware the project may use is does this hardware manufacturer participate in CCR and has this piece of hardware been tested?

Of course, in many environments, Common Criteria certification may be unnecessary. Furthermore, even in those in which it is desired, because certification can take time (and money), new products are often not certified, meaning that if you are looking for the "latest and greatest," you may not be able to find such products that are CC certified. Sometimes, the ISSMP may need to use non-certified products in order to address a particular risk; in such scenarios (in which a risk exists and certified products cannot address it) insistence on utilizing only certified products may put the organization in harm's way.

Integration with Software

A common security issue is the integration of hardware and software. Hardware that is specifically designed to work with the software being used, sometimes by having specialized drivers from the hardware manufacturer, is more secure than hardware that has to use work-arounds or must have special applications or drivers built in house. Any time extra work is required, it can introduce both extra expense in accomplishing that work and new security risks that must then be investigated and mitigated.

Most operating system manufacturers have a compatibility or certification system in place that will test and certify hardware drivers as being compatible with their operating system. Use of hardware that has passed these certification tests will give additional assurance that at least basic testing has been performed.

Some of the important questions to ask about each piece of hardware the project may use in relation to hardware/software integration are as follows:

- Is this hardware certified or tested to work with the operating system(s) that must be supported in this project?
- Is this hardware certified or tested to work with each of the commercial applications that must be supported in this project?
- Does this hardware fully support a recognized standard that the rest of the project can also use?
- Do the drivers for this hardware go through a recertification process with the operating system when updated?

Interoperability

Where integration is the ability of software to run on particular hardware, interoperability is the ability of hardware to interact and be hooked up to other hardware, often from other manufacturers, including things like networks, etc.

One factor in determining interoperability is whether the disparate pieces of hardware use a common standard, such as identical wireless protocols and/or data-transfer rates. Interoperability issues include problems such as proprietary software or firmware that is not designed to be interoperable with other products.

As is the case with integration, additional work required to make hardware interoperable typically means the incurrence of additional cost, as well as the possibility of creating additional security risks that must be investigated and mitigated.

Some of the important questions in relation to hardware interoperability that should be asked about each piece of hardware that a project may use include:

- Does this hardware support an industry standard to allow interoperability?
- Does this hardware require any proprietary support or interface in order to allow operation with other hardware required by the system?

Maintenance and Support

Maintenance and support of hardware can be an ongoing security issue for several reasons:

- People providing support may have access to sensitive information. This type of risk can be addressed in part with technical controls, but legal documents such as non-disclosure agreements, confidentiality agreements, non-compete agreements, and the like can help as well. In some environments, background checks and requirements for official government issued clearances can also reduce risks.
- Another possible risk is whether a party providing support is sufficiently knowledgeable and thorough with his or her work. In essence, the concern is whether or not the person actually doing the job knows "what he or she is doing" and "takes the time" to do the job thoroughly, flawlessly, and accurately.
- Other risks include whether the parties providing support truly understand both hardware and software maintenance requirements and scheduling, and whether an organization properly manages its maintenance plan and monitors its maintenance activity to ensure that all is properly achieved according to plan.

These factors create another balancing act to consider. There may be an impression of greater security by using an in-house maintenance team, but the team may not be as well trained and knowledgeable and, in some cases, may inadvertently cause other security issues and be unable to recognize problems that it encounters. This issue is also discussed in this book in relation to other areas of security.

Some of the important questions to ask about each piece of hardware the project may use in relation to maintenance and support are as follows:

- Who will provide the ongoing maintenance this hardware may require?
- What support will be needed to keep this hardware running correctly?
- What policies are in place to govern the people providing the maintenance and support for this hardware?
- If support is already contracted, what terms are in place, what does it cover, and how long is the contract in effect?
- What policies are in place to log and track the maintenance and support on this hardware, and what process is in place to audit those logs?
- What happens when equipment fails (which, eventually, if used long enough, it is likely going to)?

2

Security Lifecycle Management

How is equipment disposed of at the end of its usable life?

Likewise, software needs to be maintained and supported. Updates must be installed, but only after properly testing them. Often this is done in a staging environment that mimics the production systems.

Redundancy

Another important aspect to consider for hardware is redundancy. Hardware has a finite lifespan and it will ultimately fail – it is a question of "when," not of "if" – which can take down critical parts of a system. In order for one to ensure that a system functions properly in the case of a failure, there needs to be redundancy and a plan for safe failover so that security is not compromised by having to cobble together a quick fix in order to solve a business crisis. When it comes to security, preparation is key: An ounce of prevention can be worth many pounds of cure.

Remember that redundancy is not only redundancy of a particular piece of hardware itself but of whatever the hardware relies upon, like power, air conditioning, Internet connectivity, routers, physical facilities, etc.

Some of the important questions to ask about the redundancy and failover plans for each piece of hardware the project may use are as follows:

- What happens to the project if this piece of hardware goes down?
- What will be required to get the project running again without this piece of hardware, and how much time will it require?
- What happens to the project if an integral infrastructure element (power, Internet, intranet) goes down?
- What happens if the main hardware goes down, then the secondary hardware also goes down?
- Is failure of this hardware catastrophic enough that redundant hardware must be kept always ready?
- Is the redundancy provided in the same physical location or a different physical location, placing the project at a greater risk of going down completely in case of a regional issue?
- What policies are in place to log and track potential signs of hardware failure to allow early intervention, and what process is in place to audit those logs?

Physical Access

One of the cardinal rules of security is that almost anything can be compromised if an attacker has physical access to the system. With that in mind, one should examine each piece of hardware with an eye toward who should have physical access to it, and this may determine where the hardware should be installed.

Some hardware requires physical access by all users, like client machines or terminals, but access to critical hardware like servers or data centers should be limited to the people who actually require that access to perform their job functions.

Controlling access can be a bit more difficult in situations where hardware is shared by multiple projects and where hardware is housed in one site along with hardware belonging to other projects or even companies.

Some of the important questions to ask about each piece of hardware the project may use in relation to physical access are as follows:

- Who requires physical access to this piece of hardware to perform job functions relating to this project?
- Who requires physical access to this piece of hardware to perform job functions not relating to this project?
- How will physical access be restricted?
- What policies are in place to log and record check who has accessed the hardware and when and what process is in place for auditing those logs?
- What processes are in place for requesting, allowing, and denying access rights?

Operating System

Another important element in any project is the one or more operating systems on which the project will run. The actual choice of operating system is often limited to merely a selection of flavors from a single manufacturer, based on what the company's standards are determined to be.

This is not all bad because it does enforce interoperability between the different systems, but it also means that there may be occasions when the most secure operating system may not be the operating system whose use is required.

Much of this disparity can be mitigated by effective security policies and practices, but there are a lot of questions to be answered and trade-offs to be considered.

Hardening

Hardening an operating system consists of removing all nonessential tools, utilities, and other system administration options that ship with the operating system in order to reduce the potential security exploits as well as lessen the damage possible through inadvertent use of a tool or administration setting. It also includes the setting and enforcing of security policies. It is basically a way to reduce the attack surface of the system.

Some popular operating systems have a default installation that includes a lot of tools and utilities to make the use of the operating system easier, but that ease is often at odds with system security and security principles. Some manufacturers of operating systems have begun to reduce the default installation set and turn off (or allow installers to turn off) the more exploitable options by default; in a mission-critical environment, however, these features should not be relied upon.

The ISSMP should be able to help establish a baseline configuration – that is the agreed upon configuration of a system or server from which point all modifications will be considered changes. If servers, or operating systems, need to be configured differently for some reason (for example, with more of their add-ons), change management should be utilized.

Another aspect of hardening to consider is the maturity of the operating system. In general, newer operating systems have a greater number of undiscovered security holes than older, better explored operating systems.

Security and access policies are another important aspect of hardening an operating system. These policies may vary depending on the role of the machine the operating system is running on (server vs. client, for example), but many are standard security practices.

Some of the important questions to ask about each operating system in each project role in relation to system hardening are as follows:

- What are the tools, applications, and utilities of the operating system that are required to perform the assigned role for the project?
- What are the protocols and subsystems of the operating system that are required to perform the assigned role for the project?
- What other applications, utilities, tools, protocols, and subsystems can be removed without hindering the operating system's ability to perform the assigned role for the project?
- Are there any other projects or dependencies on the operating system on a specific machine that will require any applications, tools, utilities, protocols, or subsystems that would conflict with planned removals for hardening?
- Have all sample data, scripts, and applications been removed?
- Who has the ability to install new software or enable protocols or subsystems on the operating system on a specific machine?
- What policies govern what software may be installed or what protocols or subsystems may be enabled on the operating system on a specific machine, and what process is in place to enforce those policies?
- Are default user groups disabled or deleted from the operating system?
- Is a strong password policy enforced on the operating system?
- Is remote authentication used and, if so, are strong passwords required and enforced?
- Are the files and directories locked down as a default, with access granted only as needed?
- What process is in place for granting and removing access rights?
- What logging is in place to record the granting, removing, or modification of access rights, and what process is in place to audit those logs?
- Are user groups used for access control?
- What logging and auditing is in place to record system events and changes in detail, and what process is in place to audit those logs?

Patches and Updates

Vulnerability management, including the process of addressing vulnerabilities by patching operating systems and the various applications and drivers that run upon them (sometimes considered part of vulnerability management, but really it is a separate function as patches may also be needed for purposes other than correcting vulnerabilities), is an important part of securing operating systems. Most threats in the wild are patched as soon as possible, but many more systems are victimized due to not installing patches as soon as possible after they are made available.

Of course, even security conscious organizations may not patch immediately upon the release of a patch; they need time to test the patch in a staging environment before applying it to production machines. Proper change control is necessary: There must be a way of tracking changes made to systems and of rolling back any modifications that turn out to be problematic. Of course, any and all changes should be tested before being applied in production. Sometimes, if an emergency arises (for example, it is determined that a major vulnerability exists on a production system, and, if it is not patched, hackers can breach it), the process of testing must be rushed. In some cases, it may even be wise to take the production system offline while the testing is conducted. There may be rare cases in which a patch can be applied without testing (for example, in certain scenarios in which the patch was already tested in another identical system elsewhere in the organization); however, in general, even in emergencies, patches should always be tested because failure to test could lead to a patch being applied that causes system malfunctions or new security vulnerabilities. Ultimately, though, the decision whether to rush a patch without adequate testing is a business decision based on comparing the risk of exposure, the risk of downtime if a system is taken down until patched, and the risk that the patch will cause problems. Sometimes other technical countermeasures can be utilized as temporary fixes until a patch has been tested.

As discussed elsewhere in this book, there may be legal or regulatory requirements regarding the reporting of discovered vulnerabilities, so the ISSMP should also be aware of these.

Depending on the role of the machine on which the operating system is running, the application of patches can be simply and easily accomplished, as on a client machine, or it can require a scheduled downtime and negotiated timing in the case of a server or centralized resource.

Some of the important questions to ask about each operating system's patches and updates in relation to machines in each role in the project are as follows:

- What is the current policy and process for applying updates to servers or centralized resources, and how is that policy enforced?
- Is the use of automatic updates on client or desktop systems allowed or mandated?
- What is the enterprise's security policy with regard to operating system patches and updates, and how is that policy enforced?
- Is the testing of patches required before they are distributed in the enterprise, and if so, who is responsible for testing those patches?
- What logging is in place to detect noncompliance with the policy in place, and what process is in place to audit those logs?

Security Software

Another aspect to the complex security of operating systems is the use of security software. This includes firewalls, anti-virus/anti-malware software, anti-phishing technology, anti-spam technology, and other security-oriented applications. Use of well-rated and regularly updated security software is an important part of protecting and hardening operating systems. It should be noted that this type of security is needed on all computers a person utilizes, be they "classic computers" such as desktops or laptops.

Policies must be created to ensure that security software is utilized properly; simply requiring people to use it is insufficient.

2

Security Lifecycle Management

Some of the important questions to ask about security software in relation to each operating system in each role in the project are as follows:

- What is the current policy on firewalls and security software, and how is that policy enforced?
- Is the use of firewalls and security software mandatory and enforced on all systems?
- Is the use of automatic updates of the firewalls and security software mandated and enforced?
- Is the testing of updates required before they are rolled out to the enterprise, and who is responsible for that testing?
- Are firewall and security software providers reviewed on a regular basis to ensure the use of the best software for the best prices?
- When were the rules on the firewall last reviewed? Do any need to be changed?
- Is the firewall designed to "fail to deny" (as it should be)?
- Are there processes in place to ensure that change requests are handled in an orderly fashion and logged properly?

Other Security Systems

The ISSMP should also be familiar with network firewalls, application-level firewalls, intrusion detection systems, intrusion prevention systems, honeypot technology, and other systems intended to protect the network and the systems on it. Like all other security technologies, these countermeasures need to be properly selected, implemented, and maintained.

Other systems such as data loss prevention systems, compliance systems, social media active monitoring systems, and social media self-monitoring systems may also be appropriate; the ISSMP should learn about these as well.

Networks

Network security is a high priority in any enterprise, and every project that is created and rolled out has the potential to jeopardize not just the security of individual machines but also the security of the network or networks to which it is attached and through which it communicates and any data that lives on them. This is especially true because most networks connect not just to client machines but interconnect with other networks and the Internet.

Because of the greater risk and potential damage, network security deserves careful attention while carrying out risk analysis. Always be aware that the issue of networks and security applies to both wired and wireless networks, wi-fi, cellular, and any other types of networks in use by the project.

Interconnection Agreements

Interconnection agreements are the contracts between an enterprise and one or more other companies, especially telephone or Internet providers that lay out the terms of use and things like bandwidth, routing policies, customer support, etc.

Although this may seem to be something outside the realm of security, it really is not. The way the enterprise interconnects with the outside world can be the source of security issues or can exacerbate existing security flaws.

Some of the important questions to ask about each network and every interconnection agreement that will touch the project are as follows:

- What are the actual terms of the interconnection agreement, and how can they impact the project?
- What is the impact of any bandwidth limits or constraints on the project?
- What is the service level agreement (SLA) between the provider and the enterprise in regard to customer support hours, expected support hours, and uptime promises?
- What routing and security processes and procedures does the provider enforce?
- How is the connection physically and logically made, and what physical and logical security exists around the connection?
- What responsibilities does the enterprise have for content going out through the provider?
- What monitoring and logging is in place to allow auditing of traffic between the enterprise and the provider?
- What escalation paths are there for urgent security issues?

For more about interconnection agreements, please see the NIST 800-100 publication entitled "Information Security Handbook: A Guide for Managers" available at: http://csrc.nist.gov/publications/nistpubs/800-100/SP800-100-Mar07-2007.pdf

Redundancy

Like individual hardware redundancy, network redundancy is important because lack of network connectivity means that any project or system that relies on a network to convey business-critical information will go down, and clients reliant on it will be unable to connect.

While redundant connections and components for every system would be nice, cost is an issue. Rarely, if ever, will a totally separate, secondary network be available to provide redundancy for systems that are not mission critical. Instead, the ISSMP and others involved in decision making must exercise judgment to determine what parts of the network need what level of redundancy in order to prevent a catastrophic failure that results in unacceptable damage to the business.

Since not all networking components are from the same vendors made at the same time, , etc. a one-size-fits-all plan for all equipment is prone to be insufficient. Proper planning takes time.

Some of the important questions to ask about redundancy for each set of machines on each network that will touch the project are as follows:

- What are the ramifications to the project if the machine becomes unreachable by others?
- What are the ramifications to the project if the machine is unable to reach others?

2

Security Lifecycle Management

- How can the machine be made network redundant?
- Is the redundancy automatic or does it require manual intervention?
- What logging or monitoring is in place to identify a failover or the need for a failover, and what process is in place to audit these logs?

Redundancy can also be an instrumental ingredient of a business continuity plan. While such plans are discussed in more detail later in this book, at this point it is important to point out the notion that redundancy can be used to keep businesses operational when failures take place. Systems that are redundant between locations can remain up and running if one location loses power – or is even destroyed.

Likewise, authentication and authorization systems may be redundant across locations or even geographies to ensure that even if some portion of the organization's infrastructure failed, proper access can still be ensured. We always want to be able to fail to deny; without proper resilience of the authentication and authorization systems, an organization might be forced to fail to allow, or its business operations might cease in the case of a failure.

Availability

Network availability is a key attribute to protect because it doesn't matter how secure your network is if it's not up when it needs to be and users cannot make legitimate use of it. There are quite a few considerations when it comes to security and network availability, most of which are based on trying to keep the network up more than on recovery when it goes down. This does not, however, mean that there should not be any consideration toward what is needed to get the network back into operation when it fails for any reason.

Some of the important questions to ask about network availability in relation to any network the project touches are as follows:

- Is there monitoring and logging in place to detect both partial and complete network outages that might threaten the project, and what process is in place to audit those logs?
- Is there monitoring and logging in place to detect network availability threats, including attacks, that might threaten the project, and what process is in place to audit those logs?
- Are network firewalls in place, and are they using a white-list approach to limit network threats?
- What logging is in place to track changes to network firewalls, and what process is in place to audit those logs?
- Is there a standardized management policy in place for the network that uses a limited number of tools and processes to protect network availability, and how is that enforced?
- If the network does go down, in whole or in part, what is required to bring it back up?
- What is the response policy or agreement for network outages?
- If the network goes down, what impact does it have on the project?

Authentication and Authorization

Authentication is the process of validating that a party is who it claims to be, based on the identification that it has provided. Authentication is discussed in other areas of this book and in detail in the CISSP Study Guide.

Authorization refers to the allocation of resources; network authorization is, therefore, the front line of security for networks and the projects that use networks.

One aspect of authorization is to ensure that the correct permissions are assigned to the correct accounts. This also encompasses the security practice of least privilege. No account should have more permissions than the user of that account actually needs to perform his or her job functions. Permissions need to be done on a "white-list" basis, where everyone is locked out, then permissions are granted as the exception rather than removed as unnecessary.

The most neglected aspect of authorization is cross-network or cross-domain trust. All too often, this trust is done as a blanket agreement, with not enough thought or work going into determining if such a scenario is prudent from a security perspective. It can be useful to isolate extremely sensitive data or systems on their own network or domain, then grant access to that network or domain only for required users.

It might be useful for the ISSMP to learn about SAML, which is an XML-standard for communicating about authentication and authorization. SAML, for example, can be utilized to facilitate Web-based single sign-on to multiple sites (especially intranet based) by relaying authentication and authorization data. Because SAML does not care what method is used for authentication (password, multi-factor, etc.), it can be used across numerous environments.

Some of the important questions to ask about each network and authorization type that will touch the project are as follows:

- Are any alternate authentication methods (biometrics, etc.) needed, planned, or already being used by the company that will impact how authorization needs to occur?
- Does the network have a trust relationship with any other network(s), and, if so, what is that relationship?
- What logging is in place to track changes to internetwork trust relationship changes, and what process is in place to audit those logs?
- Is remote access available, and, if so, who is permitted remote network access, when, and with what authorization method?
- What logging is in place to track remote-access actions, attempted actions, and traffic, and what process is in place to audit those logs?
- Is there a policy in place for white-list permissions granting so users are only given permissions for what they really need, and how is that policy enforced?
- Is there a policy in place for granting and removing permissions, and how is that policy enforced?
- What logging is in place to track changes to permissions, and what process is in place to audit those logs?

Encryption

Encryption is another aspect of network security, and whether or not it is already in place and to what extent can have a large effect on the project, both in terms of security and required work during development. The more confidential and sensitive the information the project handles, the more important network encryption becomes. The use of encryption is often linked to particular classification levels. In some cases, it may be required due to an organization informing its customers, suppliers, or partners that all communications over public networks is encrypted. Some of the important questions to ask about encryption on each network the project touches are as follows:

- Is network traffic normally encrypted, and, if so, what encryption is being used?
- Do plans for the project include encryption of its own traffic on top of any standard network encryption?
- Does your project encrypt its own data before transmission, and, if so, what encryption is being used?
- If wireless or wi-fi is in use, what encryption is in use, and what is being done to prevent sniffing? Are there any cryptographic control standards to which, by law or contractual obligation, the organization must adhere?

Also, there should be processes and procedures in place for issuing, managing, and revoking keys.

User Policies

Policies and procedures are an important aspect of security, especially when it comes to network security. Implementing countermeasures and other risk mitigations without first establishing proper overall security policies is insufficient, and it is likely going to lead to serious problems; for security to be achieved, it must be clear how security is to be implemented and maintained, and how people are required to use security-related features. The ISSMP should be aware that some systems might operate under a waiver, and the remediation/compensating controls need to be codified into procedures and communicated to users.

Policies will vary based on the types of devices and systems being used: Desktops, laptops, tablets, smartphones, and other devices each have unique sets of risks and, therefore, demand different countermeasures or different countermeasure levels and control configurations. Environments in which people log in remotely via VPN have different needs than those where everyone works only from within the office.

User Passwords

Most networks have a policy that defines the requirements for username and password combinations that are designed to make them harder to guess or accidentally reveal to others. Unfortunately, most people are not careful enough about protecting that information, which can lead to unauthorized or impersonated access.

It is also important to realize that asking people to create overly complex passwords, or requiring them to change passwords often, increases the chances of passwords being written down and stored in insecure manners.

Some of the important questions to ask about user password policy and security for each network on which the system will be installed and the networks that have a trust relationship with the project's own network are as follows:

- Are strong passwords required and enforced?
- Are regular password changes required and enforced?
- Are passwords revealed to others, including the network administrators, or are all resets and requests automatically handled?
- Is the reuse of passwords discouraged within a brief period of time, and how is this enforced?
- Does the user have a single username and password for all resource access?
- Are password reset requests verified with the user or user's supervisor before issuing a reset?
- Are password policies increasing the likelihood of people writing down passwords and, thereby, undermining the security intended to be gained with those password policies?

Required Software

Another important aspect to maintaining network security is the set of policies surrounding required software.

In many companies, the IT department requires that specific software be installed on any device prior to it being connected to the organization's network.. In general, such software includes personal firewall, anti-virus, and anti-spyware software, as well as various applications to enable better administration of the user's hardware and software if the need to manage it arises.

Another common policy is the use of mandated firewalls and firewall policies. Since personal firewalls help increase the overall security, it's not unusual to have policies mandating their use on every system in the company.

It always bears remembering that the biggest component of policy is enforcement. If a policy is made but not enforced, it quickly becomes little more than a suggestion and will be routinely ignored.

Some of the important questions to ask about security and network policies for required software in networks that house or access the project are as follows:

- Is there a policy in place around the required use of anti-virus/anti-malware software and if so, how is it enforced?
- Is there a policy in place around the required use and settings for individual or personal firewalls and if so, how is it enforced?
- Is there software in standard use to manage and update the various machines on the network? If so, what policy is in place to enforce its installation and activation?
- Is there a policy around the installation of software updates and if so, how is it enforced?
- Is there a policy around the installation and use of non-approved software and if so, how is it enforced?
- Is there a policy around downloading software or files from the Internet and if so, how is it enforced?

Required Configuration

Besides required software, it is wise to require certain configurations of computers and other devices that are used within an organization. Having a standard baseline not only helps with security but reduces the complexity of technical support as well. Some hardening (as described elsewhere in this book) may also be appropriate. Policies for users (e.g., for what they can use the machine, and for what they cannot use it) are also a good idea. In most cases, users should also not have super user/administrator/root access to their work issued computers, and users should not be allowed to install any software that they desire without approval from the appropriate parties within the organization. In general, there will be a list of approved software; anything else requires a waiver or special permission. Technical users, and sometimes other folks, may require administrator access to certain machines, but, in most cases, the number of such machines should be extremely limited, the allowance of such access well documented, such permissions granted only for machines issued to the technical users as devices to be used by them exclusively, and, such devices should not be allowed to be connected to sensitive networks (such as production server networks).

As always, configuration management tools should be utilized if a large number of devices must be managed. These tools can simplify delivery of a baseline configuration to a system (wiping out whatever is there prior to the baseline install).

Ports and Protocols in Use

It is imperative to ensure that the security team is aware of what protocols are in use for systems within the organization and that only ports that are necessary for those protocols to function are open, as needed, for communications. Other ports should not be "listening" nor should they be open in firewalls. This is discussed elsewhere in this book in connection to firewalls.

Databases

Databases create the potential for the serious risk (and resulting repercussions) of data theft, as well as the risk of technical failures making the database unreadable and unusable. There are, of course, also risks of data integrity and of availability (that is, of data becoming corrupted or simply unavailable due to technical problems, human error, or attack). Outsourced database hosting and management, such as those that exist in cloud-based models, can exacerbate the risks of other issues as discussed in the section about cloud providers and service level agreements. Access control to databases is, of course, a major concern.

Database-related risks can have huge ramifications for a business, especially in cases where security is lax or nonexistent or where data theft occurs but remains undiscovered for a significant period of time. The costs can be anything from lack of customer confidence to having to pay for identity-theft monitoring for compromised individuals or even to pay regulatory fines.

Because multiple databases may be stored on the same server, an attack against one database used by one application could lead to a compromise of other databases. Similar problems may also exist vis-à-vis servers (virtual servers run on the same physical machines), which will be discussed later in this chapter, but are more common without the virtualization. Of course, physical and logical access to the database should be limited to approved channels and authorized parties; an n-tier architecture (as discussed elsewhere in this chapter) can sometimes assist in this regard. The ISSMP may be asked to help select a database package by providing input related to the security requirements and features, as well as to assist with planning the configuration of the database, and actually configuring it, in order to maintain security. Participation in the selection and configuration of various data reporting tools, or database access tools, might also fall within the ISSMP's realm. Likewise, helping to establish data access policies, and policies to ensure the non-repudiation of data in the database, will likely fall into the ISSMP's domain.

Access Control

Access control is the starting point for any database security. It is important to note that there are often layers of access control in each project; in which case, it is important to set each layer correctly so that a failure of one layer does not compromise access for other layers. This is another variety of defense-in-depth.

The system should not allow unauthorized parties to issue SQL instructions to the database or to even communicate with it.

All access to databases should be monitored and logged. This not only allows for catching people who do things that they should not, but it provides a proactive defense in that people who are made aware that their actions will be monitored are less likely to perform inappropriate actions.

It is also important to note that the database administrator account or accounts, which can provide tremendous access to data, are also a weak point; they must be protected to ensure that unauthorized parties, who may attempt to gain access to this account, cannot leverage it for nefarious purposes.

Stored procedures must be protected so that only authorized parties can access them, never mind execute them. Modifications to stored procedures should normally be done in a development environment and moved to the production environment by other authorized parties after proper testing; do not allow separation of duties to be undermined.

There are standards for defining access control that are also readily available. For example, XACML (and its derivatives such as GeoXACML) is a standard XML-based language for access control that allows for communication between access-control systems and implementations, even if they are from different vendors.

A common situation of special note with regard to access control of a completed project is that the members of the project development team often have full database access during development, but there have been many instances of security breaches occurring when that access persists to the live database.

Server Access

Of course, the server that houses the database must be secured. It should be hardened and should have a baseline security configuration to which the database functionality is added.

Access to the server that controls or houses the database must be controlled so only those people or applications that require access to the server actually have that access enabled. This is another case of a need for white-list permissions where everyone is locked out and then required permissions are granted as an exception.

Because access isn't a black and white situation, the type of access should also be tightly controlled, based on the actual required access needed to perform the job functions.

Some of the important questions to ask about server access control on each server that will house a database the project will use, including any backup databases, are as follows:

- Who requires access to the server in order to perform their job functions for this project, and what level of access do they require?
- Who requires access to the server for non-project-related job functions, and what level of access do they require?
- What applications require access to the server for project-related purposes, and what level of access do they require?
- What applications require access to the server for non-project related purposes, and what level of access do they require?
- What policy is in place regarding requesting, granting, and removing access rights to the server?
- What logging and monitoring is in place to track access rights changes to the server, and what process is in place to audit those logs?
- What logging is in place to track access and attempted access to the server, and what process is in place to audit those logs?

Database and Data Access

Another important access control is that of who has access to the actual database and the data contained within it. Database access must also be controlled based on the actual access required to accomplish a job function.

An additional aspect to database and data access is whether access is given to an account designed for use by applications or other servers. These accounts can create additional risk because there is a tendency to not change this connection string once it's put into place, especially if the string has been embedded within applications and/or scripts. The connection string may include confidential database access credentials that are not properly encrypted – and can be utilized by unauthorized parties to access data or even modify it. Hence, depending on what rights the account has, it can create a significant risk to the organization.

Database and data access should also be controlled with an eye toward what rights an account has. Restricting access to only required privileges (write, read, update, etc.) helps to prevent compromised accounts from further security violations. This can be trickier with databases shared by the current project and other projects where the access already given may need revision.

Some of the important questions to ask about database and data access for each database the project will use or that will share a server with a project database are as follows:

- Who requires access to the database and data to perform their job functions for this project, and what level of access do they require?
- Who requires access to the database and data to perform their job functions outside this project, and what level of access do they require?
- If the database is shared by other projects, what access has already been granted, to whom, and what level?

- What policy is in place for requesting, granting, and denying access to the database and data, and how is that enforced?
- What logging or monitoring is in place to track changes to database access, and what process is in place to audit these logs?
- What applications require access to the database and data to perform their tasks, and what level of access do they require?
- What data is being stored in this database, and what is the sensitivity of that data?
- Is the data encrypted? If so, how? Who can decrypt it? Where are the keys? Who has access to them? Who had access to them in the past?
- What data is stored in other databases sharing the same database server, and what is the sensitivity of that data?
- How is the connection information or access information stored for any applications or systems that access this database?
- How will the project access this database, and how will the connection strings and passwords be stored and changed?
- What logging or monitoring is in place to track access or attempted access of this database, and what process is in place to audit these logs?

Maintenance Plan

In order for the project's databases and database servers to remain secure and functioning properly, regular maintenance is a must. A security-conscious eye toward typical maintenance allows planning for these events in advance and prevents the use of insecure and seat-of-the-pants maintenance efforts or no maintenance at all.

Maintenance of the database server and databases can include some security risks, depending on who is maintaining the server and database and what functions they are performing.

Auditing

Auditing must be conducted to detect potential security risks and undetected security-related events and to ensure that existing policies are being enforced.

In order to conduct effective auditing, one must keep logging and records, preferably in a secure location that is not on the server itself. People who have access to a system should not have access to its audit logs and vice versa; without separation of duties, auditing can sometimes be entirely undermined. Someone must be responsible for reviewing audit logs, and there must be a policy in place for what to do if he or she detects security-related issues.

Some questions to ask about the auditing of databases and database servers include:
- What logging is in place to record server-level events like access attempts, and what process is in place to audit these logs?
- What logging is in place to record database-level events like unauthorized access attempts, invalid queries, etc., and what process is in place to audit these logs?
- What logging is in place to record network events that may be aimed at the database or server, and what process is in place to audit these logs?

2

Security Lifecycle Management

- What corporate policy is in place for the review and auditing of all logs produced by the database and server for security-related issues, and who is in charge of doing it?
- Is there a policy in place to ensure that monitoring and log auditing are being done by a party or parties who are not likely to be the source of security issues that would appear in those logs, and how is it enforced?
- What actions must take place or who must be notified if a security-related event is detected during an audit?
- Is the server at the baseline security configuration plus the database functionality, or are other services running?
- Has the baseline security configuration been changed since the server was set up?

Vulnerability Scans and Penetration Testing

Another form of auditing is to perform tests on systems to see if they are vulnerable to attack. While commercial, off-the-shelf tools are available to perform such tests, it is often best to hire a professional (as a consultant or an employee) who specializes in these types of "attacks." Remember, a penetration test that tests 98% of what it should could leave 2% vulnerabilities that cause a system and its data to be 100% vulnerable to breach.

Patches and Updates

Regular patching of the database software and the database server provides better security by keeping up to date on manufacturer-provided fixes for discovered defects, including security defects. Updating of the security software will ensure that the server has the latest signatures and detections available.

Some of the issues listed below may seem unrelated to security on the surface, but since patches and updates are vital for security, it's necessary to know quite a bit about the processes and policies around them.

Some of the important questions to ask about patches and updates to each database and server the project will use are as follows:

- Who is or will be responsible for applying patches and updates to the server and database?
- What are the ramifications of the server or database having to be rebooted or taken offline to apply patches or updates?
- Are there company policies or guidelines for patches and updates that would apply to the server or database, and how are they enforced?
- Is there auditing or enforcement of update and patch policies that would be applied to the server or database?
- Is there a requirement to failover to a redundant database or server during a patch or update to ensure minimal downtime, and how is this enforced?
- If a patch is installed, is it also added to the baseline configuration?
- Is version control being utilized to ensure that there are fixes in case of problems after a patch is installed?

Backups

Experienced professionals are familiar with the need to backup data in order to ensure that data persists even if its primary host fails. The ISSMP should be aware of security considerations surrounding backups, including related to their storage and access to them. Some of the important questions to ask about database backups for each database the product will use are as follows:

- Who is responsible for creating database backups of the database?
- Are there company policies or guidelines on making, storing, or the retention of database backups that would affect the database, and how are these enforced?
- Who can make a backup of the database on demand?
- What logging is in place for database backup requests, and what is the process for auditing these logs?
- Where are the database backups stored, and who has access to that storage?
- What logging is in place for accessing the database backups, and what auditing is in place to look at these logs?

Web Servers

More and more enterprises are moving to Web-based services (including mobile apps communicating over HTTPS) for important functions or operations, and this brings Web servers even more into the domain of a security manager who deals with the security of enterprise systems.

There are various Web server standards—and they often come with security recommendations. The ISSMP is recommended to review those related to any Web servers within the organization that he or she is serving.

This move to Web services and servers has great advantages for some business functions, but Web-based services often suffer from inadequate security.

Yet at the same time, more and more enterprises are enabling employees to work from home over a virtual private network (VPN) or to use remote access solutions to access workplace services from home via the Internet.

Server Restriction

In order to improve security, one should often restrict Web servers in ways not required by various other servers or systems. These restrictions are in addition to, rather than in place of, the normal system security measures and are intended to mitigate some of the specific vulnerabilities of Web servers, such as the ability to utilize SQL injection or buffer overflow attacks by submitting improper input into a Web form, and other forms of attacks that have become increasingly common.

Because of their accessibility, the number of vulnerabilities, and the fact they often serve as front ends to databases with valuable content, Web servers are popular targets for internal and external security threats.

121

Encryption

For all sensitive tasks, and perhaps for other tasks as well, encryption should be utilized. SSL/TLS is the standard for Web applications, and it normally is transmitted over port 443. SSL certificates must be managed and their private keys guarded to ensure that they are not pilfered and misused.

Location

The physical and network location of the Web server can mitigate one of the major risks of it being a Web server—that compromise of the one Web server can put other machines, clients of the Web server, or even the network at risk.

Because Web servers are such targets, it's good practice to not allow a server to act in the role of both a Web server and another type of server, especially a domain controller or backup domain controller. If a Web server that was also acting as a domain controller is compromised, there is a potential that the entire domain will be compromised.

Best practices for security and Web servers usually involve locating Web servers in a demilitarized zone (DMZ) where it is separated from the rest of the network, including any databases or resources it may use, by a firewall on either side. This is also a good model to use for other systems that communicate with business partners and customers. Services that are accessed after a user is authenticated may utilize systems on an internal network that are communicated to by the servers in the DMZ; external users should not communicate directly with the internal network and the systems located on it.

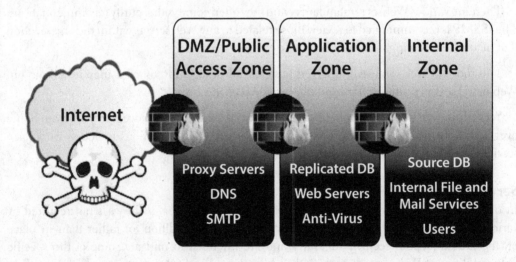

Figure 2.5 – **The Demilitarized Zone (DMZ), Firewalls, and the Internal Network**

Sometimes, using a so-called "n-tier architecture" is desired. In such a model, the Web interface and GUI, the application logic, and the database functionalities are not on the same systems, but, rather, they are logically and physically separated so that pieces can be reused on other systems. Each tier must do its own logging and security checks (e.g., authentication).

Normally, three tiers are used:

- Presentation tier (the GUI)
- Logic tier (Where the application logic is run)
- Data tier (where data is stored and accessed)

In general, the larger the number of users a system has, the more likely it uses a 3 tier model instead of 2 or 1.

Some of the important questions to ask about the physical and network location of each Web server the project will use are as follows:

- Is the Web server isolated in a demilitarized zone (DMZ) and, if so, what else is located in this DMZ?
- Is there a firewall between this DMZ and the rest of the network?
- Where is the server physically located, and who requires physical access to it in order to perform their job functions?
- What logging is in place to record access and access attempts to the physical server, and what process is there to audit these logs?
- What logging is in place to monitor the server's network access and access attempts, and what process is in place to audit these logs?
- Is the Web server also acting as another type of server or resource?
- If the Web server uses a database as a back end, are the Web server and database separated to ensure better security?
- What logging is in place to record access and access attempts that touch the firewall, and what process is in place to audit those logs?

Port Restrictions

Because a Web server is intended for a particular use, the vast array of available ports and port traffic should be limited to use or acknowledge only the ports actually needed to perform as a Web server for the project. Leaving ports open that are not required exposes the Web server to security risks from port attacks and potential software vulnerabilities in software listening on various ports.

Ports should follow a similar white-list approach to that of access control. All ports should be shut down and then only those required for the Web server to perform its tasks for the project should be opened as exceptions. The two standard ports to leave open are port 80 (HTTP) and port 443 (HTTPS).

Some of the important questions to ask regarding Web server port restrictions for each Web server used by the project are as follows:

- Are all ports other than 80 and 443 closed?
- Does the project use any other ports, and why?
- Does other software running on this machine require ports other than 80 and 443 to be open, and why?
- What logging is in place to request, approve, and log changes to port activations and deactivations, and what process is in place to audit these logs?
- What logging is in place to record port access attempts, successful or unsuccessful, and what process is in place to audit these logs?
- What is in place to protect from attacks entering via any open ports?

System Hardening

In addition to the previously mentioned operating system hardening that applies to all systems, Web servers have some specific hardening that can be done to increase security. Some of the specifics depend on what Web server software you are running, but they all have some aspects in common.

In addition to carrying out these initial hardening efforts, one should also ensure that the server configuration is kept up to date as new threats or security flaws are discovered. Any failover or redundant servers must also be examined to ensure they are as secure as the primary server. System hardening is all about decreasing the potential attack surface.

Some of the important questions to ask about the hardening of each Web server the project will use are as follows:

- What applications or utilities are installed by default that can be uninstalled or disabled without jeopardizing the project?
- What protocols or functionality can be uninstalled or disabled without jeopardizing the project?
- Are there company policies or procedures for reinstalling or activating applications or utilities, and how are they enforced?
- Are there company policies or procedures for installing or enabling protocols or functionality, and how are they enforced?
- What logging is in place to record changes in server configuration and software settings, and what process is in place to audit these logs?
- Does this Web server share duties as any other type of server or domain controller, and can it be moved to being a single purpose server to allow for more security?
- What logging is in place to record server activity and access attempts, and what process is in place to audit these logs?
- Are applications and Web services configured to run under least privileges?
- Does the project share this Web server with any other applications, websites, or Web services and, if so, do they have security concerns that can jeopardize the project's security?
- What remote access is required for the project, and who requires this access?
- What logging is in place to record remote access and remote access attempts, and what process is in place to audit these logs?

Maintenance Plan

Maintenance, in various forms, is required to keep the Web server running and secure. The constantly changing landscape of security means that ongoing maintenance, auditing, and security steps are needed to prevent a compromise of the server.

Auditing

Auditing must be conducted on an ongoing basis to detect potential security risks and undetected security-related events and to ensure that existing policies are being enforced. In order to conduct effective auditing, one must keep logs and records, in a secure location that is not on the actual server. Someone must be responsible for reviewing the logs, and there must be a policy in place vis-à-vis what to do if security-related issues are found.

Some of the important questions to ask about auditing each Web server the project will use are as follows:

- What logging is done of server-level events like access attempts, and what process is in place to audit these logs?
- What logging is done of network events that may be aimed at the server or a database or a resource it uses, and what process is in place to audit these logs?
- What corporate policy is in place for the review and auditing of all logs produced by the server for security-related issues, and who is in charge of doing it?
- What policy is in place to ensure that the party or parties that will be auditing the logs is not likely to be a source of logged security violations, and how is that enforced?
- What actions must take place or who must be notified if a security-related event is detected during an audit?

Patches and Updates

Regular patching of the Web server software and the Web server itself provides increased security by keeping up to date on manufacturer-provided fixes for discovered defects, including security defects. Updating of the security software will ensure that the server has the latest signatures and detections available.

Some of the issues listed below may seem unrelated to security on the surface, but since patches and updates are vital for security, it's necessary to know quite a bit about the processes and policies around them.

Some important questions to ask about patches and updates to each Web server the project will use are as follows:

- Who is or will be responsible for applying patches and updates to the server and Web server software, and how is this enforced?
- What are the ramifications of the server having to be rebooted or taken offline to apply patches or updates?
- Are there company policies or guidelines for patches and updates that would apply to the server, and how is this enforced?
- Is there auditing or enforcement of update and patch policies that would apply to the server?
- Is there a requirement to failover to a redundant database or server during a patch or update to ensure minimal downtime?

Open Web Application Security Project

Also known by its acronym, OWASP (www.owasp.org), the Open Web Application Security Project is an organization that seeks to improve the security of Web applications through community collaboration. It provides an online venue for learning about the security of Web applications and for related discussions. The ISSMP may wish to make use of its resources and share his or her own knowledge through this venue.

2

Security Lifecycle Management

Other Applications

Application security can be a significant source of potential risk and uncertainty, due in part to the large number of variables in play.

Applications, in this case, are intended to span not only the external software the company may purchase but also internal software.

Examining every application that presently exists is not practical. Instead, it is valuable to develop a sense for the inherent risk based on the policies for applications and applications development. A very controlled environment will tend to lead to an overall reduction of risk, while a very loose or lax environment will tend to lead to an overall increase of risk.

External Applications

One of the biggest variables is the sheer variety of applications users can and will install, given the ability to do so. It's quite common for users to innocently download a piece of software because they saw or heard about it. That piece of software may be legitimate or not, but each one introduces a set of unknown security risks to not only the user's system but also to the network and maybe the company as a whole.

Users are also prone to opening or installing files sent to them via applications like instant messenger systems or email, which can lead to even further risks.

External applications fall into three major groups: commercial software, open source software, and shareware/freeware software. Both commercial and open-source initiative software have risks (e.g., vulnerabilities in the software, infected with malware, problematic terms of service), but if the software is from a legitimate company, it usually has the advantage of a manufacturer that is interested in security testing its software and improving its security via updates or patches.

Shareware/freeware also poses risks; some shareware/freeware is well written and high quality, but some is not suitable for any kind of secure environment. Because such products may not be well documented, it is often difficult to tell the difference until time has passed and numerous reviews of offerings made by reliable parties have been created. New releases can also recreate the risks.

Some of the important questions to ask about external software coexisting with the project are as follows:

- What policies are in place governing what software users are allowed to download and install, and how are those policies enforced?
- What policies are in place governing what commercial software users are required to have installed, and how are those policies enforced?
- What policies are in place governing updating and patching commercial software, and how are those policies enforced?
- What policies are in place governing whether users can exchange files with external sources, and how are those policies enforced?
- What policies are in place governing scanning of systems and servers for security risks and issues and reporting those issues to determine what action should be taken?

- Do external applications have to pass any acceptance or approval process, and who is responsible for running this process and what are its criteria?
- What logging is in place to record what software each system is running, and what process is in place to audit those logs?

Internal Applications

Internal applications can be almost as much of a risk to security as external applications. This is due, in part, to the still prevalent misconception that internal applications have no or little need to be secure as they are in use only within the company.

Unfortunately, this is not at all the case. There are numerous cases of internal abuse of systems and data when security is not adequate for the potential risks.

In the case of very high-risk applications or data with which your project will directly interact or coexist, you may want to do some further investigation. Some simple research may give you information on how security was addressed when the internal application in question was written or updated, and, if you are lucky, you will be able to review that application's risk analysis or security plan and have a clear idea of the security landscape.

Some companies mandate the use of Secure Coding Principles for any internal application development. Secure Coding Principles can greatly increase the security of new code as it is written and reduce the overall security risk of internal applications.

Some of the important questions to ask about internal applications coexisting with the project are as follows:

- What policies are in place to govern the access to and installation of internal applications, and how are those policies enforced?
- What policies are in place to govern security during internal application development, and how are those policies enforced?
- Is a mandate in place for Secure Coding Principles, and how is that mandate enforced?
- What logging is in place to record what internal applications are installed or running on user systems, and what process is in place to audit those logs?

Project under Development

Now you move from the environment within which your project will exist and with which it will interact and focus on the actual project for which you are managing security. Some of the security focus now moves from purely being security of the finished product to security of the development process as it occurs.

Secure Coding Principles

The Secure Coding Principles by OWASP are a collection of concepts that, if properly utilized by all members of a development team (but, especially by the developers), can lead to more secure software. This is a great start to an application being secure by design, but not all development teams are willing to sign up to follow these principles.

If you can sell the development team on making the following Secure Coding Principles a requirement of the software development process, you have an immediate leg up on making the project secure (The principles are quoted here from OWASP – the most up to date version can be read at https://www.owasp.org/index.php/Secure_Coding_Principles).

Architects and solution providers need guidance to produce secure applications by design, and they can do this by not only implementing the basic controls documented in the main text but also referring back to the underlying "Why?" in these principles. Security principles such as confidentiality, integrity, and availability (although important, broad, and vague) do not change. Your application will be more robust the more you apply them.

For example, it is a fine thing when implementing data validation to include a centralized validation routine for all form input. However, it is a far finer thing to see validation at each tier for all user input, coupled with appropriate error handling and robust access control.

In the last year or so, there has been a significant push to standardize terminology and taxonomy. This version of the development guide has normalized its principles with those from major industry texts, while dropping a principle or two present in the first edition of the development guide. This is to prevent confusion and to increase compliance with a core set of principles. The principles that have been removed are adequately covered by controls within the text.

Asset Classification
Selection of controls is only possible after classifying the data to be protected. For example, controls applicable to low value systems such as blogs and forums are different to the level and number of controls suitable for accounting, high value banking, and electronic trading systems.

About Attackers
When designing controls to prevent misuse of your application, you must consider the most likely attackers (in order of likelihood and actualized loss from most to least):

- Disgruntled staff or developers
- "Drive by" attacks, such as side effects or direct consequences of a virus, worm, or Trojan attack
- Motivated criminal attackers, such as organized crime
- Criminal attackers without motive against your organization, such as defacers
- Script kiddies

Notice there is no entry for the term "hacker." This is due to the emotive and incorrect use of the word "hacker" by the media. However, it is far too late to reclaim the incorrect use of the word "hacker" and try to return the word to its correct roots. The development guide consistently uses the word "attacker" when denoting something or someone who is actively attempting to exploit a particular feature.

Core Pillars of Information Security
Information security has relied upon the following pillars:

- **Confidentiality** – only allow access to data for which the user is permitted
- **Integrity** – ensure data is not tampered or altered by unauthorized users

■ ***Availability*** – ensure systems and data are available to authorized users when they need it

The following principles are all related to these three pillars. Indeed, when one is considering how to construct a control, considering each pillar in turn will assist in producing a robust security control.

Security Architecture

Applications without security architecture are the same as bridges constructed without finite element analysis and wind tunnel testing. Sure, they look like bridges, but they will fall down at the first flutter of a butterfly's wings. The need for application security in the form of security architecture is every bit as great as in building or bridge construction.

Application architects are responsible for constructing their design to adequately cover risks from both typical usage and from extreme attack. Bridge designers need to cope with a certain amount of cars and foot traffic but also cyclonic winds, earthquake, fire, traffic incidents, and flooding. Application designers must cope with extreme events, such as brute force or injection attacks, and fraud. The risks for application designers are well known. The days of "we didn't know" are long gone. Security is now expected, not an expensive add-on or simply left out.

Security architecture refers to the fundamental pillars: The application must provide controls to protect the confidentiality of information, integrity of data, and provide access to the data when it is required (availability) – and only to the right users. Security architecture is not "markitecture," where a cornucopia of security products are tossed together and called a "solution," but a carefully considered set of features, controls, safer processes, and default security posture.

When starting a new application or re-factoring an existing application, you should consider each functional feature, and consider:

■ Is the process surrounding this feature as safe as possible? In other words, is this a flawed process?
■ If I were evil, how would I abuse this feature?
■ Is the feature required to be on by default? If so, are there limits or options that could help reduce the risk from this feature?

Andrew van der Stock calls the above process "Thinking Evil™," and he recommends putting yourself in the shoes of the attacker and thinking through all the possible ways you can abuse each and every feature, by considering the three core pillars and using the STRIDE model in turn.

By following this guide, and using the STRIDE/DREAD threat risk modeling discussed here and in Howard and LeBlanc's book, you will be well on your way to formally adopting a security architecture for your applications.

The best system architecture designs and detailed design documents contain security discussions in each and every feature, how the risks are going to be mitigated, and what was actually done during coding.

2

Security Lifecycle Management

Security architecture starts on the day the business requirements are modeled, and it never finishes until the last copy of your application is decommissioned. Security is a lifelong process, not a one shot accident.

Security Principles

These security principles have been taken from the previous edition of the OWASP Development Guide and normalized with the security principles outlined in Howard and LeBlanc's excellent *Writing Secure Code*.

Minimize Attack Surface Area

Every feature that is added to an application adds a certain amount of risk to the overall application. The aim for secure development is to reduce the overall risk by reducing the attack surface area.

For example, a Web application implements online help with a search function. The search function may be vulnerable to SQL injection attacks. If the help feature was limited to authorized users, the attack likelihood is reduced. If the help feature's search function was gated through centralized data validation routines, the ability to perform SQL injection is dramatically reduced. However, if the help feature was rewritten to eliminate the search function (through better user interface, for example), this almost eliminates the attack surface area, even if the help feature was available to the Internet at large.

Establish Secure Defaults

There are many ways to deliver an "out of the box" experience for users. However, by default, the experience should be secure, and it should be up to the users to reduce their security – if they are allowed.

For example, by default, password aging and complexity should be enabled. Users might be allowed to turn these two features off to simplify their use of the application and increase their risk.

Principle of Least Privilege

The principle of least privilege recommends that accounts have the least amount of privilege required to perform their business processes. This encompasses user rights, resource permissions such as CPU limits, memory, network, and file system permissions.

For example, if a middleware server only requires access to the network, read access to a database table, and the ability to write to a log, this describes all the permissions that should be granted. Under no circumstances should the middleware be granted administrative privileges.

Principle of Defense in Depth

The principle of defense in depth suggests that where one control would be reasonable, more controls that approach risks in different fashions are better. Controls, when used in depth, can make severe vulnerabilities extraordinarily difficult to exploit and thus unlikely to occur.

With secure coding, this may take the form of tier-based validation, centralized auditing controls, and requiring users to be logged on all pages.

For example, a flawed administrative interface is unlikely to be vulnerable to anonymous attack if it correctly gates access to production management networks, checks for administrative user authorization, and logs all access.

Fail Securely

Applications regularly fail to process transactions for many reasons. How they fail can determine if an application is secure or not. For example:

```
isAdmin = true;
try {
  codeWhichMayFail();
  isAdmin = isUserInRole( "Administrator" );
}
catch (Exception ex) {
  log.write(ex.toString());
}
```

If either `codeWhichMayFail()` or `isUserInRole` fails or throws an exception, the user is an admin by default. This is obviously a security risk.

Don't Trust Services

Many organizations utilize the processing capabilities of third-party partners, who more than likely have differing security policies and posture than you. It is unlikely that you can influence or control any external third party, whether they are home users or major suppliers or partners.

Therefore, implicit trust of externally run systems is not warranted. All external systems should be treated in a similar fashion.

For example, a loyalty program provider provides data that is used by online banking, providing the number of reward points and a small list of potential redemption items. However, the data should be checked to ensure that it is safe to display to end-users and that the reward points are a positive number, and not improbably large or growing at an unrealistic rate.

Separation of Duties

A key fraud control is separation of duties. For example, someone who requests a computer cannot also sign for it, nor should they directly receive the computer. This prevents the user from requesting many computers and claiming they never arrived.

Certain roles have different levels of trust than normal users. In particular, administrators are different to normal users. In general, administrators should not be users of the application.

For example, an administrator should be able to turn the system on or off and set a password policy but shouldn't be able to log on to the storefront as a super privileged user, such as being able to "buy" goods on behalf of other users.

Avoid Security by Obscurity

Security through obscurity is a weak security control, and it nearly always fails when it is the only control. This is not to say that keeping secrets is a bad idea; it simply means that the security of key systems should not be totally reliant upon keeping details hidden.

For example, the security of an application should not rely upon knowledge of the source code being kept secret. The security should rely upon many other factors, including reasonable password policies, defense in depth, business transaction limits, solid network architecture, and fraud and audit controls.

A practical example is Linux. Linux's source code is widely available, and yet when properly secured, Linux is a hardy, secure, and robust operating system.

Keep Security Simple

Attack surface area and simplicity go hand in hand. Certain software engineering fads prefer overly complex approaches to what would otherwise be relatively straightforward and simple code.

Developers should avoid the use of double negatives and complex architectures when a simpler approach would be faster and simpler.

For example, although it might be fashionable to have a slew of singleton entity beans running on a separate middleware server, it is more secure and faster to simply use global variables with an appropriate mutex mechanism to protect against race conditions.

Fix Security Issues Correctly

Once a security issue has been identified, it is important to develop a test for it and to understand the root cause of the issue. When design patterns are used, it is likely that the security issue is widespread amongst all code bases, so developing the right fix without introducing regressions is essential.

For example, a user has found that he or she can see another user's balance by adjusting his or her cookie. The fix seems to be relatively straightforward, but as the cookie handling code is shared among all applications, a change to just one application will trickle through to all other applications. The fix must therefore be tested on all affected applications.

Some of the important questions to ask about Secure Coding Principles for your project are as follows:

- Have the Secure Coding Principles been made into a requirement for this project?
- How often will the project be reviewed with an eye toward the Secure Coding Principles?

It should be noted that the CSSLP study guide goes into more detail on this area of security.

Environments

For obvious reasons, development of software should not be done in a production environment, and production systems should never be run in a development environment. In larger organizations, there may be multiple environments including:

- Production environment
- Staging environment
- Testing environment
- Development environment
- Disaster recovery production environment
- Disaster recovery testing environment

Human Resources

Depending on the project, personnel may need security clearances, background checks, or the like. The ISSMP should be aware of these requirements and make sure that they are adhered to.

Secure Development

Beyond the Secure Coding Principles, there are additional aspects to project security that must be considered and defined, preferably before the project development really gets under way.

Security-related requirements need to become an integral part of the project requirements, and that necessitates them being defined and agreed upon early in the process.

Define Security Quality Bar

It is important to define the security quality bar because it will serve as the basis for many decisions related to security. The security quality bar is used in conjunction with the risk analysis to define what security issues must be addressed in order to successfully complete, and deliver, the project. Often, this includes a requirement that all severe security issues be addressed prior to delivery.

The purpose of a security quality bar is to set a minimum standard for security that will help indicate when the project can be determined to be acceptable for delivery and, therefore, released. It also prevents spending a huge amount of time on trying to mitigate all security risks at the cost of the project taking far longer than usual. This security quality bar is documented as part of the risk analysis and security plan and is referenced by other project development documents.

Some of the important questions to ask about the security quality bar for your project are as follows:

- If the risk analysis is put in order of overall severity according to the project and its environment, what is the maximum acceptable risk for the project?
- If a mitigation is made, what is the new severity of that risk, and is it below the acceptable risk for the project?

Require Security Reviews

In some cases, security reviews will be a known requirement due to legal or regulatory requirements. In this case, you need to gather the development team prior to development and make its members aware of the requirements that the project must meet. Requirements should be defined up front. Periodic reviews and group discussions will take place through the development and testing process, with a final review before "going live." (Other reviews take place after going live, but they are, technically speaking, not part of the development process.)

If there is no externally mandated security review, is there a company policy in place that requires security reviews and sets the requirements the project must meet? If there is, then the development team must be made aware of them.

If there are no mandates, then a decision must be made based on multiple factors like budget, internal resources and knowledge, and the security risks of the project about whether to conduct a formal security review of the project as a requirement to it being released.

2

Security Lifecycle Management

Some of the important questions to ask about security reviews for your project are as follows:

- Is there a company policy or requirement for a security review and, if so, what are the requirements that have to be met, and who has to conduct the review?
- Is there a legal or regulatory requirement for a security review and, if so, what are the requirements that have to be met, and who has to conduct the review?
- If there is no external requirement for a security review, is the project sensitive enough to warrant a formal security review as a requirement for release? If so, what should the criteria be, and who should conduct the review?
- How many security reviews should be held?

Protect Source Code

An aspect of secure development that is often overlooked is the need to protect the source code of the project, both as it is being developed and afterward. Leaks or releases of source code can result in a huge security breach, so access to the source code should be limited to only those people who actually require that access to perform their job functions, and all other access should be denied. The standard confidentiality, integrity, and availability goals apply to source code, and methods to achieve them should be utilized.

Protect Defect Details

Another aspect to security during development is the need to protect the defect database and details contained in it, especially those relating to security. Most defect reports contain a sample of how to cause the defect to manifest itself, and exposure of that database can lead to exploitation of those defects later.

The defect database should be locked down, and only those people who require access to the defect database to perform their job functions should be given access to it. If there is a need to have other people file defect reports, it may be a worthwhile risk mitigation to set up a method just for that purpose.

Watch for common problems. Even though you are not in charge of the actual coding during development, it is a good idea to be generally aware of common security flaws to be able to watch for situations in which they commonly occur and ask the right questions about their mitigation.

These issues are broken down into broad areas for easier consumption, but this is not an expansive or exhaustive list, and it is certainly not complete. For more details and ideas, you should research the known or common security issues that may have come to light by the time you are working on the project.

The key to identifying security issues is to take the core concept of the issue and extrapolate it to cover your project. It is important to remember that overly focusing on an isolated issue or set of issues can lead to missing a similar one because it's not the same language or doesn't work exactly the same way. Here are some sample issues:

- ***Input and Information Validation Issues*** – Many security issues are related to input and stored information and how that information is handled. These issues include the following:
  - ▫ Not validating all input, all input formats, and all input sources. Nothing should be trusted or taken for granted.

◻ No graceful exit if input is not valid. Invalid or unexpected input should not cause the security to fail.

◻ Information is stored in the registry or system path, and, once stored, that information is trusted without further validation. Registries and paths can be hacked or modified.

◻ Hidden files and directories are being used for saving and retrieving trusted content without further validation. Security by obscurity is no security at all.

■ **Installation Issues** – These are issues that occur when the finished project or one of its components is installed and include the following:

◻ Risky features are enabled in a default installation. Default installations should require independent action to turn on or activate features deemed as risky.

◻ High permissions are required to install the project or component, but they are not required to execute it. This can lead to someone with lesser permissions running an application that he or she should not be able to.

◻ Installation locations are hard-coded. This leads to both always knowing where the application and its data exist and an inability to customize installation for each system.

■ **Authentication Issues** – These are issues that occur during execution of the project or its components and include the following:

◻ User authentication occurs only once or only at certain points. Once an authentication area is bypassed, the system is open with assumed authentication.

◻ Access control rules are not enforced consistently. If an access control list (ACL) is in place, it must be respected and enforced.

■ **Cryptographic Issues** – These are issues related to the use of cryptography in the project or one of its components and include the following:

◻ Custom cryptography is being used instead of tested and verified standardized cryptography.

◻ Homegrown cryptography is notoriously insecure.

■ **Information Disclosure Issues** – These are issues related to information the project or one of its components displays back to the user or files and include the following:

◻ Errors are displayed in a manner that discloses project infrastructure details. Users should be given only the information they absolutely need.

◻ Temporary files are created and data is stored in those files then later trusted with no further validation. Temporary files are easy to compromise.

◻ Crash files and logs contain sensitive information about the project. Again, no information should be disclosed that is not absolutely needed.

◻ Cached information is trusted without further validation. Caches can be tampered with and compromised.

◻ Information is disclosed that is not actually needed by the user.

■ **Execution Issues** – These are issues related to the actual execution and running of the project or its components and include the following:

◻ The project runs at an unnecessarily high privilege. If the project is compromised, that high privilege can be hijacked and used.

- ¤ The project defaults to a less secure version in case of an error or execution problem. Sometimes done for compatibility, it instead leads to risks if an error can be caused.
- ¤ Default accounts are used to run the processes. The default accounts tend to be easy to guess and misuse.
- ¤ Session cookies are weak or easily reused. This is an invitation to session replay or cookie tampering.
- ¤ Sessions are persistent. This can be a sign of a session vulnerability.
- **Output Issues** – These are issues related to the project output and how it is handled. These issues include output that can be intercepted before reaching its desired destination.
- **Common Web Server Issues** – Some issues are more common in Web servers than in other types of applications or are specific to Web servers. Some of these are as follows:
  - ¤ Server processes run at a high privilege. This means that if the process can be hijacked then other code can be run at the same high privilege.
  - ¤ Default accounts used to run server processes. These accounts are easy to guess and compromise.
  - ¤ Trust granted based on a custom packet format. Packet formats are easy to sniff and replicate.
  - ¤ Transmission of unencrypted data. Any data sent in plaintext is sniffable.
  - ¤ Hidden form fields not validated. Another case of obscurity is not security. All fields must be validated.
  - ¤ Trust granted based on transmission method. Any transmission method can be used for malicious data.
  - ¤ No validation to authorize clients. This can lead to the use of rogue or unauthorized clients.
  - ¤ Trust granted to data based on source. Legitimate clients can be subject to data hijacking.
  - ¤ Lack of non-repudiation/anti-repudiation validation. Legitimate transactions can be reversed or denied.
  - ¤ Clients not validating the server. This can lead to legitimate traffic being sent to a rogue server.
  - ¤ Clients verify only server, not data. This is another risk for session hijacking.
  - ¤ Perimeter safeguards trusted for all security. If those safeguards are defeated, the entire system is open.
  - ¤ Encryption keys stored in source code. Source code can be disassembled or copied, and keys can be found.
- **Common Database Issues** – Some issues are more common in database servers and databases than in other types of applications or are specific to databases and database servers. Some of these are as follows:
  - ¤ Database access not locked down by IP. Anyone can talk to the database server and the security risk is increased.
  - ¤ Actions taken without validation. This can lead to SQL injection or other vulnerabilities.
  - ¤ Actions and permission granted to default users. These accounts are easy to guess and misuse.

> ¤ No table access control. This allows actions that are not part of the database design to be taken on tables where that should not be allowed at all.

- **Common Application Programming Interface Issues** – Some issues are more common in application programming interfaces (APIs) than in other types of applications or are specific to APIs. Some of these are as follows:
  - ¤ Reliance on the implementation details of a particular programming language to act as implicit security.
  - ¤ Reliance on perimeter security in place of defense in depth. Once the perimeter is breached, everything is wide open.
  - ¤ API abilities open to anyone. This can lead to misuse of API abilities by other software or attackers.

Choose the Programming Language with Care

Although secure code can be written in any programming language, some programming languages are more prone to specific issues than others by virtue of the language and its programming principles. For example, someone is far more likely to accidentally create a memory leak or opportunity for a buffer overflow attack when he or she is coding in C than when working in PHP. Likewise, it is obviously more likely that there will be SQL injection risks if someone is using SQL than if data is stored in a flat file.

There are a number of languages to choose from, and the decision of language may be a done deal based on the preferences and needs of the enterprise, but there are some common language issues to be aware of.

Scripting languages, in general, are not designed to be secure. Some scripting languages, like JavaScript, have security models, but these models are designed more to protect the clients from malicious websites and not to protect the data or servers. Additionally, scripting languages are known to have a considerable number of security defects. If you intend to use a scripting language for all or part of your project, researching flaws in that particular language will give you a good idea of what to look for and what to add to the risk analysis.

Many programming languages like C and C++ give developers a huge amount of control over things like pointers, memory management, etc. The downside of this control is the increased risk of security defects in the code caused by relatively simple errors. If one of these languages is chosen, this risk should be mitigated by requiring automated or focused security code reviews to flush out these coding issues.

Some programming languages like .NET take that fine control of memory and pointers away from the developers. Although this gives less fine control, it helps to mitigate the common security flaws in code by taking care of variable, pointer, and memory management as well as buffer sizing, etc. If one of these languages is chosen for the project, there is still a risk of poor security practices in coding and mitigation that should be called out.

It should also be pointed out that there are various methodologies and protocols that one can utilize to improve the chances of producing software that will be secure. SOAP with WSS, for example, defines in a structured format how messaging can be done for object oriented programming in a way that helps ensure both confidentiality and integrity.

2

Security Lifecycle Management

137

Web Considerations

- Smart security practices for Web apps, regardless of the platform used to create them, include:
- Encryption is a must because data is, by design, being transmitted over the intranet or Internet.
- Strong validation must be used to counteract the fact that interactive Web applications are often vulnerable to input attacks.
- Server configurations must be secured and the server hardened.
- Data must be secured both in transmission and in storage or backup.
- All systems must still have up-to-date security software and the most current patches and updates applied to remain as secure as possible.
- Controls should be put in to ensure that data does not leak via social media.
- If mobile apps are created to function securely, they should not leave sensitive data on the device.

Documentation

A system is not complete until it has a good set of documentation to accompany it; hence, documentation is an important part of the SDLC. Documents usually go through multiple iterations both during development and over the course of a system's lifetime, so version control is essential.

Documentation of the project and the project security can be both a security issue and a benefit, depending on who has access to the documentation. Only those people with a requirement to have access to the system's documentation should have that access. This means that some people will need access to user guides or instructions but will not need access to development documentation or security documentation.

In general, security and development documentation should be secured in a location with limited access and never released externally to the company. Separating the documentation by security level or area can mitigate the risk of this documentation being released, but this must be weighed against the inconvenience to people who require access having to look in multiple places.

Virtualization

Another popular movement is toward virtualization, especially toward virtual machines. Virtualization can allow one computer to simulate multiple computers by creating "virtual" system resources (like RAM, disk space, etc.) for each "virtual" computer running on the same hardware. Both virtual servers and virtual desktops are becoming increasingly popular.

While virtualization technology is maturing, it is still relatively young and likely rife with undiscovered and unrealized security threats. A list of some such threats follows, but it is, by no means, complete. New problems are still being discovered. If a particular project is considering the use of virtualization, the ISSMP, or others on his or her team, should perform in-depth research into the current state of virtualization security, especially as it applies to the particular virtualization scheme the project plans to use.

Some of the security risks already raised for virtualization are as follows:

- Each virtual machine must still be treated as if it were a separate machine and its operating system and software kept updated and patched. Sometimes, organizations neglect to do this.

- Each virtual machine must still have security software installed and kept up to date.

- In addition to the software on the virtual machines, the virtualization software itself must be kept up to date and patched.

- Administrative access to the underlying server must be tightly controlled, which is sometimes complicated to do if a plethora of virtual machines are running differing tasks belonging to different business owners.

- Many questions that are simple in non-virtualization environment can become complicated and have security repercussions: For example, who gets to reboot the primary system if something goes wrong?

- Security policies regarding separation of duties can become complicated or be undermined.

- A new vector for attacks now exists between host and guest machines or even between different guest machines on the same host that may not adequately be addressed by current security software.

- Because virtual machines use the same hardware (network card, etc.) to interact with the network and resources, it may be difficult to audit logs and correctly identify traffic sources.

- Any vulnerabilities in the virtualization software may allow for communication between computers that are thought to be independent. This can expose data, systems, etc.; if the virtualization layer is compromised, all bets are off vis-à-vis the security of all systems running above it and all data on those systems.

- The lack of visibility between virtual machines, and the lack of security technologies to address virtual networks between such machines, means that some security policies might not be implemented properly, and it may be difficult to detect such violations. Network-based security technologies cannot always see the network traffic between virtual machines (in some cases, it never goes on a network): Any risks that those technologies are supposed to address might remain.

- Datasets of different classifications that do not belong on the same machines might actually be on the same machines.

- Backups of servers that run virtual machines might not implement proper security over the individual portions belonging to the virtual machines.

- Malware on the underlying server (or even potentially on other virtual machines) may impact virtual machines even if the virtual machines are running security software.

Quality Control

The project's quality control efforts can also be a source of security issues that go largely unrecognized and unmitigated. Because quality control is tightly tied to the project, it often has high-level access to the project and its resources as well as scripts, tools, hooks, or other resources designed to bypass the system's security to make testing easier. Test plans need to be created to ensure that systems consistently perform well, maintain confidentiality, availability, and integrity of all data and services, and that test results (whether good, bad, or a mix) are only available to parties to whom the delivery of such information is authorized. Remember, the leak of test data to unauthorized parties can potentially help hackers to penetrate it later on. Testing should also be done in a testing environment prior to a system being "turned on" in production.

Some of these risks can be mitigated without a huge amount of effort, but they should be added to the risk analysis and project plan.

- Test data should not include real or live data if the data is sensitive. This is a common issue in projects that use databases because there's a desire to use real data to test as close to live content as possible. This creates an unnecessary security risk because now a copy of the live database is housed in a location whose security is unknown and the access rights are also unknown. It's a relatively trivial task to create true dummy data to test with and mitigate this risk completely.

- Test hooks and code are included in the project code. This creates a risk because this test code is often designed to give access to features and functions not designed for direct access in order to test it, but the test code itself is never tested. Shipping this code creates security risks that can be discovered and used, and it might contain its own set of security defects that can compromise the project. Auditing to ensure that all test code is removed from the final version before it is released can mitigate this.

- Test users often have high-level access to the project while it's being tested, and sometimes this access is not revoked on release of the project, which creates security risks that the user can exploit later. Auditing to ensure that all test users and permissions are stripped before the project is shipped can mitigate this.

Maintenance Plan

The project's own maintenance plan may not be determined at the time the project is first designed, but there are a few things that impact security that should be kept in mind and included in the risk analysis if applicable, even as a single entry without current mitigations.

Patches

These are patches for the project itself, if needed. Some of the important questions to ask about patch control are as follows:

- How will patches for the project be handled to avoid the installation of bogus patches?
- How will required patch installation be enforced?

Code Review

Code review is essential for one simple reason: Code is written by people, and people make mistakes. When it comes to software, those mistakes can translate into functional problems and/or security vulnerabilities. Code review is the process of having appropriately trained, experienced, and qualified people review code with which they did not have prior involvement, in order to find any problems.

Code review can also detect sabotage (intentionally inserted vulnerabilities and the like), inefficiencies, and other issues.

Different models exist for code review. Sometimes code is reviewed after each module is written with a quick check for the code related to interactions between modules at the end of the project, and sometimes it is all done when all code is complete. Sometimes it is done completely manually; sometimes technical tools are utilized. Sometimes people "program with buddies" who are constantly doing code review, and sometimes no such system exists. What system to use depends on the organization's needs and resources.

Code reviews should also be done for any code changes made after an initial release. Code reviews are typically required during the initial project design and development, but when the project goes into its maintenance phase, it is common for that diligence to relax. This can create security risks when patches are released. Some of the important questions to ask about code reviews for the project's maintenance phase are as follows:

- What code reviews must take place on patches or maintenance for this project, and who has to perform those code reviews?
- What records must be kept and where on the result of code reviews and any changes required by the code review?

Threat Modeling and Risk Analysis

Threat modeling, in our present context, refers to describing the set of possible attacks against a particular computer system or infrastructure. When updates or changes are made to a project, the previously completed threat models and risk analysis may become outdated. In order to maintain security, therefore, the threat model and risk analysis must be reviewed and, possibly (if not, probably), updated.

Some of the important questions to ask about threat modeling and risk analysis for a project's updates are as follows:

- Is there a policy in place to ensure that the threat model and risk analysis are updated and mitigations are made before updates or patches are finalized and released? How is that policy enforced?
- Is there a policy on where to keep copies of updated security documents for future reference?

Service-Oriented Architecture Security

Service-Oriented Architectures (SOAs) are a model for software in which pieces of software provide application functionality as services to other applications. Because SOA is still relatively young, as well as due to some of the fundamental concepts of its design, it can be a challenge to adequately secure.

Build to the Strictest Security Bar

SOA applications have an advantage in being much smaller because the applications are typically made up of calls to different blocks of reusable code via programming interfaces. Services are designed to be as general as possible to maximize the code reuse.

This emphasis on generality is at odds with the security practices of locking functionality down to only what is required. This is made worse by the fact these services do not care who they are talking to, unlike traditional security where you need to know exactly who the user is and what the user's permissions are.

2

Security Lifecycle Management

The result is that if your project needs to use SOA and is handling sensitive data or applications, then the entire SOA and its components and services and the underlying infrastructure have to adopt the security practices of the most sensitive data or application.

Implement a Formal Change Process

SOAs are designed so new services can be added and advertise themselves in a catalog or central repository so applications can make use of them. Unlike traditional projects where code changes and additions follow a formal review process and are implemented by specific people or teams, SOAs are designed to not adhere to any of these. This can lead to rogue or insecure services sneaking in and a loss of integrity.

If your project is going to handle sensitive data or applications, then a formal process needs to be implemented and enforced for changes to existing services and additions of new services.

Enforce Authentication

Because most SOAs do not care whom they talk to, authentication often defaults to anonymous or none needed, but that violates the security concepts of knowing to whom you are talking and what they can do.

In order to implement some sort of security, the project can take one of two basic steps. The first is to move services and a supporting architecture into a separate space where the services and infrastructure can all trust each other and only each other. These underlying services and infrastructure pieces must also all meet the same basic security level.

The other possibility is to adopt a pattern of mutual distrust. This means authorization must be made and the authorization state maintained and each part of the SOA must know what services or resources can be accessed by which part of the SOA. In this case, every application trusts the SOA infrastructure and that infrastructure decides who can talk to whom and keeps logs and records of the access.

No End-to-End Security

Part of the issue with security and SOAs is that the loosely coupled nature of the SOA and its chain of processing means you really cannot follow a security path through the SOA from end to end. The components really don't know about the processing done by other components.

Right now, there is no good solution to this problem, so when you have projects that deal with sensitive data or applications, you will need to keep this in mind when deciding whether or not to use an SOA.

No Security in Standard Components

The other common issue with SOAs is the desire to reduce costs and time by using standard and premade components. The problem with this approach is that these components almost certainly do not meet any security bar and can compromise the SOA.

If your project is set on using an SOA and deals with sensitive data or applications, purchased or standard components where security is unknown or in doubt should never be used.

System Testing

Testing of the project is the point at which security risks are tested for and mitigation is either proved or disproved. It's also the time in the project development when new security risks are revealed, both while focused security testing is being done and in the course of functional and other types of testing. Testers can be the security manager's best friends and a terrific resource for exploring and analyzing security issues. A close partnership with the test team can only benefit both.

Testing and Documentation of Security Elements

Testing sets out to verify that the project meets or does not meet the specifications. Even though security issues should be a part of those specifications, it's very beneficial to push the security testing to an early part of the test process in order to catch potential security issues as early as possible.

Sometimes security testing is done with a separate test plan or as a separate part of the test cycle, but other times the security testing is integrated into the plan as a whole.

Component Testing

One type of security testing and usually the first to be performed is component security testing. This means that each component's specified security requirements are tested against the specified behavior. Gross issues where security mitigations are not put into place at all or are incorrectly implemented are often revealed at this stage.

Non security-component testing can also uncover situations where the component being tested handles some situations so poorly it becomes a security issue or where the way the component itself was implemented leads to specific security issues that then need to be rolled into the risk analysis, judged for severity, and mitigated if necessary.

Integrated System Testing

After the system is mostly functional, integrated system security can be tested. This is also referred to as end-to-end security testing and often reveals some of the more system-wide security issues or cases where reliance on environmental controls for security is not functioning as designed.

This is also the time when security issues that have to do with installation, updates, uninstalls, and such are revealed. This can encompass permissions, storage of data like passwords in the registry, and even failures in encryption.

Inevitably, this testing will reveal unanticipated security issues that must be rolled into the risk analysis, judged for severity, and mitigated if necessary.

Penetration Testing

Penetration testing is a specialized type of security testing in which a tester, or group of testers, attempts to breach a project, network, or system's security as if he/she/they were attacker/s. Penetration testing can be remarkably beneficial because it tends to uncover previously unknown or unconsidered security risks.

2

Security Lifecycle Management

Penetration testing can be expensive if outsourced, and it often requires the use of outside expert consultants; as such, as discussed in Chapter 1, obtaining budget for such a test can sometimes be tricky. Management may also take issue with penetration testing because, besides often being expensive to conduct, it can expose vulnerabilities that may create legal liabilities (such as informing customers), can impact performance of a production system, and, if not managed properly, can inadvertently create vulnerabilities in a production system.

In general, the ISSMP should be prepared to oversee security testing, both in the context of development projects and other situations. This includes vulnerability scanning, penetration testing, and other forms of security testing.

Confidential Test Data

A security issue that needs to be better recognized is the issue of using real or confidential data in test efforts. It's an all too common situation to find live data copied many times and living on various insecure servers to be used for testing, but, in the meantime, that data is severely compromised and is a huge security risk. There is no control on these database copies, and they often remain floating around long after the project is released, complete with their high security risk.

It is a relatively trivial task to generate test data that mimics live data and can be used in test efforts without the security risks associated with the use of live data. No testing should be carried out with live, sensitive data.

Insider Attacks

Another often-overlooked security issue is the potential for insider attacks. Company insiders have access to documentation, permissions, and information that the general public does not, and these insider attacks are very difficult to prevent.

Another part of the test effort should be to verify that even if an insider attempts to compromise the project, he or she will gain nothing of value. This includes things like data being encrypted, use of white-list permissions, etc.

Certification and Accreditation

One of the great unknowns when externally developed hardware or software is used in an enterprise is what security testing has taken place on these components. In many cases, an enterprise is forced to assume that none has taken place and must then choose to either accept the risk of the unknown or test it itself.

One way to relieve this additional cost and responsibility is to choose software or hardware that is certified or accredited. This allows the enterprise to know what standards the software is certified to meet and for what environments it is certified.

Most standards organizations that have a certification or accreditation process have a published list of criteria and what security testing is done and what risks are considered acceptable. Often these are built around government requirements and needs, so the standards tend to be comprehensive and carefully documented.

Furthermore, systems that have been created internally may require certification and accreditation, which much be done per policies of the organization before such systems "go live."

Developing a Business Case for New Initiatives to Integrate Security

As discussed in Chapter 1, the ISSMP may need to convince business stakeholders of the importance of information security as they pursue various projects. He or she might need to launch various security projects – or spearhead others – necessitating that he or she create business arguments and documents to help "sell security." Security is not a profit center; that is, it does not generate income for a business, and, as such, business stakeholders sometimes try to skimp on security budgets. The ISSMP, therefore, might need to present a business case – explaining what could happen to the business and quantifying the potential damage – in order to ensure that security is properly implemented.

Sometimes business units will pursue newer technologies with initiatives that can impact security. Over the past few decades, shifts from mainframes and mini computers to desktops, from client-server applications to thin-client (Web interface) apps, from desktops to laptops to mobile devices, from locally stored data and licensed applications to cloud-based storage and leased software, have all meant major changes in security risks and needs. The advent of ubiquitous "big data" analysis, the arrival of social media, the revelation of secretive government spying in the United States, the internationalization of business and the massive growth of various previously stagnant economies coupled with the dramatic rise of technical skills and cyber-armies in various previously technologically deficient regions (e.g., China), etc. are all catalysts for business projects – but they also have each had major impacts on security.

Big data creates risks in that organizations are storing a lot of information about people; if that data is stolen, it can potentially be used for nefarious purposes such as facilitating identity theft. Hence, adequate security is a must. Big data also raises privacy questions because private information about a person might be inferable from a collection of other data about him or her. And, of course, any system that allows sharing of data between organizations necessitates all sorts of security related to the storage, retrieval, and transport of data.

As alluded to in Chapter 1, for example, cloud-based technologies introduce new risks – both technological and business. There are multiple types of cloud-based architectures; most fall into one of five groups:

1. **Public Cloud** – A third party is providing services to an organization via the Internet.
2. **Internal Private Cloud** – Exactly like public cloud, except that the third party is the same party as the using party.
3. **External Private Cloud** – A cloud provided by one party to another single party with no other parties utilizing the same infrastructure.
4. **Community Cloud** – A private cloud that is shared between several parties. It may be on infrastructure belonging to the collective, to one of the parties using it, or to a third party.
5. **Hybrid Cloud** – The organization manages some resources in-house and has other resources provided to it by an external third party.

2

Security Lifecycle Management

Cloud architecture (other than internal private cloud architecture) introduces a new, substantial risk: instead of the ISSMP's organization being in control of its own security, a third party – the cloud system provider or providers whose services are being utilized – controls the security of at least some of the organization's data and systems. . The risks of insecure APIs and interfaces become much more significant as well, as might application level vulnerabilities in Web-based tools, inadequate encryption, the use of shared services, data loss, data leakage, and account hijacking. The ISSMP needs to understand how the cloud model grows these risks, methods for addressing such risks, what to demand from a provider to ensure that it is adequately secure, etc.

The ISSMP must keep up to date on technologies and trends and learn about resulting security concerns. Frequent reading of relevant publications and news sources is a great way to stay up to date, as is attending webinars and conferences, etc. Following appropriate parties on social media can also provide real-time alerts of important security-related information. (ISC)² requires that people certified as ISSMPs continue their educations in order to remain certified – but the CPE requirements should be viewed as minimum standards related to general security knowledge that emerges over a period of time; fulfilling these requirements on their own is unlikely to be sufficient to be a top performer dealing with real world, day-to-day security challenges.

Some other areas in which recent developments have led to significant projects include Single Sign-On (SSO), Bring Your Own Device (BYOD), social media, encryption of laptops and mobile device data, and PCI for securing credit card processing and transactions.

Likewise, new vulnerabilities may be discovered at any time, some of which can dramatically increase the risk to the organization of a catastrophic event occurring. The Heartbleed bug of 2014, for example, awakened many organizations to that fact that all data passing through their ostensibly secure servers was, in fact, at risk, as were all user passwords and SSL certificate private keys. Immediate rectification was necessary, meaning that security leaders, such as the ISSMP, had to quickly come up to speed, determine whether the organization suffered from the vulnerability, and, if so, where, act to address it, and inform others. While the enormity of this particular event is uncommon, vulnerabilities are not rare, and the ISSMP must be vigilant at staying up to date and acting quickly, in a well-structured manner.

If a business initiative is launched that will utilize emerging technology, the ISSMP should ensure that the security concerns are understood and discussed early on so that they are properly addressed proactively, rather than dealt with in a "firefighting" mode later on. The old adage says that "an ounce of prevention is worth a pound of cure," and, in the case of security, in whose domain it remains true that once data is pilfered there is no way to un-steal it, proper prevention may be worth many tons of reactive efforts.

Often, businesspeople hear about emerging "cool" trends or understand the business benefits and conveniences of some new product or system, but they do not realize that the technologies involved create new security risks, which sometimes render the novel offerings inappropriate for their use in a project under consideration. It is the ISSMP's job to communicate these risks to the businesspeople, along with information as to how to mitigate the risks (as appropriate).

Classifying Assets, System, and Services Based on Criticality

Not all informational assets, systems, or services are created equal. Some data may be extremely sensitive, and, therefore, the systems upon which it resides, and through which it passes, must be protected with extreme diligence even if doing so involves high financial cost. Other information may not warrant the same level of security, especially when one considers the costs associated with providing maximum protection. Likewise, some information, systems, and services may be critical for a business to operate successfully, while other information may be of less concern. Some systems must also have 100% availability with no downtime (or at least as close to this as is possible), and large expenditures to guarantee that that aim is achieved are acceptable, while most other systems do not have such a need and organizations would prefer to suffer some downtime but save a fortune. The need to ensure confidentiality, integrity, and availability is obviously far greater in the former cases than the latter. Risks to which these items are exposed may also vary.

It is for that reason, therefore, that the ISSMP must know how to classify assets, systems, and services based on the nature of the information involved and the level of criticality to the organization that owns them (or that otherwise uses them and is responsible for them). Under-protecting data puts data confidentiality, integrity, and availability at risk. Overprotecting data is a waste of money and may incentivize business units to ultimately overcut security spending – resulting in data being under-protected and, thereby, exposing sensitive information to unacceptable levels of risk. Furthermore, it is simply impractical, if not prohibitively expensive, to provide maximum levels of security for all data and systems, and doing so would likely interfere with business operations. Classification, therefore, is a must.

Many methodologies exist to classify data and systems, and organizations for which the ISSMP works may already have one or more such models in place. Classifications may use "standard" types such as sensitive, confidential, proprietary, private, critical, and public, or they may use other classification models.

It is important to realize that in some organizations, various regulations and laws may also mandate classification and even dictate the model to use; the required classes may be used on their own or in conjunction with a second model, as an overlay upon the primary model in use by the organization.

Classification of data is discussed elsewhere in this book. Some of the questions that an ISSMP might want to ask himself or herself when classifying data and systems include:

- Who is requesting the classification? If there is no business sponsor, and no business units are interested in the classification, the ISSMP needs to get executive buy in.
- Is there budget for the classification project – and to carry out security as needed based on the classifications that are established for various data? If not, it is wise to address this issue posthaste.
- Does the organization already have a classification system for data and systems in place? If so, what is it, who created it, does it conform to current regulations, does it meet current needs, who is using it, who is responsible for updating it if necessary, and what data and systems are currently classified?

■ Are there any laws, regulations, guidances, etc. that may be pertinent to the data and systems in question? If so, it is usually wise to make sure that an expert in these areas is involved with the classification project from the start. If the ISSMP is unsure as to whether or not regulations, laws, guidances, etc. may be pertinent, he or she should check with his/her compliance or legal department.

■ What exactly is to be protected? Define the scope of what needs to be classified. This includes data, systems, and services.

■ From whom are we trying to protect that material?

■ From what risks are we trying to protect it?

■ Who owns the items being classified? Is that person/organization prepared to accept the classification, the responsibility to provide adequate security, etc.?

■ Have any classification systems been used in the past, and, if so, when and why were they abandoned? Did a previous classification system fail to provide adequate security?

As long as a business is a going concern, an organization is operating, or a government is in power, it will always face threats. In fact, in today's day and age, it is often the case that at any given point in time an organization will face a large number of threats – so many that it is impractical to deal with all of them "immediately" and "fully." That is why it is important for the ISSMP to know how to prioritize threats.

Prioritizing Threats and Vulnerabilities

Prioritizing threats involves examining the vulnerabilities that may exist and the threats that they create in an effort to, in a structured way, determine priorities for addressing them so that the organization can, first and foremost, address the threats that have the potential to inflict the greatest harm. While many methodologies exist for prioritizing threats, the goals of prioritization are similar: Identify which threat agents pose the greatest risk, identify what the threat agents seek to do (as part of their threat), and how they are likely to seek to do so. These three elements are then compared with known existing vulnerabilities to identify what should be addressed with immediate concern and to help identify which countermeasures should be utilized to mitigate the risk of the threat agents that pose the greatest risk.

Technical risks are not the only aspect of threats that must be considered: What an agent is likely to seek to do is also a critical element in threat analysis. Threats fall into different categories, and agents may have completely different goals with their attacks. Some agents, for example, may seek to simply embarrass an organization, while others may seek to sabotage its operations or steal its data.

Among the parties who may be threat agents are, for example:

■ **Competitors** (e.g., business competitors, lawyers on the opposing side of a case or impending case, politicians competing in elections, etc.)

■ **Government Agents** (spies, cyber-warriors, corrupt officials, corrupt employees, etc.)

■ **Activists** (including members of radical groups, anarchists, terrorists, cause supporting activists)

- **Vandals** (e.g., hackers seeking to brag that they successfully breached a particular organization or organizations by defacing its/their website/s or social media presence)
- **Profit-Driven Criminals** (e.g., thieves, mafia/organized crime-employed technicians)
- **Lunatics**
- **Employees and Contractors** (e.g., disgruntled employees or contractors, employees or contractors paid by competitors to spy, careless employees or consultants, untrained employees or consultants, etc.). These parties know the inner workings of the organization, what valuable data it has in its possession, where it is located, and how it is protected.

Random attacks are also possible. For example, malware intended to inflict damage at some particular target may proliferate onto another network and cause performance problems or even worse. Such was the case with Stuxnet, for example.

Each class of agents includes many different actors whose motives, capabilities, and methods vary widely. Hence, when prioritizing threats, besides compiling a list of threats (which may change frequently, hence this process is not a one-time occurrence), the ISSMP should consider several questions including:

- What are the vulnerabilities (technological, business, process, etc.) that the threats may exploit to do harm?
- Who are the agents that may seek to exploit them and therefore pose a threat?
- What are their capabilities in terms of exploiting the threats? This includes considering how much financial backing they have, how much knowledge they have about the organization and its vulnerabilities, their level of technical competence and sophistication, etc.
- What capabilities are needed in order to exploit a vulnerability?
- Do the agents in question have those capabilities?
- What are the likely attacks that are most damaging to the organization?

Based on the answers to these questions, the ISSMP and his or her team can compile a chart of threats and their associated risk levels. There are many ways to display this information; tables and graphs are all valid methods. In any case, the results of the analysis should be in writing.

Once the list of threats (which includes vulnerabilities that would be exploited in order to carry out an attack) has been created and prioritized, the threats can be addressed. Remediation of vulnerabilities should proceed according to a similar plan – those that pose the greatest risk to the organization should be addressed first and with highest priority.

A plethora of technologies utilized within an organization means that many types of vulnerabilities might exist. While the list of potential risks is constantly changing and differs between organizations, and as a full list of every possible risk and vulnerability is too large for any book, the following are some specific areas of technology that, in general, should be considered as part of examining risks and weaknesses:

- Web-based application risks
- Client-based risks for thick client applications

2

Security Lifecycle Management

- Applet risks (including Active-X, Java, and Flash app related risks)
- JavaScript (client and server side)
- AJAX related risks
- Mainframe
- Malicious code risks including possible viruses, Trojan horses, trap doors, worms, keyloggers, screen scrapers, Easter eggs, data miners, etc.
- Common coding and configuration security issues including (cross-site scripting, buffer overflows, SQL Injection, bound checking problems, etc.)
- Common Gateway Interface (CGI) on Web servers
- Message oriented middleware
- Bring your own device (BYOD) risks

Mobile devices create risks as well; it is important to ensure that they have remote wipe enabled and configured, sensitive data is properly encrypted, and that security software in installed and up to date. Remember, "Smartphones" are not phones; they are computers!

Summary

While some breaches may be the result of hackers seeking to "make a quick buck," it is important to realize that the price that an organization might ultimately pay for deficient security can be far greater; businesses can literally be destroyed, and careers can be wrecked, by nefarious parties disrupting systems or obtaining the sensitive information that they house.

As such, this, the second of the five ISSMP domains, covers various aspects of security as related to defining, designing, developing, testing, implementing, and maintaining enterprise-wide information infrastructure.

The ISSMP candidate should, therefore, understand the SDLC and know how to integrate, and monitor, security as appropriate at each of its stages. She or he should also understand the role of security vis-à-vis new business initiatives, including how it relates to all of the various technical components of such efforts – from operating systems and technical infrastructure, to applications, databases, and mobile devices. Classification of systems, comprehensive knowledge of vulnerability management – including the technical aspects such as scanning and penetration testing, and the non-technical aspects, such as performing a threat analysis, prioritization of vulnerabilities and threats, and addressing vulnerabilities based on risk levels, are also important areas of knowledge.

2

Security Lifecycle Management

Domain 2: Review Questions

1. How does the need for security compare between systems developed for sale or external use and systems developed for in-house use?

    A.   Systems for sale or external use always have more security concerns.

    B.   Systems developed for in-house use always have more security concerns.

    C.   Systems developed in house require security efforts on the part of the internal security team, while those developed for external use can have security outsourced.

    D.   Both systems have security concerns that must be carefully addressed.

2. When should a project's security measures be addressed?

    A.   As close to the start of the project as possible

    B.   Only after security issues are exploited

    C.   After the initial project design is done

    D.   When the functional specifications are being written

3. Which of the following pose the greatest risk of perpetrating a catastrophic theft of an organization's valuable data without expending great resources to do so?

    A.   Foreign governments and their sponsored hackers

    B.   Employees

    C.   Activists from hacktivist groups such as Anonymous

    D.   Customers

4. How does the use of Rapid Application Development (RAD) affect security planning?

    A.   The compressed time between releases means security planning and concerns must be brought up early and stressed often.

    B.   The process of iterative development means security is built in automatically.

    C.   Security issues are more common in RAD projects.

    D.   Security issues are less common in RAD projects.

5. What security risks are associated with the use of prototyping and prototyping tools?

    A. Prototypes always allow hackers to understand what a business plans to do for security in its finished products.

    B. Prototyping helps ensure secure code.

    C. Prototyping tools write code with an eye toward that code's security.

    D. Prototypes and prototyping tools tend to generate basic and insecure code that must be carefully reviewed before use in the finished product.

6. Risk analysis is a method to do what?

    A. Find all possible security issues and how to exploit them.

    B. Gather data on the cost to mitigate security threats and the possibility of the threat being exploited.

    C. Decide how much money to spend on security.

    D. Compare risks and rewards of having a security program

7. What mitigations should be listed in a risk analysis?

    A. Only those of the project itself

    B. Only mitigations that are software or network related

    C. . Only those that can be mitigated with security technology

    D. All mitigations that apply to a risk the project has or inherits

8. How many levels of risk and mitigation must be taken into account during a risk analysis?

    A. Only the first level of identifying the risk and its immediate mitigation

    B. As many levels as needed to reach a level of mitigation that is no longer feasible

    C. Two levels—the risk and its mitigation and then the mitigation if that first mitigation fails

    D. The same number of levels as listed for maximum response times in the security plan

9. Security cost is defined as what when writing a risk analysis?

    A. The monetary costs of developing and implementing security measures, including consulting, hardware, additional software, and development process costs

    B. The productivity losses associated with time lost to implement and abide by security measures

    C. Both of the above

    D. None of the above

10. Who should review and sign off on security plans?

    A. Key players as well as anyone mandated by the enterprise itself

    B. Only those people required by the enterprise's policies

    C. Outside consultants only

    D. A third-party auditor

11. When are security reviews necessary?

    A. When legally mandated or required by company policy

    B. It depends on the project

    C. When any changes are made

    D. When a breach occurs

12. What impact can access to a project's source code have on security?

    A. It improves security because more people can look for issues.

    B. It has no real effect. There isn't much interest in enterprise in-house projects.

    C. It can compromise security and access should be limited.

    D. The source code cannot impact security. Only executable code that actually runs can impact security.

13. Who should have access to a project's bug or defect database?

    A. Everyone at the company.

    B. Only those who require access to do their jobs.

    C. It should be public.

    D. The IT support team

14. Web 2.0 projects often have more security needs in what area?

    A. Data encryption, transmission, and storage

    B. Server hardening and updating

    C. Both of the above

    D. None of the above

15. What impact does virtualization have on security?

    A. Unique risks must be taken into account.

    B. No impact. Security is treated exactly as if virtualization is not in use.

    C. Virtualization reduces security risks.

    D. The same issues as those relevant to all of the systems being run on the virtual machines combined.

2

Security Lifecycle Management

16. What is the role of security in the maintenance phase of a project?

    A. Security must be maintained by regular code and security reviews by patching and updating software and hardware.

    B. Security must be maintained by patching and updating software and hardware, and by security reviews, but code reviews are no longer necessary.

    C. Security must be maintained by regular code and security reviews, but patching is irrelevant to this issue.

    D. Security is no longer needed during the maintenance phase.

17. What is the difference between a public cloud system and a community cloud system?

    A. A public cloud involves a third party providing services to an organization via the Internet; a community cloud is a private cloud that is shared between several parties.

    B. A public cloud involves a third party providing services to an organization via the Internet; a community cloud infrastructure means the organization manages some resources available in house and has other resources provided to it by an external third party.

    C. A public cloud involves a third party providing services to an organization via the Internet; a community cloud is another word for a private cloud.

    D. They are the same.

18. What types of security testing should be done on the system to ensure that it meets its security bar?

    A. Component level security testing is more than able to validate the system's security.

    B. Component level, end-to-end, and penetration testing should all be used to validate the system's security.

    C. End-to-end security testing is the best way to validate that the system meets its security bar.

    D. Penetration testing is the best way to validate that the system meets its security bar.

19. What kind of data should be used in security testing?

    A. Mock data that follows real patterns

    B. Live data with sensitive information stripped out

    C. Live data in its entirety

    D. Live data with sensitive information stripped out

20. What benefit does using components or software that is certified or accredited bring to a system's security?

    A. Neither certification nor accreditation never has an effect on the system's security.

    B. In some cases, it can help increase the system's security level.

    C. It negatively affects the system's security.

    D. Certification can help improve security, but accreditation has no impact on security.

2

Security Lifecycle
Management

Domain 3
Security Compliance Management

In a given environment, people perform processes using technology to produce results. The results contribute to the fulfillment of objectives, goals, and missions to achieve the overall enterprise vision. There are risks to the people, processes, technology, and environment that interfere with the effective and efficient production of results. Your job as a security professional is to identify those risks and address them in an appropriate manner. One element of risk is compliance – compliance with external legislative and regulatory mandates, as well as enterprise internal compliance with policies, standards, and procedures including those for security.

Policies define appropriate behavior within the organization. Standards are a description of uniformity; they are a specification of commonality to implement and enforce policy. Procedures are a specified sequence of actions to achieve a desired end. Procedures describe a disciplined, repeatable manner for how to use the standards to implement and enforce policy. An enterprise is a unity of activity, e.g., a term to refer to the comprehensive business or business activities of a particular company or a term to refer to the comprehensive activities of a government unit (e.g., federal enterprise). Enterprise risk is the likelihood of a potential negative impact to a unity of activity.

As a security professional, you minimize enterprise risk in balance with achieving the enterprise mission by specifying security policies, standards, and procedures. Security policies reflect the compliance requirements externally imposed on the organization (e.g., legislation and regulation) as well as the internal compliance requirements self-imposed as good business practice (e.g., ISO 27001 or NIST SP 800-53). This chapter examines security operations and compliance with topics organized by people, process, technology, and environment, including a perspective of security policies, standards, and procedures to implement and enforce compliance requirements.

OBJECTIVES

Risk exposure is the degree of potential negative impact. Risk posture is an intentionally assumed position to deal with potential negative impact. Security posture is an intentionally assumed position to protect against danger or loss. Legislative mandates increase risk exposure of the enterprise via increasing its liability for noncompliance. The enterprise must decide how to position itself for compliance in balance with operational outcomes (i.e., the enterprise must define its risk posture and then implement safeguards to enforce the risk posture). Similarly, enterprise policy describes appropriate behavior within the enterprise; policy is an internal compliance requirement for enterprise employees and those doing business with the enterprise.

The objectives of this chapter are to present compliance and security operations. This includes a look at external influences on security operations (e.g., legislation, regulation) as well as internal compliance requirements that are part of security operations. We will discuss defining a compliance framework, validating it, measuring its success, and reporting on it. Additionally, we will look at compliance from various perspectives to understand what compliance is and to identify the specific compliance goals for your security department. We will look at various examples of compliance in inventory control, auditing, configuration management, penetration testing, and vulnerability testing.

KEY AREAS OF KNOWLEDGE

Key areas of knowledge for compliance of security operations are as follows:

- Security Compliance Management Program (SCMP)
- Legislation management
- Litigation management
- Enterprise Security Standard (ESS)
- Enterprise Security Framework (ESF)
- Identification of external compliance requirements
- Creation and management of internal compliance requirements
- Security policies, standards, and procedures
- Monitor for violations
- Detection
- Incident management; incident response

The Cyber Domain

There is a new domain to life, the cyber domain (i.e., there is land, sea, air, space, and now cyber). The cyber domain that most of us encounter is the Internet. This new domain has and will continue to affect the way we live, work, buy, communicate, express ourselves, socialize, make friends, form contracts and agreements, and perform transactions, e.g., banking deposits, transfers, and bill paying. The cyber domain provides a tremendous amount of benefits, as well as introduces new risks. These risks include technical failures of the infrastructure and systems we use to operate within the cyber domain as well as from those people looking to exploit this new domain for their own gain, both legitimately and illegitimately.

Many businesses now both define and use the cyber domain to interact with vendors, suppliers, partners, employees, and customers. Continued operation within the cyber domain is critical for business to survive and thrive. Therefore, examining threats, vulnerabilities, and risks to the cyber domain in business terms is good business practice. Moreover, identifying, enumerating, articulating, and addressing cyber domain risk is not only good business practice, but it may be a legislative compliance mandate.

A key differentiating characteristic of the cyber domain from the other domains is physical proximity. Traversing land, sea, air, and space requires a physical presence of some sort; the cyber domain is virtual, and access to a location, or multiple locations, across the globe is but a few keystrokes away. Safeguarding assets in the other domains was largely accomplished via physical safeguards (e.g., non-disclosure of location, lock and key, barbed wire, safes, trusted personnel to transport the asset, and armed guards). Moreover, wealth took the form of physical assets like jewels, currency, or gold. Now, bits on a hard drive represent wealth, and access to wealth is via remote means and faceless transactions (e.g., automated teller machines, banking by phone, direct deposit of paychecks, and online bill paying). While the cyber domain provides many conveniences, it also presents a new domain for crime, espionage, terrorism, and warfare. The focus of the material in this chapter is on legislative mandates governing the protection of data (bits on a hard drive) and enterprise guidance for implementation and enforcement of legislative compliance in the form of policies, standards, and procedures. Additionally, this chapter will address the complement to legislative compliance, which is good business practice, to optimize the interests of stakeholders.

Business Perspective

The business perspective boils down to two aspects: cost and revenue. The cyber domain either contributes to revenue or helps to manage costs. If you cannot express cyber activity in these terms, then step back and seriously question the validity of that cyber activity. Another way to look at this is "business need drives investments in technology." Moreover, business risk drives investment in security.

Likewise, security boils down to the same two aspects of cost and revenue. Either security contributes to revenue or helps manage costs:

- Revenue
    - Revenue generation
    - Revenue stream protection

- Cost
  - Cost maintenance
  - Cost reduction
  - Cost avoidance

Security may contribute directly to revenue generation by offering security services or mechanisms for a fee. Security may protect revenue streams, e.g., security mechanisms protecting an e-commerce site that accepts customer orders. Security may contribute to cost maintenance, (i.e., ensuring costs do not go up) for example, security mechanisms protecting cyber devices that would otherwise require manual labor and increase in payroll. Security may contribute to cost reduction by replacing manual labor with automated services; security may also reduce costs by adding protective measures that reduce insurance premiums (e.g., sprinkler systems). Security also contributes to cost avoidance. This is the main area for compliance management (e.g., adherence to external legislative mandates avoids fines and potential jail time for officers).

Risk Posture, Security Posture, and Risk Exposure

Risk posture is an intentionally assumed position on dealing with potential negative impact; the risk posture is a formal declaration of how to address risk: accept, ignore, share, transfer, or mitigate. Formally declaring a risk posture requires awareness prior to preparation. This implies that change in awareness results in changes to the risk posture. For example, awareness of a newly discovered vulnerability in the operating system (OS) that runs your enterprise desktops increases the risk exposure of the organization. You must then review your risk posture in light of this new awareness. The risk posture must change to reflect how to address this new vulnerability, e.g., mitigate the risk by installing an OS patch. Installing the OS patch modifies the security posture to return the risk exposure to an acceptable level.

The security posture is an intentionally assumed position to protect against danger or loss. The implementation of security services and security mechanisms make up the security posture. Risk posture establishes the acceptable level of dealing with potential negative impact, including that risk which is acceptable. Security posture is the safeguards that mitigate risk to reduce risk exposure to an acceptable level.

The bottom line for security is the same as any other business function: revenue and cost management. Security should contribute directly to one or more of the following: revenue generation, revenue preservation, cost reduction, and cost avoidance in terms of stakeholder currency, i.e., optimize stakeholder value. Stakeholder currency is not always literal money; at times, stakeholder currency may be lives (e.g., the military commander) or votes (e.g., the politician). In any instance, money is still a factor, but it may not be the primary factor in decision making.

As a security professional, part of your job is to determine the acceptable risk posture of the enterprise. There will always be risk; there is just no way to identify 100% of vulnerabilities and protect 100% of assets from 100% of threats 100% of the time. The presence of threats, vulnerabilities, and risk in the enterprise is like the presence of weeds in a garden. No amount of weed killer or manual effort will permanently eliminate weeds from a garden. Likewise, we must recognize, socialize (manage expectations), and deal with the reality that no amount of safeguards will permanently eliminate threats, vulnerabilities, and risk.

The point of security operations is to anticipate the risks and prepare the enterprise via enterprise policies, standards, procedures, and guidelines; defend against them using security services and mechanisms; monitor for anomalies; and respond to anomalies to discern the degree of business risk and how to best deal with that risk.

Security Core Principles

Nine security core principles[1] provide a foundational framework to implement and run security operations:

1. Confidentiality
2. Integrity
3. Availability
4. Possession
5. Utility
6. Authenticity
7. Non-repudiation
8. Authorized Use
9. Privacy

The traditional information security triad consists of confidentiality, integrity, and availability. Confidentiality is the protection against the risk of unauthorized disclosure; integrity is the protection against unauthorized modification; and availability is the protection against the risk of denial of service. Don Parker then added possession, utility, and authenticity. Possession is the protection against the risk of loss or theft; utility is the protection against the loss of the ability to use for the intended purpose; and authenticity is the protection against the risk of not conforming to reality. Non-repudiation, authorized use, and privacy round out the nine core principles. Non-repudiation is the protection against the risk of deniability; authorized use is the protection against the risk of unauthorized use of cost incurring services; and privacy is protection against the risk of disclosing personal information.

The fundamental rationale for compliance activities is traceable to these nine principles, e.g., protect the privacy of customers, avoid the disclosure of proprietary data, and avoid the theft or misplacement of valuable assets. We will next examine the perspectives of compliance and then present a framework within which to plan for and implement compliance activities in a disciplined, consistent, and repeatable manner using an enterprise security standard (ESS) and an enterprise security framework (ESF). The remainder of the chapter presents compliance in the context of security operations by decomposing operations into people, process, technology, and environment and elaborating on security services, mechanisms, and activities within each of these categories.

Compliance

Compliance is an important concept for the ISSMP to understand. Compliance means adhering to a rule or set of rules. In the case of information security, compliance refers to the rules to which people, systems, and processes are expected to comply; these are typically policies, standards, laws, guidances, regulations, or specifications.

---

1   Originally articulated in *Information Assurance Architecture as the nine IA Core Principles.*

Various industries and businesses have compliance regulations set by law or by industry. In the healthcare sector, for example:

- HIPAA privacy rules are a catalyst for many information security projects related to healthcare data and systems.
- Parties that process credit card payments are expected to conform to PCI-DSS, a security standard whose third generation requirements (i.e., PCI-DSS 3.0) is required as of January 1, 2015. PCI DSS applies to all merchants processing credit card transactions, whether based in the United States or elsewhere; however, historically, enforcement has been significantly better enforced inside the United States than in various other regions. As awareness spreads, and a greater understanding of the reasons behind the need for PCI-DSS becomes better known, enforcement will likely improve internationally.
- Financial firms may be subject to the privacy requirements of the Gramm–Leach–Bliley Act. Also, the United States Security and Exchange Commission (SEC) and many of its foreign equivalents require that public corporations not leak various financial information (for example, quarterly results) before it is officially announced.

A compliance framework is effectively an operating manual for maintaining compliance. It outlines what is needed in order for an organization to be considered compliant and what processes, systems, and controls will be used to ensure that everything adheres to the rules necessary to be followed in order to create a situation of compliance. A compliance plan is a plan to create, execute, monitor, and refine a compliance framework.

One of the important concepts of compliance is compliance validation, which is the procedure used to determine how well an official or prescribed compliance plan or course of action is being carried out. After all, implementing a good compliance program is meaningless if there is no way to see how well it is working and to correct any deficiencies. Likewise, records that document compliance, and evidence of being compliant, must be properly stored.

The procedures for validating compliance should be incorporated within the compliance framework so as to ensure that all parties seeking to be compliant utilize the same standards for verifying their compliance. (Some might argue that such a situation is necessary to be fully compliant in the first place.) The ISSMP must ensure that compliance is verified using the proper techniques.

Compliance monitoring and validation is not a one-time process but rather an ongoing operation. Employees leaving or joining an organization, new computer systems being deployed and old ones retired, new regulations being introduced and others abandoned, new businesses and product lines being created and delivered, the discovery of new technological risks and new risk agents, and all sorts of other developments can have major impacts on levels of compliance. Furthermore, because failure to comply with regulations can have serious legal implications, most organizations of a substantial size will have entire teams dedicated solely to ensuring compliance. However, not all security compliance frameworks are the result of laws; some are created by organizations simply to ensure their own security.

Regardless of the reason for establishing compliance programs, metrics should be established to measure compliance. For example, PCI requires clean vulnerability scans – this means that to be compliant, a scan must show zero problems. Metrics, which measure against a baseline, were also discussed in relation to several topics in Domain 1.

Measuring compliance, however, is not always simple. There are many different elements that go into determining a level of compliance, and they are not always as straightforward to determine as typical security metrics.

In any event, for one to establish compliance metrics, each element that is important (i.e., those discussed within the compliance framework as necessary in order to be complaint) should have an acceptable "level" defined within the compliance framework, and, during testing, a comparison should be made between the actual performance versus the pre-defined specifications. As should be obvious, it is critical to utilize the information garnered from such a study to make improvements; otherwise, performing any compliance testing is effectively pointless.

Also, when measuring compliance, remember to ask questions focused on key security controls that address the real objective of the compliance requirements and not get bogged down with other areas, disproportionally focusing on the less important matters.

Part of compliance metrics have to do with compliance itself. As noted earlier, an organization should define how it plans to test for compliance and what its compliance standards are – part of compliance testing involves making sure that the organization is meeting or exceeding those guidelines. A continuous monitoring program, as defined by NIST (http://csrc.nist.gov/groups/SMA/fisma/documents/faq-continuous-monitoring.pdf), is used to determine if the complete set of planned, required, and deployed security controls within an information system, inherited by the system, or utilized by the system continues to be effective over time in light of the inevitable changes that occur. As such, checking that the continuous monitoring for compliance is working is part of the continuous monitoring for compliance.

Compliance Perspectives

There are two sides to the compliance coin: One side is legislative mandates (what you must do) and the other side is good business practice (what you should do). The term legislative mandates herein is generic and intended to include the spectrum of legislation, regulation, directives, instructions, or other compliance requirements generated outside the enterprise. Good business practice includes those compliance requirements generated inside the enterprise with the intent of enabling or protecting enterprise people, process, technology, and environment.

Legislative mandates may drive security operations. Likewise, enterprise policy may drive security operations. The security department also generates policy, standards, procedures, and guidelines that contribute to the set of internally generated compliance requirements. Security imposes these compliance requirements on the enterprise and those connecting to the enterprise technology or otherwise doing business with the enterprise. Others within the enterprise and doing business with the enterprise are then subject to comply with these security requirements.

3

Security Compliance Management

167

These internally imposed security compliance requirements may find root in external requirements (e.g., legislation) and internal requirements (*Figure 3.1*). The internal requirements govern the behavior of both internal security operations and other enterprise internal operations; additionally, these internal requirements influence relationships with partners, vendors, customers, contractors, suppliers, and outsourcers.

It should be noted, however, that failure to follow proper business practices vis-à-vis security can expose an organization to increased civil liability in the event of a security breach.

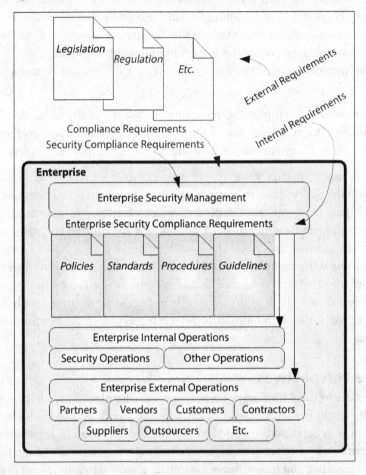

Figure 3.1 – **The effect of external compliance requirements on the enterprise environment**

Security Compliance Management Program

The Enterprise Compliance Management Program (ECMP) considers all compliance requirements on the enterprise. The enterprise security compliance management program (ESCMP) is a subset of the ECMP. The following functions apply to both ECMP and ESCMP:

■ Governance
■ Adjudication
■ Planning
■ Development

- Implementation and Deployment
- Enforcement and Disciplinary Action
- Discovery
- Analysis
- Reporting
- Correction

The ESCMP considers compliance from two perspectives: compliance *of* enterprise security guidance and compliance *with* enterprise security guidance. Compliance *of* enterprise security guidance is concerned with authoritative influences to enterprise security policies, standards, and procedures. Authoritative influences include legislation, regulation, instruction, directives, etc. Compliance *with* enterprise security guidance is concerned with the production, dissemination, awareness, understanding, and use of security guidance within the enterprise. Internal security guidance takes the form of security policies, standards, and procedures. The focus of this chapter is on both of these perspectives.

Governance

Governance identifies and enumerates all relevant security compliance requirements. These may include legislation, regulation, directives, instructions, contractual obligations, and good business practice. SCMP governance may determine that the organization will adhere to an industry standard for security management (e.g., ISO 27001) and for security controls (e.g., ISO 27002). Such adherence would be a self-imposed compliance requirement on the organization. Moreover, SCMP governance will assign responsibility and accountability for the remainder of the functions in this section.

Adjudication

At times, there will be conflict in determining the best actions to remain in compliance with security requirements. This may include claims of "this regulation applies to the rest of the enterprise but not me," *or* "but I wasn't given the budget to comply with this and unless I get the money, I'm not complying," etc. In very large organizations, there is a high likelihood of multiple security guidance (e.g., one for South America and one for Asia). Given conflicting guidance to an organization that spans both South America and Asia, formal enterprise-internal adjudication is necessary to determine applicability and precedent. Such conflicts are inevitable in medium to large organizations. The role of adjudication is to resolve these conflicts in the best interest of the stakeholders and the enterprise.

Planning

Governance determines what compliance requirements are applicable; the planning function determines the appropriate steps to take to establish and maintain compliance. The results of planning will include a list of necessary policies, standards, procedures, and guidelines that convey expected behavior within the organization to establish and maintain compliance. Planning will also determine what the enterprise will buy, build, and do to establish and maintain compliance.

Development

The development function produces the security policies, standards, procedures, and guidelines. Development formalizes the structure and content of security policies, standards, and procedures to promote readability, understanding, and compliance. Likewise, development may involve the production of a new capability, a capability that may need to adhere to enterprise compliance requirements.

Implementation and Deployment

Implementation takes the policies, standards, procedures, and guidelines and inserts them into enterprise daily activities. Deployment makes compliance part of daily operations throughout the enterprise. Deployment can be quite challenging for large regional, national, and international organizations. Part of the responsibility within deployment is to ensure enterprise awareness, understanding, and use of the security guidance. Moreover, having developed a solution, there is a need to implement that solution in the enterprise environment. Implement the solution in a test or pilot environment prior to deploying enterprise wide.

Enforcement

Now that the security guidance is out there, and there is reasonable proof that the enterprise employees, business partners, vendors, and other covered entities are aware and understand the policies, standards, procedures, and guidelines, there is the need to enforce compliance in daily operations. Enforcement requires monitoring, detecting, and responding to areas of noncompliance. The governance function also defines the enterprise response for noncompliance in the form of disciplinary actions.

Disciplinary Action

A roar from a paper tiger does little to prompt action; appropriate disciplinary action is an essential part of enforcement. There must be a disciplinary action policy that conveys the potential sanctions for policy violation. The language of this policy is important and should be reviewed by legal experts. For example, distinguishing nuances in such statements as "the enterprise *will* terminate employees who violate X," versus "the enterprise *may* terminate employees who violate X" have tremendous implications on enterprise leeway and subsequent liability over the disciplinary action it does take against an employee. The enterprise may lock itself into forced action using terms like "will take action." Circumstances vary greatly, as do intentions and culpability; making claims that the enterprise may take action provides flexibility on the part of the enterprise and also offers the enterprise protection against claims of discrimination by punished employees (e.g., "why did I get fired and they didn't?").

Discovery

Discovery elicits data regarding the actual use of security guidance. Discovery gathers the raw data to feed into the analysis function. Gathering this data may include audit logs, computer configuration data, operating system configuration data, as well as surveys and interviews of administrators and users. Predefining discovery procedures promotes efficient response to incidents, internal audits, external audits, and gathering information in support of showing compliance with legislation.

Analysis

Security imposes restrictions on operations; this is the nature of security, and its intent is good insofar as minimizing risk to the organization. However, the enterprise must be aware if the security restrictions are interfering with operations and producing the results expected by customers and stakeholders. Analysis determines the effective and efficient use of the security guidance.

Effective use shows that the guidance is actually being used and produces the expected results to minimize risk and maintain compliance as established by the governance function. Analyzing the efficient use shows whether the guidance produces expected results within acceptable operating parameters. These acceptable operating parameters may include contractual service level agreements, total cost of security safeguard operations, effect of security on network operations (e.g., bandwidth utilization, throughput), and the overall effect of security adding business value to the enterprise.

Reporting

Analysis reports go up the chain of command from operations to management and from management to adjudication and governance. The role of security must be to balance effective and efficient operations with optimal risk management. Therefore, you determine the acceptable risk posture and manage security to that risk posture and communicate threats, vulnerabilities, risk, and security in the language that resonates with the audience. If the report is going to the security operations manager, then by all means include details of firewall uptime, IDS false-positive rates, and effectiveness of remote policy management. However, a CEO is not interested in security mechanisms at all. A CEO is very interested in risk posture in terms of revenue losses, cash flow interruptions, costs, cost reduction, and cost avoidance. If the report is going to the CEO, speak in terms of risk management, managing the income statement and the balance sheet, and strategic investments in security and return on investment from security.

Correction

The results of analysis reports may show that corrective action is necessary to balance security compliance guidance and effective operations. This function revises security policies, standards, procedures, and guidelines accordingly to achieve an optimal effective and efficient balance between producing results and managing risk. Modifying security guidance is the first step, but more important is to ensure that enterprise personnel and other covered entities are aware, understand, and are modifying their behavior to comply with the security guidance.

Awareness of Legal and Regulatory Requirements

Work with your legal department to discover all the relevant legislation that pertains to your organization. There are likely national and local laws that affect the way your organization does business; which particular laws that apply to you depend largely on what type of business, the location of the business, and where the business provides customer transactions. Some of these laws may conflict in their guidance, and you will need a qualified legal opinion on which law takes precedence.

3

Security Compliance Management

Legislation awareness also provides a scope of concern for you as a security professional. Is your concern all legislative compliance? No, that is the purview of the legal department. Your scope is legislation that has implications for security operations. The next two sections briefly introduce examples of security-related legislation.

Legislation Management

Legislation management is part of a comprehensive security compliance management program. Legislative management identifies all applicable security laws and regulations to your organization. This includes all local ordinances (e.g., fire regulation) and county, city, state, and national laws. The purpose of legislation management is to avoid infractions by complying with the legislation. Examples of security legislation in the United States are the Healthcare Insurance Portability and Accountability Act (HIPAA), Final Security Rule (FSR), and Sarbanes-Oxley.

A View of the HIPAA Final Security Rule

The HIPAA FSR specifies three categories (administrative, technical, and physical), each with subcategories, and each subcategory has implementation specifications as seen the following excerpt:

Appendix A to Subpart C of Part 164 – Security Standards: Matrix
Administrative Safeguards

- Security Management Process
    - Risk Analysis
    - Risk Management
    - Sanction Policy
    - Information System Activity Review
- Assigned Security Responsibility
- Workforce Security
    - Authorization and/or Supervision
    - Workforce Clearance Procedure
    - Termination Procedures
- Information Access Management
    - Isolating Healthcare Clearinghouse Function
    - Access Authorization
    - Access Establishment and Modification
- Security Awareness and Training
    - Security Reminders
    - Protection from Malicious Software
    - Log-in Monitoring
    - Password Management
- Security Incident Procedures
    - Response and Reporting
- Contingency Plan
    - Data Backup Plan
        - Data must be backed up so as to ensure availability.

- Data must be secure when backed up: encrypted, physically locked up, and protected with administrative controls.
  - Disaster Recovery Plan
  - Emergency Mode Operation Plan
  - Testing and Revision Procedure
  - Applications and Data Criticality Analysis
- Evaluation
- Business Associate Contracts and Other Arrangement
- Written Contract or Other Arrangement

Physical Safeguards

- Evaluation
  - Facility Access Controls
  - Contingency Operations
  - Facility Security Plan
  - Access Control and Validation Procedures
  - Maintenance Records
- Workstation
- Workstation Security
- Device and Media Controls
  - Disposal
  - Media Re-use
  - Accountability
- Data Backup and Storage

Technical Safeguards

- Access Control
  - Unique User Identification
  - Emergency Access Procedure
  - Automatic Logoff
  - Encryption and Decryption
- Audit Controls
- Integrity
  - Mechanism to Authenticate Electronic Protected Health Information
- Person or Entity Authentication
- Transmission Security
  - Integrity Controls
- Encryption

The legal language of the legislation needs interpretation to ensure full compliance and understanding within the enterprise; however, the HIPAA FSR provides a pretty good idea of the scope of security measures required.

A View of Sarbanes-Oxley

Sarbanes-Oxley is an act "to protect investors by improving the accuracy and reliability of corporate disclosures made pursuant to the securities laws, and for other purposes."[2] Section 404 drives cybersecurity activity and reads as follows:

SEC. 404. Management Assessment of Internal Controls.

(a)   RULES REQUIRED. – The Commission shall prescribe rules requiring each annual report required by section 13(a) or 15(d) of the Securities Exchange Act of 1934 (15 U.S.C. 78m or 78o(d)) to contain an internal control report, which shall –

(1) State the responsibility of management for establishing and maintaining an adequate internal control structure and procedures for financial reporting; and

(2) Contain an assessment, as of the end of the most recent fiscal year of the issuer, of the effectiveness of the internal control structure and procedures of the issuer for financial reporting.

(b)   INTERNAL CONTROL EVALUATION AND REPORTING. – With respect to the internal control assessment required by subsection, each registered public accounting firm that prepares or issues the audit report for the issuer shall attest to, and report on, the assessment made by the management of the issuer. An attestation made under this subsection shall be made in accordance with standards for attestation engagements issued or adopted by the Board. Any such attestation shall not be the subject of a separate engagement.

So, what is an "adequate internal control structure"? What constitutes an adequate assessment? An assessment by whom and with what credentials? Does the direction seem a bit vague to you? It should because it is. The scope of required controls is not nearly as specific as that in the HIPAA FSR.

To avoid being arbitrary in your approach to determining, planning, and implementing adequate safeguards, find an industry security standard applicable (or most closely applicable) to your organization and work on customizing that standard for your specific needs. This customized standard becomes your enterprise security framework. Then record all legislative compliance activities in the context of the enterprise security framework (ESF). See the section on enterprise security framework for more details on the ESF concept.

Litigation Management

Legislative management addresses compliance with legislation and attempts to avoid litigation through safeguarding against the occurrence of incidents. Should an incident occur (e.g., disclosure of a database full of personal medical information), the result is likely going to involve litigation, i.e., appearance before prosecuting lawyers and a judge. Become familiar with laws applicable to your organization that address the sentencing of organizations (e.g., in the United States of America, there is The Federal Sentencing Guidelines–Chapter 8 Sentencing of Organizations). There is a culpability calculation to determine the amount of potential jail time for officers and the amount of potential fines. The lower the culpability score, the lower the potential jail time and fines. The guideline puts forth two main areas for calculating culpability: an ethics program and a security program.

---

2   Sarbanes-Oxley, p. 1.

You achieve lower culpability through higher preparation, raising awareness throughout the enterprise, training the enterprise, and generally instituting acceptable practices surrounding ethics and security. The complement to legislative management is litigation management, where the intent of litigation management is to minimize the negative effects on the organization in the event of an incident that leads to litigation. Both are compliance management challenges, and the effective implementation of both optimizes stakeholder value.

Effective compliance management and litigation management require a disciplined, repeatable approach to enterprise security management that includes an enterprise security standard (ESS) and enterprise security framework (ESF). The following sections provide insight into many other business benefits to identifying, creating, implementing, and deploying the use of ESS and ESF within an enterprise.

Enterprise Security Standard

There are many compliance requirements driving the structure and content of security operations. Some of these are external legislation and regulation, and some of these are generated internal to the enterprise. Security management includes the generation of various compliance reports in the context of these many compliance drivers. The enterprise security standard (ESS) is a list of all applicable security controls grouped by families. For example, NIST SP 800-53 contains security controls (*Table 3.2* is an excerpt) grouped by security control families (*Table 3.1*). Selecting or developing an enterprise security standard helps manage security planning, assessment, and reporting in the context of these various compliance drivers. What enterprise security standard should you choose?

Identifier	Family	Class
AC	Access Control	Technical
AT	Awareness and Training	Operational
AU	Audit and Accountability	Technical
CA	Security Assessment and Authorization	Management
CM	Configuration Management	Operational
CP	Contingency Planning	Operational
IA	Identification and Authentication	Technical
IR	Incident Response	Operational
MA	Maintenance	Operational
MP	Media Protection	Operational
PE	Physical and Environmental Protection	Operational
PL	Planning	Management
PS	Personnel Security	Operational
RA	Risk Assessment	Management
SA	System and Services Acquisition	Management
SC	System and Communications Protection	Technical
SI	System and Information Integrity	Operational
PM	Program Management	Management
Source:	NIST SP 800-53 Rev. 3, Recommended Security Controls for Federal Information Systems, August 2009, p. 6.	

Table 3.1 – **NIST SP 800-53 Security Control Classes, Families, and Identifiers**

There are many standards from which to derive an ESS including National Institute of Technology (NIST) Special Publication (SP) 800-53, Recommended Security Controls for Federal Information Systems; International Standards Organization (ISO) 27002, The Code of Practice for Information Security Management; and many others. You can use the standard as is or customize the ESS from other compliance requirements included in security legislation (e.g., Healthcare Insurance Portability and Accountability Act [HIPAA], Sarbanes-Oxley, and European Union Directive on Data Protection). Some of these industry security standards are free and some charge a purchase or licensing fee. How do you choose the best security standard?

The best choice is completely situational dependent. Some questions to ask in determining the best industry security standard as the foundation for your ESS are as follows:

1. **Is your organization critical infrastructure?**
   - Examine your national definition of critical infrastructure and determine if your organization falls under that description. Then look at your national security standards to see if they offer a good starting point for your ESS.
2. **Do you have a need for an internationally recognized certified security management?**
   - If so, consider the ISO 27000 series for your organization.
3. **What legislative mandates apply to your information technology and overall security posture?**
   - Use these legislative mandates to either create or enhance the ESS.
4. **What best supports the way you do business?**
   - For example, if the nature of your business is financial, then seek an industry standard most applicable to financial organizations.

Once you have chosen a baseline ESS, review it to see if it covers all the security categories and controls applicable to your enterprise. If so, great; if not, look at the other security compliance requirements and add categories and controls until all your enterprise security needs are accommodated within the ESS. The ESS should find a basis in an industry standard and then apply additions or modifications to reflect relevant legislative mandates and good business practice as determined by your enterprise security governance.

The ESS may be based entirely on an industry security standard, e.g., ISO 27001, Information Security Management System (ISMS). ISO 27001 subsequently references ISO 27002, The Code of Practice for Information Security Management. An organization may then become ISO 27001 certified to prove that it adheres to at least a minimal security standard. NIST SP 800-53 is also a good foundation for an ESS. The structure of the ESS becomes the foundation for the enterprise security framework (ESF).

Enterprise Security Framework (ESF)

Separating out the control families and their respective controls provides an outline of the ESS. This outline then becomes a framework for enterprise security.[3] This framework may be specific to your organization and may not exist elsewhere in that exact same way. That's okay

---

3 For more information on a frameworks approach to security, see *Information Assurance Architecture* by Keith D. Willett, Auerbach 2008.

because each organization's security needs are slightly different. However, even though the specifics may vary, the principles and the methodologies surrounding the use of an ESF apply to all organizations.

The ESF then becomes the structure for all enterprise security documents including planning, assessment, and reporting. The use of a common framework among all these documents enables easy referencing among the various document types; all the information for a given family or a given control is in exactly the same place in the framework throughout all documents. Moreover, if consolidated reporting is necessary, simply copying columns from one framework-based table to another is very straightforward because all families and all controls appear in exactly the same row throughout all documents. The administrative and reporting implications of using an ESF-based security management process are far reaching in efficiency, cost savings, and reporting capabilities.

Note: For many seasoned security professionals, it takes up to one year for the frameworks approach to sink in. They hear it and they can rationally acknowledge it, but it takes time to internalize it and get to the point where the light bulb goes on and they experience the "aha – I get it!" moment.

From a compliance perspective, now that you have your enterprise security framework (ESF), cross-reference the ESF with all applicable security compliance requirements. For example, if you are a European medical company with a wholly owned subsidiary registered and doing business in North America, you are likely subject to HIPAA, Sarbanes-Oxley, and your home country's data protection legislation. Cross-referencing all these to your ESF will enable you to have a single security management plan that shows alignment to multiple compliance requirements.

Enterprise Use of ESF

To better understand the enterprise use of ESF, consider the following questions and answers.

What Is the ESF?

The ESF is a list of security controls grouped under categories that comprehensively represents security in your organization. There is no universal ESF. You may choose a security standard on which to base your ESF and stay exclusively with that standard, or you may choose a security standard as a foundation for the ESF and tailor the ESF to better meet your organization's needs.

Who Uses the ESF?

Enterprise security professionals use the ESF to help with planning, assessing, tracking, and reporting enterprise security activities.

What Do You Do with ESF?

Generate tables and templates for enterprise security documents. These security documents are for security planning, management, assessment, activity tracking, and aligning architecture, systems engineering, security controls, security technologies, standards, and configuration guidance. The power of a frameworks approach is the ability to have a single format (a single structure) within which to achieve security governance, adjudication, management, development, and operations.

Why Use an ESF?

Using an ESF provides a standard, disciplined, repeatable approach for recording enterprise security planning and assessment details, tracking projects and activities, and reporting security activities. A common form and flow among all these types of documents provides for easy discovery of details; any personnel may go to any document and know exactly where to find details for a particular security category or security control.

- For example, a new security manager reviews the latest security assessment results and sees that a lot of gaps exist between current access control practices and access control guidance in the ESS. The next question for this new manager is "what are we doing about closing these gaps?" The new manager then finds the latest security project activity report and looks at the details under access control. Both reports use exactly the same framework, and access control details appear in exactly the same place.

- The key point of using an ESF is to separate structure from content. Align the structure with business activities (e.g., the enterprise architecture, if one exists). The structure remains constant as the content evolves. The security planning activities for this year are different from those for last year and next year. Those specific planning activities are but one of many content details that evolve within the structure. Since all relationships to other business activities are from the structure, those relationships remain constant. As new content enters the structure, that content immediately inherits the relationship to the structure.

When Does ESF Apply?

ESF applies to any enterprise security activity for planning, assessing, tracking, and reporting. You can generate many types of report templates for many types of target audiences, all using the same enterprise security framework, including compliance details across as-is, to-be, and transition from as-is to to-be.

How Do You Use ESF?

Use the ESF as a basis for defining methodologies and templates for enterprise security planning, assessing, tracking, and reporting. All methodologies will then focus on a common framework for structure and content. All templates will follow a common look and feel. The result is a standard, disciplined, repeatable approach to enterprise security that will result in consistency from user to user and across multiple projects and activities.

The use of an ESS and ESF provides a focal point for recording external security compliance requirements as well as internal security requirements. Generating a traceability matrix from the ESF to external security requirements that may include legislation, regulation, local ordinances, etc. will help you be comprehensive and provide evidence of due diligence. Generating a traceability or tracking matrix of all enterprise security policies, standards, and procedures will also ensure comprehensiveness on the part of generating guidance for appropriate behavior within the organization; again, this provides evidence of due diligence on the part of the enterprise.

A View of NIST SP 800-53 as an ESS and ESF

"Why NIST SP 800-53? My company is not a United States Civilian Federal organization, so why do I care about NIST standards?" First, it is an industry standard, which is a lot better than being arbitrary in your approach to enterprise security planning. Second, it is free and easily obtainable. Third, it probably won't apply to your organization 100% because it will either contain too much or too little security for your specific circumstances. However, it is a good starting point to create an enterprise security framework that is specific to your enterprise. Is NIST SP 800-53 the best for your organization? Only you can answer that by examining the nature of your business and the enterprise security needs. NIST SP 800-53 is a good starting point; however, it is one of many choices for good starting points.

NIST SP 800-53 (SP 800-53) provides families of security controls (*Table 3.1*) and groups specific security controls under each family. Table 3.2 provides a sample of security controls from the SP 800-53 Access Control family.

If you use the controls in *Table 3.2* as part of your security management program, they would become part of your enterprise security framework, and you would then perform planning and implement, assess, and audit against these controls. Moreover, you could cross-reference these controls with applicable legislative guidance like HIPAA and Sarbanes-Oxley. Part of the overall security management plan would include an applicability statement (e.g., AC-11 Session Lock is part of our Sarbanes-Oxley compliance because it ...) and then provide specifics for how it contributes to compliance.

Control No.	Control Name
AC-1	Access Control Policy and Procedures
AC-2	Account Management
AC-3	Access Enforcement
AC-4	Information Flow Enforcement
AC-5	Separation of Duties
AC-6	Least Privilege
AC-7	Unsuccessful Login Attempts
AC-8	System Use Notification
AC-9	Previous Logon (Access) Notification
AC-10	Concurrent Session Control
AC-11	Session Lock
AC-12	Withdrawn
AC-13	Withdrawn
AC-14	Permitted Actions without Identification or Authentication
AC-15	Withdrawn
AC-16	Security Attributes
AC-17	Remote Access
AC-18	Wireless Access
AC-19	Access Control for Mobile Devices
AC-20	Use of External Information Systems
AC-21	User-Based Collaboration and Information Sharing

3

Security Compliance Management

179

Control No.	Control Name
AC-22	Publicly Accessible Content None
Note:	NIST has left some control references with a notation of "Withdrawn." To maintain a consistent enterprise security framework, use the same control references as appears in the NIST guidance, including all Withdrawn controls.

Table 3.2 – **Security Controls for Access Control (AC)**

ESF as a Common Alignment Structure

A comprehensive view of enterprise security includes and aligns the security architecture, systems engineering, technology, standards, and configuration guidance for security (*Table 3.3*). The architecture provides an alignment with business drivers; systems engineering provides both an enterprise systems engineering (ESE) and traditional systems engineering (TSE) perspective; technology provides a selection of specific vendor and product information; standards provide situational dependent guidance to narrow technology selection; and configuration guidance specifies how to implement the technology to achieve the enterprise security vision. *Table 3.3* provides a template for completing this alignment using only access control security controls as an example. The actual ESF will contain the same information for all security families and all security controls.

Control No.	Architecture	Systems Engineering	Technology	Standards	Configuration Guidance
AC-1					
AC-2					
AC-3					
AC-4					
AC-5					
AC-6					
AC-7					
AC-8					
AC-9					
AC-10					
AC-11					
AC-12					
AC-13					
AC-14					
AC-15					
AC-16					
AC-17					
AC-18					
AC-19					
AC-20					
AC-21					
AC-22					

Table 3.3 – **Applied Use of the ESF (Access Control Excerpt)**

People

In a given environment, people perform processes using technology to produce results. People are the most critical resource in the fulfillment of the enterprise mission. Considerations of people subject to compliance or in support of compliance management include the following:

- Awareness, training, and education
- Policy, standards, procedures, practice
- Compliance document dissemination
- Metrics

The reasonable person judgment is a subjective measure of negligence and standard of care. For example, assume ABC Inc. has a duty of care to protect personal information of customers, and a list of customer information appears on a third-party public Internet site. A subsequent investigation shows that the information was stolen by a disgruntled employee and posted online in order to damage the reputation of ABC Inc. and put the company at risk for litigation. The investigation also shows that ABC Inc. has an exemplary security management program and that this employee was in a position of trust and violated that trust. There is an argument that ABC Inc. implemented adequate safeguards according to the reasonable person judgment. While this may limit or eliminate legal action, it does little to recover the loss of reputation to customers. Damage still occurs to ABC Inc. but less than may otherwise have occurred without a security management program.

Part of this reasonable person judgment is the hiring of security professionals. Even though legislation may not explicitly require the hiring of security professionals, it is good business practice to do so. In the event of an incident where your organization may be held liable, the organization may show due diligence and avoid accusations of negligence by hiring qualified security personnel. Security, information assurance, and cybersecurity are all highly specialized areas. The ability to install and configure a firewall is a good skill, but it hardly qualifies you to write an enterprise security management plan. The latter ability requires training, education, and experience in business, risk, technology, and security.

The other part of this reasonable person judgment is addressing the non-security professionals within the enterprise through a security awareness and training (SAT) program. The objective here is to make people aware of security, make sure they understand the implications of being secure, and ensure that they are actually complying with security policies, standards, procedures, and guidelines.

For the enterprise to comply with security, you must disseminate security requirements within the enterprise. The documents that convey this information are in policies, standards, procedures, and guidelines. A policy is a statement of objectives for appropriate behavior. A standard specifies what to use to implement and enforce policy. A procedure specifies how to use a standard to implement and enforce policy. A guideline is less formal than the previous three and may offer more suggestions than more emphatic statements of "thou shall." The term guidance refers collectively to policies, standards, procedures, and guidelines. The following sections describe security guidance in more detail.

3

Security Compliance Management

People and Compliance

The bottom line for compliance is to drive the behavior of people; the compliance document puts forth guidance for appropriate behavior. Legislative guidance describes appropriate behavior in the name of the greater good of society. Enterprise policy describes appropriate behavior in the name of the greater good of the enterprise. Some enterprise policy will reflect legislative compliance; other enterprise policy will reflect good business practice to optimize stakeholder value.

Enterprise Role of Policies, Standards, Procedures, and Practice

Policies provide a description of acceptable behavior for those within the enterprise and, at times, for those doing business with the enterprise. Policies may be thought of as enterprise law. They reflect both external mandates on appropriate behavior as well as internal mandates for good business practice as determined by executives and upper management. Standards are a description of uniformity; they are a specification of commonality to implement and enforce policy. Procedures are a specified sequence of actions to achieve a desired end of effective and efficient use of standards to implement and enforce policy. Policies, standards, and procedures describe what should be; actual practice is reality. For enterprise personnel to behave as they should requires awareness and training. Moreover, when assessing for compliance, you should assess the presence and quality of policies, standards, and procedures, plus assess actual practices to ensure that they reflect the intent of the documentation.

Security Policies

Security policies provide a description of acceptable behavior with the intent of minimizing risk to the organization – risk that may occur in the form of legislative and regulatory compliance, technical risk, environmental risk (e.g., clean and safe work environment), and the execution of processes and tasks. Security policies define appropriate behavior within the enterprise to establish compliance with security-related legislation, regulation, and internally imposed security controls. The security governance function determines the scope that security policies should address as well as the appropriate breadth and depth of security policies.

Policy Structure and Content

The structure is the outline of topics that will appear in the policy. All policies should follow a similar structure so that all employees know where to look for particular details. The policy content will vary according to what the policy addresses. The following is a sample policy structure:

Dates
Date issued, date effective, and date revised

Sponsor
Statement of management commitment

Purpose
Scope
What the policy applies to
Who is subject to adhere to the policy?

Definitions
Clarify terms to ensure reader understanding

Authority, roles, and responsibilities
Include office responsible and official responsible (by title if not actual name)

Include who implements, who enforces, and an adjudication contact to resolve conflicts with policy details

Implementation and enforcement
Reference to repository containing associated standards and procedures

Reporting requirements
The content of security policies will address a variety of areas. The following is a partial list of potential enterprise security policies in no particular order:

- Configuration Policy
- Configuration Management Policy
  - Change Management Policy
- Inventory Management
- Portable Media Policy
  - Enterprise Issued
  - Personal (PDAs, iPods, flash pens, cameras, portable hard drives, cell phones, thumb drives, digital recorders)
- Wireless
- Access Control
  - Privileged access (e.g., root, administrator)
  - Remote access
- Portable Media
- Software
- Media Disposal
- Pre-hire
- Contracts and Agreements
- Incident Response
- Disciplinary Action
- Authentication
- Encryption
- Virtual Private Network (VPN)
- Anti-malware
- Acceptable Use
- Software Licensing
- Network Traffic Management
  - Inbound
  - Outbound
  - Priority
- Information Classification
  - Proprietary
  - Confidential
  - Public
- Non-disclosure Agreements

The following sections elaborate on details of some security policies.

Security Policy General Practices

Policy management includes the following:

- Policy generation
    - Policy structure and content
- Policy dissemination
- Policy awareness, understanding, and compliance
- Policy enforcement

The governance process determines relevant external compliance requirements as well as appropriate behavior that represents good business practice within the organization. Policies capture the details of this appropriate behavior and convey the details to all employees and contractors. Policy generation is an enterprise-internal administrative aspect of compliance management. To help facilitate ease of reading and understanding, develop a standard policy structure. This means that all policies will have the same or very similar sections in the same order. The content of all policies should include acceptable and unacceptable behavior in clear language.

Policy dissemination is making the policies available to personnel and other covered entities. This may mean an explicit push of the policy to each employee and contractor, e.g., email attachment. Dissemination may also be a passive pull of the policy document from a policy repository located on an intranet website. Good policy management will record the review and acceptance of the policies by all personnel, including contractors; this record shows the person is aware of the policy. Subsequently testing knowledge of the policy and when and where the policy applies will capture understanding of the policy. Monitoring for policy infractions will capture policy compliance.

The first challenge is the development of the policy; the second challenge is enforcing the policy. Policy enforcement will occur at the management and operations level of the organization. Some policy enforcement will be automated (e.g., firewalls will enforce the appropriate use of the Internet, and disabling USB ports will enforce a policy prohibiting the use of thumb drives). Other policy enforcement is administrative, such as exposing new employees to indoctrination procedures that adequately prepare them to function effectively and securely within the organizational environment.

Access Policy

Access policy describes the ability to enter, obtain, or use information, information technology, or a facility. The access policy describes the access group, action group, resource group, and relationship. The access group is the collection of users to which the policy applies. The action group is the collection of activities performed by the user on the resources. The resource group is the collection of physical or virtual entities covered by the policy. Resources may include documents (e.g., contracts), computers, software applications (e.g., order entry), and command sets (e.g., database backup commands are available to a backup operator but not access to the database administration commands). The relationship describes the association among resources, users, and actions.

Access policy should distinctly cover privileged access. The UNIX operating environment has a root account and Windows has an administrator account. Both root and administrator accounts allow the user privileges to perform certain tasks that no other user can perform. These tasks include configuring the system for efficient operations and secure operations. Modifications of these configuration settings without the skill to understand the implications or modifications of these configurations with the explicit purpose of subverting security are both undesirable. The access control policy should restrict the number of privileged accounts and the assignment of privileged accounts to qualified users, and restrict their use in operations.

Users without an explicit need for a privileged account should not be assigned one. Any user assigned a privileged account should be vetted through an approval process that includes multiple people reviewing and approving the account assignment. Each person who possesses a privileged account should have at least one other account with normal user capability. They will then use the privileged account for tasks explicitly requiring the inherent permissions of that account and use the regular user account in everyday, normal activities. The number of existing privileged accounts, the password strength associated with them, and the actual use of privileged accounts should be part of the security audit process.

By default, privileged accounts have standard names like "Administrator." A good practice to hinder casual misuse attempts is to rename these default accounts as something else that blends in with the structure of usual user accounts. For example, if the practice is to use the first letter of the first name coupled with the first seven letters of the last name, then rename the privileged account using a fictitious name, and make it an innocuous fictitious name like jsmith, not something associated with privilege like gwizard. There are relatively simple ways around this for a knowledgeable hacker, but there are simple ways around a front door lock to a knowledgeable thief. Simple deterrents deter the simple, but they are deterrents nonetheless.

One way to bypass the above is to be aware of security identification numbers (SIDs). Windows creates a SID for each user and computer account. UNIX uses a unique identification number (UID). The same SID is used for all administrator accounts, and there are other commonly known SIDs that can aid a hacker in identifying accounts. Microsoft, for example, provides one set of SIDs for Windows at the URL http://support.microsoft.com/kb/243330. The Windows user account control (UAC) function runs all applications in user mode, regardless of the privileges of the user executing the command. Knowledge of these technical specifics will help articulate access control standards. For example, all enterprise financial systems operating under the Windows operating system will activate and enforce the use of a UAC to limit the running of applications under privileged accounts. Policy states the intent, and standards describe what to use to implement and enforce the intent. The section on access control provides more details.

Remote Access Control

The access control policy should include a section on remote access. The remote access policy applies to all employees, contractors, vendors, business partners, and agents that connect to the enterprise network from outside enterprise-owned facilities. Access may occur using a personally owned device or a company-issued device. The policy should restrict remote access privileges according to job function and business need. Access to email may be the only necessary remote access. Others may need access to the internal network (the intranet) for services offered via the internal website. This is distinct from others who need intranet access for purposes of connecting to internal database or application servers.

Remote access control addresses technical privileges, business privileges, as well as personal responsibilities on the part of the remote user. The same responsibilities exist for remote access as exist for on-site use. This means limiting the line of sight to the remote computer, password protection, authentication process, screen lock, securing the communication path (e.g., virtual private network), and acceptable use of the remote computer to avoid malware entering the enterprise via remote connection.

Authentication

Authentication is the validation of the user presenting an identity credential. That is, the user presents a claim of identity (e.g., user ID) and then some verification that he or she is the valid owner of that identity. Authentication may occur in many ways, including something the user:

- **Knows** – e.g., a password or personal identification number (PIN)
- **Has** – e.g., a secure token, identity card with embedded radio frequency identification (RFID)
- **Is** – e.g., biometric (fingerprint, retina scan)
- **Does** – e.g., written signature metrics (some consider this a subset of *Is*)
- **Is Located** – e.g., Global Positioning System (GPS) coordinate validation (some consider this a subset of *Is*)

The use of two or more of these in a single authentication transaction is known as multifactor authentication, or strong authentication. A secure token is a small device in the possession of the user that displays a random number sequence that synchronizes with the authentication server. Upon login, the user enters his or her ID, then a PIN plus the number sequence as the password. The password is always changing and is generated by a combination of something the user knows (the PIN) and something they have (the secure token). Theft of the token is not enough for the thief to gain access. The use of a secure token is an example of strong authentication.

Authorization

Authorization is the validation and approval of a claim of privilege. Authenticating an identity is a separate and distinct process from authorizing an activity. The possession of a valid identity credential and proving that it indeed belongs to the presenter does by default equate to permission to perform an activity. Privileges may be embedded in the identity credential, or there may be a privilege database that contains a list of permissible activities. The individual may be assigned specific activity privileges, or the user may be assigned a role with which certain privileges are permitted by default.

For example, a new employee presents his or her identity credential at the card reader leading into the main lobby. The user authenticates this claim of identity by entering a PIN. The card reader system authenticates the identity (i.e., yes, this is John Doe); a default privilege by virtue of being an employee is permission to enter the main lobby. John Doe then goes up one flight of stairs and attempts the same sequence of events to enter the data center. The card reader may authenticate the claim of identity (i.e., yes, this is John Doe) but deny entry because John does not have the explicit privilege to enter the data center, nor is John assigned a role that has the privilege to enter the data center.

A log is made of this entry attempt. A once or twice attempt is likely a mistake on the part of John and does not warrant any further investigation. Ten attempts within 24 hours plus other attempts at unauthorized entry in other parts of the building are indicators that further investigation is prudent. Establishing authentication, authorization, logs, log review procedures, anomaly detection, and further investigation of anomalies are all part of a comprehensive security management program to establish and maintain compliance.

Network sniffers and other monitoring devices have the potential to intercept network traffic. This includes the message exchanges during logon, password entry, and authentication/authorization. Authenticate over an encrypted link to hide the sending of user IDs and passwords.

Encryption

Having established a connection via a successful login, protect the subsequent exchange of data (data in transit) from interception using encryption. Encryption is the transformation of plaintext to ciphertext. Plaintext is the native form of a language like the sentence you are reading now. The transformation of this plaintext into ciphertext uses a key and an algorithm to modify the text into a format that can be read only by those who possess the key to turn ciphertext back into plaintext.

For example, assume the key to be "+1" and the algorithm to be an alphabet shift to the right. Applying this algorithm to the word ENCRYPTION results in FODSZQUJPO, or the shifting of each letter to the right by one. The decryption process applies the associated decryption key of "–1" to the encryption algorithm, which is to shift the alphabet minus one space to turn FODSZQUJPO back into ENCRYPTION. This is a very simple encryption process and is easily broken by cryptography professionals. This is why you should always choose the strongest form of encryption possible to make it very difficult to break the encryption.

The use of encryption on data at rest and in transit is one method to protect data from unauthorized disclosure. If during the course of normal operations your organization discloses protected data, and the investigation shows that you do not use encryption and that the disclosure could have otherwise been avoided if encryption were in place, your organization needs a really good reason for not having put encryption in place. There are valid arguments for not having encryption due to cost, complexity, or lower priority than other security investments; however, omission by oversight is not a valid position. Conscious omission with the rationale of business priorities is a valid position. Hence the usefulness of the ESS and ESF to provide a checklist of considerations and a place to record current situation (as-is), future situation (to-be), current projects (transition), and future plans for all of security, as budget allows.

It is important to realize that various legal or compliance requirements might dictate that encryption of a certain minimum standard is necessary for certain data or activities. It might also prohibit the storage of certain data, even if such data were to be encrypted (e.g., credit card CVV numbers by a merchant).

3

Security Compliance Management

Virtual Private Network

A virtual private network (VPN) is an encrypted link between network nodes. Traffic traversing this link inherits the encrypted properties of the link. This means that the end-user PC does not have to encrypt the in-transit traffic at the application level because the VPN accomplishes this for the user. A VPN may exist between routers or may be an application on the end-user PC that establishes an encrypted network connection to the enterprise for secure remote use. SSL-based VPN technology, which has become increasingly popular over the past decade, allows similar functionality to be established from computers running only a Web browser with a plugin (Active/X, Java, etc.).

Acceptable Use

Acceptable use policies define what usage of particular items are acceptable. Such policies normally explain restrictions on the use of computers and other electronic devices, as well as restrictions vis-à-vis accessing other networks and websites. The purpose of such a policy is threefold: to avoid productivity wasters, to avoid potential litigation against the enterprise, and to avoid malware entering the enterprise and other security risks. Productivity wasters include dating sites, sports sites, auction sites, and other sites that offer activities, that, while perhaps useful, have no benefit to the organization and simply waste employee time on activities that, at least vis-à-vis the organization, are non-productive. Accessing material on hate sites, porn sites, and pirated software/movies sites may also place inappropriate material on enterprise computers or networks, or display material within the enterprise that may offend others and may lead to lawsuits against the enterprise for allowing such activity (for example, a sexual harassment lawsuit, a claim that the firm is using unlicensed software, etc.). Productivity wasters may be allowed (for example, during nonworking hours or as long as they do not waste too much time) in the interest of preserving employee morale or some other justification. Activities that are likely going to ultimately lead to potential litigation should be restricted at all times.

Likewise, activities that could lead to the introduction of malware into the enterprise network, or to other security problems including the leakage of data from the enterprise, should also be restricted at all times. This may include restricting the download and installation of executable code, the use of file sharing systems (e.g., music sharing), accessing sites with a history or reputation of introducing spyware, and the use of USB storage devices. The technical restriction of all such activity may interfere with valid business functions (e.g., the use of USB storage devices). At the least, the appropriate use policy should call for employee awareness and training on the responsible and secure use of enterprise information technology.

Wireless Policy

Publishing an access policy that also incorporates wireless access is better than maintaining two separate policies for access control. The point is to publish wireless policy details somewhere to ensure the appropriate use of wireless technology and, more importantly, to avoid the misuse of wireless technology. Wireless networks are available for connection to anyone within range of the wireless access point. Many wireless signals extend beyond enterprise office space, buildings, and campuses (see the "War Driving" section for detecting this). For that reason, appropriate guidance is necessary to govern the presence, configuration, and actual use of wireless networks. Wireless policies should cover the registration of access points, the allocation of channels, and security and access control.

Wireless access point (WAP) registration records WAP details in a database. If a WAP is detected that is not in the database, it is likely a rogue access point. The presence of a rogue access point may be an enterprising, but misguided, employee trying to set up a valid business application. A rogue access point may also be set up by a would-be attacker looking for access to the network from close physical proximity but not physically on enterprise property.

Multiple WAPs may lead to conflicts over channel allocation. The channel allocation portion of the wireless policy will cover which channels are available and which should be used. Wireless policy covers both the secure and efficient use of wireless networks within the enterprise.

Wireless Security

The security and access control portion of the wireless policy covers the restriction of network access to authorized personnel and the prevention of unauthorized disclosure of data traversing the wireless network. Securing wireless networks is achievable via machine access code (MAC) access lists, isolating the wireless network from other networks, and encrypting the wireless transmissions. Access lists restrict access to the wireless network to known entities. Isolation of wireless networks keeps wireless traffic off wired networks and limits the potential damage through unauthorized access. Preventing unauthorized disclosure is accomplished using wireless encryption schemes like wired equivalent privacy (WEP; note: WEP is not an acronym for wireless encryption protocol) and Wi-Fi Protected Access (WPA and WPA2).

WEP is specified in the IEEE 802.11b Wireless Fidelity (Wi-Fi) standard. WEP suffers from less than acceptable encryption (due to both small key size and flaws in the way the encryption is implemented) and, today, it can be easily cracked with readily available software. WPA superseded WEP in 2003, which at the time implemented only part of the then-pending standard IEEE 802.11i. In 2004, WPA2 implemented the full IEEE 802.11i standard. (For more on this, please see: http://en.wikipedia.org/wiki/IEEE_802.11i-2004 .) Implementing wireless encryption is normally necessary; it is important to remember to ensure that the implementation is adequate to satisfy compliance requirements. The use of a weak encryption method (e.g., WEP) may not satisfy the requirements of customers or provide a good defense in situations in which data was disclosed or in which a prosecuting attorney challenged a claim that the firm practiced Due Care.

Portable Media Policy

Portable media includes personal digital assistants (PDAs), iPods, smartphones, tablets, flash memory sticks, cameras, portable hard drives, digital recorders, tapes, floppy disks (they are still used in some environments!), DVDs, CDs, etc. There are valid business uses for all these devices, and policy should enumerate valid business uses and restrict all others. Many portable devices have the potential to record and store vast amounts of data. These portable devices are also easily lost or stolen. This policy is a difficult balance between empowerment, well-intentioned productivity, and the restriction of use to avoid being tomorrow's national news headline for disclosing sensitive customer data.

3

Security Compliance Management

The valid business use of portable media may include the use of portable devices to store sensitive data. Policy may require the use of encryption to protect data in the event of loss or theft and the secure removal of sensitive data from these devices, which are procedures beyond the standard delete command.

Personal Property Use Policy

A supplement to the portable media policy, as well as other policies, is the use of personally owned technology versus organization-issued technology. The use of organization-issued USB devices, portable hard drives, tapes, CDs, floppy disks, etc., may be fine. However, the use of personally owned devices may be restricted or prohibited. Personal devices include everything in the previous list plus PDAs, iPods, iPhones, flash pens, digital audio recording devices, and portable storage devices like USB thumb drives, cameras, PCs, and laptops. These devices are capable of storing electronic files, and even under the best of intentions they pose a threat to disclose proprietary or sensitive information. The use of personal devices may disclose data because personal devices may not have the same security software and devices.

The use of personal devices on enterprise networks may introduce malware, also from the lack of the same security software installed on enterprise-issued equipment. Many of these devices initiate an automated startup procedure when connected to a PC. If these personal devices connect at any time to enterprise PCs and the personal device contains malware, that malware has now been introduced to the enterprise environment. For example, a thumb sucker attack is the installation of malware on a USB thumb drive and leaving that thumb drive lying about. A person picks up the thumb drive and, wanting to know what is on it or whom it belongs to, plugs it into a PC. The automated startup software initiates and installs the malware on that PC, and the enterprise network is now compromised. Cameras may take pictures of sensitive areas like data centers and data center security. Cell phones may be tracked via global positioning (GPS). PDAs can store large amounts of data as can USB storage devices. Personal laptops are often not as secure as enterprise PCs.

Enterprise policy governing the possession and use of personal property should reflect the sensitivity of the data and the environment. Legislative compliance requirements that require the protection of personal information or financial information should influence these policies. Moreover, the enterprise competitive environment should also influence the details of policy. Corporate espionage is not just an interesting dramatic movie plot. There are real dollars at stake in a globally competitive marketplace. The desire to save millions of dollars on research and development and to accelerate time to market by years if not decades is a strong motivation to compromise competitor security. The use of personally owned devices makes theft of information easy.

Again, you as a security professional have a difficult balance of restricting behavior to protect stakeholder interests but empowering employees to use the best tools available for the greatest level of productivity.

Software Management Policy

The software management policy covers software procurement, tracking, and audits. The purchase of software includes two components: the physical media and the number of licenses. The physical media may be used many times; however, each installation receives a unique license. Good software procurement ensures that the organization receives the appropriate number of licenses and optimizes software costs including initial purchase and ongoing maintenance fees. A large organization often enters into multiple separate agreements for the purchase of the same software. This leads to multiple contracts, multiple purchase orders, and a premium fee for separate purchase and maintenance agreements. Consolidating all these into a single contract optimizes costs.

The procurement process also ensures the appropriate purchase of server licenses as well as client licenses that connect to the server. The number of client licenses may be for installations or for simultaneous connections. This calculation can be a bit tricky, but it is necessary to optimize costs to the organization.

Have your legal department review software license agreements to ensure that you and your organization understand the implications of accepting the license. Inadvertently agreeing to a software vendor's right to monitor or audit software use or install spyware may impose unacceptable risk to the organization. If the license agreement is too restrictive on your organization or too liberal to the vendor, you may attempt to get the vendor to modify its license agreement with you, or you can find a new vendor.

Tracking software installations is necessary to ensure that all installations are indeed being used and that software licenses are not exceeded. If a user receives a new PC and needs software moved from the old PC to the new one, the software is installed on the new PC and the use of the seat license is recorded. The software should also be uninstalled from the old PC and the seat license returned to the license pool; otherwise, the organization is paying for a license that is no longer in use. Software tracking should maintain records of the location of the physical media as well as the licenses.

Software auditing provides a validation of the software packages installed. The data from a software audit shows what software packages are installed and, if the software is approved, software that is provided by the organization, or, if it is unapproved, software that was inadvertently or illegally installed by the end-user. Additionally, the software audit will validate the number of licenses currently in use as well as the versions of software in use. Older versions may contain vulnerabilities taken care of by patches or later releases.

Media Disposal Policy

Planning for the disposal of media via policy, standards, and procedures is more about the data on the media than the media asset itself. The purpose of the media disposal policy is twofold: first, to ensure that any sensitive data is not disclosed during or after disposing of the media, and second, to ensure that the data may indeed be discarded and that it is not primary data necessary to retain under legislative compliance requirements.

Media disposal addresses how to discard old, outdated, or broken media that store data. A standard delete process only removes a pointer and does not remove the actual information from the media. Even reformatting a disk may leave ghost images of previous data that may be recovered. The media disposal policy should address all media but especially media that stores sensitive information. Sensitive information includes any information whose unauthorized disclosure may cause harm to the enterprise, its officers, or its stakeholders. This includes proprietary information as well as information that may be protected under litigation, e.g., personal health information (PHI).

Consider the use of an authorized service to handle the disposal of media. The service understands the procedures and the appropriate steps to take to degauss (the process of eliminating a magnetic field), reformat, or physically destroy the media. The disposal process should be formal and include the assignment of roles, responsibilities, and accountability handling media disposal. This means that employees do not take it upon themselves to dispose of media, but rather they transfer the media to the in-house personnel responsible for media disposal and document the transfer. The media disposal personnel then document the media handling from receipt through actual disposal.

If your organization does business with third parties that store your sensitive data, business agreements should include provisions for secure handling and appropriate disposal of the storage media.

Contracts and Business Agreement Policy

A contract is a meeting of the minds for the exchange of promises to perform or refrain from performing some act. The result of a contractual agreement may be a product or service. The contract may also specify certain characteristics that the product or service must possess. These characteristics may include an operational feature or operational performance parameters. The following are examples of contracts and agreements:

- Service level agreements (SLAs)
- Contractor agreements
- Business partner agreements
- Vendor agreements
- Managed security service providers

The contracts and business agreement policy specifies certain attributes that must appear within any contract or business agreement. The motivation behind these attributes may be good business practice or to comply with a legislative directive. The HIPAA FSR is one law that specifies the need for business agreements to address the protection of PHI.

Service Level Agreements

As discussed in Chapter 1, a service level agreement (SLA) is an agreement between a service provider and a service consumer, or between service providers. The SLA records common understanding about the services provided and the performance parameters within which to provide the services. Sections of the SLA include the following:

- Service Definition
- Warranties and Performance Measurements
- Problem Management
- Customer Duties
- Disaster Recovery
- Termination

Performance measurements include time of initial response, time to produce result, and billing details. Performance measurements also include service availability specified as up time (e.g., no less than 99.9%) or down time (no more than X minutes per year). The SLA should clearly specify penalties for falling below expected performance and termination given repeated or sustained performance violations.

Problems will occur; this is a given. Preplanning for problem management is good business practice. Problem management includes notification, evaluation, escalation, adjudication, resolution, and follow-up action to implement the resolution. The service provider has the duty to provide the service within acceptable performance; however, this may only be possible if the service consumers fulfill their own duties. Clearly specify these duties to help with problem resolution (i.e., the root cause is more clearly identifiable to be with the provider or the consumer).

Part of the benefit of engaging an outside service is the responsibility of guaranteeing that the service resides with the provider. In the event of disaster, the consumer doesn't care from whom or from where the service is provided so long as the consumer receives the result within acceptable performance parameters. Specify these performance expectations as part of disaster recovery, including acceptable down time to allow for service swap from one location to another.

As the last paragraph alludes to, the use of an outside service transfers responsibility from the enterprise to a supplier. To be successful at this, the enterprise needs good outsourcing relationship management (ORM). Outsourcing may include any activity that is not the core expertise of the organization. For example, Small Tools, Inc. likely has a core expertise in the manufacturing of handheld tools. Their expertise is not likely to include information security. Hence, they may outsource to a managed security service provider.

Managed Security Service Providers

With the complexity of technical security coupled with the increase in cyber threats, many companies have opted to outsource security to managed security services providers (MSSPs). MSSPs offer security services that would otherwise be unaffordable to medium and small companies due to cost or be unattainable due to resource limitations like qualified security personnel. Many companies view security as a core need, if not a core capability, and hesitate to turn over so much control to a vendor. However, the economies of scale make the cost of using an MSSP very attractive, and the proliferation and sophistication of attackers require highly specialized personnel, infrastructure, and procedures.

As competent and as trusted as the MSSP may be, good business practice dictates that no company yields complete control of its networks to another organization. There is still a need to maintain in-house expertise to ensure that the organization's interests are accurately conveyed to the MSSP and that the MSSP acts accordingly to protect those interests. In-house efforts are still necessary to produce security policies that govern MSSP activities and performance.

Develop confidentiality agreements with the MSSP. The MSSP will have intimate knowledge of your operations and confidential information. Moreover, your organization should develop incident response policies and procedures that influence the specifics of the

MSSP business agreement. This is still your network and your responsibility. Operations, monitoring, detection, notification, and resolution may be outsourced, but the security responsibility is only shared, not abdicated.

The Cumulus Assessment Module (CAM) assists with the evaluation of SLA fulfillment (i.e., it verifies that the MSSP lives up to the performance agreements with your organization). *Figure 3.2* shows the CAM architecture with inputs of SLA details, data distribution parameters, and statistical probe measurements, as well as output of Cumulus Point (CP) balance over time. Every service will have measurable, quantitative properties such as the amount of resource usage, number of resource accesses, and the length of time it may be used; these quantitative properties are known as parameters. The service agreement specifies expected performance in terms of these parameters as well as specified acceptable deviations from expectations; acceptable performance and acceptable performance deviations are described as the corridor. Deviations outside of the acceptable range (i.e., leaves the corridor) result in a penalty as determined by the penalty function.

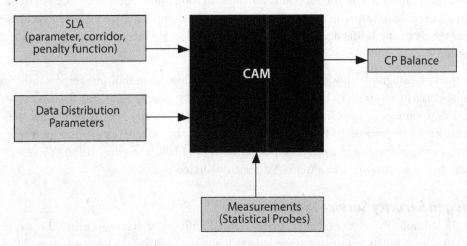

Figure 3.2 – **CAM architecture**

CAM also uses measurements from the operating environment that may include a full set of measurements over a period of time, statistical probes, or statistically prepared values. The data distribution parameters describe how to interpret the measurement data. The CP output describes how the SLA has been fulfilled.

Contractor Agreements
A contractor is not a direct employee of the organization but has the same responsibilities as employees, including the need for awareness and compliance with security-related policies. The policies will make contractors aware of relevant legislation and regulation with which they also must comply. The same policy repository should be available to both direct employees and contractors to ensure full access to all relevant policies at all times.

Business Agreements

Business agreements are appropriate for vendors, suppliers, original equipment manufacturers (OEMs), and contractors. A chain is as strong as its weakest link. This is a sentiment that HIPAA FSR reflects in its requirement for business agreements that include the safeguarding of personal health information (PHI); PHI is a special case of personally identifiable information (PII). PII is the general term for data that may disclose the identity of an individual; PII is the main concern in privacy-related legislation and regulation. PHI is PII with respect to any medical details, including billing, treatments, and prescriptions. Unauthorized disclosure of PHI or PII may result in a lawsuit against the owner and custodian of the data. The data owner may be your organization, and the business agreement may be with a custodian of the data. The custodian may take possession of the data for processing (e.g., medical billing outsourcer).

To limit liability for your organization, you want to show due diligence for the protection of your data by having business agreements that state responsibilities on the part of data custodians. A business agreement may include the following sections:

- Definition of Terms
- Permitted Uses and Disclosures
- Non-disclosure
- Safeguards and Reporting
- Mitigation and Enforcement

Your legal department or a business unit may have the final say on the structure and content of the business agreement. The sections above are exemplary to spark discussion between you as the security professional and the legal department to ensure that the business agreement conveys the intent to secure your organization's data.

Define all terms for a common understanding. Explicitly state the permitted business use of data and the permitted disclosure of data. For example, an outsourcer for human resource (HR) services may need to share employee information with a subcontractor who processes payroll. The HR services company will have to share employee information with the payroll company, so it makes no sense to prohibit them from sharing the data with anyone. Likewise, provide specifics for non-disclosure, even if it is a simple statement to the effect of "anything not explicitly listed as a permissible disclosure is prohibited."

The safeguard section does not have to enumerate specifics but simply state expectations that the data custodian will provide appropriate administrative, physical, and technical safeguards to prevent unauthorized disclosure according to X, where X may be an industry standard or legislative compliance requirement. The reporting section of the business agreement may require the data custodian to report security incidents, their effect, and the outcome of the incident and subsequent investigation. Additionally, the reporting section may require the data custodian to report within X days any unauthorized disclosure of your organization's data.

The mitigation section addresses the need for security practices that minimize risk to your organization's data. The enforcement section gives you the right to examine the custodian for compliance with the business agreement. Other business agreement sections may be necessary according to circumstances.

Incident Response Policy

An incident response policy will establish the need for preparation and planning to monitor for, detect, categorize, and respond to incidents. In addition to the standard policy sections, the incident response policy will include details for initial reporting, triage, escalation, mitigation and containment, investigation (e.g., root cause analysis), restoration, and ongoing reporting.

A single incident response policy often makes more sense than multiple incident response policies. There will be a lot of information in common among all incidents. The single incident response policy may address multiple types of incidents, including the following:

■ Denial of service
■ Malicious code
■ Unauthorized access
■ Inappropriate use
■ Forensics

Incident response policies must account for compliance requirements. Reporting times, notification rules, etc. all may be impacted by laws and regulations, or by industry standards and norms. Reporting requirements are also discussed elsewhere in this book.

Some organizations are only concerned with maintaining effective operations, and the focus of incident response is to restore operations and also to minimize the potential of incident recurrence. Other organizations may wish to pursue prosecution in the event of an attack, disgruntled employee, or corporate espionage. Successful prosecution will include forensic activities that establish and preserve the chain of evidence. If this is the case for your organization, ensure that the incident response policy includes the need to engage qualified cyber forensics expertise. If one is seeking prosecution, in order to preserve the potential to submit valid evidence for legal proceedings, specific preparations are necessary prior to touching the affected system. The cyber forensics experts will be aware of these preparations.

The section on incident response in Domain 5 provides more details on incident response that implement and enforce the incident response policy.

Digital Policy Management

Digital policy management consists of the following:

■ Digital policy infrastructure
■ Digital policy manager
■ Policy repository
■ Digital policy client
■ Policy decision point (PDP)
■ Policy enforcement point (PEP)

The discussion of security policies to this point has referred to documents. Digital policy management (DPM) is the automated enforcement of policy on the network. A digital policy infrastructure is the collection of policy managers, policy clients, PDPs, and PEPs. The DPM administrator translates written policy into digital policy and reflects that written policy in parameters within the digital policy manager. Digital policy takes the form of being either rule based or role based and uses attributes associated with users and objects to make decisions based on policy (e.g., authorization decisions).

The digital policy manager provides direction to the digital policy clients that are distributed throughout the enterprise network. For example, the DPM administrator may enter in parameters to a firewall policy manager that reflect the enterprise policy on Internet traffic. That policy manager then disseminates the digital policy to all firewalls containing the digital policy client throughout the enterprise to ensure consistent and expedient enforcement of the Internet access policy.

Policy enforcement points (PEPs) enforce policy decisions made by the policy decision points (PDPs). In other words, PDPs decide yes or no and the PEP enforces that decision and informs the user. The PEP is a software process running on the system attempting to be accessed. When a user tries to access a file, database, application, or service on the system, the PEP passes the user attributes on to the PDP. The PDP compares the user attributes to the permissions described in the digital policy repository and makes an authorization decision, yes or no, for access. The PDP passes the decision to the PEP, which in turn informs the user.

A security compliance management program establishes the association of compliance drivers with enterprise policy. Digital policy management is a technical implementation and enforcement of enterprise policy. Capturing these relationships within the ESF will show a clear association of compliance requirements and the implementation of services and mechanisms to enforce those compliance requirements.

Security Standards

Security standards are a description of uniformity to minimize enterprise risk in balance with fulfilling the enterprise mission. Standards may reflect a choice of technologies (e.g., a firewall standard may provide a choice of two vendors and two products); additionally, a standard may reflect how to implement a particular technology (e.g., configure the operating system in this manner, or set up packet filtering in the firewall in this manner). Categories of security standards include the following:

- Hardware
  - Computers
    - Servers
    - Desktop PCs
  - Infrastructure
    - Routers
    - Switches
    - Network interface cards (NICs)
    - Cables
  - Storage media
    - CDs, DVDs, tapes, floppy disks, hard drives
- Software
  - Operating system
  - Applications
    - Word processing, spreadsheet, presentation software

3

Security Compliance Management

- Configuration
  - Hardware
  - Software
- Security mechanisms
- Firewall, anti-virus, anti-spam, anti-spyware, intrusion detection system (IDS), intrusion prevention system (IPS)

Standardized server configurations enable easy setup and integration into the data center. Standard desktop configurations enable easy purchase, setup, and installation of desktops for new employees. A standard desktop environment enables the creation of software images with standard software applications. There is no need to test the applications because they are known to work efficiently within the standard desktop configuration.

Standards will address how to approach homogeneous versus heterogeneous environments. A homogeneous environment uses all of the same types of hardware and software, typically all from the same vendor; a heterogeneous environment will vary hardware and software among different vendors. Benefits to a homogeneous environment are volume purchase agreements, site licensing, help desk efficiency, the ability to provide standard configurations, and ease of creating a standard desktop image. A major drawback of a homogeneous environment is once an attacker learns to exploit one vulnerability, he or she may exploit the same vulnerability elsewhere in the enterprise. A heterogeneous environment purchases the same functionality from multiple vendors; for example, the firewall used for Internet connectivity may vary from the firewall used to separate business units, or routers from different vendors handle local area networks (LANs) versus wide area networks (WANs). This increases the expenses to manage multiple vendor equipment and applications, but it does provide an increase in security.

Defense-in-depth is the use of multiple security devices from the edge of the network to the core; defense-in-breadth (a term less commonly used but definitely still relevant) is the use of multiple types of security devices within each layer. A heterogeneous environment supports the concept of defense-in-breadth. Another example is the use of multiple anti-malware applications because the anti-malware signature files may vary among vendors, and the use of multiple anti-malware applications filters a wider variety of malware. Note: Defense-in-breadth also includes extending security beyond the enterprise to vendors, partners, contractors, etc.

Security Management Standards

Many times, people are in violent agreement because they are saying the same thing in different words but, due to communication issues, do not understand one another. For example, speaking of security concepts and characteristics can get quite confusing and frustrating when debates start over the definition of risk or the exact nuance of vulnerability, or people use the terms without clarifying to one another to what they are actually referring. One method of overcoming this is to introduce a common language. There is emerging work by NIST that provides standards for articulating security concepts and characteristics. This work includes Common Vulnerabilities and Exposures (CVE) for common identification of vulnerabilities, Common Configuration Enumeration (CCE) to define secure configurations, Common Platform Enumeration (CPE) for a structured information technology naming scheme, Common Vulnerability Scoring Systems (CVSSs) for scoring all CVE vulnerabilities, eXtensible Configuration Checklist Description Format (XCCDF) for specifying a language to write security checklists, and Open Vulnerability Assessment Language (OVAL) to provide an industry standard for security content across all security tools.

The National Vulnerability Database (NVD) "is the U.S. government repository of standards based vulnerability management data represented using the Security Content Automation Protocol (SCAP). This data enables automation of vulnerability management, security measurement, and compliance" (http://nvd.nist.gov/, last accessed March 2009). The SCAP project within NVD has more details on CVE, CCE, CPE, CVSS, XCCDF, and OVAL.

Vulnerability management is also important from a compliance standpoint, as:

The presence of vulnerabilities that remain unaddressed when methods for directly mitigating against them (e.g., by applying a patch) exist can render an organization that was otherwise compliant with some standard or regulation to be non-compliant. Failure to patch can also increase civil liability in case of a breach.

If a vulnerability exists for which no patch is yet available, actions should be taken to prevent the vulnerability from being exploited. This may entail, for example, disabling a particular service. Failure to take preventative action can lead to breaches and, in certain circumstances, potentially render an organization that was otherwise compliant with some standard or regulation to be non-compliant. Failure to take action can also increase civil liability in case of a breach, although, perhaps, if the method for preventing the problem is not obvious, the liability risk may be less than it would be in situations in which a patch that existed was not applied.

Awareness of such standards will help you decide what aspects of security monitoring, analysis, and reporting may take place automatically versus manually. The ability to elicit configuration details from information technology may provide a real time feed into a view of the enterprise security posture and the enterprise risk posture, and the details may support many audit efforts.

Security Procedures

Security procedures are a specified sequence of actions to achieve a desired end of effective and efficient management of business risk. Security procedures describe a disciplined, repeatable manner in which to use the security standards to implement and enforce security policy. Some security procedures are explicitly for information technology professionals and security professionals. Other security procedures are for other enterprise personnel. Security procedures may include the following:

- Installing new PCs using the standard desktop image that includes operating system configurations and applications explicitly for security purposes
- Discarding old PCs, hard drives, and other media
- Backups (type and frequency)
- Backup storage (legislative requirements for retaining transaction data)
- Pre-hire procedures, e.g., background and reference check
- New hire procedures, e.g., establish unique identity for access control

3

Security Compliance Management

Security Guidelines

Security guidelines are less formal than procedures, but they provide a general idea of intent and how to achieve that intent. If the enterprise security department has a particular goal in mind but doesn't really have a specific manner in which it desires to see that goal achieved, meaning that leaving the means to achieve the end is up to the individual, then capture that intent in a guideline.

Security Practice

Despite all the enterprise policies, standards, procedures, and guidelines, there remains a difference between what the organization prescribes to do (documents) and what the organization actually does (practice). Evaluating the documents to ensure that the right directives exist to motivate behavior is critically important for good business practice and to show due diligence for an effective security program (remember the need for both legislative and litigation management). Even after evaluating the documents, one still needs to evaluate actual behavior to ensure it complies with the documents.

Evaluating behavior means interviews, observations via shoulder surfing (i.e., looking over the shoulder of an employee to verify secure practice), and hands-on verification that security measures exist are being used, and they are being used according to policy. The sections on vulnerability management and penetration testing provide more detail on evaluating security practice.

Compliance Document Dissemination

Dissemination of these compliance documents is a challenge for many organizations. Factors to consider are the number of people to receive the documents, the physical location of the people, the duration (effective shelf life) of the documents (i.e., how often they change), and the access to technology of the people to receive the documents. Printing and physically mailing the documents is not likely to be a good choice, unless you have a non-technical workforce without access to computers.

The most cost-effective method is to place the documents on a document server with a Web interface and provide access information via email. Now that people know where to get them, they need to know when they need them. An awareness campaign is one method that will work well for general security information like preparing people to be aware of social engineering. Other documents may be situation specific and require more focused communication with managers and require the managers to engage the appropriate personnel for awareness and training.

For dissemination purposes, consider the usefulness of the following for your organization:

- Compliance resource center
- Compliance management system
- Record-specific employee access
  - *Note: consider non-repudiation and the non-deniability principle*
- Record employee reading and acceptance

A compliance resource center is a single point to store the latest version of all policies, standards, procedures, and guidelines. A compliance management system will help with version control, keep records of old compliance documents, and be able to track who checks out or otherwise downloads compliance documents. This latter will help with recording specific employee access, which is necessary to prove that employees are indeed aware of a particular policy that all employees may be required to read. Further, the compliance management system may support recording digital signatures to verify employee reading and acceptance of enterprise compliance documents.

Metrics

The purpose of metrics is the objective evaluation of value to the organization in terms of business need, and solution existence, effectiveness, and efficiency. That is, define what we need, discover if the things we need exist, determine if they are producing the results we expect, and analyze if they are producing the results we expect within acceptable performance parameters. Determination of what we need is the baseline of comparison for all other metrics. Defining what we need includes the type of safeguards (determined from a risk assessment/ analysis), the depth of safeguards (e.g., perimeter and core safeguards), placement of safeguards (e.g., number and location), and performance parameters (e.g., bandwidth utilization, bandwidth throughput, mean time between failures, and annual down time allowance).

Existence Metrics

Examine the risks, threat space, asset space, and the vulnerability space to determine what safeguards the organization needs. The enterprise risk posture expresses the manner in which to address each risk: accept, ignore (which is really implicit acceptance), share, transfer, or mitigate. The safeguards necessary to implement and enforce the risk posture consist of a to-be security posture. The discovery of security services and mechanisms the organization currently has in place provides an as-is security posture. Comparing as-is to to-be provides the security posture gaps. Establishing safeguard priorities via a business impact analysis (BIA) and assigning budget and schedule to priorities is the gap closure plan. An effective gap closure plan is an intelligent allocation of resources to establish an enterprise security posture that balances empowerment to fulfill the mission with risk mitigation to ensure legislative compliance, employee safety, and optimize stakeholder interests.

The gap closure plan will include what to purchase, implement, test, deploy, and operate for users to perform tasks that achieve the enterprise mission and fulfill the enterprise vision. Existence metrics compare the as-is posture to the to-be posture. Existence metrics may track how many safeguards are in the budget, how many are ordered, and how many are received, tested, deployed, and in current operations.

Effectiveness Metrics

The fact that the enterprise has a safeguard and it was deployed into the field does not necessarily imply that the safeguard is producing expected results. The safeguard may be inoperable, or it may not be providing what the end-user or operations manager expected it to provide. Moreover, a safeguard may have been effective in the past, but a new threat may compromise its effectiveness in the present and future. With respect to technology and process, effectiveness metrics track the operational state of the safeguard and whether the safeguard is producing the expected results.

3

Security Compliance Management

For example, with respect to security training, awareness, and education, effectiveness metrics may track the dissemination, awareness, understanding, and use of security policy, standards, procedures, services, and mechanisms. Dissemination metrics may track how many emails went out notifying employees of a new policy or safeguard. Awareness metrics may track how many employees opened up the email, with the assumption that if they opened it, they are now aware. Follow-up tests, quizzes, or surveys will measure employee understanding of the material. Audit logs and transaction logs will provide measures of actual use. Training metrics may include actual performance on a test.

Remember, awareness and training are not identical. Awareness is a state of mind that influences behaviors, while training provides a fixed body of actual knowledge, When it comes to awareness, any knowledge taught is irrelevant if it does not cause the person being made aware to modify his or her behaviors in a certain desired fashion. When it comes to training, if the person knows the material, the training is normally considered successful, even if he or she does not apply it when desired – in which case, awareness needs to be improved.

Efficiency Metrics
A safeguard should produce a desired result, and it should do so within acceptable operating parameters. Service level agreements (SLAs) reflect these acceptable operating parameters and may include bandwidth utilization, response time, quality of communications, error reporting, notice of performance degradation, and notice of hard failure.

Process
In a given environment, people perform processes using technology to produce results. Security operations processes subject to compliance or in support of compliance management include the following:

- Configuration Management
- Records Management
- Vulnerability Testing
- Outsourcing
- Incident Management
- Problem Management
  - Error and problem control
- Prioritization Techniques
- Backups
- Auditing

Configuration Management
Configuration management (CM) is the process of managing changes in hardware, software, firmware, and documents throughout the product lifecycle. The purpose of CM is to enforce discipline around modifications and provide the ability to roll back to previous versions in the event of difficulties in implementing the modification or adverse results stemming from the modification. Configuration management consists of a combination of practices that include the following:

- Library Management
- Patch Management
- Change Control

Library Management

A library management system (LMS) provides enterprise resource administration for a repository of artifacts that include the following:

- Software
- Source code
- User documentation
- System documentation
- Test data
- Project plans

The CM library management system should provide for the storage and retrieval of library artifacts; provide for sharing of artifacts among individuals and groups within the library; provide for the storage and recovery of archive artifacts (e.g., old versions); provide service functions to check artifact status, verify the presence of all built items, and integrate changes to form a new baseline; ensure the creation of products from the baseline library; provide for the storage, update, and retrieval of CM artifacts; produce CM reports; and support traceability requirements throughout the lifecycle.

Critical business decisions may ride on the integrity and accuracy of the library artifacts. An important feature of the CM LMS is to ensure only authorized access and authorized modification to library artifacts within the LMS. Similarly, the LMS should also control the introduction of modified and new artifacts. One function of the LMS is to collect many artifacts that may be aggregated into larger documents or larger software applications. Trust in the low-level artifacts to contain the correct details and produce the correct results is very important. Multiple libraries may be necessary to accommodate different types of artifacts like financial documentation or software development source code. Multiple libraries may also be necessary to accommodate the diversity of material and to provide different types of security controls.

Patch Management

Patch management involves methodically directing the administration of software and hardware updates that intend to provide additional features, fix bugs, or eliminate vulnerabilities. Patches are modifications to software to fix bugs, design flaws, and close up security holes. Patches may cause problems as well as fix problems, especially when patches are applied to operating systems or system utilities upon which other applications depend. The software applications (e.g., accounting software) may have been developed to work around a particular operating system (OS) flaw. When the OS flaw is fixed, the application may no longer work because it expects the flaw that is no longer there. These types of scenarios make unconditional installation of software patches problematic.

Good business practice is to create a test system, install the patch, and test critical applications to ensure they work with the patch installed. If they do not work, this becomes part of the decision process to install a patch or not. If the patch fixes an egregious security hole but renders key applications unusable, the enterprise must decide what takes precedence ... operations or security – not always an easy choice. The potential for negative effects of installing patches is the reason patch management is associated with change control.

Patch management software, as available from various vendors, may assist an organization with management and deployment of patches. Patch management software has four functions:

1. Facilitates patch download to a central location
2. Repository of patches
3. Patch testing
4. Patch database

Downloading patches from the vendor to a central location saves on bandwidth that would otherwise be necessary to support downloading from the vendor to each individual desktop. The central repository may then facilitate the forced installation of patches throughout the enterprise from within the enterprise. Patch management software provides a means to test patches prior to deployment throughout the enterprise. The patch management software also provides a database of software, current versions, and patched systems that provide input to overall enterprise situational awareness.

Part of the benefit of creating a policy and standards for a common desktop environment (CDE) is to facilitate the capability to "test once, deploy many." If a patch works well with the CDE, then deploying the patch enterprise-wide should not create problems. The CDE is a standard that enumerates permissible software and operating system settings. Managing PCs enterprise-wide is greatly simplified, though still far from simple, if you implement and enforce an enterprise CDE standard.

Patch Management, Risk Posture, and Security Posture

The enterprise security posture is the aggregation of all the safeguards and precautions that mitigate risk. The enterprise risk posture is the formal articulation of an intentionally assumed position on dealing with potential negative impact. Awareness of a new vulnerability does not change the security posture (i.e., no safeguard or precaution is any different than it was). Likewise, this vulnerability awareness does not change the risk posture (i.e., the enterprise still has the same stance on risk that it did before). Risk exposure does not change either; in other words, the enterprise has the same degree of risk exposure. What does change is the risk awareness, which is the level of conscious knowledge of potential negative impact. This new awareness starts a sequence of events that evaluates risk exposure (e.g., yes, this vulnerability does indeed represent a high degree of risk exposure to the enterprise), evaluates the risk posture (e.g., yes, we should modify our risk posture to mitigate this risk), and modifies the security posture accordingly (e.g., we will install a patch to eliminate the vulnerability).

The reason for distinguishing among security posture, risk posture, risk exposure, and risk awareness is to point out nuances of consideration for installing the patch. Often, installing patches is like squeezing jelly; every time you tighten up one area of your fist, jelly shoots out another. Installing the patch may take care of the risk you are now aware of, but it may introduce new risk to other parts of business operations. How do you know if this happens? One method is to set up a test lab, install the patch on a mirror of the production system, and test the effects on system and application operations. Another is to install the patch directly on the production system and be prepared with back-out procedures. Establishing a test lab requires an investment of time and resources. Using a test lab is the most prudent approach from a risk management perspective. Installing patches on the fly in production may be necessary to respond to a critical operations need. If this is the case, the best risk management method is to be prepared to back out the patch as quickly as possible if something goes wrong.

A change to the security posture is the addition or detraction of a safeguard or safeguard feature; for example, adding an intrusion detection system (IDS) increases the security posture by adding an additional defense-in-depth security mechanism. However, presenting the security posture to executives has no meaning to them. Honestly, a CEO could not care less about a security posture in terms of firewalls, IDS, anti-malware, and security awareness training. What a CEO does care about is risk posture that includes how you as a security professional are handling potential liability issues via legislative compliance. Your understanding of the nuances around security posture and risk posture will help you articulate the security story in words desirable and understandable by the audience across operations, management, and governance.

Change Control

A change is an event that results in a new status of one or more aspects of the enterprise. Enterprise aspects include people, process, technology, environment, policy, standards, procedures, and guidelines. Controlling change within the enterprise results in the predictable impact of modifications on operations and productivity with minimal disruption and efficient use of resources involved in the change. The overall process of change control is different from the information technology use of revision control, version control, and source control (collectively referred to herein as version control for simplicity). Change control is for quality management and ensures forethought; version control traditionally applies to software development environments, but it is finding new uses in knowledge management applications. We will first look at change control as an enterprise process for managing the impact of modifications on policy, standards, procedures, practices, people, process, technology, and environment; change control is for technology but not only technology. Change control roles include the following:

- Change initiator (CI)
- Change sponsor (CS)
- Change owner (CO)
- Change administrator (CA)
- Impact assessor (ImA)
- Change manager (CMgr)
- Task owner (TO)
- Change control board (CCB)

The CI initially requests a modification and is the same person who will ultimately confirm the completion of the modification. The CS provides business approval for the change. The CO monitors and manages the change through acceptance of the CI and closure. The CA assesses the change request, monitors progress through the CO, and ensures acceptance by the CI. The ImA analyzes the enterprise impact of the change. The CM guides the overall change process, acts as a point of escalation for the CO, and interacts with the CCB to review and process change requests, especially in the event of emergency changes. The TO receives direction from the CM and performs activities that implement the change. The CCB is a management group that reviews the change process and specific changes that may affect enterprise operations.

The CCB is a committee of stakeholders affected by the proposed change. The CCB makes the final decision on whether or not to implement the change. The authority of the CCB should be such that its decision regarding the change is final and binding. Members of the CCB should include a representative from security. Any change to the organization requires a review of the risk to the enterprise environment (e.g., physical), processes (e.g., operations), people (e.g., safety), and technology (e.g., ability to produce desired results). The security representative can assist with risk identification, risk implications, and risk mitigation. The change control process consists of the following steps:

- Initiate
- Analyze
- Plan
- Build/implement/test
- Deploy
- Outreach
- Close

The CI initiates a change request via formal submission. The CI and CS work together to provide as much detail as possible in the formal submission, including classification of the change (e.g., people, process, technology, environment, policy, etc.), scope of impact on enterprise operations, impact on enterprise bottom line (e.g., cost and revenue impacts), cost of change, and benefit of change; the formal submission also identifies a CO as the primary contact for the CI and CS. Note: Distinguishing these roles helps identify necessary change control steps and accountability. The roles may be virtual, meaning any particular individual may be assigned multiple roles.

The CA and ImA analyze the change request with respect to enterprise impact, including risk, risk mitigation, operational impact, cost, and benefit. The CA identifies all stakeholders in the claim request, including those impacted by the change (e.g., the operations manager). The stakeholders all provide input to the change plan, which provides details on budget, schedule, milestones, areas affected, work breakdown structure (WBS), resource list, resource assignments, etc. The plan also provides for the ability to back out changes in the event of unforeseen difficulties.

The change request delivery team then follows the plan and proceeds to build, implement, and test the changes. These are accomplished in a controlled environment or a small production environment to discern the nuances of introducing the change with high efficiency and low impact to operations. The lessons learned from this step will make deployment throughout the enterprise much more cost effective. The CM oversees those performing tasks (the TO) that implement the change; additionally, the CM oversees the entire change process, including outreach to stakeholders.

Outreach to those parts of the organization affected by the change should begin in the building phase and proceed throughout implementation, testing, and deployment. Engaging people early on will make them feel like part of the process and increase the likelihood of their adopting the changes. At the very least, outreach should include awareness and training post-deployment to ensure that operations personnel know about the change, what it means to them, how it affects their jobs, and how to use the change effectively.

Closure of the change request is the result of successful implementation. Also, a decision to back out the change and regress to the initial pre-change state may or may not result in closure. Backing out a change may be an interim step to implementing the change differently and accommodating an unforeseen impact. A final decision to back out the change because it is the wrong business decision may also result in closure of the change request.

The following are examples of modifications requiring change control:

- Operating system upgrades
- Policy modifications
- Network infrastructure renewal

Operating system upgrades have the potential to affect all the underlying software applications that run the organization. A formal change process is necessary to manage the introduction of the new operating system in a controlled manner to ensure full knowledge of the organizational impact.

Policy modifications come from executives and upper management. Many times, policy changes rarely find their way into operations because it is assumed that the decree of upper echelons is known and acted upon simultaneously with the policy change. Any change in policy must find its way to operations in order to have any real impact on the organization. In an analogy, consider the difference between a law and the ability to enforce that law. The citizenry needs to be aware that there is a new law; the police and judicial system needs to be aware that there is a new law and what that means insofar as monitoring for violations and adjudicating violators. The same applies to changes in enterprise policy. The change control process will help facilitate the application of new policy throughout the enterprise, especially in operations to implement and enforce the new policy.

Network infrastructure renewal includes a refresh of all routers and switches. The enterprise impact is huge and IT operations need to analyze the implications of introducing new versions from the same vendor or swapping out for new vendor equipment all together. The formal change process will help identify technical and business implications of either decision.

Version Control

Version control is the management of multiple revisions of a file, where the file may be source code, a written document, an engineering diagram, an architectural blueprint, etc. The purpose of version control is to track changes and to provide the ability to restore or reference previous versions. If updates to a system cause problems, for example, the version control system (VCS) facilitates and simplifies the process of "rolling back" to an earlier version of the system.

This same concept of version control or revision control applies to knowledge management systems (KMS). A KMS supports the creation, capture, storage, dissemination, comments, and modifications to knowledge within the enterprise. A KMS facilitates the learning organization where information belongs to the enterprise and is made available to the enterprise via information technology. This is contrary to information belonging to an individual, residing on an individual hard drive, and lost when the individual leaves the organization.

3

Security Compliance Management

207

Records Management

The ISO 15489: 2001 Information and Documentation–Records Management standard defines records management as "the field of management responsible for the efficient and systematic control of the creation, receipt, maintenance, use and disposition of records, including the processes for capturing and maintaining evidence of and information about business activities and transactions in the form of records."

Records

The word "record" as a noun means a document or other entity that preserves information. The 44 U.S.C. Chapter 33 Section 3301 defines records as "all books, papers, maps, photographs, machine readable materials, or other documentary materials, regardless of physical form or characteristics, made or received by an agency of the United States Government under Federal law or in connection with the transaction of public business and preserved or appropriate for preservation by that agency or its legitimate successor as evidence of the organization, functions, policies, decisions, procedures, operations, or other activities of the Government or because of the informational value of data in them."

ISO 15489: 2001 defines records as "information created, received, and maintained as evidence and information by an organization or person, in pursuance of legal obligations or in the transaction of business."

The International Council on Archives (ICA) Committee on Electronic Records defines a record as "a recorded information produced or received in the initiation, conduct or completion of an institutional or individual activity and that comprises content, context and structure sufficient to provide evidence of the activity."

Records Management Process

Records management activities involve the entire lifecycle of records, including creation, storage, retrieval, use, and disposal.

The goal of records management is to manage organizational information so that it is timely, accurate, complete, cost effective, discoverable, accessible, and usable. Protect records in accordance with their value to the enterprise and the cost it would take to recreate them. The records management process includes the following with respect to records:

- Identify
- Classify
- Label
- Store
- Preserve
- Track
- Disposition

It is important to realize that the focus of records management is data, not the media on which data resides. Media management is still important, but it is different from records management in that media is the physical entity on which the record is stored, not the information contained on the physical object. The physical lifespan of the media is, therefore, a different concern from the legal life or useful life of the data. Of course, physical concerns must also be addressed; otherwise data may become lost or corrupted.

Record Retention

Record retention refers to retaining a piece of data even after its period of primary use. The objective of retention is to have the information available if needed.

A retention period is the amount of time that an item must be kept. Laws, regulations, or standards might define the retention periods for particular data. For example, the IRS (http://www.irs.gov/Businesses/Small-Businesses-&-Self-Employed/How-long-should-I-keep-records) requires that various documents be retained for different periods of time after filing a tax return.

With the rapid decrease in the cost of electronic storage space, one might think that it is best to retain all records forever; however, such reasoning is incorrect for several reasons:

1. The retained data must be managed, and retaining unnecessary items can complicate management and cause necessary data to become difficult to find.

2. In the event of legal matters, materials might be demanded during "discovery" phases or the like; if extra material exists, it can create extra costs and potentially give extra information to an adversary. The same is true vis-à-vis government investigations.

3. Retaining too much information can lead to insufficient attention and care being given to the items that must be retained.

Identify

Identify what records are necessary to manage. The organization's mission and operations will provide this insight, as well as legislative mandates for record keeping and record retention. Such legislative mandates may be for financial data, commercial transactions, contracts, and customer/patient data. Understanding the enterprise mission, mission needs, and operational needs is part of identifying records to manage. You need to understand what records require access, when, why, performance requirements, and format.

There are various roles surrounding records management, including the producer of records, owner of records, custodian of records, and user (consumer) of records. Owners have the responsibility for classification of the record, which determines who may access the record when, how, and for what purpose. Producers of the record are in operations; producers accept input, perform some process to aggregate and manipulate the input, and produce a resulting record. The consumer may receive the record in a number of ways, either directly from the producer or from an intermediary repository. The intermediary repository has custodianship of the record for as long as it maintains a copy. Custodianship has responsibilities to handle the record according to owner specifications.

The consumer may receive the record via explicit subscription, which is a push of the information directly to the consumer. Consumers may receive the information via implicit subscription, which is a registration for type of information versus an explicit result, and the record happens to fall under that information type. The consumer may search and find the information in a repository, e.g., knowledge base, database, or Internet or intranet website. Enabling awareness of records and getting the records to those with the need to know requires effective classification, labeling, and storage.

A complement to need-to-know is need-to-share. The creation of extremely useful records is worthless if the existence of the record is kept secret and access to the record is overly restricted. Need-to-share is a paradigm shift where the producer of the record has a duty to advertise the existence of the information and provide access to the information. An extremely important note is that need-to-share does not replace need-to-know (i.e., need-to-share does not equate to a right to know). Both paradigms work in complement to more effectively manage the production and consumption of information to fulfill the enterprise mission. Need-to-share equates to advertising what you have and making it available; need-to-know equates to providing access to only those who need the information to perform a valid business function.

Classify

Record classification promotes effective finding of information as well as secure access to that information. Library science provides for the coding and organizing of records by subject, key words, and actual document address (e.g., international standard book number [ISBN]) to help consumers find records relevant to their need. Security classifications code records to restrict access only to those with authorization to access.

Security classifications for information artifacts may include a subset of the following: public, sensitive, proprietary, confidential, secret, top secret, official use only, restricted, or unclassified. The set of security classifications is organization specific in both the number of distinctions and the naming convention. Caveat: Keep the security classification system as simple as possible to promote understanding, simplify the ability to appropriately label records, and enforce the security restrictions using both automated and manual means.

Label

To implement and enforce record classification requires effective labeling. Labels may be physical and appear in document headers, footers, on the front of document folders or binders, on file cabinets, or on other physical media storing records (e.g., tapes, CDs). Labels may also be virtual additional digitally encoded information associated with the record. The most popular form of virtual labeling is metadata, or attributes about the data.

Metadata is information about the record and may include both library science and security classification details. Metadata may also contain information about the record that assists with integrity checks like record size. Moreover, metadata may assist consumers in making a judgment call regarding the confidence consumers put in the record content. Details like the producer, the date of creation, and subsequent modifications all contribute to consumer confidence levels in record accuracy and timeliness.

A further challenge is to ensure that metadata actually refers to the record it claims to and that the metadata itself is accurate, or at least unchanged from its original creation. This requires a binding of metadata with data in a manner that provides a high level of confidence that they belong together, and the consumer can have a high level of trust in the integrity of both. This may be accomplished via metadata crypto-binding, which is the application of cryptography and digital signatures to associate the record and its metadata with high assurance.

The Dublin Core Metadata Initiative (DCMI) is an organization that promotes interoperable digital metadata. The Dublin Core Metadata Element Set is a vocabulary of fifteen properties for use in resource description:

1. Contributor
2. Coverage
3. Creator
4. Date
5. Description
6. Format
7. Identifier
8. Language
9. Publisher
10. Relation
11. Rights
12. Source
13. Subject
14. Title
15. Type

The actual use of these fifteen properties, a subset of the properties, or an extension to these properties is dependent on enterprise need and plans for automation. For example, the implementation and enforcement of digital policies require data on which to make access authorization decisions. Metadata, or attributes, must be associated with subjects (e.g., users, computers, applications, utilities) that request access, and to objects (e.g., database, documents, servers) to which subjects request access. The Dublin Core fifteen properties have no classification property. This is one example of extending the Dublin Core to accommodate security aspects of digital policy management.

Store

Records storage may be either physical (e.g., paper) or virtual (e.g., digital media). Records storage is subject to both internal and external compliance requirements. Internal requirements will help protect and preserve records that are important to enterprise operations and continuity. External requirements include legislative mandates governing the type of data to keep and the duration to keep it (e.g., financial data must be stored in a readily accessible format for a period of no less than seven years). Records storage may be for imminent use or archived for the potential of future access. The retention period is determined by the needs of the enterprise and by legislative mandates.

Records storage also provides access to records in a manner necessary for effective and efficient operations. For example, manual storage of physical records does not promote real time access to a distributed workforce; scanning paper records to digital images or via digital optical character recognition (OCR) makes more sense. Records storage also requires an environmentally controlled environment to preserve the integrity of the media.

3

Security Compliance Management

Preserve

Record preservation involves maintaining the record in a usable format. Preserving the record is a separate concern from preserving the media. For example, if the record preservation requirement is for 25 years, and the CD media that stores the record has an effective life of 15 years, then the record must be transferred from the initial CD to another CD to maintain the record in a usable format for the required 25 years. Media preservation may require special environmental controls for temperature and humidity to ensure optimal media life. Verify that off-site storage facilities have the appropriate environment and procedures to preserve records to the standards you require.

Moreover, record preservation includes protection from inadvertent physical destruction from fire, flood, harsh weather like hurricanes, earthquakes, civil unrest, terrorist acts, and acts of war. This may require special equipment like fireproof safes and special rooms with sufficient physical safeguards.

Another concern is the storage of records on media that can no longer be accessed on current technology; for example, floppy disk drives (i.e., readers and writers) are no longer common, and records on this type of media should have long-since been copied to newer technology media to ensure record access. This same concept applies to the use of CDs and DVDs – they are disappearing from laptops, and will ultimately disappear nearly entirely (as have floppy disks).

Digital preservation is a discipline that studies whether electronic records can be retained and remain accessible and readable over time. Accessing and reading electronic records requires appropriate versions of both software and operating systems. The rate of change in technology can quickly render older digital media inaccessible. An example of a digital preservation organization is the Public Record Office Victoria (PROV) in Melbourne, Australia. PROV published the Victorian Electronic Records Strategy (VERS), which includes a standard for the preservation, long-term storage, and access to electronic records.

Track

Tracking records involves maintaining knowledge of their location, possession, and lifecycle state. Tracking the location of records is necessary to know where primary and secondary copies reside for backup and access purposes. Tracking possession of the record involves tracking circulation, both cyber and physical. Tracking the lifecycle state of the record includes the current usefulness of the record to the enterprise, if the record is on a viable media (i.e., the media is not yet close to degrading beyond use) and if the record qualifies for destruction.

Tracking records also includes monitoring the access and use of records. Legislative compliance may require knowing who has access to, who has accessed, who has used, and when they used the record. Creating an audit log of these details may be useful to provide these details to legal authorities. Maintaining circulation history will help this. Circulation is retrieving, tracking, and returning the physical media on which the record resides, e.g., paper, microfiche, or CD. Circulation records may be manual or take advantage of an automated records management system that assigns a bar code or radio frequency identification (RFID) to the media, and scans of removal and return track the circulation. Tracking cyber circulation involves maintaining a log of record retrieval or download. However, once a record is retrieved via cyber means, circulation is very difficult to track. Some circulation management practices distribute only numbered hard copies to individually accountable people. Others may view the physical record but must check it out from the individual and return it without making copies.

Disposition

Record disposition includes the destruction and transfer of records. Maintaining records is an expense to the enterprise; destroy unnecessary records when in compliance with both external and internal requirements for record maintenance. Record transfer may be to an archive, museum, or private party. Document the destruction or transfer of records to maintain a history of enterprise possession and of the enterprise fulfilling its duty to effectively protect record details by destroying or transferring them in an appropriate manner. This includes a record of the manner of destruction such as burning, shredding, or pulverizing the storage media, and details of the record transfer, including new owner or custodian, date, and continued responsibility of the enterprise to the record, if any.

Physical and Virtual Records

Physical records are those that exist in a tangible format like paper or microfiche. Virtual records are digitally recorded records like bits on a hard drive, tape, floppy disk, or CD; virtual records are also known as electronic or digital records. There is a distinction between a virtual record and the physical media on which it resides. Managing the record is very different from managing the physical media, as the previous sections describe.

Virtual records require a computer or other technology to access and view them. Maintaining the content, context, and structure of a virtual record is much more difficult when the record has no physical existence. Tampering with original physical records is difficult to accomplish without detection, whereas tampering with virtual records is much easier. Virtual records take up far less space than physical records, and backing up virtual records is far easier and less expensive than making duplicates of paper records and storing them in multiple locations.

Vulnerability Management

Vulnerability management consists of the following:

- Advisory services
- Vulnerability testing
- Vulnerability management metrics

Advisory Services

Vulnerability advisory services will notify you of newly discovered flaws in hardware and software that are susceptible to attack. A good resource to research vulnerabilities and related services is the Common Vulnerabilities and Exposures (CVE). "CVE is international in scope and free for public use. CVE is a dictionary of publicly known information security vulnerabilities and exposures" (http://cve.mitre.org/index.html, last accessed March 2009). The vulnerability management section of CVE provides a list of vulnerability management services and products, including notification services. US-CERT (http://www.us-cert.gov/, last accessed April 2009) is another vulnerability advisory service. Most importantly, you should tap into your hardware and software vendor advisory services (e.g., Microsoft, Cisco, etc.).

Part of managing risk exposure is the use of advisory services to become aware of new risks. Advisory services will notify you of new vulnerabilities. Now that you, and the rest of the world, are aware of these vulnerabilities, your risk awareness just changed, and you need to analyze the enterprise effects. Have the additional vulnerabilities increased risk to the enterprise? You then examine your risk posture to determine the best option to address this new risk: accept, ignore, share, transfer, or mitigate. A new risk posture that includes risk mitigation for this vulnerability implies the need to modify the security posture to reduce enterprise risk exposure.

Vulnerability Testing

Vulnerability testing is the discovery of the degree of susceptibility to damage or attack. Cyber vulnerability testing consists of a variety of activities, including the following:

- War dialing
- War driving
- Network scanning
- Network probing
- Penetration testing

War Dialing

War dialing involves discovering all the phone number ranges of a given organization, plugging them into an automated system, and dialing them to see if you get a modem on the other end. Yes, companies still have modems hooked up. Many of the unauthorized modems were back doors for employees' convenience to work remotely, and they still exist as vulnerabilities to unauthorized network access.

War Driving

War driving involves literally driving around a campus or facility to detect wireless access points and ranges of potential connection. War driving technology can be combined with a Global Positioning System (GPS); by driving roughly in concentric circles around the facility, the technology records the outer limits of the wireless signal and superimposes it on a map. The results show how far from the facility a wireless signal extends and where it may be detected, meaning if the wireless signal extends to an open field, overlaps with other office buildings, overlaps with residential houses, or overlaps with a school.

Network Security Scanning

Network security scanning is the methodical review of the enterprise's computing infrastructure for the presence and effectiveness of the safeguards to protect against danger or loss. Network scanning validates the security posture of the network by testing for appropriate configurations in firewalls and the presence of unauthorized software applications, utilities, and background processes, e.g., the unauthorized presence of file transfer protocol (FTP).

Scanning the network both externally (outside trying to get in) and internally shows the potential for an attacker to get into the network and what the attacker may accomplish once inside. External network scanning initiates from the Internet or business partner network to simulate the path of an attacker. Internal network scanning initiates from inside the enterprise network to simulate attacker capabilities once inside the network.

Network scanning includes mapping the network, system identification, OS identification, port scanning, and probing. Network mapping notes that a system exists along with IP address or addresses; the goal of mapping is to create a "map" of the network and the resources it contains. System identification will attempt to discern system names that may give a clue to their function (e.g., R&D Server or Accounting). OS identification will provide insights into potential vulnerabilities. Port scanning will show what ports have active software ready to respond. Probing will discern what software applications reside behind those ports without trying to actually use the applications. An attempt to actually use applications is part of penetration testing.

Penetration Testing

Penetration testing is the next potential step after network scanning. Network scanning gives you a good idea of what is there; penetration testing gives you an idea of what is accessible. Variations on penetration testing include soft and hard testing. Soft testing attempts penetration but only to the point of showing the capability to penetrate. Hard testing goes further and attempts to take systems down or otherwise use them in subsequent attacks. Hard testing has much greater potential to interfere with enterprise operations. Most companies do not opt for hard testing because of this danger. This is understandable from a certain perspective, but when is it better to find the vulnerabilities: under a controlled attack that can be stopped immediately or under a true adversary attack that will continue to wreak havoc until you figure out how to stop it? As a security manager who arranges for penetration testing, you must negotiate with business operations and management to determine an acceptable level between soft and hard testing so you get actual details of where you are strong and where you are not. You can't fix a problem if you don't know you have one.

Physical Scanning

Physical scanning is the literal walking around a facility and reviewing for vulnerabilities. This includes attempting entry through conventional means (e.g., lobby) and less conventional means (e.g., loading dock). Physical vulnerability checks include checking doors that should be locked, trying out common codes on cipher locks (e.g., 31415 [pi]), throwing something under a door that is open via a motion detector on the other side, specifically trying doors on data centers and wiring closets, and social engineering your way past the security guard or secretary. Personal experience shows that if you look like you belong and carry yourself with confidence, you are rarely challenged no matter what you're carrying or where you're going. The lesson here is for you as the security professional to make employees aware and train them to politely challenge unknown personnel for identification and their local point of contact to verify that their presence is for valid business purposes.

Vulnerability Management Metrics

Metrics surrounding threats, vulnerabilities, risk, and security are difficult. There is no inherent metric to gauge how much more or less secure you are today than yesterday. Metrics for these areas are mostly artificial metrics that provide indirect insight into effectiveness. An example of an artificial metric is the calendar. There is no inherent metric within the universe to measure natural progression. Humanity assigned meaning to repetitive actions of sunrise, sunset, and seasonal cycles to provide a common reference point to coordinate activity. An artificial metric is okay as long as it is applied consistently to provide a meaningful reference. We as an industry have yet to produce good, generally applicable metrics for threats, vulnerabilities, risk, and security.

Despite the lack of a universal security metric system, you are still responsible for attempting to generate meaningful metrics for your organization. Easy metrics involve measuring counts (number of things) and time. You may count known threats against your organization, known attacks against your organization, number of events, number of incidents, and time to effectively respond to incidents. Example metrics include the following:

- Time required to
    - Discover an event from time of event occurrence
    - Triage to determine that event is a security incident
    - Respond to incident
    - Discover source
    - Isolate source
    - Restore business functionality
    - Discover root cause
    - Fix root cause
    - Restore source of incident to normal operations
- Number of identified vulnerabilities
- Number of assets with these vulnerabilities
- Estimates on security maintenance of these assets
    - Number of vulnerability notices from services
    - Time to evaluate enterprise risk posture
    - Time to implement patches or new safeguards
    - Cost of safeguards
- Effectiveness of security posture in achieving desired risk posture
- Use information from vulnerability scanning and penetration testing

From an investment management perspective, use metrics to track the number of security mechanisms necessary (e.g., 20 firewalls), the number actually purchased, the number delivered, the number installed, and the number currently in operational order. Use network scanning to determine how many firewalls actually have the operating configuration as specified in policy. These same types of metrics apply to all security mechanisms.

After receiving a vulnerability notice from an outside service, determine the number of systems with this vulnerability. If you decide upon a patch or other means to mitigate this new risk, track how many patches have been installed. Many of these metrics may seem somewhat mundane, but they do provide business value in tracking vulnerabilities, risks, and mitigation efforts.

Outsourcing

Outsourcing is the subcontracting of a business function or business process outside the enterprise. Most organizations that outsource do so for cost savings or to subcontract non-core competency. The cost savings is an obvious answer; if someone else can do it better and cheaper than you can, then by all means outsource. Outsourcing non-core competency also makes sense so as not to get distracted from core business operations (e.g., a manufacturer of power tools likely does not have organizational experience and expertise in IT and security). Outsourcing part or all of IT and security allows the manufacturer to focus on what it is good at - making power tools. This manufacturer then avoids distracting upper management and executives with in-house concerns over IT and security. Does this mean that the manufacturer transfers responsibility and accountability for IT and security? No! It means it transfers operations; the manufacturer remains accountable to stakeholders (e.g., stockholders) and is still responsible to ensure that the outsourcer does the right thing.

Your organization must retain in-house expertise in IT and security to manage the outsourcer relationship. Outsourcing does not eliminate in-house practice, but it can reduce it dramatically. The discussion of outsourcing consists of the following:

- Outsourcing Misconceptions
- Managing Outsourcing
- Outsourcing Performance Standards
- Outsourcing and Compliance
- Outsourcing Best Practices

Outsourcing Misconceptions

- **Misconception –** IT expenses will immediately be reduced. Remember, you still need in-house IT expertise, and the cost of running IT is expensive even if outsourced. Even if the expense of outsourcing is equal to in-house IT, there still may be the benefit of transferring operation of a non-core business practice.
- **Misconception –** Vendors use best practices. First, "best" is in the eye of the beholder. Vendors are in business to make a profit just as you are. They are likely to use adequate practices over best practices. For the most part, you really should not care what they use as long as you have a solid business agreement and clear SLAs. You are looking for a result. If you are getting it, great; if not, you need to get into their business and find out why.
- **Misconception –** Off-shoring offers huge savings. As previously stated, your organization still has responsibility to manage the outsourcing arrangement. Off-shoring now introduces foreign workers in a different time zone. Don't underestimate the language and cultural barriers to using off-shoring. Is it a viable business alternative for cheaper labor? Yes, in many cases. Is it a guaranteed method for cost savings? Absolutely not! Remember the difference between price and cost. The price of the labor may be less; however, the cost of managing the relationship, managing communications across time zones, the expense of communications across wide geographic areas, and customer [dis]satisfaction all contribute to the total cost of off-shoring.
- **Misconception –** Vendors are better/faster/cheaper than internal IT. An outsourcer may not have competent employees, nor does it necessarily have more up-to-date equipment. An outsourcer business model may result in higher cost for IT than your own business model. The decision to use an outsourcer, therefore, should be made only after performing significant "homework" that includes asking hard questions regarding the outsourcer's ability to (a) provide equal or better results than the firm itself could deliver,

(b) provide results according to your performance parameters, and (c) do so at an equal or lesser cost than maintaining operations in house.

Managing Outsourcing

Outsourcing is an investment. It is an investment in external fulfillment of a function important to your organization. As an investment, you expect a return on it. Managing outsourcing ensures that you get the return on investment you expect.

The outsourcer is now a critical part of your organization's success. Negotiate agreements that ensure performance effectiveness and efficiency. Effectiveness means they produce the results expected. Efficiency means they produce the results expected within acceptable performance parameters. A service level agreement (SLA) may enumerate these performance parameters, specify minimal acceptable levels of performance, and specify rewards for beating expectations (e.g., performance bonuses) or penalties for not meeting expectations (e.g., reduced payment or nonpayment). Your outsourcing arrangement will exist according to the agreements you negotiate, so understand your choices carefully and their implications to your financial bottom line.

Outsourcing Performance Standards

Effective outsourcing requires an ongoing relationship; outsourcing is definitely not a "buy it and forget it" purchase. An outsourcing agreement should contain at least the following:

- The objectives for outsourcing
- Description of the outsourcing relationship
- Level of service expectations
  - SLA parameters
  - SLA measures
- Acceptable variations to performance agreements (if any)
  - For example, seasonal fluctuations in business volume
- How to benchmark service performance
- Performance reports
  - Structure
  - Content
- Who may request performance reports

Performance standards establish your organization's expectations of the outsourcer and the quality requirements for the outsourcer. Performance metrics should be contractual obligations of the outsourcer to your organization. Clearly establish performance standards to help the outsourcer understand your objectives and to help you track the activities of the outsourcer to be sure you are getting what you are paying for.

Outsourcing and Compliance

The outsourcer commits to your organization to perform certain tasks within certain efficiency parameters. So, how do you ensure that they are doing what they say within the SLAs you agreed upon? One method is to audit third-party compliance. The purpose for third-party audits is to ensure that the outsourcer documents its internal controls to support legislative and regulatory compliance. Examples of industry standards for third-party auditing are SAS70 and SSAE16.

SAS70

For nearly two decades, the Statement on Auditing Standard 70 (SAS70) developed by The American Institute of Certified Public Accountants (AICPA) was a popular auditing standard.

"SAS 70 is an auditing standard designed to enable an independent auditor to evaluate and issue an opinion on a service organization's controls. The audit report (i.e., the service auditor's report) contains the auditor's opinion, a description of the controls placed in operation, and description of the auditor's tests of operating effectiveness (if the report is a Type II)."

Table 3.4 shows the differences between a Type I report and a Type II. A Type I report describes controls at a specific point in time. A Type II report includes the service organization's description of its controls plus detailed results from testing the service organization's controls over a six-month period.

SAS 70 was replaced in 2011 by the Statement on Standards for Attestation Engagements (SSAE) No. 16 (SSAE16).

Section Contents	Type I Report	Type II Report
1. Independent Service Auditor's Report, i.e., audit opinion	Included	Included
2. Service organization's description of controls	Included	Included
3. Information provided by the independent service auditor; includes a description of the service auditor's tests of operating effectiveness and the results of those tests	Optional	Included
4. Other information provided by the service organization	Optional	Optional

*Table 3.4 – **SAS70 Section Contents***

SSAE16

SSAE 16, which became effective in mid-2011, is a popular standard, currently in use, for auditing service organizations.

SSAE augmented the prior SAS70 standard in several regards. It more closely mirrors international standards such as ISAE 3402, and it also establishes a new Attestation Standard (AT801), which standardizes matters related to the examination for auditors.

A copy of the SSAE 16 standard can be ordered from the AICPA's online store at http://www.cpa2biz.com. It is publication number 023035. More information about SSAE16 can be found at http://ssae16.com.

Outsourcing Best Practices

"Best practices" is a term that sounds good, but at best it is vague and in the eye of the beholder; that is to say, best practices is a relative concept to expectations and business need. However, in keeping with the spirit of the term, there are some features of outsourcing that increase the likelihood of success, and we may refer to these success factors as outsourcing best practices; these include the following:

3

Security Compliance Management

- Relationship between key management personnel
- Measurable objectives
- Formal committees
- Incentives and penalties
- Periodic review meetings
- Training vendor personnel
- Bridging cultural differences

The quality of the relationship of key managers between your organization and the outsourcer contributes greatly to the overall success of the outsourcing engagement. This relationship begins with the negotiation of the service level agreement (SLA). The objective negotiation is to get the best deal for your organization; however, the reality of a successful business arrangement is that you have to make a profit and so does the other party in the negotiation. Establish a professional, congenial relationship between your organization and the outsourcer. An adversarial relationship may win a short-term benefit in one-sided SLAs, but it is counterproductive in the long run. Forcing the outsourcer into an untenable profit margin just threatens to put the outsourcer out of business, which is bad for everyone, including your organization, which is now dependent on outsourcer performance.

Negotiate clear, measurable objectives that represent your operational needs, then enumerate and explain these objectives in the contract and SLAs. These will provide an objective list of expectations and provide for objective measurements to gauge performance. Both your organization and the outsourcer know exactly where they stand with respect to receiving and delivering expected services.

The term governance relates to the establishment of performance criteria. Your organization will have an executive board and upper management that will perform a governance role for the enterprise. Likewise, there is a governance role of upper management for establishing outsourcing services and performance criteria. Part of this governance role is establishing adjudication bodies and procedures. There will be conflicts between your organization and the outsourcer. These conflicts won't necessarily be adversarial; a conflict could be a misunderstanding of a vague portion of the contract or clarification of poorly worded performance criteria. Establishing committees or adjudication boards consisting of representatives from both parties to identify, resolve, and escalate these types of issues will go a long way in quickly resolving misunderstandings or disagreements.

Establish performance-based pricing for the outsourcer. When they have skin in the game of producing quality results, they are more likely to deliver. Incentives apply for performance above expectations, and penalties apply for performance below expectations. Establish a schedule of periodic review meetings; they should be frequent and formal in the review of performance criteria and review of actual performance. Understanding the challenges and business needs on the part of both parties is critical to managing expectations, identifying gaps in performance, and working together to optimize the outsourcing relationship.

Part of the reason you are hiring the outsourcer is for its ability to provide a lower cost service and a higher level of expertise. Part of the contract between you and the outsourcer may include expectations of hiring and maintaining qualified people within the outsourcer. This may include notification to you of employee turnover rates, hiring of key people, loss of key people, and a training program to maintain expertise within the outsourcer. This training may include technical expertise as well as business expertise where the outsourcer commits to learning more about your business and how to align its operations in support of your industry.

Many outsourcing agreements occur between organizations in different countries (e.g., off-shoring). Cultural differences can contribute to conflict between organizations. Expectations of problem resolution in a country where personnel leave at the end of a shift despite the state of operations can be quite frustrating. Don't assume that any performance level is implied in the contract; clearly state expectations that also consider cultural differences. Also, don't underestimate the potential impact of language differences. Even people who speak the same language, in theory, may have different understandings for specific words or phrases. Technical operations by nature involve subtle nuances that may be lost during language translation, due to the misunderstanding of idioms or terms, or among people using a secondary language to their native tongue. Many serious problems have developed as a result of miscommunications caused by outsourcing to overseas countries, even when people in such locations speak English. Therefore, be sure to include a mutual awareness/training program that addresses company backgrounds, cultural expectations and practices regarding work, and especially the type of work involved in the outsourcing relationship.

Managed Security Service Providers

Outsourcing security to a managed security services provider (MSSP) makes sense if security is not your organization's core competency, security resources are difficult to come by (e.g., qualified personnel), and the expense of security is less with the MSSP than you can provide in house. Outsourcing security does not at all mean the same thing as abdicating all responsibility for security. Your organization must define an enterprise fit for security, and an enterprise role and relationship to other parts of the business. An MSSP may implement security to your specifications and operate security more cost effectively - but still to your SLAs, which provide effective risk management and business value.

Technology

In a given environment, people perform processes using *technology* to produce results. Security operations technology that is subject to compliance or is supportive of compliance management includes the following:

- Inventory management
- Access control
- Anti-malware
- Operating systems

Inventory Management

Inventory management, or inventory control, is the set of policies, standards, and procedures to maintain optimum inventory levels, track the location of enterprise assets, and schedule inventory replacement. From a technology perspective, inventory management includes hardware, software, and configurations and all those aspects necessary to provide effective and efficient business operations. From a security perspective, the purpose of inventory management is to prevent the loss of equipment (e.g., misplacement), facilitate the recovery of equipment in the event of disaster or failed equipment, prevent the violation of software licensing agreements, and prevent the unauthorized installation of hardware and software and unauthorized modifications to configuration settings.

Effective inventory management addresses legislative compliance requirements, e.g., the ability to track the location of systems with healthcare information or track systems with corporate financial data. Moreover, inventory management is addressed in most industry security standards like ISO 27002 and NIST SP 800-53. Inventory management addresses the possession and availability of core security principles.

Also, effective inventory management is critical for patch management. When you receive notice of a newly discovered vulnerability and an accompanying patch to fix that vulnerability, inventory management shows you how many systems are affected and their location. Such knowledge translates into resource planning, scheduling, and cost for patch installation.

Hardware

The enterprise invests a lot of money in hardware, and the ability to track the location and status of this investment is good business practice. More importantly, the loss of the asset may not be nearly as costly as the loss of the business function that the asset provides. Hardware tracking includes servers, PCs, and components like network cards and video cards, networking equipment like routers and switches, information technology security devices like firewalls and intrusion detection systems, and so on.

Inventory control may apply to all enterprise assets and not just information technology. Useful details to track in an inventory management system include the following:

- Computer name
- Computer model
- Serial number
- Supplier, so you know who to go to for questions, service, updates
- Date acquired, to track mean time between failure (MTBF)
- Warranty dates, to manage enterprise expense in the event of failure
- Location, to know where to go for problem response
- Function, including technical function and business function
- Assigned user
- Owner or accountability, to know who to call with questions or requests
- MAC address for automated inventory check

The Simple Network Management Protocol (SNMP) and Cisco Discovery Protocol (CDP) are two examples of software that may retrieve MAC addresses and validate against the inventory database. Missing MAC addresses prompt further investigation to determine if the equipment is faulty, turned off, or missing. Having an individual contact name and email accountable for the hardware enables an automated email message with a copy to the help desk.

Software

Software inventory management enables tracking of how many of application X are installed on enterprise systems, what this number is compared to the number of licenses purchased, the location of original software installation media and license keys, what versions are installed, whether these versions need patching to mitigate the latest vulnerability notice, whether it is time to upgrade, etc.

Tracking software helps with adherence to licensing agreements and digital rights management (DRM). An unauthorized copy of copyrighted software or media in soft form opens the enterprise to liability issues. Knowing the contents of PCs, servers, and portable media helps avoid potential litigation against the enterprise.

Policies inform employees of the organization's right to inventory software and media contents for review. Additional policies should provide potential disciplinary action for finding unauthorized software or media. Such unauthorized software may introduce malware to the enterprise network as well as put the enterprise at risk for hosting illegal material like illegal music or video files.

Many end point security solutions (those running on individual PCs, smartphones, tablets, etc.) bundle anti-malware, anti-spam, anti-phishing, personal firewall, and intrusion detection technologies. An additional feature includes the implementation and enforcement of whitelist, blacklist, and greylist software applications. A whitelist is an enumeration of all permissible applications; a blacklist enumerates all impermissible applications; and a greylist enumerates applications that may be run under certain conditions. Maintaining a blacklist could be quite an effort - a list of all those software programs not permitted to execute on that platform. An easier approach is to list all those software programs that may be run and exclude anything not on the list; this is the classic "anything not explicitly permitted is denied." Software inventory will check for the presence of unauthorized applications and is a complement to the whitelist filter, which blocks the execution of unauthorized applications.

Software Licensing

A software license is permission granted from the software publisher to a company or individual to use a piece of software under certain conditions. Software licenses are legal instruments and are binding among parties to the agreement. Nearly all software applications are licensed rather than sold, meaning you have permission to use the software, but you do not own the software. Tracking and monitoring licenses is necessary to remain in compliance with licensing agreements (e.g., end-user license agreements [EULAs]) and legislation governing use of software.

Typically, one license is required per computer. A per-seat software license is based upon the number of users who may use the software. Some server software will provide the ability to purchase a license for a number of simultaneous users, meaning that 100 users may have the client software installed, but only 20 may access the server simultaneously; simultaneous user licenses are also known as concurrent user licenses. Note that server licenses and client licenses may be separate purchases and tracked separately in software inventory. Enterprise licenses permit the installation of software on a network server and allow access by all employees. Enterprise licenses may involve an annual license fee plus a maintenance fee. Not all license agreements are the same, and they may vary within the same vendor as well as among different vendors.

Many software license agreements will specify that they are nontransferable. This means that you may not resell the software. You may sell the media on which it resides, and you may sell a piece of equipment that has the software installed (e.g., private branch exchange [PBX]) but not the license that provides the next owner the right to use the software. The new owners may have to purchase their own license, their own "right to use" from the software vendor.

The traditional method of installing from the original software media (e.g., physical CD) has largely been replaced by push deployment across the network. This software deployment push method allows for faster software deployment as well as facilitating keeping track of software installed and license counts. Installer packages coupled with group policies provide the ability to selectively install software on end-user PCs. This ensures that only personnel who need the software receive the software.

Many software deployment tools provide the ability to track usage. Tracking software installed and license usage helps the organization maintain legal compliance and thus avoid liability issues; it helps with cost management by not over-buying licenses for personnel that do not need the software, and it facilitates efficient patch deployment. Some applications (e.g., Microsoft Remote Desktop) will not allow the application to launch if there are insufficient licenses. Some applications create audit trails when license limits are exceeded (e.g., Microsoft Terminal Server).

Some software packages may use usage meters to track actual use of the software. A software license with a usage meter does not limit the number of users, but it monitors the usage and charges according to volume of use. Another type of license is shareware or freeware. The name of this type of license is misleading because even though the software is available for free downloading from the Internet, the use of the software is often on a trial basis after which the user is expected to pay for a license to continue to use it.

The Business Software Alliance (BSA) is an organization that represents the commercial software industry and promotes the reporting and prosecution of software theft. The Canadian Alliance Against Software Theft is another example similar to the BSA. The Recording Industry Association of America (RIAA) is a trade group representing the recording industry. The RIAA is involved in the licensing and royalties within the recording industry. Scanning enterprise systems for the illegal storage and sharing of video and audio recordings is necessary to avoid liability for hosting such activity.

Digital Rights Management (DRM) is an enforcement mechanism for access control and what can and cannot be done with a software file, audio file, video file, or document file. Copyright law prohibits unauthorized copies of digital files or other media (e.g., audio tapes, video tapes). DRM extends beyond this to restrict the number of viewings or restrict copies to certain types of devices; e.g., Sony restricts the copying of some music files from the music CD to a hard drive.

Software piracy is a romantic phrase that veils the reality of the situation (i.e., software theft is a crime). Licensing is a serious issue, and the rise of watchdog organizations and litigation against violators requires good software license management. The level of culpability goes up with explicit intent to steal software as well as with negligence in taking reasonable steps to avoid being an unwitting host for illegal activities. Any organization is only expected to do so much to avoid illegal activities, but you must do at least that much. Working out exactly what to do, resourcing allocations to do it, and budgeting allocations is a matter of discussion among information technology, security, executives, governance, and legal departments.

Configuration Settings

Tracking hardware and software is good but not enough. The configuration settings of the hardware and software are also necessary to track. These settings enable appropriate functionality as well as restrict other functionality. The functionality restrictions are to safeguard the systems and the data residing on the systems. Unauthorized modification of these settings may place the enterprise at risk by permitting unauthorized remote access, exfiltration of data, installation of unauthorized software, use of unauthorized devices such as USB drives, etc.

Policy will state the need for standard configurations, and standards will articulate the parameters and the parameter settings. Configuration tracking will elicit these settings from servers, PCs, and other devices and compare them against the standard. These configurations may be related to general operations or specifically to security. One example of a security configuration tracking methodology is Security Content Automation Protocol (SCAP). SCAP is a method to enable automated vulnerability management and policy compliance evaluation. Many software vendors are developing SCAP-compliant applications.

Policy may require enterprise-wide configurations for workstations, servers, user configurations, application settings, database settings, and more. These settings may be modified to optimize performance and to optimize security. A major goal of the configuration policy is to normalize the enterprise on a common operating environment to ensure interoperability, consistency for redundancy and recovery, and optimal network traffic flow.

In addition to compliance evaluation, tracking configuration settings is good business practice to ensure consistency throughout the organization as well as to have a record of settings in the event of disaster recovery. Getting the hardware and software installed and reconfigured is time consuming, and attempting to remember the configuration settings is not nearly as productive as simply restoring settings already captured.

Virtual Machines

Virtual refers to that which is not real (not tangible) but exhibits qualities as if it was real. A virtual machine (VM) is not a real, tangible machine but a simulated device to perform some activity. A key characteristic of a virtual machine is containment, meaning that the software running within the VM cannot reach beyond the VM; the VM is its entire universe. Containment includes not reaching beyond the hardware assigned to the VM, as well as the abstractions within the hardware like random access memory (RAM). Containment has implications to security and to compliance: Software and data on one VM must remain separate and distinct from those on other VMs running on the same hardware platform. A practical ramification of this is that if malware were to be present on one VM, it should have absolutely no impact on other VMs running on the same hardware. Even performance should not be impacted (other than excess performance that was not guaranteed to begin with), as each VM should be allocated specific subsets of resources and not be able to exceed them.

Two general types of VMs are a system virtual machine and a process virtual machine. A system virtual machine has a single hardware platform with multiple OS installations, each

3

Security Compliance Management

sharing the underlying hardware. A process virtual machine runs as a software application within an operating system. The process VM then provides an environment to execute code, e.g., a software business application. The process VM abstracts the underlying OS and hardware from the business application; hence the same business application may run on a variety of OS and hardware combinations. A key benefit of using system VMs is to leverage single hardware platforms to house many OS instances running a variety of applications. A key benefit to using process VMs is to write software applications that may execute on any hardware environment.

It is important to understand that virtual machine technology creates significant complexity and security challenges. Virtual machines are not tangible like real, physical machines, and, as a result, they may reside "hidden" while not running. They may be missed during assessments, audits, or the process of checking physical inventory. A virtual machine may pose a threat if unnoticed because scans for vulnerabilities may bypass non-running virtual machines. Unauthorized virtual machines may allow hackers to perform all sorts of nefarious actions. Inventory management should keep track of all hardware that host virtual machines and the number, type, and business function of each virtual machine. Checks should be made for any unauthorized virtual machines that might have been placed within an organization's infrastructure – running or not running.

Virtual machines also create issues vis-à-vis licensing. Third-party software running on a virtual machine must be licensed; the licensing requirements vary from vendor to vendor, and from contract to contract, but, in general, the software will need to be licensed, so unless an unlimited license, or site license, has been obtained, some form of software and license tracking will be necessary. Virtual machines may be created and deleted, further complicating matters.

Virtual machines also need to have patches applied so as to remain secure – so patch management must account for virtual machines, not just physical machines. A secure baseline needs to be established, updated, and maintained to be current so that new instances of virtual machines are instantiated in a secure state; you do not want VMs to be vulnerable when they "go live."

Information Inventory

Keeping track of physical assets is one part of inventory management. Various compliance requirements may dictate specifics as to how well physical assets must be tracked, both to know what an organization has and what it does not have. This not only ensures that appropriate systems are in place, but it also helps ensure that rogue systems, or deficient systems (e.g., unpatched computers) are not present.

Another part is tracking information, specifically sensitive information that resides on the PCs, servers, or other storage media. A large part of compliance with litigation is to ensure the proper handling of employee and customer (or patient) information, e.g., personally identifiable information (PII). Moreover, tracking information will help maintain a record of data sensitive to your organization like financial data, employee lists, research and development plans, strategic plans, or engineering plans.

Develop an information classification scheme that includes information sensitivity and information criticality. Sensitivity classifications may include categories such as public, proprietary, private, sensitive, or restricted. Public information is available for general access, whereas proprietary is intellectual property. Your organization may not use these specific classifications but, rather, choose those appropriate to distinguish the variety of information.

- **Criticality** classification may include essential, nonessential, primary, and derived.
- **Primary** information is the root source and may often be a unique source; the loss of primary information may cause severe loss to the organization.
- **Derived** information is an aggregate from primary sources; the loss of derived information may be annoying, but it is not devastating to the organization.
- **Essential** information is critical to operations; nonessential is still important, but it is not critical for the enterprise to fulfill its mission.

Develop standards and procedures for media labeling and handling that use the information classification scheme. Such a scheme on physical labels and on virtual labels (e.g., metadata) will help in determining access, modification, deletion, and media disposal.

Inventory Management

Good inventory management practice includes the following:

- Inventory lists
- Software libraries
- Inventory report
- Inventory audit

Maintain an automated inventory management system that retains lists of hardware and software as well as configuration setting details. Establish a software library to manage the distribution of both the software media (disks, CDs, DVDs, documentation) and to track licenses. If a person moves from one computer to another and their software moves with them, there is a need to track the removal of the license from one system and the installation on another. Be sure to account for the removal so you are not paying for a license that is not in use.

Generate a comprehensive inventory report at least once per year that includes an evaluation of current information against expected information. Provide answers to following questions:

- Do we have what we think we have?
- Is it where it belongs?
- What can we anticipate to refresh over the next fiscal year?
- Are we within our license agreement?
- Are we finding any unauthorized software?
  - ¤ Are there patterns to the unauthorized installations? (Note: A pattern may show that a particular application has business value and people have taken it upon themselves to add it to their desktop. This is good feedback to operations.)
- Are we finding any unauthorized hardware (e.g., rogue wireless access devices)?
- Are we licensing too much software (i.e., are we paying for licenses that are not in use and not needed)?

Inventory management tells you what you think you have. It is a good idea to periodically (once a year is a commonly suggested frequency) verify what you have via a physical inventory. The goal is not only to know that you have and what you need but to ensure that no unexpected items are present; rogue systems, software, or devices could be spying on the organization, stealing data, corrupting files, or performing other undesired, sinister functions.

Put eyes and hands on assets and validate the information you have recorded in the inventory management system.

Access Control

Access control is fundamental to effective security and includes the following categories and examples:

- Physical access
  - Building, floor, office, wiring closet
  - Identity card, possession of a combination for a cipher lock, possession of a physical key
- Technical access
  - Remote access
  - Wireless access
  - Application access
  - Password, PIN, biometric, smart access card
- Identity and authentication
- Privilege and authorization
- Identity credential
- Privilege credential

There are many security constructs that do not fit exclusively within people, process, technology, or environment, and access control is one of those. People are assigned identity credentials to gain access to physical space and technology. Technology (e.g., a computer or specific application) may also be assigned an identity credential. The identity credential is authenticated to prove that the presenter of the credential is indeed who or what the credential claims them to be. Usually, privileges are coupled with identity; a privilege is the ability to do something. The claim of privilege is authorized prior to allowing the action. For example, a claim of privilege is to enter the front door of the corporate office. Corporate policy states the need to present an identity credential and authenticate that the identity belongs to the bearer of the credential. The implementation and enforcement of this policy is the identity card reader that also requires the entry of a personal identification number (PIN) known only to the employee; this is two-factor authentication via something the employee has (the identity card) and something the employee knows (the PIN). The privilege to enter the front door is inherent in being a current employee bearing a valid identity credential.

Privileges are associated with identity either individually (i.e., to that specific identity) or via a role also assigned to that identity. As a continuation of the example above, entry into the lobby and past the security desk usually means you can enter the elevator and exit on your office floor. Additional presentation of an identity/privilege credential may be necessary to enter your office space. Subsequent presentation of a different identity/privilege credential may be necessary to log on to your computer. The identity/privilege credential may be the same one used to enter the building; entry into your office or logon to the computer just requires an additional presentation and reentry of a PIN. The authentication/authorization process then checks your ability to perform the action requested and denies/permits according to the privileges assigned to your identity.

Perhaps a completely separate identity/privilege credential is required to log on to the computer. For example, an identity card with an embedded radio frequency identification (RFID) chip may provide access into the building, but a smart card is necessary to log on to the computer. A smart card has integrated chips in the card and metal contacts to transmit data through a reader connected to or embedded in the PC. Use of a smart card may also require the entry of a pin or presentation of a biometric (e.g., fingerprint) for multifactor authentication.

The use of multiple identity/privilege credentials and multifactor authentication depends entirely on the enterprise business need. If your business is a high visibility target such as a government installation or a bank, your security practices warrant such strong safeguards. If yours is a small business of little international importance and of little attractiveness to criminal elements, then adjust the strength of safeguards accordingly. Organizations of any size must also consider the legislative mandates that govern how to protect the data they process. For example, a small medical billing company of little international import and low criminal attractiveness is still responsible for protecting PHI to at least the minimal degree required by legislation.

Anti-Malware

Malware is a contraction of the phrase "malicious software." Malware is a category of software that intends to cause harm or intends to commit an unlawful act, the key word being intent, which differentiates malware from a software bug. Malware consists of viruses, worms, spam, phish, spyware, root kits, Trojan horses, backdoors, spyware, bots, keystroke loggers, zombies, and more. What is the business purpose of anti-malware? To keep out malware of course! Well, actually to keep out malware is a technical purpose, not a business purpose. The main business purpose of anti-malware is to protect intellectual property and maintain regulatory compliance for the protection of data (e.g., PII and PHI).

Most malware intends to infiltrate a system and provide a communications channel to the originator. This communications channel may provide access into the enterprise network or provide a data exfiltration pathway. This provides an illicit communications channel to exfiltrate proprietary or sensitive data. The loss of proprietary data may threaten the very existence of the organization, e.g., knowledge of a pending business agreement that is then subverted, or knowledge of a new engineering design that is then copied and a competitor undercuts the cost because it didn't have the research and development expense. Malware includes the following:

- Virus, Worm
- Spam, Phish
- Spyware
- Root Kit, Trojan Horse, Backdoor, Easter Eggs, Zombies, Keystroke Capture, Screen Capture

3

Security Compliance Management

- Bots and Botnets
- Outbound Traffic and Exfiltration

Anti-malware includes the following:

- Anti-virus, Anti-spyware
- Host-Based Intrusion Detection
- Firewall
  - ◻ Web Application Firewall, Personal Firewall, Proxy Firewall
- Content Filter
- Cross-Domain System (CDS)

The sections below elaborate on some malware and anti-malware safeguards to provide examples of business threats, technical threats, and technical functionality.

Anti-malware both prevents and detects malware on a system (e.g., server, PC, gateway, firewall, or workstation). An example of anti-malware is anti-virus (AV). Virus software follows a signature pattern. This may include a file name or more likely a sequence of binary codes. The binary code sequence may represent executable code or data used by the executable code to entrench and spread. AV software contains a signature file containing binary sequences of known virus software. Managed AV software pushes updates to all instances of the AV software throughout the enterprise. These updates may include software executable updates to enhance the capability of the AV software as well as signature file updates to reflect new viruses.

AV software may filter the transmission of files (e.g., email) or check existing files prior to use (e.g., Internet downloads or sneaker-net transfers). Note: Sneaker-net transfers are files copied via floppy disk, CD, DVD, USB thumb drives, Bluetooth, etc., and they are hand carried from one computer to another.

Defense-in-depth will use anti-malware as one type of defense. Defense-in-breadth may employ multiple anti-malware applications. One AV software package may detect a virus that another will miss. Employing one vendor's AV software on the email server and another AV software on PCs, workstations, and servers may provide protection against a wider array of virus software. Be careful, though, not to install multiple AV software packages on the same system because they may use common OS configuration parameters with different settings and hence interfere with each other's operation.

Depending on technical infrastructure, the effective use and regular updating of anti-malware software may require the active participation of users;.if that is the case, be sure to include a discussion of the importance of anti-malware, and how to ensure it is updated regularly, to user security awareness and training programs.

Botnet Awareness

A bot is a term for software robot; exposure to bots is one type of vulnerability. Successful penetration of a PC by a bot makes that PC part of a botnet, or a network of software robots. Botnets are usually associated with malware or malicious activity. Malware in spam or phishing campaigns or embedded Trojan horses in downloads implant a bot on an unsuspecting Internet user. That bot may then transmit to other computers on the Internet according the direction of the master program (bot controller, also known as a bot herder) directing the bots.

The bot may lie dormant until invoked by the controller. Bots may forward spam, thus hiding the originator's identity. A bot controller may perform a denial-of-service attack by invoking thousands of bots to begin forwarding packets to a single Web server, thus bringing it down because it is unable to respond to the volume of network traffic. For example, given two major online retailer competitors that make 50% of their profits the two weeks before Christmas, how would competition be if one were to bring the other down during this time? First, the attacker may gain market share because consumers give up on the other site and transfer their business. Second, the one being attacked may not be able to sustain itself the following fiscal year due to lack of profit during a critical revenue generation period.

Bots are in essence software tools that adhere to RFC 1459 Internet Relay Chat (IRC) Protocol: tools that may be a means applied to any end. Bots may forward keystrokes to the controller or intermediary collection repository; keystroke logging may result in identity theft. Bots may act in coordination with each other in a distributed denial-of-service attack. Bots may provide an entry point to install malware or a launching point to distribute malware. Like any other tool, the application is dependent upon the wielder.

Creating a Botnet

A botnet operator or botnet controller sends out viruses or worms. These may be in email (e.g., spam, phish), embedded in downloads, or retrieved via other malware. The bot, now installed on the unsuspecting PC, then logs into a particular server. This server may be an intermediary device or the actual bot controller. A spammer may then purchase access to the bot from the bot operator. Instructions are sent from the IRC server to the bot on the infected PCs, causing the bots to send spam. Variations on this theme are known as spambot, click fraud, and spamdexing.

A spambot collects email addresses to build mailing lists. Targets for spambots include websites, newsgroups, special interest groups, and chat rooms. Consider the attractiveness of such a capability to the manufacturer of Techno-Wonder-Widgets (TWW). They can tap into TWWlovers.net, retrieve all emails of TWW lovers, and target market them with tailored advertisements. While this may seem like good marketing, the invasion of PCs with bot malware is certainly less than moral if not illegal.

Click fraud is related to pay-per-click advertising, where a legitimate user clicking on a Web ad generates a fee from the advertising company to the host of the Web ad; the more clicks, the more revenue generated by the Web ad host. Click fraud is the engagement of a person, automated script, or other software that imitates a legitimate user clicking on the Web ad and artificially inflates the fees paid to the Web as host. Bots are one method of accomplishing click fraud.

Spamdexing manipulates the relevance and prominence of search engine results. All search engines use key words and frequencies to both find and order the presentation of search results. The increase in online retail competition also creates an increase in competition for customer attention, especially in search engines. Spamdexing simulates search activity with key words and site selection that artificially push certain results to the top of the list so they appear on the first page of search results rather than later pages to which most users will not scroll.

Cyber Swarm

When bees swarm in attack, one bee sets the swarm in motion with an alarm pheromone; subsequent bees attack, sting, and set off additional alarm pheromone. The pheromone calls additional bees to the attack; likewise, for both attack and defense purposes, a bot may call other bots to action. If a system is under attack, a bot may retaliate (defend) against the source of the attack while calling other bots to swarm against the same source. Each individual bot may be more or less insignificant, but 10,000 bots may result in a denial-of-service, or 10,000 bots with variations of activity (e.g., each attempting variations on ports, protocols, services, and applications) may succeed in overwhelming cyber defenses. Such retaliation assumes accurate attribution of the attack, which is not always simply the source of the packet. Also, the legalities of such retaliation are highly questionable. Therefore, such defensive swarming is not recommended. The same principle of cyber swarming applies in offense where one bot succeeds in penetration and calls subsequent bots to swarm on the victim.

Botnet Employment

In analogy, consider that a bot may act like a virtual soldier. Like soldiers, bots may group together in units like battalions or squadrons. Each group may play a tactical role in a larger strategic picture where tactical roles may be diversionary, denial, and objective execution. Diversionary tactics draw attention away from the objective by adding noise over the signal; it can be very difficult to distinguish extraneous activity from the real threat. Denial is the removal of key functions like the ability to detect an anomaly (e.g., a denial-of-service attack against a firewall and intrusion detection system). With extraneous noise coupled with denial of key monitoring devices, execution of the actual objective becomes much harder to detect. The point is to draw your attention to the sophistication of malware as a tactical element in an overall strategic attack. Such offensive capability on the part of the adversary requires a heightened awareness and defensive capabilities on your part as a protector of the enterprise.

Botnet Prevention

Bots and botnets pose a threat to the enterprise in a direct attack or incidental attack, or they introduce liability as a host of botnet activity, even as an unwitting host. Botnet prevention includes anti-malware, intrusion detection systems (IDSs), intrusion prevention systems (IPSs), and honeypots.

By nature, botnets are extremely varied in source and capability; therefore, simple IP address filtering is unlikely to be successful. Passive operating system (OS) fingerprinting may offer a clue to the source system. Passive OS fingerprinting is also known as TCP/IP stack fingerprinting because certain parameters within the TCIP/IP stack, specifically layer 4, are configurable, and the standard default values may vary from OS to OS. Collecting and reviewing these values provides insight into the source OS of the bot. Note: This same concept applies to an adversary seeking to understand your OS types. Firewalls may be configured to take advantage of OS fingerprinting to detect a botnet attack.

Rate-based IPSs monitor network behavior, establish a baseline of "normal" behavior, and detect variations from normal. These variations may offer insight into an active attack including denial-of-service or distributed denial-of-service attacks from botnets.

Outbound Traffic and Exfiltration

Exfiltration is a military term for exiting and is the opposite of infiltration. Data exfiltration is the unauthorized transmission of data out of the organization. Some malware will search for files that contain key words in the title or content and then send that file to a predefined location. Therefore, monitoring outbound traffic is a concern for security operations. Compliance reasons for monitoring outbound traffic include potential damage to enterprise reputation, loss of proprietary information, and potential legal liabilities. For example, if a botnet penetrates the enterprise networks and sends out spam with illegal material (e.g., child pornography), the enterprise may be held liable for negligence in preventing the outbound message.

Use security software to monitor outbound traffic using content filtering. Upon detection, the software can generate an alert to the security department or Help Desk and may even initiate an auto lockdown of the source system. Monitoring data in transit that is in plaintext format is difficult enough because of the volume of data to check. Monitoring encrypted transmissions or peer-to-peer applications is particularly difficult.

Web Application Firewalls

An application firewall is a software-based firewall that limits access of software applications to operating system services; this may include hardware access. Hardware firewalls restrict data flow across the network but do not control the activity on a system like the execution of an operating system command.

Web application firewalls (WAFs) are safeguards for websites to protect them against attacks. WAFs are deep packet-inspection firewalls and are designed to prevent attacks that network firewalls and IDSs do not address. Though available for about 10 years, WAFs are not widely deployed and only recently found a growth market with the introduction of the Payment Card Industry Data Security Standard. WAFs look for attack signatures for specific attacks as well as abnormal behavior that does not fit into normal traffic patterns.

WAF operations involve looking for data attacks that use special characters or wild cards to change data. Also, WAFs look for logic content attacks, which go after command strings or logic statements, and for targeted attacks, which focus on accounts, files, or hosts.

Many businesses provide an online presence for customer convenience, including banking and other financial transactions, order placement that includes entry of credit card information, and the entry of PII to facilitate transaction completion and order fulfillment. The addition of WAFs is part of a comprehensive security program that is necessary to comply with legislation governing the protection of PII.

Operating Systems

Operating system installations out of the box include many technical vulnerabilities. These include standard user accounts, default passwords, default software application activation, default use of background processes, and default configuration settings. Without modification, these offer easy exploitation points for an attacker with knowledge of that OS. Therefore, research the OS choices for your organization for commonly known vulnerabilities and how to eliminate those vulnerabilities, and otherwise configure the operating system to be more secure. Make these changes part of a standard software image or include them in procedures for OS installation.

Eliminating vulnerabilities inherent in default installations is the first step. An additional step is to harden the OS by eliminating all unnecessary functions, i.e., all functions not explicitly required for the OS to produce the required business result. Limiting OS boot-up functions, processes, background jobs, and utilities vastly reduces the vulnerabilities of the OS and of the software applications running on the OS. Moreover, limiting OS functionality makes it easier to monitor and detect anomalies on the OS, e.g., detecting an unauthorized utility as a clue to a potential intruder.

While no legislation is likely to dictate how to protect operating systems, and no legislation should, the legislation will imply this need. Internal policies will reflect the intent of legislative direction, and OS installation and configuration standards will provide direction on how to implement and enforce policy. Situational awareness services and mechanisms that include vulnerability scanning and log analysis will provide monitoring of configurations to ensure that the production systems conform to enterprise standards. This is the path from external compliance requirements to internal compliance requirements to compliance enforcement to compliance monitoring.

System Hardening

System hardening is the elimination of known vulnerabilities, exploits, and generally turning off or uninstalling unnecessary functions. Each operating system, each version of the same operating system, and each patch release of the same operating system may have a different procedure for hardening the system.

Disabling unused services will require OS parameter changes at the kernel or registry level, or modifications to services that initiate or run at startup. Some operating systems (e.g., Microsoft) will provide all administrator software as part of the standard installation process. This is good in that it provides the administrator with everything he or she may need, but it is bad in that it provides every inherent vulnerability that malware may exploit. Other operating systems (e.g., UNIX) provide only the bare essentials in the standard installation and require the administrator to install any other applications needed.

Disable unnecessary ports and protocols that may respond to connection requests or port probes, or invoke connections that are not part of the system's core function, e.g., disable port 80 if the system will not initiate HTTP connections. Change standard account names like "Administrator" to resemble the common user ID structure. Change all standard passwords for any installation out of the box. Disable all unnecessary accounts. In general, when in doubt, disable or uninstall and wait for a reason to enable or reinstall. Users will let you know if they need a particular functionality.

Environment

In a given *environment*, people perform processes using technology to produce results. Security operations environments subject to compliance or in support of compliance management include the following:

- Physical security

- Campus
- Building
- Lobby
- Loading dock
- Floor
- Room
- Office
- Workstation
- Windows
- Special purpose areas
  - Data center
  - Wiring closet
  - External service demarcation points
    - Phone
    - Data
    - Water
    - Electric
- Secure facilities according to government standard
- Secure facilities according to legislative mandate
- Secure facilities according to internal standards

Despite the focus on cybersecurity, physical security remains a critical factor in an enterprise security management program. Physical security starts with the perimeter of the campus and of the building, including driveways, landscaping, lighting, entrance gates, doors, loading docks, and windows. Loading docks are especially important because there may be high traffic of non-enterprise personnel. Invited guests come through the front door, but most intruders will not. However, personal experience in physical security testing shows that if you look like you belong or that you are there for some particular reason, you are rarely challenged even if entering through the front door; a suit, tie, briefcase, and obscured badge holder of conforming design go a long way as challenge deterrents.

Physical Security

The scope of information and information technology security includes all information in any form. This means information on computers, tapes, and disk drives, as well as on paper, in file cabinets, or in briefcases. Physical security is every bit as important as cybersecurity; why bother breaking through the firewall when all you have to do is walk through the loading dock to the data center with a thumb drive or steal backup tapes?

Legislative compliance for the protection of PHI and PII applies to physical security. Additionally, the safeguard against crime and corporate espionage is good business practice if these threats apply to your organization. Consider that if you have something worth stealing, then someone is likely willing to go to some lengths to steal it. The point of security is to make the cost of stealing it prohibitively high in both the expertise required to steal it and the equipment costs to perpetrate the theft. For example, if the board of directors or the CFO of the organization hold sensitive meetings about strategy and finance, then consider holding those meetings in an inside, windowless room to prohibit eavesdropping through the glass.

3

Security Compliance Management

HIPAA Physical Safeguard Requirements

HIPAA Physical Safeguards include the following:

- Evaluation
  - Facility Access Controls
  - Contingency Operations
  - Facility Security Plan
  - Access Control and Validation Procedures
  - Maintenance Records
- Workstation
- Workstation Security
- Device and Media Controls
  - Disposal
  - Media Reuse
  - Accountability
- Data Backup and Storage

Similar to cyber access controls, facility access controls require the issuance of an identity credential (e.g., a picture identity card). Policy may state the need to present the identity credential upon access to an automated card reader or to a security card or both. The access privileges associated with the identity credential may restrict access to certain parts of the facility: For example, the average employee does not need access to the data center or to wiring closets; therefore, only privileged individuals or privileged roles have access to these areas.

Physical safeguards address the need for contingency operations within cold, warm, or hot backup sites. A facility security plan establishes emergency procedures, e.g., pre-established meeting places in the event of building evacuation, a call plan to notify of emergency or establish whereabouts, and emergency responsibilities such as safely powering down critical equipment.

HIPAA is especially sensitive to workstation placement and display screen visibility. Processing PHI on a PC visible through a heavily traveled public area (e.g., shopping mall) violates the PHI protection requirements of HIPAA. Physical security also addresses device and media controls that include media disposal, media reuse, accountability, and data backup and storage.

Media disposal includes the discarding of old backup tapes, hard drives, thumb drives, laptops, and any other device that may store enterprise data. Consider engaging a disposal service to apply the appropriate technology and procedures for preparing the media for disposal. Degaussing may be fine in some cases; in other cases, nothing less than physical destruction is acceptable. Media reuse within the organization is a good cost-saving method; however, be sure the media is appropriately erased, reformatted, or degaussed according to the previous use. Passing on old storage media to HR is fine but not if it still has the CEO's strategic plans still stored on it.

Provide accountability for media possession and location. For example, the issuance of laptops requires tracking who has them, who is accountable for their safety and whereabouts, and actually tracking the location (e.g., on enterprise property or off enterprise property) is prudent to track a valuable physical asset. More importantly, track the business use of the asset to understand the business implications of asset damage or loss. Losing a laptop is bad enough; losing a laptop with client PII is far worse. Controlling and tracking data backups will help discern if the loss of primary data is the loss of the only copy (i.e., knowing there is a backup) and how old the backup is compared to the date of data loss.

NIST SP 800-53 Physical and Environmental Protection

NIST SP 800-53 Rev. 3 provides 19 physical and environment protection controls: [4]

1. Physical and Environmental Protection Policy and Procedures
2. Physical Access Authorizations
3. Physical Access Control
4. Access Control for Transmission Medium
5. Access Control for Output Devices
6. Monitoring Physical Access
7. Visitor Control
8. Access Records
9. Power Equipment and Power Cabling
10. Emergency Shutoff
11. Emergency Power
12. Emergency Lighting
13. Fire Protection
14. Temperature and Humidity Controls
15. Water Damage Protection
16. Delivery and Removal
17. Alternate Work Site
18. Location of Information System Components
19. Information Leakage

These physical access controls correspond closely with HIPAA but not exactly. HIPAA calls for contingency operations under physical safeguards, whereas NIST SP 800-53 provides an entire control section on contingency planning. Similarly, SP 800-53 provides a separate section on maintenance controls that includes maintenance records. The use of SP 800-53 as a foundation for the ESS and ESF provides for the planning, implementation, and tracking of a comprehensive security program and may trace to various compliance requirements, including HIPAA. Even though the compliance requirements may call a safeguard something different or categorize it differently from SP 800-53, there is usually a mapping from SP 800-53 to the legislative compliance requirement. Moreover, if the legislative compliance requirement contains a safeguard not in SP 800-53, then add that to your ESS and ESF to customize your situation.

---

4   NIST SP 800-53 Rev. 3, Appendix D.

Government Standards

Some government standards will prescribe physical security for sites where top-secret activities occur. Often, site configurations will be rated for secret activities, top-secret activities, or beyond. Seek out relevant government standards that may apply to your particular situation. Or, if your organization is a high visibility target for corporate espionage or organized crime, you may benefit from researching government standards and incorporating them into your own security management program.

The big focus here is on information leakage from paper documents, cyber data, and conversations in house, on a phone, or on video-conference equipment. The methods to illicitly obtain information are many and varied; likewise, so are the safeguards.

Managed Security Services

If you use managed security services (MSSs), then you must also consider the environment of the outsourcer. Your operations, data, reputation, and survivability now also depend on efficient and secure outsourcer operations. This means that you need to understand and influence their operations to ensure that they represent your organization's best interests.

Address MSS physical security requirements in the business partner agreement and SLAs. Also, provide the ability for you to assess the MSS environment for compliance with the business agreement.

Local and Distributed

If your organization transports data off site, then physical security requirements apply to physical transportation. This includes the type of media, protection of data on media, protection of media in transport vehicles, procedures for the driver, and media checkout/check-in procedures. Be aware that your domestic laws may vary from foreign laws where you have operations; the use of encryption may be fine in the United States but not fine at all in some eastern countries. This applies to both businesses operations in the local country as well as organization employees traveling in that country.

Mission Assurance

In a given environment, people perform processes using technology to produce *results*. The results are the achievement of the business purpose and the fulfillment of the business mission. The successful execution of a software program may contribute to the fulfillment of the business mission, but successful execution is not the business mission. Safeguarding the data center may contribute to the business mission, but a safe data center is not the business mission.

The traditional focus on information assurance (IA) or computer security is on the technology, i.e., ensuring the software application runs and the data center is safe. As the material herein shows, technology is certainly important but is far from the only consideration. Another habitual focus of information assurance and security is on information technology, or IA and security for their own sake – a "build it and they will come" approach to developing software and purchasing hardware. In other words, if we produce a wonderful solution, surely there is a problem out there that needs us. The amount of time and money wasted on this misconception is huge. Worse, the credibility of IT and security professionals is far less than it should be for lack of proposing solutions and budgets in terms of business value. Enterprise operations exist to produce a result, the bottom line of which is to optimize stakeholder interests. Business need drives the need for technology; business risk drives the need for security. There is no justification for investment in security without a corresponding business risk that it addresses. The enterprise mission is not to be more secure; being more secure ensures the ability to fulfill the mission.

Mission assurance involves safeguarding the fulfillment of a specific task with which an individual or group is charged and accepts as their main purpose. Mission assurance is an emerging formal practice to identify key people, process, technology, and environment that fulfill the mission and then to align security operations with these key resources. Understanding the mission will help you as a security manager to prioritize the following: security investments, operations decisions, budget allocations, hiring decisions, incident response, and overall security management in the context of the mission. This will help you articulate the business value of security and provide you with the ability to make intelligent resource allocations for security in terms of business value. Mention of mission assurance here is to make you aware of the concept and to spark your personal research into current mission assurance practices.

Summary

At this point, you should be familiar with the following topics covered in this chapter:

- The differences between and the complementary nature of legislation management and litigation management
- The use of an ESS as a foundation for all enterprise security planning
- The use of an ESF as a common construct for planning, tracking, and assessment of documents
- External security compliance
- Internal security compliance
- Manage outsourcing
- Software compliance
- Incident management and incident response
- How to apply the concepts to operational security daily activities

The key take-away from this chapter is the need for a disciplined approach to compliance management of security operations. This disciplined approach starts with identifying an enterprise security standard and developing an enterprise security framework from that standard. The ESF then becomes the outline within which to record all security planning activities, development projects, and current practices. Develop a traceability matrix from the ESF to compliance requirements. Because the traceability is from the ESF structure, the content within the ESF inherits the traceable relationships. This is the best way to track a single activity that may satisfy multiple compliance requirements. This is also the best way to identify gaps, which is when an ESF area traces to a compliance requirement and that ESF area has no current activity, no development activity, and no plan related to that area.

References

DOE-NE-STD-1004-92, *Department of Energy Guideline Root Cause Analysis Guidance Document*, February 1992 (standard is currently inactive, but still useful).

ISO 15489: 2001 *Information and Documentation–Records Management*, September 15, 2001.

NIST SP 800-53 Rev. 3, *Recommended Security Controls for Federal Information Systems and Organizations*, August 2009.

Reichl, Peter and Wolfgang Haidegger, *The Cumulus Assessment Module as General SLA Evaluation Mechanism for Telecommunication Services*, Telecommunications Research Center (FTW), Vienna, 2004.

Willett, Keith D., *Information Assurance Architecture*, Auerbach Publications, June 2008.

Domain 3: Review Questions

1. Cyber vulnerability testing consists of which of the following activities?

    A. War driving and war dialing

    B. Network probing and network scanning

    C. Penetration testing

    D. All of the above

2. Which of the following statements is true?

    A. The main benefit of using an MSSP is to turn over all responsibilities and wash your hands of the entire enterprise security burden.

    B. MSSP relationships can be more casual because most MSSPs are willing and capable to take on the enterprise security responsibilities.

    C. Operations, monitoring, detection, notification, and resolution may be outsourced, but the security responsibility is only shared, not abdicated.

    D. When using an MSSP, in-house security efforts are no longer necessary.

3. What is the intent of metrics?

    A. Objective measurement of the enterprise risk posture

    B. Objective evaluation of value to the organization in terms of business need

    C. Determine if operations are performing within SLAs

    D. Objective measurement of the enterprise security posture

4. An emerging formal practice to identify key people, process, technology, and environment that fulfill the mission and then to align security operations with these key resources is known as what?

    A. Enterprise risk management

    B. Enterprise security management

    C. Risk management

    D. Mission assurance

5. Given the existence of enterprise security guidance, and that enterprise employees, business partners, vendors, and other covered entities are aware and under stand the policies, standards, procedures, and guidelines, there is a need to enforce compliance in daily operations. Enforcement requires which of the following?

    A. Monitoring for noncompliance

    B. Detecting and responding to noncompliance

    C. Both a and b

    D. None of the above

6. Which of the following statements is false about the Enterprise Security Standard (ESS)?

    A. You can develop an ESS from an industry security standard or from security legislation or both.

    B. The structure of the ESS becomes the foundation for the enterprise security framework (ESF).

    C. To save money, and since the ESS is unique to each organization anyway, developing the ESS from staff experience, though somewhat arbitrary, is an acceptable practice.

    D. The enterprise security standard (ESS) is a list of all applicable security controls grouped by families.

7. Which of the following statements is true about incident response?

    A. Some potential members of an incident response team are senior management, legal, corporate communications, and operations.

    B. Incident response team (IRT) and cyber incident response team (CIRT) are similar phrases for the same organizational function.

    C. The news media will print what they want anyway, so it is okay for anyone on the security team to speak to them about security incident details.

    D. All cyber incidents are unique and upon detection are immediately escalated to subject matter experts (SMEs).

8. Which of the following statements is false?

    A. In a given environment, people perform processes using technology to produce results.

    B. Security is a support structure of safeguards for cost management and never contributes to revenue generation.

    C. A key differentiating characteristic of the cyber domain from the other domains is physical proximity.

    D. The complement to legislative compliance is good business practice.

9. What is the purpose of a service level agreement (SLA)?

    A. The SLA is only used as a formal agreement between the enterprise and external service providers to establish services, performance parameters, and financial penalties for performance outside of specified parameters.

    B. The SLA records common understanding about the services provided and the performance parameters within which to provide the services.

    C. The SLA specifies performance measurements in terms of thresholds, e.g., number of transactions per hour, available bandwidth, and downtime tolerances.

    D. The SLA is a formal agreement that specifies pay for performance within operations departments.

10. What is the enterprise risk posture?

    A. Intentionally assumed position of safeguards throughout the entire organization

    B. The probability of specific eventualities throughout the entire organization

    C. The aggregation of all the safeguards and precautions that mitigate risk

    D. The formal articulation of an intentionally assumed position on dealing with potential negative impact

11. What is data exfiltration?

    A. The unauthorized use of USB devices

    B. The unauthorized transmission of data between departments

    C. The unauthorized transmission of data into the organization from a service provider

    D. The unauthorized transmission of data out of the organization

12. Which of the following groups is not representative of the nine core security principles?

    A. Nonrepudiation, possession, utility

    B. Authorized use, privacy, authorized access

    C. Confidentiality, integrity, authenticity

    D. Availability, privacy, utility

3

Security Compliance Management

13. Which of the following is true about a Security Compliance Management Program (SCMP)?

 A. Governance identifies and enumerates all relevant security compliance requirements. These may include legislation, regulation, directives, instructions, contractual obligations, and good business practice.

 B. The planning function determines the appropriate steps to take to establish and maintain compliance. The results of planning will include a list of necessary security technologies to insert in IT operations.

 C. Implementation takes the policies, standards, procedures, and guide lines and inserts them into information technology systems. Deployment makes compliance part of daily operations throughout the enterprise.

 D. The role of adjudication is to resolve conflicts in the best interest of enterprise senior management and executives.

14. Which of the following is false about system hardening?

 A. System hardening is the elimination of known vulnerabilities, exploits, and generally turning off or uninstalling unnecessary functions.

 B. Each operating system, each version of the same operating system, and each patch release of the same operating system may have a different procedure for hardening the system.

 C. Disabling unused services will require OS parameter changes at the kernel or registry level, or modifications to services that initiate or run at startup.

 D. None of the above.

15. What is the difference between legislative management and litigation management?

 A. Litigation management is the use of lobby groups by senior management to establish working relationships with the local judiciary, and legislation management is the use of lobby groups with Congress to influence the content of security laws.

 B. Legislative management attempts to avoid litigation, and litigation management intends to minimize the negative effects on an organization in the event of an incident.

 C. Litigation management involves establishing working relationships between senior management, security personnel, and the enterprise legal department, and legislative management is the result of this working relationship.

 D. Litigation management comes before legislative management.

16. Which of the following is a true statement about digital policy management (DPM)?

    A. A digital policy infrastructure is the collection of policy managers, policy clients, PDPs, and PEPs.

    B. DPM is the process of creating and disseminating information technology (IT) policies.

    C. DPM is the automated enforcement of policy on the network.

    D. None of the above.

17. The most dangerous type of malware is

    A. A spear phishing attack because it targets a specific weakness in people.

    B. A zero day exploit because it tries to exploit unknown or undisclosed vulnerabilities.

    C. A physical breach because it is the hardest to see coming.

    D. An insider threat using a USB thumb sucker attack because of unique knowledge of the enterprise.

18. Which of the following statements about bots is false?

    A. A bot is a type of malware that performs a specific function as directed by the bot herder.

    B. A bot is a term for software robot.

    C. Successful penetration of a PC by a bot makes that PC part of a botnet.

    D. A bot has a limited lifetime, typically less than 60 days, and must perform its nefarious activities before it removes itself from the infected system.

19. What is the purpose of security policies?

    A. To provide a description of acceptable behavior within the enterprise

    B. To clearly convey the uses for security services and mechanisms within the enterprise

    C. To exert control over the organization by the security department

    D. To provide a description of acceptable behavior with the intent of minimizing risk to the organization

20. A privately held restaurant chain in New Jersey, USA is likely thinking about its compliance needs. Which is likely to apply?

    A. HIPAA

    B. GLB

    C. PCI-DSS

    D. SEC rules

3

Security Compliance Management

Domain 4
Contingency Management

As the old adage states, "failure to plan is planning to fail," and, yet, unlike the other domains in this book, this domain is dominated by the concept of failure. The secret is to understand what might cause that failure and plan to mitigate against it. If businesses operated in a static world, identifying such cause and effect scenarios would be a relatively simple activity. However, businesses operate in a dynamic environment where internal and external changes conflate to provide complex and multiple perspectives. Businesses grow, expand, contract, divest, and redirect their operations operating in local, national, multinational, and global arenas; technology advances change their modus operandi; adversaries present themselves no longer as the bored student looking for the fun of "breaking and entering" but under the guise of organized crime funding extraordinary activities. Legislation, passed to protect employees' and customers' privacy, increases the need for vigilance and protection of corporate systems, applications, and data in their four states (in situ, in flight, in backup, and in archive).

One of the greatest challenges facing the ISSMP, whether serving as a chief security officer (CSO), a chief information security officer (CISO), an IT security officer (ITSO), or any other senior position responsible for ensuring that a business is able to function under any condition, is to convince the board of directors of that need and of its importance.

Unfortunately, security, business continuity, and disaster recovery are often considered "business overhead," which does not contribute to the "bottom line." It is your role to serve as a security evangelist and convince the board that without the necessary forward planning, the impact on the business could be catastrophic and potentially fatal.

The tools we use for this are risk assessment and business impact analysis. These are not simply mathematical calculations but require an element of qualitative and quantitative analyses to assess the likelihood of any impact to business operations and revenue generation. It is, therefore, no longer sufficient for you to be technical experts in communications or systems architecture or applications development or data storage, protection, and privacy: The ISSMP must also understand the business, its strategy, and its core assets. Whether you have responsibility for the business continuity or disaster recovery, or your role is of a more technical

249

nature, understanding how each area contributes to continued success (the business needs to understand the technology, and the technology needs to understand the business) is necessary. Understanding the impact of an event or incident to business assets at a tactical or operational level is well rehearsed during the CISSP and SSCP; however, at the strategic level, we need to take the wider pan–business view to explore end-to-end processes rather than view activities in silos.

Accordingly, this domain takes a strategic view of business continuity, disaster recovery, and continuity of operations, extending the discussions of those during your CISSP and SSCP.

This domain provides step-by-step guidance of the stages involved in managing the activities involved in the strategic decision-making processes to develop the following:

- The planning, design, and development of emergency response, business continuity, disaster recovery, and continuity of operations plans, including:
  - *Personnel notification*
  - *Communications*
  - *Logistics and supplies*
  - *Documentation*
  - *Business resumption planning*
- Security awareness programs to facilitate the coordination and marketing of the plans
- Restoration of the business functions following an emergency/incident

The domain is formed into two sections:

1. The first section considers the business and the planning for the development of the business continuity, disaster recovery, and continuity of operations plans including the people, processes, planning—the what and the why.

2. The second section considers each of the components in isolation—the how.

Each of the discussions relates to the general perspectives and should be tailored to meet the requirements of your own business, your market sector, and the size of your organization, shaping each to meet your own specific context.

The primary concern for the ISSMP is to ensure integrity, availability, and confidentiality at all times (Figure 4.1). Developing appropriate strategies, policies, and plans to support the three tenets is key to promoting organization sustainability.

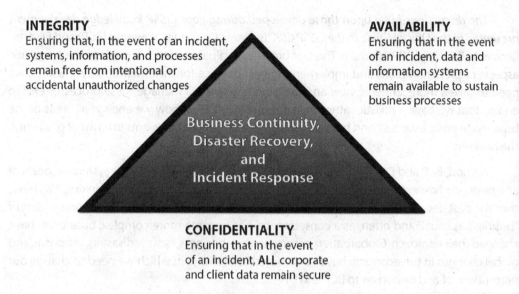

INTEGRITY
Ensuring that, in the event of an incident, systems, information, and processes remain free from intentional or accidental unauthorized changes

AVAILABILITY
Ensuring that in the event of an incident, data and information systems remain available to sustain business processes

Business Continuity, Disaster Recovery, and Incident Response

CONFIDENTIALITY
Ensuring that in the event of an incident, **ALL** corporate and client data remain secure

Figure 4.1 – Developing appropriate strategies, policies, and plans to support the three tenets is key to promoting organization sustainability.

The business continuity planning (BCP) and disaster recovery planning (DRP) domain explores the concepts, principles, and pragmatic steps for planning and executing proper BCP and DRP, and it discusses the business impact analysis and risk management and the development of enterprise recovery strategies (Figure 4.2).

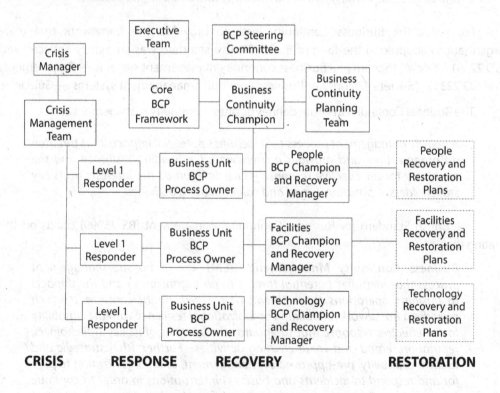

Figure 4.2 - **Roles, relationships, and responsibilities**

The discussions build upon those developed during your CISSP knowledge development presented in the Official Guide to the CISSP CBK "Business Continuity Planning (BCP) and Disaster Recovery Planning (DRP)" domain. This text provides a valuable reference guide to the pragmatic aspects of preparing plans and implementing best practice for their invocation. As ISSMPs, we need to take a more strategic view and examine how we will manage these processes end to end so that we have a holistic rather than a reductionist view, how we engage all areas of the business to ensure success, and how we can mitigate the impact of events in terms of protecting the business.

A priori, BCP and DRP were considered to reflect only the information systems aspects of any business; however, recent events have contributed to redirecting our thinking. We have, over the past decade, become more reliant on technology; it has become an integrated part of "business as usual" and often, as a consequence, has become more complex; businesses have changed their approach. Globalization, e-commerce, e-business, natural disasters, terrorism, and global changes in the economy have contributed to the ways in which we need to change our perceptions of and responses to BCP and DRP.

The terms business continuity and disaster recovery are widely used throughout the business and security communities, and yet there is sometimes confusion as to their respective definitions. IDG (idgconnect.com) defines business continuity as:

> *... the processes and procedures an organization puts into place to ensure that essential functions can continue during and after a disaster. Business continuance planning seeks to prevent interruption of mission-critical services, and to reestablish full functioning as swiftly and smoothly as possible.*

For years, the Business Continuity Institute provided the framework that many organizations adopted in the form of BS 25999; this standard was ultimately replaced with ISO 22301 - "Societal Security — Business continuity management systems — Requirements" and ISO 22313 - "Societal Security — Business continuity management systems — Guidance."

The Business Continuity Institute defines business continuity management as:

> *A holistic management process that identifies potential impacts that threaten an organization, and provides a framework for building resilience and the capability for an effective response which safeguards the interests of its key stakeholders, reputation, brand and value-creating activities.*

The British Standard for Business Continuity Management (BS 25999) builds on this, stating that:

> ***Business Continuity Management (BCM)*** *– Is a holistic management process that identifies potential threats to an organization and the impacts to business operations those threats, if realized, might cause, and which provides a framework for building organizational resilience with the capability for an effective response that safeguards the interests of its key stakeholders, reputation, brand and value-creating activities. Further, [the] strategic and tactical capability, pre-approved by management, of an organization to plan for and respond to incidents and business interruptions in order to continue business operations at an acceptable pre-defined level.*

The Disaster Recovery Institute International provides the following definitions:

Business Continuity – *The ability of an organization to provide service and support for its customers and to maintain its viability before, during, and after a business continuity event.*

Business Continuity Management – *A holistic management process that identifies potential impacts that threaten an organization and provides a framework for building resilience with the capability for an effective response that safeguards the interests of its key stakeholders, reputation, brand and value creating activities. The management of recovery or continuity in the event of a disaster. Also the management of the overall program through training, rehearsals, and reviews, to ensure the plan stays current and up to date.*

ISO 22031 defines the terms as follows:

Business Continuity – *the capability of the organization to continue delivery of products or services at acceptable predefined levels following disruptive incident.*

Business Continuity Management – *a holistic management process that identifies potential threats to an organization and the impacts to business operations those threats, if realized, might cause, and which provides a framework for building organizational resilience with the capability of an effective response that safeguards the interests of its key stakeholders, reputation, brand and value-creating activities.*

Each of these views is helpful in its own right and may reflect the view of your own organization.

In summary, we can define the difference between BC and DR as the availability of the business processes.

BC has a recovery speed that can be almost imperceptible in that the disruption to service is so brief that users of the system may not even notice that part of the system has failed. BC plans identify possible consequences of incidents and provide mitigation activities to keep the business active. To achieve this state, we can employ in-chassis operating systems and application redundancy, server clusters, traffic management software, redundant paths and network components, redundant arrays and components, and tools that offer continuous backup.

The costs for employing such high levels of redundancy may be high; however, where the systems are safety critical, such as fly-by-wire aircraft, nuclear power plant systems management, etc., or where human life would be at risk, typical configurations may have triple redundancy to ensure the best possible continuity of service.

DR, on the other hand, recognizes that there has been a break in service, a lack of availability. The DR plans provide for the recovery of the business processes within a planned downtime. The DR plan focuses on using an alternative operating base that may not be a complete duplicate of the original. We will look at how we approach the development of each of these plans and the strategic implications of our choices.

As ISSMPs, we need to take a strategic approach to address the aspects of BCM to ensure the ongoing management of the following:

- The business continuity plan to ensure that it is always current and available

- Management of operational resilience and process availability within an organization, with the aim of ensuring that the organization experiences the minimum possible day-to-day disruption

To achieve this, we need to ensure that we have the following:

1. An enterprise-wide business continuity strategy

2. Communication and coordination across the business units

The content of this domain extends the discussion from that held in the CISSP literature, providing more detail from a management perspective. For the benefit of readers, and particularly of those readers whose primary activities are not in the business continuity or disaster recovery arena, refresher points have been included.

TOPICS

Contingency management refers to the process by which contingency plans are created, established, managed, and utilized; as discussed in the Official (ISC)² Guide to the CISSP CBK, it is the process of establishing actions to be taken before, during, and after a threatening incident.

Contingency management plans are designed to prevent serious incidents that could disrupt information services, and to ensure that information services – including the security of information services -- can recover and continue to provide service even in the event of some serious "incident" or series of incidents. Business continuity and disaster recovery planning, as discussed in detail throughout this domain, are significant elements of contingency management.

Security managers play a critical role in the continuity of business operations. As many organizations are critically reliant on their information systems infrastructure, the need to ensure that computer systems are operational, and continuously meet the needs of the business, is an important requirement for security managers, risk officers, and auditors. This domain looks at the broad picture of business continuity—keeping the business operational. It also looks at the more focused aspect of disaster recovery—restoring the information systems themselves. Information security managers also have the responsibility of continuing to provide operational support for the organization; this includes potentially help desk and user support, control center management and coordination during an incident and rehabilitation from backup of data, configurations during an incident, and documentation.

OBJECTIVES

The CISSP-ISSMP candidate should be able to:

- Understand the concepts of enterprise business continuity planning and disaster recovery.

- Understand enterprise recovery strategy development.

- Understand project planning.

- Understand the design and development of plans.

- Implement and market plans.

- Understand restoration planning.

4

Communications & Network Security

Contingency Plans

This section explores the different types of plans that may form a library of documentation to provide for continuity of business operations.

Types of Plans

Within the domain of BCP and DRP, we need to develop a library of plans that collectively reflect all aspects of the business and the different perspectives affected by an event or incident. To provide the detail for each of these plans, we need to understand the Sustain, Protect, Recover/Resume trefoil (see *Figure 4.3*). How we view each of these three "leaves" will be organization, context, and culturally dependent. However, we can take as a measure and direction the business drivers that guide our organization, aligning with our risk appetite. It is key to remember that these are all living documents. The threat vectors and risk appetite frontiers are dynamic and fluid. The more agile we can make our policy planning, the greater benefit we can derive and the more responsive we become.

The next section provides an example range (but not definitive list) of possible business drivers that might influence your strategic considerations. We must always remember that business continuity, disaster recovery, and continuity of operations strategies and plans are not optional extras and are not independent of the core business objectives and strategy. Everything we do is to keep the business delivering and generating revenue by keeping our internal and external customers confident and our suppliers all through the supply chain engaged.

Business Drivers

The benefits of developing comprehensive business continuity and disaster recovery plans include the following:

- Minimizing potential economic loss
- Decreasing potential exposures
- Reducing the probability of occurrence
- Reducing disruptions to operations
- Ensuring organizational stability
- Providing an orderly recovery
- Minimizing insurance premiums
- Reducing reliance on certain key individuals
- Protecting the assets of the organization
- Ensuring the safety of personnel and customers
- Minimizing decision making during a disastrous event
- Minimizing legal liability

Plan	Purpose	Scope
Business Continuity Plan (BCP)	To provide procedures to sustain core business operations while recovering from significant disruption	Addresses business functions, accommodating information technology in the context of supporting the impacted business processes
Business Recovery Plan (BRP)	To provide procedures for recovering business operations immediately following a disaster	Addresses the business processes and is not information technology focused
Continuity of Operations Plan (COOP)	Identifies and establishes procedures and capabilities to sustain an organization's essential, strategic functions for a limited period of time while reparation takes place (usually a time limit of 30 days)	Addresses the organization's mission-critical functions and is not usually information technology focused
Continuity of Support Plan (COSP)	Establishes instructions or procedures that describe in detail how, in the event of a significant disruption, to sustain general support systems and major applications.	This plan addresses the information technology system disruption and is not business focused
Disaster Recovery Plan (DRP)	Provides details of procedures to facilitate recovery capabilities at the original or another permanent site	Often information technology focused; implemented when maximum tolerable downtime has been exceeded and in response to long-term effects
Incident Response Plan	Defines the strategies to detect, respond to, and limit the consequences of incidents that can impact the business	Focuses on information security responses to incidents affecting systems or networks
Occupant Emergency Plan	Provides coordinated procedures for minimizing loss of life or injury and protecting property damage in response to a physical threat	Focuses on personnel and property particular to the specific facility and is not business or IT focused
Emergency Response Plan	Provides details for protecting employees, visitors, contractors, and anyone else in the facility in the event of an emergency	Focuses on life safety, incident stabilization, and conserving property when possible.

Table 4.1 – **Library of plans that collectively reflect all aspects of the business and the different perspectives affected by an event or incident**

Continuity of Operations Plan

As discussed in the *Official (ISC)² Guide to the CISSP CBK*, a COOP is a document that describes the procedures and capabilities needed to sustain an organization's essential strategic functions at an alternative location to its usual place of operations for a period of up to thirty days.

Understanding BCP and DRP

In *Figure 4.3,* we identify the different plans in our library. Each entry shows the focus of the plan and the perspective, whether a business focus or a technical focus. Each of the plans should:

- Be developed in consultation with the key stakeholders as appropriate.
- Be developed in alignment with core business objectives.
- Take account of the business risk appetite.
- Mitigate current threat vectors.

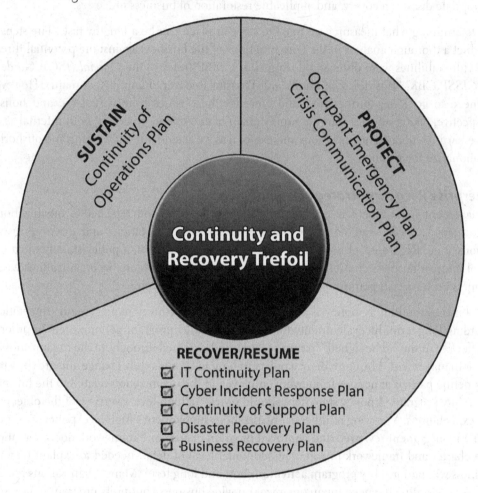

SUSTAIN
Continuity of
Operations Plan

PROTECT
Occupant Emergency Plan
Crisis Communication Plan

**Continuity and
Recovery Trefoil**

RECOVER/RESUME
☑ IT Continuity Plan
☑ Cyber Incident Response Plan
☑ Continuity of Support Plan
☑ Disaster Recovery Plan
☑ Business Recovery Plan

Figure 4.3 – **Positioning of the library of plans that collectively reflect all aspects of the business and the different perspectives affected by an event or incident**

What should be clear from this list of conditions is that we are reminded that each of the plans must be considered as living documents. As core business objectives, key stakeholders, risk parameters, and threat vectors change, we must update the library of plans.

The next section examines the concepts of policy development and the content and production of policies and plans from a generic perspective. The formal approach to development provides a baseline for inclusion, and these may be adapted to meet your organization's needs.

Policy Development and Strategy Planning

Some organizations have no BC or DR plans at all. True to say that many have been created and placed on a shelf to collect dust, only to see the light of day during an audit or if an incident occurs (when it is too late to ensure that the plans reflect the current processes and systems in place). However, in our dynamic climate, as organizations grow from local to national to international and beyond or merge with or take over other organizations, downsize, outsource, or offshore, we need to reconsider our strategic plans to promote secure business continuity, appropriate disaster recovery, and applicable restoration of business processes.

Determining what measures we need to have in place can be a lengthy task. The steps to conduct a thorough analysis of the core functions of the business against the potential threats and vulnerabilities were discussed during your CISSP (refer to the *Official (ISC)² Guide to the CISSP CBK*, "Business Continuity and Disaster Recovery Planning" domain). However, we need to go a step further now and consider these issues from a strategic and holistic perspective, taking into account the supply chain of end-to-end processes, both internal as we move toward federated organizations and external as we extend our outsourcing and offshoring to rationalize the business.

Enterprise Recovery Strategy Development

Management involvement is not the only driving force behind repeatable, organizational performance. Short, concise policy statements also set expectations and drive consistent performance. Regardless of the size or culture of an organization, a policy statement can be a tool to drive business continuity program performance, particularly in organizations where business professionals perform planning in a decentralized manner.

A business continuity policy is a document written to convey management expectations regarding long-term, lifecycle-oriented business continuity program performance. In order to be effective, it should be signed, communicated, and enforced throughout the organization by senior management. The contents of a policy statement should rarely change and are such that they define particular actions from every employee in the organization related to the business continuity program. A policy statement should provide a high-level overview of the objectives and expectations. A growing number of organizations supplement a high-level policy statement with a management reviewed and approved program charter and framework documentation. The charter and framework provide the additional level of detail needed to explain how the business will perform key program activities, short and long term. Many organizations remain skeptical regarding the need for an organization-wide business continuity program policy, so it is important to understand the benefits of authoring and approving one.

A well-written policy that describes the program's key role players and their responsibilities provides clear expectations for business continuity personnel, senior management, key program contributors, and all other employees. A policy prevents the need for the program to waste valuable time reinventing itself year after year. Instead, it allows the organization to align its culture and operations around a single, simple, and repeatable vision for organizational resiliency and recoverability.

Because many business continuity programs fight for attention among all the other priorities of an organization, a business continuity program's worst enemy can be inconsistent execution.

Consistent execution provides the basis for a program to integrate with the organization's strategy, operations, and even other risk management disciplines. In many cases, a program's effectiveness is only as strong as its weakest link. For example, a program that consistently updates plan documentation but fails to perform exercises or train its personnel continues to take on unnecessary business risk. Policy statements set organizational and management objectives, which in turn provide the necessary motivation to complete needed business continuity activities and remove such risk.

Business continuity program benchmarking can be challenging. When one is comparing a variety of program capabilities and elements across the organization, it can be difficult to evaluate progress or performance; however, the policy can serve as that internal benchmark for management's review of the program. Each year, a policy should be reviewed and re-evaluated in light of the strategic vision management sets for the organization and the business continuity program. This process of reviewing and updating the policy, when necessary, provides an up-to-date and measurable benchmark for how the business continuity program aligns with the organization's goals. When the cliché "what gets measured gets done" holds favorably with senior management, the business continuity program can leverage its policy to provide a measurable evaluation of the program's performance.

Business Continuity Policy

A business continuity policy is a document that provides a high-level overview of the organizations' policies regarding BC and DR. This document can be quite short because it is not the actual BC or DR plan, just a high level overview of policies. Typically, policies will include items such as the goal of having the BC/DR policy, definition of what the policies are, clear delineation of who is responsible for the policy (for creating, approving changes, for implementing and enforcing it, etc.), what the repercussions are for people and groups who do not obey the policy, and how the organization will check that people obey it (i.e., how does it measure compliance with the policy). A business continuity policy can also play the important role of helping to create vision for organizational continuity and recoverability, especially when there are no dedicated BC or DR personnel. The policy, when communicated across the entire organization, provides a common set of expectations.

The policy should be created in conjunction with all business units impacted, and with the legal and HR departments.

Objections to developing a business continuity policy are often culturally driven. In many cases, objections to policy statements occur because the organization has few policies governing other business activities. These concerns are understandable in organizations that do not have policies in the format described above or cultures where policy alone does not have the power to create change. In these situations, less formal methods of communicating expectations may suffice, even if the tool is not a formal policy statement. A management-approved alignment to a standard may be the answer or a less formal email or letter from a senior executive. Overall, it may take some creativity, but a management-approved mandate is necessary to build a repeatable program that consistently executes necessary program elements, enables performance measurement, and clearly communicates program expectations.

Whether or not an organization historically creates policy statements, leadership should consider developing formal business continuity program expectations. When it is done right, all of an organization's stakeholders align behind a common set of expectations. Competition in the marketplace and reliance on intrinsic information systems are critical elements that are driving organizations to recognize the need for business continuity and disaster recovery to support continuity of operations. Accordingly, many now employ teams of dedicated business continuity and disaster recovery professionals. Establishing management expectations by focusing on the core business functions is critically important to the successful development and adoption of any business continuity and disaster recovery policy.

Aligning BC and DR Policies with the Human Resource Policy

The importance of aligning the BC and DR policies and plans with human resource (HR) policies cannot be emphasized enough.

Part of the dilemma in planning for business continuity is the myriad of human issues to be dealt with—the human resource policies and procedures that impact employees involved in the response to disaster. Human resources encompasses so many factors that it is difficult to identify and plan for all the issues in a logical manner. However, using the phases of the BC and DR plans, we can identify four key phases:

1. Pre-disaster (planning phase)
2. Emergency response (what do you do when the event occurs?)
3. Recovery (what do you do while you are in the process of using that part of your plan which recovers your business?)
4. Post-recovery (what are the long-term recovery issues?)

Pre-Disaster Planning Issues

There are two principles that are very important. The first is communicating expectations. More than any function within an organization, the human resource function is the keeper of the organization's expectations. It is usually through the human resource office that company announcements are made and company policies are announced that, in fact, the will of executive management is enforced. It is through the human resource office that we would expect very clear goals, guidelines, and expectations set out for employees regarding business continuity. This should be communicated as part of an employee handbook. The handbook should:

- Discuss continuity.
- Describe the expectations of the company regarding the employee being present and helping to restore the business in the event of a disruption.
- Describe the employee's responsibility for notifying management of conditions that may lead to a disruption of work, e.g., fire extinguishers that are not charged, exit lights that are burned out, or other obvious possible hazards.

BC and DR should also be covered as part of the induction program. Clearly communicating expectations for employee response is the most important element of pre-disaster planning.

The second principle involves planning for an emergency work environment. There are many issues to be resolved during the planning phase that will impact your recovery plan execution. For example, your recovery plan may call for employees to be relocated at an alternate site in another town or another state. When the personnel arrive:

- Where will they live?
- How will their living costs and needs be cared for?
- How will they be paid?
- Will they work normal or extended shifts?
- Will they get overtime for extended shifts?
- Will they get compensatory time?

Exploring alternatives and preparing strategies in advance will promote a smoother transition in the event of an incident occurring.

Emergency Response and Occupant Emergency Planning

When one is planning for the emergency response phase, there are a number of issues to be discussed. The important one for human resources is readiness. While other parts of the organization are evacuating and beginning the recovery response, human resources is expected to be prepared and functional as a critical business unit.

One of the first issues for the human resources function is employee life and safety, and even fatalities. You must have some way within your organization to know where employees are and what has happened to them. Any event that affects the building to the extent that you may have to invoke your business resumption plan may have also caused injuries or fatalities. Questions to be asked include the following:

- Who is responsible for calling the emergency services?
- How will first responders get into the building?
- What is the company's role once employees are evacuated?
- What is the company's responsibility to find safe haven or medical treatment for employees?

In your organization, whose responsibility is it to ensure an employee's safe passage to a hospital? Is it the role of HR or the role of the employee's manager?

Another human resources issue has to do with notifying families of injured or missing employees. Some companies leave it up to the individual supervisor; others leave it to human resources to contact the family in any kind of event, whether it is a fatality or an injury. It is important that human resources have the recovery items it needs to do this job.

How the incident is communicated to the outside world is also important. Clearly there will be communication with the media. Protecting the corporate image is important; however, it may be the first notice families of employees have that an emergency has occurred. So the issue then becomes, "How do we notify families in a conscientious way?"

Part of the issue is communicating with and accounting for employees. How do you know that all of the employees are out of the building? If you don't have a very effective emergency response program that has regularly scheduled fire drills and floor monitors and those sorts of things, you may have a lot of work to do. It is vitally important for that to be done.

Recovery Issues

To ensure maximum engagement by individual employees in the event of an incident, you should involve them in the planning process and tell them at the business unit level what is expected of them during business recovery, and how they are expected to respond. Involving the employees, at a variety of levels, in planning the response will ensure excellent ideas and an effective response; after all, they work at the operational level and will have a clear understanding of the layout of their work area and of people's habits and activities that may not be officially recorded elsewhere.

During recovery, your organization will be working in an "organizationally altered state." For example, you may have very altered work schedules, some very different than you normally have. Some plans call for recovery teams to work longer days but fewer days per week, to avoid burnout. Such changes need to be reflected in the payroll system or in leave balance calculations, or absentee reports.

The work being processed in an emergency response is usually the most critical work; thus a change to shift patterns, extended days but shorter weeks, may be more effective and result in greater productivity.

Locating an HR team at the command and control center optimizes efficiency, reducing the need for communications and having a single point of contact for employees and families, and reducing duplication and the potential for ambiguity.

More importantly, it immediately creates a presence for carrying out the plan, specifically:

- Notifying employees when their business units are expected to resume partial or full activity.
- Filling critical vacancies through temporary services.
- Coordinating employee assistance for those employees impacted by the outage.
- Providing management with issues and concerns that may need their attention regarding employees.

During recovery, the human resource function also will be called on to assist employees in a heightened manner. What kind of assistance might you plan for? The literature is replete with all kinds of company assistance programs that organizations have put together to handle major cataclysmic events, including the following:

- Emergency food
- Emergency cash
- Providing cash
- Storage of household goods

These factors are important to have considered in the recovery plan. The extent to which employees' basics needs and those of their families are taken care of will determine the extent to which the employee is able to focus on recovering the business.

Post-Disaster Issues

In the post-disaster environment, there are a number of human resource issues that are better considered in advance as, alongside the practicalities of managing staff, the issues often carry fiscal implications. At a time when the organization will be experiencing a high level of spending to recover the business, unexpected added costs would not be welcomed. If members of staff are not part of the recovery team and therefore not working, there should be a clear statement of policy regarding pay, leave, and benefits cover for the duration.

While often overlooked, the human resource part of business recovery is a vital link between the employees who produce the recovery and the plan that guides it. However, very little in the development of a business recovery plan can be ignored by human resources. Careful consideration of the issues will allow those planning a business recovery to protect and support its most critical resource — its employees.

Project Planning

The term "project planning" for business continuity is anathema. A project implies a specific start and end date, a budget, and a set objective. However, the concept of BC and DR is that it is a continuous process, rarely is there a budget set, and further, how can we measure the quality of our plans until the worst happens? However, we can take the principles and apply them well in order to provide us with a structure or framework. Thus, our project plans are not the business continuity and disaster recovery plans themselves but the formulation of those plans at the outset.

Our project plan needs to identify the major phases and the activities that comprise individual phases, the resources required to undertake the different activities, and the governance to apply quality controls to the project. The governance should identify the reporting structure, all of the documentation to support the project, the schedule of meetings and who will attend them, the risks and issues associated with the project, and the deliverables.

The Process for Developing the Plans

A top-down view in *Figure 4.4* provides four distinct stages in the development of business continuity plans.

Understanding the organization requires a strategic understanding of the core business functions, the organization's risk appetite, and the information technology infrastructure that supports the business.

Each of the plans as identified in the previous section should be considered as living documents. As a consequence, we should not see their creation as linear but as cyclic.

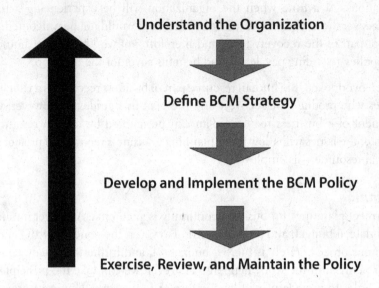

Understand the Organization

Define BCM Strategy

Develop and Implement the BCM Policy

Exercise, Review, and Maintain the Policy

Figure 4.4 – **The four distinct stages in the development of business continuity plans**

Figure 4.5 illustrates a more detailed lifecycle for the continuous development and communication of strategic policies to mitigate business risks and address vulnerabilities in a dynamic environment where threats are constantly changing.

Further, each of the activities identified in the cycle is also cyclic and repetitive in nature. You will notice that each of the activities has communication with the central monitor, control, and communicate. The Business Continuity Security Steering Group, discussed on the next couple pages, should undertake this function.

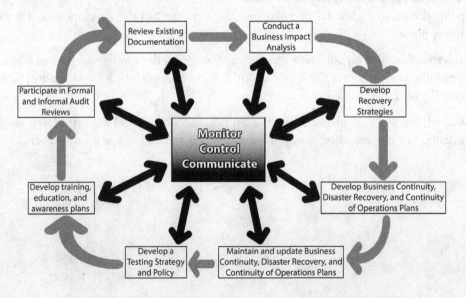

Figure 4.5 – **Detailed lifecycle for continuous development and communication of strategic policies to mitigate business risks and address vulnerabilities in a dynamic environment where threats are constantly changing**

Project Reporting Structure

Business continuity and disaster recovery impact business processes across the organization. Accordingly, it is appropriate that the project team should comprise representatives from each business process area defined in *Figure 4.6*. To demonstrate sponsorship and support, the BC and DR project team will report to a steering committee. The BC and DR project team may be led by a nontechnical project manager as the team itself will comprise business and technical experts from each of the business divisions. Representatives will differ according to the structure of your organization.

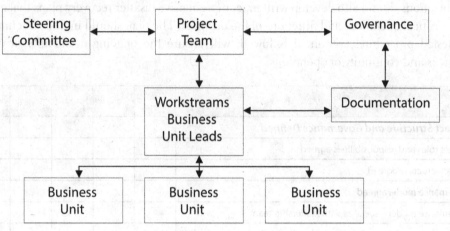

Figure 4.6 – **Business continuity and disaster recovery project reporting structure**

Steering Committee

The purpose of the steering committee is to provide a strategic, holistic view of business continuity, disaster recovery, and continuity of operations across the enterprise. The scope and mandate of the steering committee should be clearly defined in the terms of reference. These should be developed in full consultation with representatives from the business, the technical, and the security domains across all elements of the organization.

Business Managers

Business managers are key to any business continuity, disaster recovery, and continuity of operations. They understand the prioritization of the impact to the business of the loss of any operational component at whichever layer of the security "onion" the component may reside. Their role is to advise on the impact of a "systems" failure to the business on fiscal, human, reputation, and operating activities. Accordingly, they should determine strategic priorities where conflicts of priorities arise.

Stakeholders

Other stakeholders may include customer-facing managers, business development managers, and third-party managers.

The Business Continuity and Disaster Recovery Project Steering Committee

In order for business continuity and disaster recovery to receive support within your organization, it should have champions and sponsors at the highest level. The steering committee should comprise senior managers from the business and technical areas of the business to ensure that all areas of the business are protected.

The Project Team Identification of Roles, Responsibilities, and Accountability

Disaster recovery planning involves more than off-site storage or backup processing. Organizations should also develop written, comprehensive disaster recovery plans that address all the critical operations and functions of the business. The plan should include documented and tested procedures, which, if followed, will ensure the ongoing availability of critical resources and continuity of operations.

Project BC and DR Plans Key Milestones	Owner	Planned Start	Actual Start	Planned Finish	Actual Finish
Project Structure and Governance Defined					
Project roles and responsibilities agreed					
Project structure agreed					
Governance model agreed					
Governance model—socialize with leadership team					
Governance model—socialize and sign off with Steering Group					
Risk management plan—review with Project Team					
Risk management plan sign-off at Leadership Team					
Risk management plan sign-off at Steering Group					
Communications and Engagement plan sign-off at Leadership Team					
Communications and Engagement plan sign-off at Steering Group					
Risk Analysis					
Scope risk appetite					
Business impact analysis					
E2E process risk assessment					
Data Gathering					
Due diligence planning workshop					
Review evaluation criteria					
HR input to evaluation criteria					
Commercial input					
Financial input					
Operations input					
Legal input					
E2E service input					
Systems input					

Project BC and DR Plans Key Milestones	Owner	Planned Start	Actual Start	Planned Finish	Actual Finish
Development of Plans					
Develop Business Continuity Plan					
Develop Disaster Recovery Plan					
Develop Continuity of Operations Plan					
Develop Business Recovery Plan					
Test Plans					
Desktop—Operational Processes					
Desktop—Tactical End-to-End Processes					
Desktop—Strategic					
Live Exercise					
Training, Education, and Awareness					
Plan and build workshops					
Deliver workshops					
Review evaluation criteria					

Table 4.2 – **An example of the stages and activities you might consider for inclusion when developing the business continuity and disaster recovery project plans**

Business Continuity Plan and Disaster Recovery Plan—Project Planning

Developing the plan is a seven-stage process. However, you should remember from your CISSP that this is not a linear process but an iterative one, and that there should be continuous feedback between the stages.

Develop Contingency Planning Policy

While some may be tempted to miss this stage, it is probably the most important of the seven steps. According to the National Institute of Technology (NIST) description, the "policy provides the authority and guidance necessary to develop an effective contingency plan." Gaining the "authority and guidance necessary" is vital to the success of the planning venture because without these, you do not have a sponsor.

The policy statement is about effective communication between management and those responsible for developing the plan. Using the business goals as drivers for the project promotes and supports the level of financial and other resources the effort commands and guides the people who are to be responsible. The policy statement provides the planners with the information they need to work out options that can achieve the organization's goals. It also provides a basis for planners to communicate back to management either their success or the need to reassess the goals or the resources, should that be necessary.

This is an iterative process and may require several attempts and discussions to ensure that the appropriate level of engagement with the appropriate stakeholders has been entertained to achieve the desired outcomes. It is possible that you will need to re-evaluate the policy and scale down goals, scale up resources, or attempt some radical rethinking.

4

Contingency Management

Objectives

Establish the types of disasters you are going to cover in your plan. Recall from your CISSP the types of disasters you may experience. Not all will be relevant to your organization. For example, you may not operate primarily in a geographic location that experiences earthquakes. However, in this era of global sourcing, off-shoring, and global operations, there are few organizations that may not be affected in some way either directly or at some point in the supply chain. Remember, different threats require different types of solutions, but all will involve people, systems, and data, and all business continuity, disaster recovery, and continuity of operations solutions will require the same level of integrity, availability, and confidentiality as your production sites.

In establishing your plan, you must also consider your intended recovery time objectives (RTOs). This may not only be for operational purposes. As a manager taking the strategic business perspective and not merely the tactical and operational views that you took as a CISSP or SSCP, you need to consider damage to reputation, shareholder views and stocks, and share values. There may also be governance, compliance, regulatory, and legislative challenges that you must accommodate in your considerations, for example, any service level agreements to which you have signed up with your customers. Not meeting delivery deadlines could incur penalty payments. Breaching the security of your data could lead to prosecution under the Data Protection Act or the Patriot Act, as applicable.

Your plan should, therefore, prioritize the end-to-end processes that must be transferred to the new operations site. These will be defined within the scope.

Scope

The scope of the plans may be challenging to establish if your organization is a complex, multifaceted one. You need to clearly identify the various components of the plan to establish which entities will be covered. For example, will only IT hardware and software systems be covered? Will you include the different layers of staff involved and non-IT systems between the IT infrastructure and the external functions that depend on them all?

In general, it is helpful to break up an organization's overall DR plan into a number of more limited and simpler plans. An outside-in approach works best, with the internal resources covered by one plan becoming the source of external requirements for the next level in.

It is timely to remind you of the defense-in-depth that was covered on your CISSP. This is summarized in *Figure 4.7*.

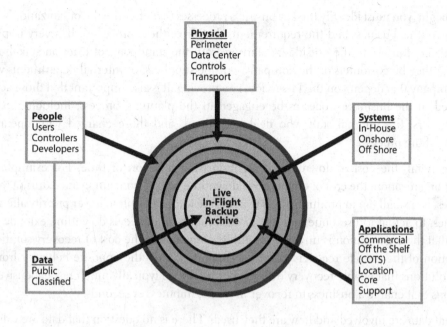

Figure 4.7 – **Defense-in-Depth model, a layered approach to security**

You should, however, establish the maximum level of resources that the plan can command during preparation, implementation, testing, and maintenance. You should ensure that you include constraints on all relevant resources: financial, staffing, equipment, space, etc.

You will also need to establish who is responsible for the various components of the plan and their level of authority. Identifying who has the right to make final decisions and what the appropriate reporting structure is will be key.

It is important that the policy statement and the entire plan are recorded. The policy will not only guide the initial development of the plan, it should also guide maintenance and review in the future, since it states the purpose and the expectations for resources on an ongoing basis. The plan will provide a written record of the stages and activities to achieve the policy. Recording both in a central location will ensure that appropriate persons may access them as and when required. Refer to the Governance section for the types and purpose of documentation.

The Business Impact Analysis (BIA) Process

The business impact analysis (BIA) helps to identify and prioritize critical IT systems and components. The purpose of this step is to ensure that you are protecting everything that you need to protect, without wasting resources on systems that are of secondary importance. The goal is to determine what must be recovered and how fast; this information will be used to develop recovery strategies. The output of this step is a prioritized list of critical data, roles, and IT resources that support your organization's business processes, together with maximum outage times for each of the critical systems.

To begin, you must identify the key business processes that underlie the organization's ability to carry out its business and the requirements that drive these processes. It is very important that this be done from the outside-in, starting from the standpoint of external stakeholders, whether they be customers of the company, outside suppliers, or internal departments within the company that depend on the IT services you provide. It is also important that those actually involved in the business processes be engaged in the planning process, including external stakeholders, the internal staff who deal with them, and those charged with operational support of the process.

In general, the cost of downtime is an increasing function of time. For example, in a typical organization, the cost of email server downtime ranges from annoyance during the first minutes, to a small dip in productivity as workers are forced to shift to lower priority alternative activities, to actual lost revenue and loss of customer confidence as downtime extends to the point that the organization is unable to fulfill its obligations. The cost of recovery solutions as a function of the time to recovery that they support exhibits the opposite behavior from the first. Solutions that enable recovery over days or weeks are typically much less expensive than solutions that enable a business to recover in hours, minutes, or seconds.

What data are involved and how are they used? There is no question that data are valuable. However, your organization has generated and stored so much data that to consider loading all of the data, for DR in particular, would require storage on terabyte storage devices and be a lengthy process to recover it all. Part of your considerations should, therefore, be to establish exactly what data are required by the prioritized core business functions and ensure availability for that subset. Ask questions, such as the following:

- How do I determine the relative value of the data?
- How will the value of the data change with time or classification?
- Will the value impact where the data are physically stored?

Remember that your data are commercially sensitive, and depending on the work of your organization, they could be politically or nationally sensitive with a high security classification. Thus it is important that whatever measures your plans offer for the availability to the data, you retain the level of confidentiality.

Table 4.3 represents a sample data classification and data placement profile according to corporate priorities.

Priority and Category	Subcategory	Cached	Online	Offline Archived	Offline Vaulted
1 Business Value					
	Customer applications and data				
	Customer support (data produced internally/externally, accessed, processed, reporting, updated)				
	Operations (business, technical, operational data)				
	Internal (payroll, benefits, employee data)				

Priority and Category	Subcategory	Cached	Online	Offline Archived	Offline Vaulted
2 Access Frequency					
	Day-to-day				
	Monthly				
	Periodic within or at yearly intervals				
	Longer than 1 year				
3 Cost and Risk					
	Utilize current infrastructure (leverage investment in hardware, software, personnel)				
	The risk is overtaxing resources				
	Outsourced infrastructure (including overtaxing and access security)				
	Shared responsibility (supply chain partners)				
4 Retention Period/Compliance Policy					
	Day-to-day				
	Monthly				
	Periodic within or at yearly intervals				
	1, 3, 5, … year intervals				

Table 4.3 – **Sample Data Classification and Placement Profile according to corporate priorities**

Data that are used or generated in the process must be accounted for separately from equipment and roles. Unlike a system or role, data cannot be replaced and often cannot be repaired. It must, therefore, somehow be copied and the copy later used to restore the data. You should consider as well the role each process plays in the lifecycle of the data: Which process creates the data, which processes use it, and where and through which process is it stored and maintained?

We are therefore taking an end-to-end view of the data and the processes that contribute to the data life. You should note that the points of division between layers or processes are different for different organizations. Examples of criteria that may be used to determine how best to subdivide the overall process into systems and subsystems include departmental lines; oversight, maintenance, and management roles; substitutability by manual or other systems; complexity and size; and, of course, common sense.

One helpful way to work through this phase of the task is to perform a mental or actual walkthrough of each process, with the participation of all those who are normally involved. This can help ensure that you do not miss critical dependencies that may not be immediately obvious. I have found that taking a roll of wallpaper and mapping the dependent processes and sub-processes focuses the mind and facilitates the walkthrough of different elements of data.

This dependency chart will also illuminate which of the components are critical to the system and the order in which they should be recovered if an incident occurs.

The result of this outside-in phase of the analysis is, for each business process, a complete list of systems involved, points of contact between systems, and performance and availability requirements at each point.

The Inside-Out Analysis

The inside-out phase focuses on resources that are required in each layer in order to provide the services that have been identified in the previous phase. Beginning from the deepest system or layer, list all IT and infrastructure resources that are required for them to function. Next, for each of these resources, determine the impact of a disruption in the availability of the resource on the functioning of the system and its ability to deliver the services on which outer layers depend. In particular, determine the maximum allowable outage time for each resource before it causes unacceptable disruption in essential functions—essentially, the point at which the availability of the system falls below the most stringent requirement of all the systems that depend on it. Be sure to include in the analysis any indirect impact that may occur through related or dependent systems.

The cost for any outage can be calculated using a variety of data. For example, if you are processing customer orders, you can calculate the total value of historic order levels against your recovery time objectives. Remember to add in any penalty payments.

What are the points of contact between the current process or system and any other systems on which it depends? The answer to this question gives us the next layer of the onion and how it interfaces with the current one. For example, the sales process may involve personnel working with a customer relationship management (CRM) system. The point of contact there may be via a Web portal into the CRM application.

The CRM application is itself a system that may consist of Web servers, CRM application servers, and database servers, all with the portal as a point of contact with the sales process. Later you may consider the CRM layer and its points of contact with, for example, the storage systems, if they are administered separately. At the end of the chain, of course, are basic infrastructure resources and systems such as electric power, telecommunications connections, and environmental control systems; these must be considered as well since they may well be impacted by some of the disruptions for which contingency planning is being undertaken.

What are the critical roles in the process? The point of this information is twofold. First, in many cases these roles must be taken into account for recovery. If a process requires the intervention of a person for monitoring, management, analysis, or maintenance on a regular basis, how long can the process run without that role in a crisis? For IT systems, in particular, there may be IT administrator roles that will play a critical part both in the recovery and in running systems for the duration of the crisis. The second reason these roles are important is that the people in them represent critical sources of information for determining system dependencies and requirements. These are the people who must be closely involved both in this phase of the planning and in subsequent testing.

Essentially, the same analysis should be performed for data and roles. Again, what is the impact that results from unavailability or loss of data or from the inability of someone to fulfill a specific role? In the latter case, this may occur because the person is injured or otherwise prevented from performing his or her duties, but it may also be a result of the lack of access. After natural disasters (e.g., Hurricane Sandy), terrorist attacks (e.g., September 11th), or medical pandemics (e.g., SARS outbreak in 2003), people might be quite capable of working but unable to do so because they lack access to the resources they need.

Carrying out this sequence of analyses yields, in effect, a full chart of dependencies that runs from the outermost layer of business processes to the innermost layer of core infrastructure on resources, people, and data. This is a very valuable tool for later test development and maintenance and should be included in the disaster recovery plan in the System Description and Architecture section described later. Once this analysis is complete, it is time to develop recovery priorities for IT systems and individual components, beginning with the latter. This task is straightforward if the work described in this section has been done thoroughly because the priorities follow naturally from the outage impact and allowable outage times recorded for each component. There are many possible scales that may be used for labelling priorities, from a simple high-medium-low qualitative scale to a numerical scale to a scale more focused on business impact, such as "customer-facing high" versus "management and control" versus "low priority maintenance." Whatever scale you use, it is important that the scale be uniform across all systems based on business impact. In some cases, it may be all right to use a different scale internally within a process or system, as long as system-level values remain mutually consistent.

Recovery priorities must be developed at the system level as well. Consistency is obviously vital—it will not work for one system to have a higher priority than another system on which it critically depends, unless it can continue to function without the dependency at an acceptable level. It is convenient to transfer system level priorities to a Master System Information Form (SIF), which lists each system together with a very brief description of its purpose, the recovery priority, maximum outage time and business impact, major dependencies on other systems, and a brief description of the recovery strategy after it has been developed in Step 4.

Planning, Designing, and Development of Plans

The planning process for developing the business continuity plan (BCP) and the disaster recovery plan (DRP) is not too dissimilar to any other project planning activity.

- *Step 1* – Develop the Planning Policy Statement
- *Step 2* – Conduct a Business Impact Analysis
- *Step 3* – Identify Preventative Measures
- *Step 4* – Develop Recovery Strategies
- *Step 5* – Develop the Plan
- *Step 6* – Plan Testing, Training, and Exercises
- *Step 7* – Plan Maintenance

Step 1: Develop the Planning Policy Statement

Consensus by executive board members and a collective understanding that there is a need for business continuity and disaster recovery is a realization that does not come easily within many organizations, yet it is critical for continuity of operations and mitigation against loss of business. This realization often comes too late. Take for example the IRA bombing at Canary Wharf in February 1996. The immediate damage to buildings was estimated at £85 million. The consequential loss to businesses that were unable to continue operations following their evacuation has never been reported. None, however, had the ability to move operations in a timely manner. After 9/11 – just half a decade later – businesses without plans in place suffered similar failures.

The point is that the "it will never happen to us" attitude is highly problematic.

The Planning Policy Statement should identify the organization's overall contingency objectives and provide a framework and the individual responsibilities for contingency measures. These measures fall into a number of categories and will vary from organization to organization depending on culture, political stance, market sector, and whether it is public or private sector. The following are examples of what you might include but is by no means a definitive list.

Aligning to your ethics as a CISSP, clearly a primary inclusion should be to protect human life. Thus your policy needs to identify this as a priority statement.

Minimizing loss and risk to the organization and maximizing the ability to recover will naturally form a part of your policy plan, as without either of these there will be no business. This may sound obvious, yet how many times do we overlook the obvious while focusing on what are actually less business-critical issues?

We live in a litigious world where alleged breaches of contract and subsequent fiscal penalties can lead to the demise of organizations that do not have the ability to pay. Further, in the U.K., inappropriate handling of information can lead to fines by the Information Commissioners Office and consequential brand damage which could, with the right planning policy, have been mitigated; thus maintaining customer confidence and goodwill can be critical to business continuity.

So, in our policy plan, we need to define from a strategic perspective what is at stake if we fail to plan. We can identify from a holistic perspective an overview of a preliminary business impact analysis. Different incidents will affect different organizations in different ways and to greater and lesser extents.

Finally, we need to think about a recovery strategy. Consider what would be most appropriate for your organization structure. Perhaps you work in a global organization; you might consider a recovery strategy that employs resources from across the globe rather than in a similar geographic location. Of course, your recovery strategy will reflect the maturity, the size of your organization, and the nature of your business.

Developing the strategic policy plan will not be an easy task and will require input and agreement from all board members. Your role will be to convince each of its importance to the continued survival of your organization. However, once completed, you can then start the journey to develop the granular level of detail that will give your policy life.

4

Step 2: Business Impact Analysis

The rationale for undertaking the construction of business continuity and disaster recovery plans is based on the precept that at some point in time something may occur that will affect the business, potentially leading to damage to brand reputation, financial loss, or loss of human life. The consequence of such outcomes can be mitigated to some extent, as discussed during your CISSP education.

This section starts with a refresher to re-familiarize your understanding of risk, risk management, and possible risk strategies that could influence the development of your plans.

Determining Critical Needs

To determine the critical needs of the organization, each department should document all the functions performed within that department. An analysis over a period of two weeks to one month can indicate the principal functions performed inside and outside the department, and it could assist in identifying the necessary data requirements for the department to conduct its daily operations satisfactorily. Some of the diagnostic questions that can be asked include the following:

1. If a disaster occurred, how long could the department function without the existing equipment and departmental organization?
2. What are the high priority tasks including critical manual functions and processes in the department? How often are these tasks performed, e.g., daily, weekly, monthly, etc.?
3. What staffing, equipment, forms, and supplies would be necessary to perform the high priority tasks?
4. How would the critical equipment, forms, and supplies be replaced in a disaster situation?
5. Does any of the above information require long lead times for replacement?
6. What reference manuals and operating procedure manuals are used in the department? How would these be replaced in the event of a disaster?
7. Should any forms, supplies, equipment, procedure manuals, or reference manuals from the department be stored in an off-site location?
8. Identify the storage and security of original documents. How would this information be replaced in the event of a disaster? Should any of this information be in a more protected location?
9. What are the current microcomputer backup procedures? Have the backups been restored? Should any critical backup copies be stored off site?
10. What would the temporary operating procedures be in the event of a disaster?
11. How would other departments be affected by an interruption in the department?
12. What effect would a disaster at the main computer have on the department?
13. What outside services/vendors are relied on for normal operation?
14. Would a disaster in the department jeopardize any legal requirements for reporting?
15. Are job descriptions available and current for the department?
16. Are department personnel cross-trained?
17. Who would be responsible for maintaining the department's contingency plan?
18. Are there other concerns related to planning for disaster recovery?

The critical needs can be obtained in a consistent manner by using a user department questionnaire. The questionnaire focuses on documenting critical activities in each department and identifying related minimum requirements for staff, equipment, forms, supplies, documentation, facilities, and other resources.

Offshoring Risks

Simple communication is possible without trust, but collaboration is not. High-value activities require trustworthy environments. The good news is that the need to distribute trust is highly recognized, resulting in numerous initiatives to create both new technologies and new social mechanisms. Technology tends to take the lead, with legal and other social mechanisms following.

The term "community of trust" (CoT) refers to a sociotechnical construct that meets the communications and security needs for ongoing sharing of sensitive data across the Internet between multiple organizations. Built on top of the existing enterprise and the Internet, but not limited to any particular subset of it, a CoT provides the social conventions and technical standards necessary to support substantive collaboration, ensuring that initial conditions for trusted collaboration are met and maintained.

Concerns about controlling conditions of data use have grown as data become easier to copy. A growing risk since the introduction of the Xerox machine, data misuse exploded as a concern in the 1990s. Inexpensive computers, a ubiquitous network, and high-capacity personal storage devices make this goal exponentially more difficult to attain than it ever was in the past.

There is, then, a need to develop the strategy to ensure that your BC policy and plans for your organization accommodate a growing number of requirements for external access to sensitive organizational information.

In the rush to save costs through outsourcing and take advantage of new business models, we have often forgotten one of the most fundamental aspects of risk. The less you know about something, the riskier you must assume that it is. Furthermore, postmodern philosophies about moral relativism have made it somewhat politically unacceptable to suggest that some groups of people cannot be trusted as much as other groups. This flies in the face of human experience that universally puts family relationships ahead of community relationships, with a culturally dependent set of increasingly less-trusted communities arranged almost hierarchically beyond that. Within each recognizable community exists what Francis Fukuyama refers to as a "radius of trust;" outside of that radius, people feel a lesser obligation toward others.

In terms of a distributed communications model of any kind, the greater the degree of separation, the harder it is to predict what other people will do. If you misinterpret your relative standings within the perceived radius of trust, you are going to underestimate the likelihood that you will come to harm.

With all other factors equal, the farther you get from your data center, the greater the information-related risk. Technical compatibilities and differences in legal climate also create unanticipated risk. The greater the degree of separation, the more effort that must be put into ensuring that the collaboration partners can be trusted and that communications are reliable.

Business impact assessment (BIA) is a fundamental part of the BS 25999 standard. It provides the basis upon which all of the other activities are driven. It is therefore essential that the right mechanisms exist within the owning organization to ensure that BIA is addressed in a controlled, consistent, and robust manner.

Identification of Critical Activities

Describe here how the organization identifies its business critical activities (BCA). In this context, these are all the activities that, should they fail, would represent an impact to the delivery of the goods and services provided to your organization or its business partners. *Table 4.4* provides an example of the typical level of detail required.

Supporting Activities	Impacts Resulting from the Disruption of the Activities	Maximum Tolerable Period of Disruption (Recovery Time Objective [RTO])	Recovery Priority and Critical Activities (Priority 1 = Critical Activity [Mission Critical Activities (MCA)]	Relevant Dependencies for Critical Activities	Determine Supplier BCM Where BCAs Are Dependent	Critical Activity RTO	Resources Required by BCAs for Resumption
Key operation facilities (e.g., estate inventory including facilities provided, business operations housed, and technical infrastructures)							
Transport/logistics (e.g., vehicles, tools, spares, fuel, materials inventory data, and location of documentation)							
Key Systems Documentation of end-to-end processes of core business systems, conceptual and physical							
Test facility Test environment before restoration of business processes							
Provision of people (e.g., loss of key personnel or critical mass due to industrial action, pandemic flu)							
Supply management (e.g., inability to maintain supply chain)							
Suppliers/sub-suppliers (e.g., loss of main or sub-supplier)							

Supporting Activities	Impacts Resulting from the Disruption of the Activities	Maximum Tolerable Period of Disruption (Recovery Time Objective [RTO])	Recovery Priority and Critical Activities (Priority 1 = Critical Activity [Mission Critical Activities (MCA)]	Relevant Dependencies for Critical Activities	Determine Supplier BCM Where BCAs Are Dependent	Critical Activity RTO	Resources Required by BCAs for Resumption
Operational environmental management (e.g., loss of building or use of building)							
Information and communications (e.g., fixed voice [incl. internal], mobile [incl. messaging], information access [inc]. intranet, Internet, and extranet])							
Incident management capability							
CERT teams, IRM teams							

Table 4.4 – The typical level of detail required to identify business critical activities (BCA)

Threats and Vulnerabilities

In the past you may have evaluated a generic structure based upon the model provided by the Common Criteria for IT Security Evaluation in *Figure 4.8*. This model shows the relationships between the different elements. However, we have to remember that as our systems have become more complex over time, as objects are reused by different subsystems, and as systems are distributed across distributed systems, sometimes geographically dispersed, that a single threat can impact a number of assets with differing outcomes. What may appear as a minor risk to one asset could have a significant impact on another. Thus, evaluating the threat against the end-to-end processing of any given asset will provide a truer reflection of the level of risk. For obvious reasons, such a process is an important predecessor to designing BC and DR plans.

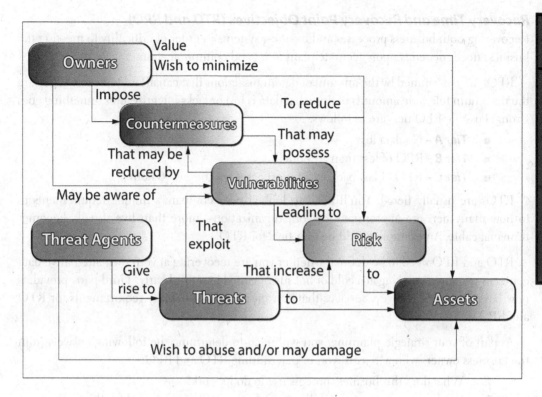

Figure 4.8 – **Generic structure used to evaluate threats and vulnerabilities**
(Common Criteria for IT Security Evaluation, ISO, 1998.)

Critical Business Processes

Business functions, processes, activities, and systems can be classified as core or non-core. The core business functions, processes, activities, and systems are those without which the business would collapse. The non-core business functions, processes, activities, and systems are those that provide support and improve effectiveness and efficiency, but, whose loss would impair productivity, not cause the collapse of the business. Thus, we should focus our primary attention on the design, development, and delivery of BR and DR for the core business functions. These become our critical systems.

Once the critical needs have been documented, management can set priorities within departments for the overall recovery of the organization. Activities of each department could be given priorities in the following manner:

- ■ **Essential activities** – A disruption in service exceeding one day would seriously jeopardize the operation of the organization.
- ■ **Recommended activities** – A disruption of service exceeding one week would seriously jeopardize the operation of the organization.
- ■ **Nonessential activities** – This information would be convenient to have but would not detract seriously from the operating capabilities if it were missing.

Recovery Time and Recovery Point Objectives (RTO and RPO)

Recovering both business processes and business systems in order of criticality to meeting the business needs depends upon accurate plans and good communication.

RPOs are determined by the amount of data/transactions that can afford to be lost. They are the maximum tolerable amounts of time that data is lost or lacks integrity after something goes wrong. Possible RPO tiers are as follows:

- **Tier A –** No data loss
- **Tier B –** RPO of less than 24 hours
- **Tier C –** RPO of last backup (in most cases will be 24–36 hours)

RTOs are usually tiered. You'll need to look at your company's unique requirements as to how many tiers are appropriate for your organization—more than five usually becomes unmanageable. An example would be four tiers for RTO.

RTO and RPO need to be defined whether you are recovering at your own alternative data center or you are recovering at a cold or hot site operated by a third party. Third-party providers now have advanced recovery services that can meet high availability requirements for RTO and RPO.

As part of your strategic planning, you will need to determine the following answers from the business owners who will assist you in determining RTO and RPO:

1. What does this business process use to do its work?
2. What resources (people, skill sets, and other tools) are needed for this process to continue to function in a disaster scenario?
3. What vital information flows through this business process, either from another process or to another process? What other business processes are dependent on the activities of this process?
4. What activities of the process can be done manually, if needed? What manual work around procedures could be put in place to minimize either the financial or nonfinancial impacts?
5. What would be the direct financial loss to your company if this business process were not available for 24 hours? One week? Three weeks? How is this loss calculated? What components contribute to this loss?
6. Does this business process have business cycles? Would a significant loss to your company be different at different times of the year? What months are critical? Are there times of the month that are more critical than others?
7. What is the business recovery plan? Are there subject-matter experts outside the affected area who could process the work if critical employees are not available?
8. What are the negative impacts of the following nonfinancial concerns if this process does not function for 24 hours? One week? Three weeks? Do your disaster recovery time objectives meet your business requirements? What will the impact be on the following areas:
   a. Cash flow (generation of revenue)
   b. Public image
   c. Shareholder confidence
   d. Financial reporting

  e. Managerial control (for example, approval levels)

  f. Productivity

  g. Competitive advantages

  h. Industry image

  i. Customer service

  j. Vendor relations

  k. Legal/contractual violations

  l. Regulatory requirements

  m. Employee morale

  n. Consumer confidence

9. For each day of outage, how long will it take to handle the backlog of work, in addition to other daily work, when this process is back in operation?

10. What expenses would be incurred if this process were disrupted?

  a. Temporary employees

  b. Emergency purchases (supplies, office machines, etc.)

  c. Rental/lease of equipment

  d. Wages paid to idle staff

  e. Overtime

  f. Temporary relocation of employees to alternate business recovery location (assume not working from home)

11. What other vulnerabilities and exposure exist with this business process?

In most circumstances, the definition of RTO and RPO will be an iterative process. There is no absolute formula. There is also a negotiation process with the business owner to balance the risk with the cost. That is, there may initially be a requirement for a short RTO and RPO. But after weighing the costs of the solution, the business owner may accept a longer RTO and RPO that would be less costly. How much risk is the business owner willing to take for what cost?

As with other business continuity plan components, an annual review of the RTO and RPO requirements should be done to capture changes to both the business environment and the systems environment.

Risk Assessment and Management

While risk assessments were discussed in general in Domain 1, they are also pertinent to the topic of contingency planning. Of course, if your organization does not already have a risk strategy, you should take the time to work with the risk managers and address this need. Most large organizations have risk registers that identify the risks in business terms, the consequences of those risks (usually financial and damage to reputation), and mitigations. The mitigations are translated into activities that can in turn be audited to ensure that they have been implemented and are achieving the perceived results. (See *Figures 4.9* and *4.10*)

If we choose to accept the risk and do nothing, we will need to prove that the level of risk, the probability of an attack, and the level of damage have been calculated, and that a cost/benefit analysis has been conducted for all possible control mechanisms to provide evidence to demonstrate that the value of the asset does not justify the cost of protection. In such instances, it is important to have recorded, auditable proof that can be presented should the event occur.

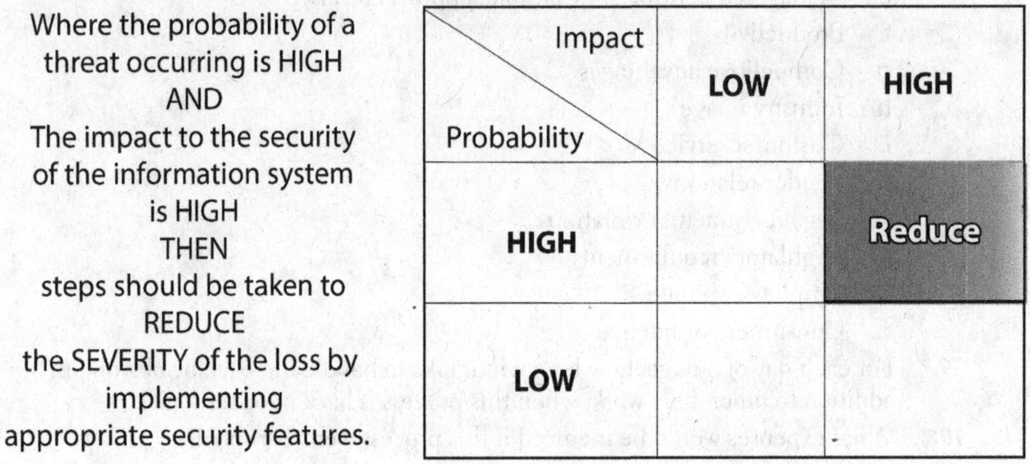
Where the probability of a threat occurring is HIGH AND The impact to the security of the information system is HIGH THEN steps should be taken to REDUCE the SEVERITY of the loss by implementing appropriate security features.
Impact
Probability
LOW
HIGH
HIGH
LOW
Reduce

Figure 4.9 – **Risk Reduction Matrix**

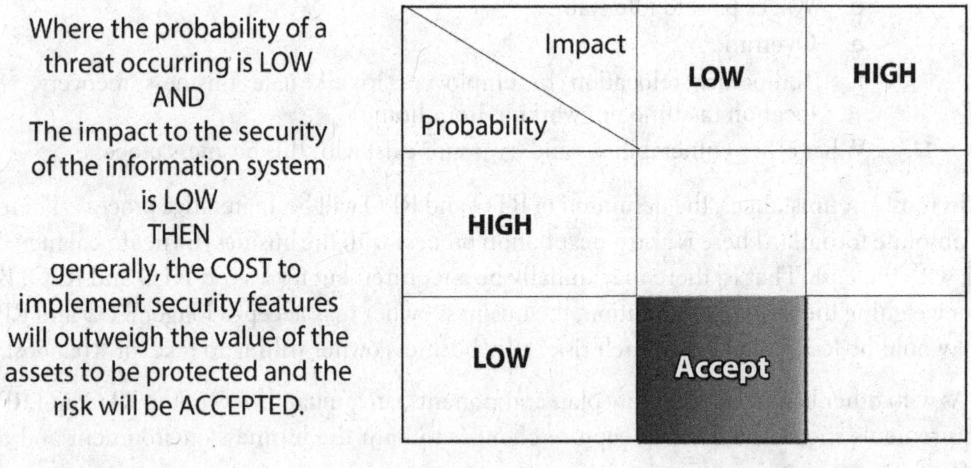
Where the probability of a threat occurring is LOW AND The impact to the security of the information system is LOW THEN generally, the COST to implement security features will outweigh the value of the assets to be protected and the risk will be ACCEPTED.
Impact
Probability
LOW
HIGH
HIGH
LOW
Accept

Figure 4.10 – **Risk Acceptance Matrix**

Many organizations today develop "heat maps," as shown in *Figure 4.11*. These maps consist of a grid and use color coding to reflect the level of risk an activity poses to the organization.

The number of squares on the grid is indicative and not prescriptive. You should design the grid according to your own needs. The bold line represents your organization's risk frontier. The risk frontier will flex depending on your organization's risk appetite, the external threats you are currently facing, and your business strategy. The squares immediately below and/or to the left of the bold line should be amber; any risks plotted in these squares require mitigating. They will of course be your second priority after you have addressed the mitigations for any risks plotted above or to the right of the bold line—the risk frontier.

4

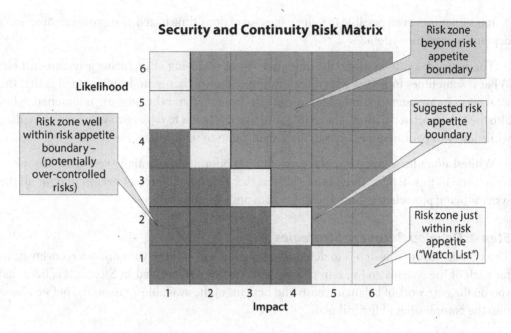

Security and Continuity Risk Matrix

Likelihood

Risk zone well
within risk appetite
boundary –
(potentially
over-controlled
risks)

Risk zone
beyond risk
appetite
boundary

Suggested risk
appetite
boundary

Risk zone just
within risk
appetite
("Watch List")

Impact

Figure 4.11 – **Heat map**

Step 3: Identify Preventative Measures

A simple formula for estimating the financial risk associated with a given type of disaster (and thus how much is worth investing in a plan to mitigate that risk) is $R\$ = P \times C \times T$ where P is the probability that the disaster will occur; C is the hourly or daily cost of downtime in lost productivity, lost revenue, etc.; and T is the time that systems are expected to be down. For example, if the probability of a major hurricane hitting your place of business in the next 3 years is 20% and it will cost you roughly $100,000 per day that you are down and you expect that you are likely to be down for a week, then your financial risk is $0.2 \times \$100,000 \times 7 = \$140,000$.

One way to minimize this risk is to reduce T, the time you are down; that is basically the purpose of the disaster recovery planning exercise. However, it is not the only way. The risk can also be reduced by reducing the probability that the disaster will occur or by reducing the cost that will be incurred if it does. Both of these are types of preventative measures. It is very often the case that the cost of preventing a problem is far lower than the cost of fixing it after it occurs.

Measures that reduce the probability of a disaster occurring range from fairly drastic, like physically moving the organization out of reach of threats such as hurricanes or floods, to the fairly mundane, such as ensuring that regular maintenance is performed on critical systems; that redundant components are built in; that sensors are installed to monitor environmental factors; that performance monitors are installed to give early warning of server malfunction; even something as simple as keeping plastic tarps available to throw over computer equipment to protect it from water damage.

It is sometimes even possible to reduce the cost of downtime by reducing your organization's dependence on the system.

The basic idea is to examine the potential win of removing or replacing a system entirely. What is sometimes forgotten when new equipment and systems are implemented is that the total cost of any system includes not just the up-front cost and the ongoing maintenance but also the risk associated with it. There are times that it is better to replace a system with one that, while lower in performance, exposes the organization to significantly lower risk.

While I don't have any particular procedure to offer, it is potentially very useful to spend some time in this step for all types of disasters that you wish to protect against and for all the systems being protected, at both the full-system and component levels.

Step 4: Develop Recovery Strategies

The primary task of this step is to determine how you will achieve your disaster recovery goals for each of the systems and system components that were identified in Step 2. It is here that you do the core work of balancing costs and benefits of the available approaches, before diving into the complexities of the full plan.

This step is not about selecting specific vendors, determining exact costs, or developing detailed procedures. Rather, the purpose in this stage is to select the types of solutions that you will use and to determine the scales of the costs involved. Thus, for example, you may determine that a small, critical subset of systems requires a fully mirrored and staffed alternate site ready to take over in minutes, while other systems can utilize a more traditional backup strategy that trades longer recovery time for much reduced expense.

There are several considerations to keep in mind as you work through this step. First, this is the point at which it becomes important to consider exactly what types of disasters you need to prepare for and to classify them by the extent and type of impact they have. The reason is straightforward—the recovery strategies available to you necessarily depend on from what you must recover. Focused failures such as a hardware component failure or a water leak affecting a couple of servers are very different matters than a site-wide disaster like a flood, fire, or regional blackout. In one, it may be possible to depend on a vendor to deliver a replacement. In the other, an alternate facility may be required.

The second consideration that arises from this is the need to consider solutions of differing breadth of coverage. Obviously, a solution that can address a site failure will serve as well to recover from failures of individual systems or components. There are a number of reasons not to depend on a single system-wide solution to address all issues, however. The most obvious is that such a solution is certainly costly to implement and probably costly to activate; the disruption from failing-over all of your systems to a secondary site is unlikely to be commensurate with a problem arising from failure of a single component.

There are two other reasons to not just consider but actually to implement several alternative approaches that address different levels of problems. First, no matter how good your planning and testing are, depending on a single solution, especially a complex one, means that your recovery is all or nothing. Anyone with much experience in complex systems knows that this is not a good idea. It is much better to have a series of backup solutions so that if one fails another is in place to recover at a greater, but still not completely devastating, cost. Second, alternative solutions that are actually implemented can give you significant flexibility in responding to an actual disaster. For example, if a problem occurs in the middle of a business day, it may be important to go immediately for an expensive solution in order to recover quickly, but if it happens at night or over a weekend, you may be able to institute slower but less disruptive or less costly recovery procedures.

A final consideration is that you need to take into account the particular characteristics of the infrastructure, human, and data aspects of recovery. Each of these must be considered differently, with different fundamental drivers of the decision of what type of solution to invest in and how much to spend.

Infrastructure is the simplest. While there may be more or less significant costs involved, the salient characteristic of infrastructure is that it can be replaced. A server can be replaced with another server, an alternate provider can be found for network connectivity, and so on. In many cases, the replacement system need not even be an exact duplicate, as long as it interfaces with other components and systems in a compatible way: Manual systems may replace IT-based automated systems, or you may be able to temporarily outsource an internal system. The fundamental driver when considering recovery strategies for infrastructure is typically that of cost versus performance.

People (roles) represent a more difficult factor. Particular roles usually require special skills and knowledge. If a recovery strategy requires, for example, that a given role be duplicated at an alternate site, there may be additional costs associated with hiring or training personnel to fill that duplicate role. Similarly, the recovery solution itself may require special training or skills. The key driver for the consideration of recovery strategies from the standpoint of roles, then, is the degree to which they require you to duplicate or acquire special skills, which then impacts the long-term cost of hiring and training.

Finally, data are potentially the most difficult issue because data are usually unique; it is not generally possible to replace data with other data that have the same or similar properties. Either you have it or you don't. The driving question from the standpoint of data, then, is how much data are you willing to lose? It is also important here to recall that data may not only be destroyed, for example, through the loss of the system it is stored on, but they may also be corrupted through user or administrator errors or through deliberate sabotage, for example, by malware.

This step consists of reviewing each of the systems characterized in Step 2 and determining the system- and component-level strategies to apply that can achieve recovery within the maximum outage time, while remaining roughly in the bounds of budget and other resource constraints that have been established. In considering cost, characterize the total cost of a solution, which means not only the cost of any hardware, software, or services purchased but also the level of disruption caused by installation and the ongoing costs in both money and personnel to maintain and test the solution.

Keep in mind too that the different systems are not independent of one another and in many cases require that the recovery strategies be compatible. This may be a minor consideration for purely local solutions, but if you wish to set up an alternate site, you need to ensure that all the systems on which a given system depends are also duplicated. For example, if you wish to have a failover system for your email servers at an alternate site on the other side of the country, in addition to the email server you will need facilities to house the server, power, network connectivity, sufficient bandwidth to operate throughout a crisis, access or personnel to maintain the facilities and the servers, DNS servers and other auxiliary systems that are critical to the operation, etc. When you are done, add a brief summary of the recovery strategies for each of the systems on the master system information form.

Step 5: Develop the Plan

This step is the culmination of all your work. It is not, unfortunately, an easy step, but neither is it too complicated, as long as you have been thorough in the previous steps and you approach it systematically.

The outcome of this step is both a documented plan and the completed implementation of all the infrastructure required to enable the plan. The documentation includes background information on the assumptions and constraints that went into making the plan, as well as written documentation on specific procedures. The implementation side includes purchasing and installing hardware and software, setting up alternative locations, contracting for alternative sources of network or other communication services, and so on.

This step is a major project all by itself, even if the previous steps have been carried out perfectly. It will require a significant amount of time on the part of the person or team responsible for leading the development of the plan, but it will also require time and effort by everyone whose systems are involved because their expertise will be required both to develop recovery procedures and, of course, to test them.

We will cover all aspects of the plan, roughly following the organization suggested in the NIST guide. The organization itself is not important—that should be adapted to best serve your needs—but all the types of information I will discuss should be present in the plan. The sections we will use are as follows:

1. Introduction
2. Operational Overview
3. Notification/Activation Phase
4. Recovery Phase
5. Restoration Phase
6. Appendices

For each section, I will briefly discuss its contents and the purpose for their inclusion, then review some of the major issues or potential pitfalls to keep in mind, and finally offer some suggestions on how to approach the actual development of that section.

Keep in mind that this part of the work in particular is likely to be iterative. As you select specific solutions and work out step-by-step procedures, you may discover new dependencies, errors in your initial assumptions, or simply that your planned approach exceeds the resources available, so that you need to revisit and re-evaluate your recovery strategies and perhaps even your recovery targets. In fact, you may wish to do this deliberately in preparing the entire plan—to make several passes through all of the steps in this guide but starting with a much shallower effort and deepening gradually. This approach can significantly reduce the likelihood of surprises that entail rethinking major parts of your plan.

4

Plan Section 1: Introduction

The main purpose of this section is to document the goals and scope of the plan, along with any requirements that must be taken into account whenever the plan is updated.

Preparing this section is simple because it is essentially the planning policy statement that you prepared in Step 1. You may as well just include its contents verbatim here. This is also an appropriate place to include the record of changes made to the plan whenever it is updated.

Plan Section 2: Operational Overview

The purpose of this section is to provide a concise picture of the plan's overall approach. It contains essentially two types of information:

1. A high-level overview of the systems being protected and the recovery strategies employed

2. A description of the recovery teams and their roles

The section provides a context for understanding the plan as a whole. It should be possible to read just the introduction and this section and have a good idea of the overall approach to disaster recovery for all the systems involved.

Once again, you have already prepared the first type of information in this section during the previous steps: the business impact analysis and the development of recovery strategies. An easy way to do this part of this section is simply to include a copy of the Master System Information Form (SIF), which lists all the major systems with individual SIFs and annotates them with recovery priority, maximum outage time and business impact, major dependencies on other systems, and a brief description of the recovery strategies employed. It is recommended that you include all the individual SIFs in an appendix of the plan as well. These serve as a useful reference during reviews of the plan and ensure that all information is together during future updates.

The operational overview should also contain a description of the teams that will be responsible for activating and carrying out the plan. Detailed information on the teams and the succession plan will be prepared in the next section, so the information here should be brief, probably no more than a list of key teams and roles together with a few words describing their role in the overall recovery plan. It is probably best to develop this part after completing all of this phase of the work to ensure that it reflects the actual structure of the recovery teams after all decisions have been made.

Plan Section 3: Notification/Activation Phase

This is the first of three plan sections that document actual recovery operations. According to NIST Publication 800-34, this section defines the initial actions taken once a system disruption or emergency has been detected or appears to be imminent. This phase includes activities to notify recovery personnel, assess system damage, and implement the plan. At the completion of this phase, recovery staff will be prepared to perform contingency measures to restore system functions on a temporary basis.

It is common for organizations to plan this phase inadequately. Most of your work on the plan is focused on the actions that you must take to recover. It is very easy to forget that declaring the emergency and deciding that it is time to initiate operations under the disaster recovery plan can be difficult and require advance planning as well. In fact, there is a very natural tendency, absent clear guidelines, for people to delay action until they are "certain" that the disaster is imminent or is bad enough to react. Unfortunately, by the time certainty is achieved, it is generally too late. This section must answer the following questions:

- On what basis will the decision to activate the plan be made?
- What information is required?
- What additional guidelines are there for making the decision?
- Who is responsible for performing the damage or threat assessment that will provide the information above?
- What restrictions or guidelines are there for how long the assessment may take or how certain the information must be?
- Who is responsible for the go/no-go decision?
- What are the rules of succession, if that person is not available?
- How will teams be notified?
- How will recovery teams communicate?

There are several things that should be kept in mind when preparing this section of the plan.

- When preparing guidelines for the activation decision, account for the fact that there is a natural tendency to be conservative in assessing risks to avoid being seen as an alarmist if the feared damage does not actually happen.
- Wherever possible, provide clear, positive, and specific guidance on when the person in charge should or should not activate the plan.
- Make sure that the person responsible for decisions is in a position to know what he or she needs to know. For example, if the decision requires knowledge of conditions at a site, it is best to designate someone located at that site, in case communications are impossible.

In fact, communication is a key aspect that must be carefully thought through. Depending on the type and scale of the disaster, common means of communication, such as cell phones, email, and landline phones may not be operational. Either alternative methods must be developed, like satellite phones or radios, or local teams need to be empowered to make decisions autonomously and be given the tools they need to implement those decisions.

This section may be an appropriate place to keep contact information on each team member; alternatively, it may be included as an appendix. Keep in mind that you can never have enough contact information. Especially for key recovery personnel, you may wish to include work and home phones and email addresses, faxes, cell phones, neighbors, relatives, etc.

This is the first point in the development of the plan where you must design actual procedures to be followed during a crisis. It is impossible to develop good procedures of any complexity without playing them out. For this reason, it is critical that the procedures developed for this section be tested in actual use, just like the recovery procedures themselves. It is also useful, during the development of the plan, to role-play a crisis, preferably with the people who will actually be involved, in order to think through the necessary steps.

Plan Section 4: Recovery Phase
This is the second of the three major sections documenting actual recovery operations, but it is the one that most of us have in mind when we talk about a DR plan. This is the section

4

of the plan that documents in detail the solutions to be used to recover each system and the procedures required to carry out the recovery and restore operational capabilities.

The organization of this section is simple. For the organization as a whole and for each system individually, the plan identifies a sequence of recovery goals (for example, to restore Internet connectivity or to switch email services to a backup system at a secondary site) and provides documentation on the procedures required to accomplish each of them. Procedures may be as simple as a couple of bullets, or they may be many pages of instructions and checklists, depending on the complexity of the recovery solution and, of course, of the system.

There are two aspects to your work in developing this part of the plan: Actually implementing solutions that align with the recovery strategies you identified in Step 4 and then documenting the procedures required during recovery. Implementing your recovery strategy is, of course, the major work here. This includes everything from evaluating and purchasing hardware and software solution components, designing and implementing the solution around these components, equipping alternate sites for your systems, negotiating with managed service facilities, vendors, and IT consulting companies, and so on. To lay out everything, you need to know what would require a substantial book just for this discussion. Further, in this dynamic environment, details could be out of date as soon as published. Therefore, you should take the generic concepts and keep yourself up to date through conferences, research, and general awareness through networking.

You may also wish to consider outsourcing some or all of this work to a professional services organization that specializes in disaster recovery system development—although it is important to understand that it will still take a lot of effort on your part to ensure that they have the information they need about your organization.

Whether you are doing all of it yourself, outsourcing parts, or outsourcing everything, it is a good idea to utilize other resources to help ensure that you understand the options available and the trade-offs involved.

There is no substitute for action in this phase — do the recovery and write down what you did. Then do it again following the instructions, and see if they are correct and complete. It is important that the level of detail in the instructions corresponds to the level of knowledge of the least knowledgeable personnel who might need to carry them out. To minimize disruptions, you can simulate or role-play much of the doing, and procedures for individual subsystems can be worked out independently.

Nevertheless, it is extremely important that both final documentation and final testing include full-scale tests as they are expected to occur during a real crisis. This is the only way to discover subtle intersystem dependencies that might otherwise be missed.

It is very important to highlight any points in the procedures that require coordination with other teams or other systems. This is information that should be easy to see by skimming quickly over a given procedure. If the procedure is long and complex, it may be helpful to include an overview of the major steps in an introductory section or to break out some of the details into separate checklists or sub-procedures. Of course, while completeness and correctness are key, the shorter and simpler the procedure, the better. Remember that these procedures will be carried out in a high-stress environment, in which mistakes and confusion are much more likely than during a practice run.

Plan Section 5: Reconstitution Phase

This is the last of the three sections of the plan that document actual operations, and it is again one that does not immediately leap to most peoples' minds when thinking about disaster recovery planning.

Disasters eventually end and there is a need to return operations to normal. Per the NIST guide, in this phase "recovery activities are terminated and normal operations are transferred back to the organization's facility. If the original facility is unrecoverable, the activities in this phase can also be applied to preparing a new facility to support system processing requirements."

There are two reasons why it is very important to think through and document reconstitution procedures just as carefully as recovery procedures. The first is that it will help you ensure that the solutions you select are supportive of a relatively painless return to normal. A solution that gives you easy recovery, but makes it hard to get back, is not a particularly good solution.

The second reason is even more important. Even though stress levels may be lower during the return to normal, doing it without well-documented and well-tested procedures risks mistakes that can transform the return to normal into another disaster. The type of content and suggestions for preparing it are the same as for the recovery section, so I won't repeat them here.

Plan Section 6: Appendices

The appendices should contain any information that:

    a. Is necessary as reference material during recovery
    b. May be necessary during any revision of the plan
    c. Documents legal agreements. Examples include the following:

- Team contacts
- Vendor contact (including off-site storage)
- Standard operating procedures (SOPs) and checklists for system recovery or processes
- Lists of equipment, system requirements for hardware, software, firmware, etc.
- Vendor SLAs, reciprocal agreements, etc.
- Description of/directions to alternate site
- Worksheets used to develop the plan

Step 6: Plan Testing, Training, and Exercises

Testing a business continuity plan can be difficult. Simulating potential threats to your business can be time consuming and expensive. However, testing your business continuity plans will help show whether you have covered all angles, and whether your plan is achievable. In addition, it can increase your business and trading partners' confidence in your business' ability to recover from disruption. Tests are also useful to raise staff awareness of the plans.

You can test whether staff can function without access to data cheaply and easily. Such tests can also help to check that other sources of data, such as backups or archives that are held off site, are sufficiently up to date.

How often should plans be tested? At some point, usually around 12 months after the plan has been developed, you should carry out a real restore of data—use data that has been backed up to get your system fully operational again—and attempt to work without premises or files. This will help to establish the following:

- Whether your expected timescales for recovering key business applications are realistic
- How prepared staff are for putting the plan into action
- Whether any third parties or service providers who are integral to the plan are ready to respond

You should ensure that any test you undertake, whether technical (relating to the operation of the IT systems) or nontechnical (relating to all associated activities), has clear objectives. For example, measure the time needed to get your main IT system running following a disruption or to test how long it takes to contact all key personnel in the event of a disaster. This will enable you to measure the success, or otherwise, of each exercise and highlight areas in need of further attention.

Any initial testing should be followed by further tests on a regular basis. In particular, details of any changes to IT systems should be included in the plan, and tests should be undertaken on the new systems.

Over time, things change. Hardware components are replaced, software is upgraded, networks are reconfigured, data sizes grow, and people come and go. All this is a normal part of the life of an IT environment. And all of it can impact the performance of your disaster recovery systems. Although these systems were fully tested when first installed, the dynamic nature of the environment makes it critical that testing continues to take place regularly and that personnel training be up to date. There are many different types and levels of testing. Generally speaking, they span two key dimensions: scope and realism.

Test Scope

Scope refers to the degree to which you are testing a full system, individual components of a system, individual platforms, or end-to-end business processes. It is necessary to define the boundary – and identify the external links feeding data to and receiving information from – the bounded system.

Ensure that you have mapped all of the components, the people involved, the applications used to process the data, and the platforms upon which the processing takes place.

All systems have customers and suppliers whether they are internal or external to your organization. Where possible, include your internal customers and suppliers because they will be able to provide you with valuable information, and their presence will assist in developing their understanding of how your systems work and where the challenges lie in the event of an incident.

External customer-facing representatives should also be present wherever possible. Their input to helping you understand the business consequences of your actions will also be invaluable. You may not be fully conversant with the details of the service level agreements and any penalty payments that may arise as a result of downtime.

Book an appropriate location and invite representatives for all processes involved in the scope. Where you have outsourced processes, on shore or off shore, it may not be possible for those representatives to be physically present. You therefore need to set up conference call facilities to enable them to participate.

Where your end-to-end business process is complex, you may find that while the individual components have developed BC and DR plans, there has never been an opportunity to test multiple component failure. The results of conducting such an exercise can be very revealing. Each component lead will vie for priority restoration, not fully understanding where their component fits into the end-to-end business process. Further, your RTOs for each component may not be realistic. Using project management tools for dependencies and critical path analysis will reveal the actual maximum downtime, which is clearly not the sum of all RTOs, as some components may be recovered concurrently while others have dependencies and can only be recovered consecutively or contiguously.

Tracking and mapping the component recovery during the test will provide you with valuable information to update your BC and DR plans. Furthermore, evidence of proper testing, and of achieving acceptable results for those tests, may be required by management and may need to be provided to auditors and/or regulators. Additionally, reporting on the testing and its results – and preservation of such reports – is almost certainly going to be required by the business continuity and disaster recovery steering committee.

Realistic Testing
Realism refers to the degree to which you are performing exactly the procedures that you would during a disaster—a classroom role-playing test in which you talk through steps without actually doing them is one extreme, and a full execution is the other. In both cases, one side of the spectrum tends to be less expensive and less disruptive to day-to-day operations, but also less reliable in its results.

In general, it is a good idea to do a mix. Less disruptive tests can be carried out more often. Problems found and fixed that way avoid the typically higher impact and cost of finding the issues during a live test. The NIST guide states, "It is important that a test never disrupts normal operations." We would modify that. If never disrupting normal operations means never performing a full disaster recovery exercise, then it is necessary to occasionally disrupt normal operations. Such disruptive tests should be kept to a minimum, perhaps once or a few times a year, as long as component and subsystem testing are carried out more regularly. It is important to remember that it is always less expensive to expose yourself to the cost of a full test in a planned way than to discover during a disaster that a subtle missed dependency leads you to being unable to recover at all. I should note finally that it is important to be thinking about the testing side of your plan throughout the previous steps because testing represents a significant part of the total cost of your disaster recovery plan. In particular, when considering particular solutions and vendors, make testability part of the evaluation process.

Proper training is equally vital. Training in disaster recovery procedures should be considered part of the regular orientation of new hires if they have any role at all in implementing the plan. Key disaster recovery personnel should undergo frequent enough training that they are intimately familiar with the procedures that they will have to carry out under the plan. As noted in the NIST guide, ideally they should be trained well enough that they can execute their responsibilities without the aid of the actual disaster recovery plan document.

Step 7: Plan Maintenance

If it is worth the money and effort to develop a disaster recovery plan, it is also worth the effort to ensure that the plan accurately reflects current requirements and systems. Otherwise, it is only a matter of time before the two diverge sufficiently to put your capacity to recover from a disaster in real jeopardy. For the most part, this step is beyond the scope of this document, but I offer one thought. There are three natural points at which the plan can be reviewed: during testing, in a regular annual or semi-annual review devoted specifically to the task of review, and when changes are made in either the IT systems being protected or in the business processes they support.

The first two fall directly under the purview of those responsible for disaster recovery planning and so can be planned for directly. The last requires that consideration of the impact of changes on the disaster recovery plan be introduced as a standard consideration in procedures that are outside the scope of direct concern of those responsible for the DR plan. As a result, it requires that, one way or another, those responsible for changes in the systems take on a certain level of responsibility for DR plan impact. While this may be difficult, it makes maintaining a correct DR plan significantly less costly than discovering changes later, through testing or an annual review.

Contingency Management Summary

This section has considered the steps and challenges in developing the project plans to develop the business continuity plan and the disaster recovery plan.

Third-Party Dependencies

Vendor Support Services

Having support services from your major vendors in place adds strong value to disaster recovery planning. For example, specific managed hot standby sites or on-site services with rapid response times can significantly ease disaster recovery. Key questions regarding vendor support include the following:

- Are support contracts in place?
- Has the disaster recovery plan been reviewed by the vendors, and are the vendors included in the escalation processes?
- Does the vendor have sufficient resources to support the disaster recovery?

Most vendors have experience handling disaster situations and can offer additional support. Many organizations offer a wide range of service and support solutions and can often assist with limiting downtime in the case of an unexpected outage.

Recovery Strategies

Methods of recovery might include the following:

- Carrying out activities manually until IT services are resumed
- Staff at an affected building moving to another location
- Agreeing with another business to use each other's premises in the event of a disaster
- Arranging to use IT services and accommodation provided by a specialist third-party standby site

Types of Contingencies

1. **Multiple Processing Centers** – This option involves constantly using multiple facilities with failover in between them. If one goes down, the others pick up the load.

2. **In-House** – The option with the least risk, but potentially the most expensive, is to set up an in-house contingency. Such a facility could be put in for office space, warehouse space, production environments, and any other needed facility resource.
   - ◘ Some advantages of this option would include the following:
   - ◘ Facility is built to the exact required specifications.
   - ◘ Facility can be accessed without time constraints on occupation.
   - ◘ Testing can be facilitated at any time or at any activation level.
   - ◘ Some disadvantages would include the following:
   - ◘ Cost of the facility
   - ◘ Depreciation of additional assets
   - ◘ Maintenance and update requirements

3. **Third-Party Contracts:** Computing facilities that have a varying degree of space or hardware in place to facilitate a recovery.

4. **Cold Site:** Usually consisting of a shell or computer room space with minimum or little equipment already on the floor.

5. **Warm Site:** Computing facility that has some equipment available, although it may not be powered up and running. Some special equipment may need to be procured. Systems and applications have to be set up and installed.

6. **Hot Site:** Computing facility that matches your hardware/software/network requirements and is loaded with your operating system. The equipment is up and running at all times and, normally, secondary backup sites are available. This is similar to the multiple processing centers approach except that the hot site does not run unless there is a failure at the primary site.

7. **Reciprocal:** If an organization enters into an agreement to assist another part of the organization or a totally separate organization, then this is termed a reciprocal arrangement. Such agreements for reciprocal recovery ensure that should one site be affected, the facilities of the other become available to the agreeing party. It should be noted that when one business relocates to another, the impact of the disaster is sometimes exported to that second business.

	Ownership		
Recovery Time	**In-House**	**Contracted**	**Ad-Hoc**
Months	• Rebuild or relocate	• Extend commercial recovery site contract (if permitted)	• Rebuild, rent, or purchase
Weeks	• Prefabricated buildings on site • Adapt buildings from other users	• Expansion at recovery site • Contracted prefabs and mobile units	• Furnished offices • Subcontract processes
Days	• In-house recovery site • Budge-up • Home-working	• Commercial recovery site • Reciprocal agreements • Mobile facilities • Subcontract processes	• Managed officers (if available)
Hours	• Diverse locations with staff redeployed from other tasks	• Relocate a small team only to contracted commercial recovery site	• None
Immediate	• Diverse locations	• Initiate contracted service agreements	• None

Figure 4.12 – **Time to recover options**

Recommendations

Site

Selecting a location for your disaster recovery site is an important decision. Too near your site of operations and the DR site could be impacted by the same event as that which required the move in the first place such as climate or environmental disasters, political uprisings, war, or loss of utilities or services. However, selecting a site in a different geographic location requires logistical considerations such as the availability and movement of human resources.

IT

Restoring your IT systems as discussed earlier in this domain requires an understanding of the business needs. Ensuring that you first accommodate the recovery of your core business processes is critical. The type of site you choose will be based upon the considerations presented in the list of contingencies in the previous section.

The key point for the systems aspect is to ensure that all infrastructure and software versions are the same as those used at the production site. You will need to work with the head of IT to ensure that all versions are compatible. It is all too easy to neglect upgrades across sites, especially where budgets are tight or there is a lack of resources.

Where you have elected to use an alternative in-house site, clearly its operations will need to continue; thus you need to ensure that the system also has appropriate processing capability to provide a normal service and not a degraded service. If this is not the case, you need to include in your plan which of your processes has priority and the volume of transactions that can be accommodated, and whether or not the DR host will have to reduce its own processing to accommodate the transferred processes.

If you can offer only a degraded service, you need to work with the business unit owners who then need to communicate with suppliers and customers in the supply chain (whether internal or external). In turn, they will need to communicate with their suppliers and customers to reduce the flow of transactions and mitigate any breach of service level agreements penalty payments.

Communications

In any incident or minor or major disaster recovery, communications is a critical activity. The nature of the incident may restrict the types of communications media available, so your plan must provide for alternatives. Mobile devices and cellphones – or, in cases of network outages, satellite phones – can be used in place of landline communications. Radio-wave based communications can also work; Ham radio, "Walkie Talkie" type devices, and CB radios, long since disappeared from our society, still work. However, bandwidth may become congested if the incident affects more than your own organization and will degrade quickly. The following are a couple of suggestions to promote continuity of communications:

1. Ensure that you have an established communications plan. This should include a list of contacts (a communications tree works well with each nominated person contacting two or maybe three other people—this passes the message expeditiously). You should also have determined who will communicate with external bodies: the emergency services, the press/media, families and other relatives, customers, and suppliers. Prepared scripts are also useful. As previously discussed, the timing and frequency of the communications are also critical, and you need to judge the balance of providing too little or too much information, too often or too infrequently. This is a matter of judgment when the incident occurs.

2. Ensure that your key communicators have immediate access to mobile devices and that the batteries for the devices are always charged.

Roles and Responsibilities

Planning for any incident, large or small, requires an understanding of the type of response required. Training, education, and awareness of response activities instill preparedness, and rehearsing the teams provides some confidence for effective resolution.

Incident handling involves receiving, triaging, and responding to requests and reports, and analyzing incidents and events. These activities can include, for example, the following:

- Taking action to protect systems and networks affected or threatened by intruder activity
- Providing solutions and mitigation strategies from relevant advisories or alerts
- Looking for intruder activity on the network
- Patching or repairing security breaches on the system
- Evaluation of data loss either logical or physical
- Theft of IT or communications components
- Each of the above example incidents may impact the business to a greater or lesser extent.

4

Emergency Operations Center

Regardless of the type of plan you have prepared from the previous discussion, an identified emergency operations center provides a focal meeting point for face-to-face management of the incident. Your selection of the venue is important. The operations center should be fully equipped and provide for secure and confidential discussions. At a minimum, you should provide for a communications infrastructure with internal and external connections, and access to all business continuity and disaster recovery plans, communications plans, and a directory of useful telephone numbers.

As the event may be of lasting duration, it will also be important that forms of refreshment are available.

Crisis Management Team

Many organizations have adopted a three-level approach; whether these are called "Level 1, Level 2, and Level 3 responders" or Bronze, Silver, and Gold teams or bridges, the labels are irrelevant and contextual within your own organization. However, the activities they perform and the decisions they take are predefined and based on operational, tactical, and strategic decision making.

As the incident occurs, it should be recorded and reported to the appropriate lead for the Level 1, Bronze, Operational level, who will attend the scene of the incident. The level of damage is assessed. If the incident cannot be resolved in accordance with the incident management plan and requires escalation, the lead will contact the appropriate lead for the Level 2, Silver, Tactical level responders, who will invoke plans for ensuring business continuity or a move to disaster recovery. At this point, normally the Level 3, Gold, Strategic team will be notified of the situation and be prepared in case of the need for further escalation and intervention.

Thus, the chain of command to deal with the event is established. While this is a generic description, it is impossible to be more precise because each organization will prepare its own incident response plan according to size and strategy, organization structure, and culture. You should therefore prepare an appropriate incident response plan to meet your own organizational needs. The following is a sample team description:

- **Team Manager** – The team manager has overall responsibility to ensure that business objectives are met during a response. He or she is also responsible for communicating status to senior management.
- **Technical Lead** – The technical lead is charged with assessing the impact on the technology infrastructure. He or she is also responsible for containment and recovery activities as they relate to information processing technology. The technical lead supervises the following members of the incident response team (IRT):
  - One or more network engineers
  - One or more programmers
  - One or more server engineers
- **Public Relations** – This person is responsible for communicating with investors, the press, and other outside entities.

- **Security** – Security encompasses facility, personnel, and information security. If these are separate departments, each should be represented on the incident response team.
- **IS Support** – The support team can assist with containment, establish alternate methods of information processing when primary systems or network paths are disrupted, and assist with system recovery tasks.
- **Facilities Management** – Responsibilities for resolving power issues, locating and coordinating the move to alternates, and structural assessments and repair fall here.
- **Labor Union** – If an organization's employees are represented by a union, getting union leadership to the table can help diffuse a possible reaction to unusual management decisions and provide employee perspectives of events.
- **Representatives of Critical Business Functions** – When a single process fails, it might be enough to have one or two administration or operations teams represented. However, a catastrophic event requires a broader scope. Prior to any event, representatives from critical areas of the organization should be identified, including the following:
  - Payroll
  - Accounts receivable
  - Human resources
  - Legal
  - Other financial services
  - Clinical services
  - Production management
  - Transportation

Once the team members are identified, they should meet to begin building an incident response plan (IRP). The plan should include all activities related to containing and mitigating effects and improving future response. The plan is then used to train the team.

Thorough training produces a team that reacts to events quickly, without confusion. It helps ensure that all members understand their responsibilities, the roles of others, and team cooperation when it's needed most.

Reflection on Developing the Policy

We have identified the various component parts for the tactical and operational implementation of our strategic policy. The culture and structure of your organization will influence your policy design. Your organization's risk appetite will influence your recovery approaches. Wherever you are in the world and however large or small your organization, the following collection of "keep its" provides generic guidance for achieving success.

Keep It Simple

The policy should be clear and concise. It should be stated as briefly as possible without omitting any vital information. Long-winded policies are more difficult to understand, less likely to be read, and harder to implement.

Keep It Understandable

Develop a good policy that is understandable and actually makes sense within the context of the organization. As the aphorism from the world of business states, there are two types of people: those who don't manage what they understand, and those who don't understand what they manage.

In the realm of information security, business continuity, and disaster recovery, sense can only be achieved if the person writing the policies has a grasp of the concepts as well as the organization's structure and purpose.

Keep It Practicable

Regardless of how succinct and understandable a policy might be, if it is not possible to practice, it is worthless. An example of this would be the implementation of a policy requiring processing to be transferred to a site that has neither the same version of the production site software nor the spare capacity to process the transactions. An example related to incident response might be a policy stating that members of a response team have to be reachable 24 hours a day, even though no reliable means of contact is provided by the company except when the members are at work. Policies that are not practicable are not only, by definition, ineffective, but then an organization's employees quickly ignore them.

Keep It Cooperative

Good business continuity and disaster recovery policies are cooperative in that they are crafted and maintained with the input of all relevant departments within an organization. Where incident response is concerned, departments such as legal, human resources, public relations, audit, and information technology all have to contribute to the creation and review of policy documentation. During an incident response, it is very likely that some or all of these departments will play a significant role in the management of the situation. If relevant departments have not given their endorsement for a policy, the policy is sure to experience problems during implementation. Prioritization of activities should be done in advance and not at the time of the incident.

Keep It Dynamic

Finally, any useful business continuity and disaster recovery policies are dynamic and need to be capable of changing and growing with an organization: It would be negligent to create policies and believe that the needs they serve today will be adequate in the long run.

No organization wants to appear as though they have a weak information security posture. Such an appearance can tarnish the corporate image, precipitate lawsuits, attract unwanted hacker attention, and damage good will. Yet there is no such thing as foolproof security: Sooner or later, all organizations must respond to a security incident. The speed and decisiveness with which an organization can mount its response will determine whether or not a serious incident turns into a nightmare. If the response is methodical and well-orchestrated, invariably the incident will be controllable.

A poor response capability may lead to financial and public relations trouble at least and penal repercussions at worst. This risk can be managed by devising an effective incident response policy from the outset. Such a policy's documentation will consist of the following sections: background, definitions, incident classification, reporting, business continuity, process flow, and example incidents.

Background

All policies need to have a background section in order to explain the motivation and purpose driving the policy. For incident response, the objective is somewhat obvious: to adequately respond to electronic incidents that take place within an organization's purview. This background not only identifies the objectives of the incident response policy, but it also provides the context within which those objectives will be met.

Definitions

The policy should define exactly what an incident is. The answer to that question is contingent upon your organization's goals and priorities. However, a starting point would be your organization's policies, International Standards Organization (ISO) accreditation, and applicable legislation, regulations, guidances, and generally accepted best practices.

Another item that requires definition is the role of the computer emergency response team (CERT). An incident response policy will not be practicable unless there is someone who puts that policy into action during an incident. The CERT must be a highly skilled and available group. Members should represent expertise within the various information systems belonging to an organization, be on call 24 hours a day, and be capable of responding within a nominal amount of time. There should be backup available for when members are out of town or on vacation (succession planning).

Members of the CERT need to be familiar with the fundamentals of gathering and handling computer evidence. In the United Kingdom, you should be familiar with the ACPO (Association of Chief Police Officers) Guidelines. Following these procedures will save time later should the incident be found to be of a prosecutable nature. You can never go back and recreate a crime scene, especially a technology-based crime scene. Mishandling evidence will create a loophole and the guilty may escape justice.

Incident Classification

To be effective in managing its incident response process, an organization should create an event classification system. Such a system will enable the filtering of background noise from items that are more serious. One effective approach is to assign events a degree of urgency and then further assign a priority ranking to anything of high urgency. Incidents that fall into the low and medium urgency classes may be logged, with medium events being examined later on by a system administrator. High urgency events would be treated immediately. This response would require the attention of other relevant departments and groups.

An escalation list should be used for all incidents. Such a list designates responsibilities for incidents in which the degree of urgency increases as the incident progresses. As an event increases in urgency and priority, an appropriate individual further up the escalation list is contacted. Ultimately, for incidents of the highest urgency and priority, the CERT is activated.

As an incident escalates, it is likely that departments other than network administration will need to become involved. Executive management will have to be very careful to not hamper the CERT's ability to do its job, e.g., by assigning it unreasonable or time-consuming chores. The legal and public relations departments may also need to become involved. If the situation warrants it, executive management should be prepared to contact law enforcement.

Note that an organization's information system vendors should be included on the escalation list. In particular, relevant vendors should provide a 24-hour contact and be given such a contact at the organization. It is also recommended that some type of information security service level agreement be included in any contract between an organization and its vendors.

Reporting

Before, during, and after an electronic incident, various kinds of data will be gathered. How will these data be processed, and to whom will they be presented? Very little beyond intrusion detection system and server audit logs will be available for reporting during normal business operations. However, when an incident is being managed, there is a great potential for additional information. For example, evidence that might be collected, additional log data, and documentation of the incident can all contribute to the data available. After an incident has passed, there will no doubt be new information pertaining to the aftermath: what the incident has cost the organization, what resources will be needed to fully recover, etc. It's important for the incident response policy to outline when reports are generated, what they will contain, and to whom they will be made available.

Invoking Business Continuity

In the event that a serious IT incident should take place, a decision to halt certain information systems may need to be made. For example, during a denial-of-service attack, it may be better to undergo a self-imposed service outage, a graceful and controlled shut down, rather than wait for an overwhelming flood of service requests. Of course, in doing so, the business continuity plan, and in extreme cases, the disaster recovery plan, will be invoked. The incident response policy should identify who such key decision makers are and under what circumstances specific decisions should be made. The converse is also of importance. The policy should identify who should be allowed to re-enable a service and under what circumstances. Answers to these questions will exist within the context of your organization.

Process Flow

Now we come to the heart of the incident response policy; it is within the process flow that the steps for response are outlined. The flow should start wherever an incident comes into being, and then trace the incident via the classification system up to the point where the CERT and other departments are notified. It is a good idea to use both a written description and a diagram to describe the incident response process. Reading pages of text in an emergency situation will lose effectiveness. Brevity and schematic formats are much clearer and easier to follow. You should be mindful of our earlier discussions regarding supply chains, both internal and with external entities. Where systems are connected through extranets to customers, suppliers, or outsourced suppliers, you need to follow the process flow from end to end.

Triage

The concept of triage is similar to that employed in the medical environment. The plans that you have designed and developed, and may even have tested either through a desktop, walkthrough exercise, or a simulation, cannot, however comprehensive, account for every single possible dimension. In the event of a real incident that requires the invoking of the plans, you should assess the impact of the incident and the consequences.

Prioritize those systems that have been least affected and allocate a resource to repair. Identify those systems on your critical list and prioritize remedial action to either relocate processing to your DR site or implement corrective action through your BC plan.

Emergency Response

A key part of the BC and DR plan development process is to review the types of disruptive events that can affect the normal business process. There are many potential events that can occur and the type, probability, and impact must be assessed. These include natural disasters, such as environmental and ecological, and man-made disasters such as terrorist and political. Considering each in isolation will provide one set of plans; however, it is important to also recognize that events do not always occur in isolation. Therefore, plans should account for multiple and related events. For example, following a natural disaster such as a flood, organizations should also prepare for human activity such as theft from looters.

Natural and weather-related incidents will be geographically focused and have a potentially high impact on your business continuity with regard to human availability, loss of utilities, demands on local resources, and access and egress to the surrounding areas. Resources such as fuel and transport may become in short supply (if available at all); thus pre-planning and arrangements will be critical to your business continuity and disaster recovery. The next sections consider examples of events.

Tornadoes and Hurricanes

Traveling at speeds in excess of 50 miles an hour, tornadoes can cause significant structural damage to buildings and severe injuries or death to humans.

Hurricanes generate winds in excess of 60 miles an hour, bringing strong winds and torrential rain. They can lead to flooding, again causing structural damage to premises, both business and domestic. Consequently, there may be direct and indirect impacts to the continuity of your business. If your employees' homes have been affected or there has been a loss of human life in the family, their first priority will be to their relatives and not to work. While your organization may not be directly affected, your employees, suppliers, and customers may be, thus impacting your business.

Freezing Conditions and Snowstorms

Snowstorm conditions can include blizzards, strong winds, freezing temperatures, and snow drifts. Employees may be unable to travel. The snow and ice can impact basic utilities such as lighting and communications. Buildings may collapse under the weight of the excessive snow. Persons trapped may suffer injury or death from hypothermia.

4

Floods

The source of a flood can be torrential rain, melting snow, tropical storms, swollen rivers, or poor drainage systems. Water damage to buildings and equipment can lead to incapacity for long periods of time. Extended impact can lead to power failures, loss of transport, and potentially result in injury or loss of life.

Drought

A prolonged lack of rainfall can have a devastating effect on humans, livestock, and vegetation. Although these conditions are seasonal in some geographical locations, in some areas of the world, severe droughts can have a significant impact on businesses that rely on water for their business processes, such as manufacturing.

Earthquakes

Earthquakes are caused by shifts in the earth's rock plates that cause movement of the earth's upper surface. The Richter scale is the best-known scale for measuring the magnitude of earthquakes. The magnitude value is proportional to the logarithm of the amplitude of the strongest wave during an earthquake. A recording of 7, for example, indicates a disturbance with ground motion 10 times as large as a recording of 6. The energy released by an earthquake increases by a factor of 30 for every unit increase in the Richter scale. *Table 4.5* gives the frequency of earthquakes and the effects of the earthquakes based on this scale.

Severe earthquakes can destroy power and communication lines and disrupt utilities. They can destroy road and rail networks, disrupting travel. Additionally, landslides, damage to dams, and aftershocks can hinder rescue efforts. Humans may be trapped in buildings or be injured by falling debris such as glass and building materials.

Richter Scale No.	Number of Earthquakes per Year	Typical Effects of This Magnitude
<3.4	800,000	Detected only by seismometers
3.5–4.2	30,000	Just about noticeable indoors
4.3–4.8	4,800	Most people notice them, windows rattle
4.9–5.4	1,400	Everyone notices them, dishes may break, open doors swing
5.5–6.1	500	Slight damage to buildings, plaster cracks, bricks fall
6.2–6.9	100	Much damage to buildings: chimneys fall, houses move on foundations
7.0–7.3	15	Serious damage: bridges twist, walls fracture, buildings may collapse
7.4–7.9	4	Great damage, most buildings collapse
>8.0	One every 5 to 10 years	Total damage, surface waves seen, objects thrown in the air
Source: http://www.matter.org.uk/Schools/Content/Seismology/richterscale.html		

Table 4.5 – **Frequency of earthquakes and their effect**

Communications

In the event of any incident requiring the need to invoke a business continuity or disaster recovery plan, communications within the organization and to all impacted external parties are key. It is therefore important to ensure that you have a properly thought out communications plan. You must identify beforehand (and, as part of your plan preparation,) who will take responsibility for all communications and the message you want to convey. The critical issue is to reduce alarm, putting the minds of employees, suppliers, customers, and all other stakeholders (shareholders, etc.) at ease. You also need to ensure that you have an appropriate communications plan that provides for interaction with emergency services and government bodies (local and national).

Communications Plan

Communications is concerned with several elements, all equally important:

- **The Content** – What do you want to say? Are you actually saying something by omitting details?
- **The Medium** – How are you going to deliver the message? In a press interview? Written or verbal?
- **The Delivery** – Why are you delivering the message? What are your expected outcomes?
- **The Timing** – When do you deliver the message? How often should you repeat it or provide updates?
- **The Audience** – Who are you expecting to listen? Will a single message reach out to all, or do you need different messages for different audiences?

First impressions count: If you deliver the correct message in the correct way to the right audience and achieve the desired effect (i.e., reducing any exacerbation of the situation and producing a calming, reassuring impact), then confidence in the organization will be sustained. However, a negatively received message can only add to your damaged situation.

Thus, your plan should identify the most appropriate person to deliver the message in the correct format with the right level of detailed information using a medium relevant for the intended audience. Let us consider a sample of scenarios.

1. An explosion at your plant:
   - Who do you need to inform?
   - Who is the best person to make the initial communications?
   - How do you communicate with the emergency services?
   - How do you communicate with the families of your employees?
   - How do you communicate with the public in the vicinity impacted by the incident?
   - How do you manage the internal communications to employees to ensure continuity of operations?
2. A hostage situation:
   - With whom do you share the incident information?
   - What action can you take?
   - What assets have been impacted? People? Physical assets?
   - How do you communicate the information to the public? How much information do you share to protect those involved? How do you communicate to those relatives directly involved?

        ¤   How do you work with government agencies?

        ¤   How do you communicate with the hostage takers?

3.   Flooding of key computer site:

        ¤   Which vendors need to be contacted to assist in equipment cleanup?

        ¤   Who should be hired to dry out and clean documentation?

        ¤   What action is needed to clean and restore the facility?

        ¤   How long will it take to repair or replace critical resources?

        ¤   Will it be necessary to activate an alternate site for critical system processing?

        ¤   Public Relations

The importance of the public relations aspect of the plan varies with the scope of the incident. Major incidents will attract the media. In this case, it is necessary that the incident be explained by an experienced spokesperson in a straightforward manner. Efforts to fool the media will surely fail and serve to worsen the image of the organization. It is important that a single voice speaks for the organization in order to avoid contradictions and misunderstandings; hence the organization should ensure that vis-à-vis the firm and its disruption and recovery, one, and only one, person is authorized to speak with the media and that everyone else is instructed not to speak with the media. The reputation of the organization is at stake, so this is an important activity.

Vendors

During any incident that results in a severe disruption of a data processing facility, emergency vendor support will be necessary to maintain processing continuity and conduct restoration procedures. All vendors that will be needed to help satisfy requirements should be placed under contract to provide emergency services. Vendors normally involved include providers of backup storage; contractors for alternate site processing; experts in water, mold, smoke, and fire cleanup; and those providing critical equipment repair or replacement. In the event that personnel will be required to move to an alternate site, vendors to provide transportation, office, and living space, etc., may be required.

Utilities

Electrical power is probably the most critical utility to the operation of data processing mechanisms. Alternate sources of power should be investigated and contracted for. It is important to review BC and DR plans for available power companies and ensure that your requirements are included. Forward-thinking organizations often acquire portable power generators for use as emergency power when all else fails. Critical systems should be linked to an uninterruptible power source to provide continuity of service during short outages.

Lessons learned from previous major incidents have identified the loss of voice communications as a serious handicap during the response and recovery phases. Therefore, it is important to consider the probable loss of the primary phone system as well as the impairment of mobile and cellular communications. When considering handheld radios for backup, one should ensure that they are located in convenient and secure places for distribution and have spare batteries and training in their use available. Finally, the need for fresh water and HVAC should be determined, particularly in areas likely to be flooded or have high humidity.

External Agencies

Government, both local and regional, can play an important role in your ability to recover from a wide area incident. They will be responsible for helping their constituents and, unless you can convince them otherwise, may be tempted to commandeer your critical resources, such as transportation, utility equipment, and facilities to support the populace. Consequently, it is important to communicate your recovery requirements to local and regional authorities and be included in their BC/DR plans.

Recovery Plans

Priorities identified in your business impact analysis must be clearly communicated to all of the stakeholders in the organization in order to counter attempts to increase personal priorities during the heat of response/recovery efforts.

Key personnel need to be able to communicate directly and effectively with each other in order to ensure that response/recovery procedures are carried out as planned. Therefore, communication equipment/facilities must be assigned to them on a priority basis.

Logistics

Transportation to relocate personnel and materials from the damaged site to the alternate site must be pre-planned. Also, transportation needs to be arranged to move items required from off-site storage to the alternate processing site expeditiously. This is a critical function to enable the continuity of services in accordance with the BCP. Procedures in the BCP related to transportation should include best estimates of the numbers of personnel to be transported, the volume of material to be moved, services payment, and reimbursement of expenses. Contracts with vendors for transportation services should be prepared that commit the vendor to the required level of support.

Facilities at the alternate site will be required to provide personnel workspace, IT and office equipment, and a dedicated meeting room. At the alternate site or nearby, prearrangements for temporary shelter with showers, exercise facilities, and medical care should be made.

Data backups in support of critical systems can be kept at the alternate site or in an off-site facility. The backup and off-site storage facility should feature the same environmental characteristics as the primary facility. This includes physical security, temperature, humidity, power, and fire suppression controls, etc. The stored data should be used in operational tests to ensure that all anticipated items are there and in a computer-readable form. The location of off-site data storage is an important consideration. The facility must be available 24 hours a day and in an easily accessible location far enough from the primary location to avoid being involved in the same geographical disaster (usually about 25 miles). Communications procedures necessary to access the facility must be included in the plan as well as identification of those personnel authorized to retrieve items.

Communications network priorities to support the transmission of data for critical systems must be agreed upon and included in the plans. As an example, initial emergency data communications could be through cable, satellite, or fiber optic services that are widely available, or, in severe cases, even via dial up.

Supplies required for recovery operations must be identified and placed in off-site storage to be available for movement to the alternate site. Items to be included on the list are as follows:

- Hard and soft copies of the BCP, DRP, and other plans
- Contracts for recovery and restoration support
- Office supplies, forms, and stationery
- Spare parts, equipment, tools, etc.
- Financial supplies, such as checks, credit cards, and petty cash
- Documentation, such as inventory lists, wiring diagrams, operating manuals, etc.
- Flashlights, cameras (digital and video), handheld radios, spare batteries, etc.

Equipment not already in place at the alternate site that is required to support critical system continuity of operations must be made available. Some organizations are able to stockpile excess equipment or used equipment that is not yet obsolete at an organization storage facility. Otherwise, vendor agreements to provide equipment on an emergency basis must be executed, but only after determining that the vendor is likely to be able to provide the necessary items in the event of a situation requiring such a delivery. The ability to move stored equipment or obtain vendor-supplied equipment to be quickly available at the alternate facility must be included in tests of the plans. It is also important to test any communications mechanisms that would be utilized in the event of a disaster to notify the storage facility and relevant vendors of the situation; tests should confirm that such communications links properly function 24 hours a day, 7 days a week, 365/6 days per year.

Plan Implementation

Implementing the developed plans requires coordinated action by all of the personnel involved in the response, recovery, and restoration phases of the plans. This coordination can only be achieved and maintained by regular and thorough testing of the plans. It must be ensured that all key personnel and their backups are thoroughly trained and involved in plan tests so that they are confident in their ability to perform their roles.

Testing

Once the draft BC and DR plans have been developed, they should be fully tested to ensure that they will be effective.

Methods

There are basically five types of tests listed in order from the simplest to the most complex.

1. Checklist is a test involving a meeting of the key stakeholders and plan participants who review the plan contents to agree that all issues have been adequately addressed.
2. Structured walkthrough is a more thorough review that includes the plan procedures by the plan participants and team leaders to ensure that they understand their roles and the interfaces and that the plan will work as expected.
3. Parallel testing is essentially an operational test of the plan that includes the operations recovery team, critical system users, and observers to ensure that the systems being recovered will run at the alternate site. Off-site storage data and software should be utilized to ensure that it is sufficient and usable. Hot

site contracts should include adequate testing time for this purpose, and all critical systems must be tested on a regular basis.

4. Simulation is a comprehensive test involving the vendors, all critical systems users, and all teams and participants with designated backups. Usually this is scenario driven to provide everyone involved with an example of what would transpire during an actual recovery. The players include the executives who would man the Emergency Operations Center and control the simulated recovery. Only materials from the off-site storage facility should be available to participants. The simulation should include a rehearsal of all actions up to the actual movement of employees or equipment and materials to the alternate site. This test is a confidence builder that enables all concerned to experience role-playing in preparation for an actual disaster.

5. Full interruption involves actually shutting down normal operations and relying on the recovery procedure accuracy and personnel to provide continuity of operations. This can be dangerous for large organizations because of the possibility of precipitating an actual disaster, so it is not recommended except in unusual circumstances.

Schedule

The scheduling of tests is an important consideration because it involves the required participation of several key personnel, but it should not generally be allowed to interrupt or otherwise impact normal operations. Tests should be conducted frequently enough to ensure that changes to critical systems, equipment, facilities, and personnel do not make continuity/recovery plan specifications obsolete. Many organizational changes can adversely impact plans, but most often it is changes to contact information or personnel that are a problem. The test schedule should be published well ahead of time to enable key personnel to adjust their personal schedules in order to be available. Each scheduled test should include a test plan that identifies the test objectives, scope, time requirements, participating personnel, location, etc.

Approval

Since tests involve the participation of several personnel, management approval should be obtained before publishing the schedule. Executive management must approve expensive tests such as simulation and full interruption.

Success Criteria

How can you ever know when you have been successful? The basic purpose of testing is to discover potential problems either in the ability of the plan to meet the recovery time and recovery point objectives or the readiness of personnel and materials to execute the plans effectively. Therefore, the purpose is to identify problems. If no problems are experienced, something is wrong with the testing procedure. It is best to start small with testing until most of the problems are resolved in order to minimize wasted employee time. More elaborate and complex testing should follow to thoroughly ensure that interfaces and overlapping requirements are accommodated. One of the most common problems is assigning key personnel to more than one team. This usually doesn't work well because of the overlapping need to be in more than one place at the same time.

Reporting

Reporting the results of testing is very important for several reasons. One is that it keeps management aware of the program and its need for continued support. Another is that it provides information for maintaining the plans. It can also be evidence for auditors to show progress and viability of the planning process.

Plan Feedback and Update

Documentation of plans must be kept updated to accommodate personnel changes, equipment upgrades, critical system changes, and facility movements. The updates should be centrally coordinated to maintain consistency. If test results show that aspects of the plans are inadequate, the planning team should meet and develop modifications.

It is extremely important that strict version control be established for all plans to ensure that all participants of response and recovery operations are using the same procedures and guidelines.

Training, Education, and Awareness

All members of staff should be aware of the importance of business continuity planning. Training and awareness are important to make sure that the staff fully understands the plan and the role they will play in it.

Awareness can range from simple knowledge of the assembly points should the building have to be evacuated, to the exact role each member of staff will have in the event of a disaster or unexpected event.

Awareness training should be undertaken on a regular basis and be included in any staff induction programs.

Training in emergency response skills needs to be provided for those personnel assigned to teams involved in damage assessment, rescue operations, safety evaluations, etc.

Staff who will have specific responsibilities for the recovery of IT systems should be given further technical training. This will ensure that they are able to recover systems and applications quickly and efficiently.

Changes to the plan may require the retraining of key personnel and additional testing to ensure that the changes result in anticipated improvements.

Any third parties who have a critical role in your business continuity plans should be part of this awareness training. If, for example, you have set up office-sharing arrangements with another business, then they need to know the procedures you will follow if your own office becomes unavailable.

You might also wish to consider training for any member of staff who may need to talk to the media in the event of a disruption or incident. This is particularly important if the reputation and public perception of your business are key to its ongoing success.

Audit

The auditors have a special role to play in BCP and DRP. They should review the plans to ensure that they reflect the industry best practices, and they should observe the plan tests and report on the effectiveness of plan implementations. Audit findings should be appropriately addressed in plan updates. Also, the auditors evaluate the plans for compliance with legislation and organization policy. The audit role provides due diligence with their assurance that due care is completely addressed.

Restoration

Depending on the cause of the disaster, restoration of the primary facility could be fairly easy or very complicated. Of course, it is wise to prepare for the worst case based on your threat analysis that was previously completed.

The primary objective of restoration is to return the primary facility and equipment to normal full operations. The facility and equipment must first be cleaned of water, smoke, or fire contamination. The damaged equipment must be repaired or replaced and water-soaked documents salvaged. There are vendors that can repair and salvage equipment and documentation. Quick action is required to limit water damage and minimize mold. Equipment should not be restarted until the equipment vendor declares it safe to do so; otherwise, insurance protection could be voided.

The primary facility should be operated in parallel with the recovery site to ensure that processing is successful. After completion of this step, the recovery site is decommissioned, and the restoration completion report to management, users, and stakeholders can be issued.

Survivability

After the creation of a business continuity and disaster recovery plan, the ISSMP may be called to participate in the determination of an organization's survivability and resilience capabilities. This is a form of testing the aforementioned plan. It is also possible that such a study will be ordered prior to, or during, the creation of a plan.

It is extremely important to understand that survivability and resilience are not one and the same, and that the ISSMP should ensure that the organization for which he or she is performing a capability determination study understands the difference and has acceptable levels of both.

Survivability refers to the physical survival of systems and information. Clearly, organizations, and their disaster recovery planners and team members, want to ensure survivability. But, doing so is not normally sufficient to address continuity risk. An organization that suffers a disaster with a great deal of successful "survival" may still be unable to continue operations. Individual systems may survive, but without proper resilience, the business may be unable to function. Resilience refers to the survival of the capabilities to perform and deliver at an acceptable level despite challenges to normal operations. Survival is, in fact, a subset of resilience.

The need for survival and resilience – and the capabilities for addressing such needs – can vary widely between organizations. Some entities may have single points of failure with little or no fault tolerance and find such a situation perfectly acceptable, especially after examining the cost of redundancy or other countermeasures against failures; others may have tremendous redundancy in place as part of robust contingency plans intended to ensure as-close-to-zero-downtime as possible. The need for designing appropriate plans was discussed earlier in this domain.

Once plans are in place, however, it is important to determine how well they actually deliver survivability and resilience through testing and analysis. In most cases in which an ISSMP will be involved, resilience, not simple survival, is the goal. While there are multiple methods of measuring how well these two are delivered, one can, at a high level, think of these as being defined by the answers to the following question, where X is every anticipated failure type analyzed one at a time:

If a failure of type X took place, how long would it take, and how much would have to be spent, to guarantee the same level of availability, integrity, and confidentiality as existed prior to the failure, or at least at an acceptable level? This calculation is sometimes known as the measure of restoring "goodness."

Some types of anticipated possible failures may not be addressed; those should be described in the plan as reflective of the limitations of the scope of the plan.

There are no standard metrics to measure resilience, and the answer to this question is usually not just a single measure of time and money. Often it may be expected that those running determination tests will produce charts and documents describing what resources will be able to recover to what level and when, and scenarios for multiple types of disasters and failures will be described. Information as to how quickly a particular system or service can be restored from non-functioning to a degraded and unacceptable level, and from such a level to a degraded but acceptable level, and from an acceptable level to a normal level, is important for business owners to understand.

Likewise, if there are costs associated with the recovery, business system "owners" need to understand as such. Perhaps recovering to a normal level quickly is not desired if doing so will involve high cost, when recovering to a slightly degraded, but still acceptable, level can be done at much lower cost. Cost in this case means not only financial outlays but other costs as well. For example, if employees will need to be relocated after a disaster instead of being with their families in order to fully recover operations, such a recovery may have an unacceptably high cost in terms of ill will and employee morale. Any costs related to recovery, therefore, should be spelled out clearly in the documentation produced.

When Disaster Strikes

Professionals who prepare disaster recovery plans usually hope that their work serves to create a feeling of safety and security but that their plans never need to be put into action other than during tests. Humans, however, often fail to anticipate extraordinary events. Unforeseen events occur more often than one might think – and cause unexpected disruptions. In the New York area, for example, between 2001 and 2013, the 9/11 attacks, a major area-wide power failure, an October snowstorm, and Hurricane Sandy each presented a different set of severe challenges for many organizations and millions of people in the United States. Terrorist attacks in the United Kingdom and Spain have also caused major disruptions in public transportation and other services, forcing various operations to resort to emergency procedures. History tells us that many more disaster recovery plans will actually be activated than one might expect, and, therefore, it is critical that the ISSMP be able to not only contribute to the design and testing of a plan but also to play the appropriate leadership role in the recovery process.

If disaster recovery planning was done properly, the recovery process should flow according to plan, almost as if actors were acting out the script of a movie. As such, the ISSMP should ensure that everything goes according to the pre-defined plan. However, as mentioned earlier, there are sometimes circumstances that are unanticipated and, despite the best efforts in planning, are not accounted for in a disaster recovery plan. The job of the ISSMP in such a scenario includes ensuring that security is in no way compromised by efforts to address the unforeseen circumstance as part of the recovery.

4

Contingency
Management

Summary

In this, the fourth of five ISSMP domains, we discussed the critical need for proper contingency management. Disasters and other business disruptions will happen, and organizations that wish to survive and flourish must be prepared. The ISSMP candidate should understand the different types of relevant plans that an organization might need, and possess strong knowledge regarding the planning, design, development, implementation, and testing of the appropriate plans. He or she should be able to determine existing resiliency capabilities and address any challenges to the processes involved, be prepared to coordinate with other relevant stakeholders, understand a business impact analysis, and be able to guide a recovery. The ISSMP should also be able to understand, address, and manage third-party dependencies and security roles in case of an emergency, and be able to manage the maintenance, testing, and updating of any plans as needed.

References

NIST SP 8003-53 Rev. 3, *Recommended Security Controls for Federal Information Systems and Organizations*, August 2009.

Domain 4: Review Questions

1. Which one of the following is not a benefit of developing a disaster recovery plan?

    A. Reducing disruptions to operations

    B. Training personnel to perform alternate roles

    C. Minimizing decision making during a disastrous event

    D. Minimizing legal liability and insurance premiums

2. A business continuity policy should be reviewed and reevaluated

    A. Annually in light of management's strategic vision

    B. Biannually in preparation for an audit review

    C. Whenever critical systems are outsourced

    D. During implementation of system upgrades

3. Which of the following is a key phase of BC and DR plans?

    A. Damage assessment

    B. Personnel evacuation

    C. Emergency transportation

    D. Emergency response

4. The vitally important issue for emergency response is

    A. Calling emergency services

    B. Protecting the corporate image

    C. Accounting for employees

    D. Employee evacuation

5. The third stage in the development of business continuity plans is

    A. Define Business Continuity Management strategy.

    B. Exercise, review, and maintain the policy.

    C. Understand the organization.

    D. Develop and implement the BCM policy.

6. Which one of the following is not required for understanding the organization? Understanding the organization's

    A. Organization chart

    B. Risk appetite

    C. Information technology infrastructure

    D. Core business functions

7. Key milestones in developing the project plan and governance include all of the below except

    A. Risk analysis

    B. Data gathering

    C. Audit approval

    D. Training, education, and awareness

8. The output of a business impact analysis is

    A. A prioritized list of critical data

    B. A prioritized list of sensitive systems

    C. The recommendation for alternate processing

    D. The scope of the business continuity plan

9. When a critical system cannot function at an acceptable level without input from a system on which it is dependent, which of the following statements is incorrect?

    A. The system on which it is dependent is at a higher priority.

    B. The system on which it is dependent is at a lower priority.

    C. The system on which it is dependent is at the same priority.

    D. The critical system feeds a lower priority system.

10. People based threats include

    A. Theft, whitelisting, industrial action

    B. Industrial action, blacklisting, pandemics

    C. Pandemics, theft, industrial action

    D. Pandemics, call forwarding, theft

11. Risk acceptance is usually most appropriate when

    A.   Impact is high and probability is low.

    B.   Probability is high and impact is low.

    C.   Impact is high and probability is high.

    D.   Impact is low and probability is low.

12. Heat maps reflect the level of risk an activity poses and include all of the below except

    A.   A suggested risk appetite boundary

    B.   Proposed risk countermeasures

    C.   Risk zones

    D.   Color coding

13. A System Information Form contains all of the following information except

    A.   Recovery priority

    B.   Maximum outage time

    C.   Dependencies on other systems

    D.   Recovery point objective

14. The Notification Activation Phase of the BCP/DRP includes

    A.   A sequence of recovery goals

    B.   Activities to notify recovery personnel

    C.   The basis for declaring an emergency

    D.   The assessment of system damage

15. Documenting recovery procedures is for

    A.   Implementing recovery strategy

    B.   Highlighting points requiring coordination between teams

    C.   Outsourcing disaster recovery system development

    D.   Providing instructions for the least knowledgeable recovery personnel

16. The primary purposes of testing are to

    A.   Satisfy audit requirements.

    B.   Check that sources of data are adequate.

    C.   Raise staff awareness of recovery plans.

    D.   Prove the ability to recover from disruption.

17. Plan maintenance should be scheduled

    A.   After testing to account for hardware or personnel changes

    B.   In anticipation of audit activity

    C.   When changes are made to protected systems

    D.   When changes are made to supported business processes

18. Communications is a critical activity during the response and recovery phases of an incident. The communications plan must provide

    A.   Alternative types of communications media

    B.   A list of contacts reachable through a communications tree

    C.   Alternative communications service providers

    D.   Immediate access to mobile devices for key communicators

19. An Emergency Operations Center must be provided to centrally manage the incident. It should include

    A.   A provision for secure and confidential discussions

    B.   Office space for recovery team leaders

    C.   Access to all BC and DR plans

    D.   Forms of refreshment for EOC personnel

20. Thorough training in plan activities helps ensure

    A.   All team members understand their responsibilities.

    B.   All team members understand the roles of others.

    C.   Team cooperation.

    D.   Plans are current.

Domain 5
Law, Ethics, and Incident Management

A security manager may be responsible for many investigations, resolving ethical queries, and ensuring that the organization is responding appropriately to security incidents. He or she must also be aware of, and, at times, help the organization comply with, various regulations and laws. In this role, a security manager is expected to know about the current legal environment, the rules of evidence, trustworthy forensic actions, and how to conduct an investigation in a credible and effective manner, protecting the organization and individuals from undue harm or danger. A security manager is also often required to assist in the establishment, communications, and enforcement of ethical standards and guidelines.

OBJECTIVES

- The impact of laws that relate to information security
- Global privacy laws
  - Customer
  - Employee
- Legal footprint of the organization (e.g., Transborder data flow)
- Export laws
- Intellectual property laws
  - Trademark
  - Copyright
  - Patent
  - Licensing
- Manage liability (e.g., downstream and upstream/direct and indirect)
- The incident handling and investigation processes
- Establish and maintain incident handling process
- The financial impact of incidents and investigations to senior management
- Management issues as they relate to the (ISC)² Code of Ethics

KEY AREAS OF KNOWLEDGE

According to the Candidate Information Bulletin (CIB)/Exam Outline, the ISSMP candidate should be able to:

- Understand, and lead, the security incident handling process.

- Identify and understand domestic and/or international laws that pertain to information systems security and their ramifications vis-à-vis information, information systems, and information security.

- Understand forensic procedures.

- Understand professional ethics.

This domain incorporates the management of the domain covering legal, regulatory, compliance, and investigation issues within information technology, as well as the security incident management process; these areas of knowledge address computer crime and civil issues in law, as well as the ethical issues surrounding the management of information systems. This domain has an international focus and addresses the general points of law that are found across many jurisdictions. This is a conceptual look at the issues and concerns from a management perspective. As such, it does not address the technical issues of how to implement controls to address these concerns and processes within an organization.

Information Security Laws

The Internet is fundamentally a means of communication. Issues with law that have arisen because of the Internet are, thus, a result of the differences between communication in the physical world and communication using the Internet. Contractual negotiations are the result of a series of communications that create a legally binding agreement, which holds true on the Internet as well.

The foremost dilemma with the study of electronic law is the complexity and difficulty in confining its study within simple parameters. Internet and e-commerce do not define a distinct area of law as with contract and tort law. Electronic law crosses many legal disciplines, each of which can be studied individually. Examples of a range of areas of law that touch upon electronic, e-commerce, and the Internet can be seen in the following pages.

Much of the main focus of Internet-related law is on the regulatory trends in the United States, which are often indicative of future trends in other countries. Of course, cultures vary dramatically between nations; behavior that may be acceptable in some areas of the world may be a capital offense in others. As such, it is impossible, in this book, to address every nation's laws as they pertain to information security. Most Western nations, however, will have laws that will resemble, to some extent, the American laws discussed below, and it will be the laws of the United States of America that will serve as the guiding point for this domain.

Some of the primary Unites States laws that influence information technology security are:

The Gramm-Leach-Bliley Act

The Financial Modernization Act of 1999, or the Gramm-Leach-Bliley Act (GLBA or GLB), delineates stringent requirements for financial institutions to secure any and all personally identifiable customer information that is stored. A "financial institution" is roughly classified to comprise tax agents, mortgage brokers, banks, credit unions, and possibly merchants. A customer is defined as a consumer who "obtains, from a financial institution, financial products or services which are to be used primarily for personal, family, or household purposes, and also means the legal representative of such an individual" (US Code Title 15 > Chapter 94 > Subchapter I > § 6809). The GLBA has three requirements that direct the compilation, disclosure, and securing of confidential financial information (such as in a database) and the application of this data. These are as follows:

1. **Safeguards Rule** – Stipulates that financial institutions must implement security initiatives to protect confidential information.
2. **Financial Privacy Rule** – A financial institution must provide a privacy notice to the customer both when their relationship is established and on an annual basis.
3. **Pretexting Protection** – Prohibits access to personal private information without proper authority, e.g., social engineering.

The U.S. Attorney General enforces Gramm-Leach-Bliley. It has provisos for penalties up to $100,000 for each violation. Civil penalties of up to $10,000 that directly attach to the officers and directors of the organization can also impact the financial institution.

The Health Insurance Portability and Accountability Act

The Health Insurance Portability and Accountability Act (HIPAA or the Kennedy-Kassebaum Act) was implemented as law in 1996. The sections relevant to information security, and to people working with information security, fall primarily into Title II of this law (known as Title II: Preventing Health Care Fraud and Abuse; Administrative Simplification; Medical Liability Reform) and impact security as follows:

- **The Privacy Rule** – Defines patient medical records or protected healthcare information (PHI) and controls the use and disclosure of PHI, necessitating well-built measures to certify patient privacy.
- **The Security Rule** – Defines three security measures required to protect electronic protected health information (EPHI)
  - Administrative, e.g., policies and procedures
  - Physical, e.g., access to equipment or facilities
  - Technical, e.g., electronic safeguards

The Security Rule also balances the Privacy Rule by defining administrative, physical, and technical security safeguards required to protect PHI. Security standards are defined for each of these groupings. Additionally, HIPAA provides rigid sentences for those who violate it, including criminal prosecution.

The HITECH Act

The 2009 HITECH (Health Information Technology for Economic and Clinical Health Act) is intended to promote and expand the use of information technology in the American healthcare system.

In 2013, updates were made to HIPAA specifically related to security requirements and breach notification regulations, based on the HITECH Act. The definition of "significant harm" – as utilized to define scenarios in which reporting must be done – was expanded so as to include scenarios that under the original regulations would not have been included as reportable incidents; situations in which an organization cannot prove that harm would not occur to a person are reportable under the new law; there is no need to prove that harm did occur as was originally required under HIPAA prior to the passage of HITECH.

Additionally, parties not included in the original HIPAA regulations – for example business associates of parties handing medical data – were now included. Likewise, the penalties for failing to protect the privacy of PHI were increased (i.e., they are now more severe). However, the length of time that PHI is protected was shortened from forever to fifty years.

The Sarbanes-Oxley Act

The Sarbanes-Oxley Act (or "The Public Company Accounting Reform and Investor Protection Act of 2002") is typically called SOX or Sarbanes-Oxley. SOX was enacted "to protect investors by improving the accuracy and reliability of corporate disclosures made pursuant to the securities laws, and for other purposes" (Sarbanes-Oxley Act 2002). SOX was created in reaction to a perceived lack of public trust in the accounting industry that occurred as a consequence of various high-profile accounting scandals, such as Enron, that came to public attention early this millennium. SOX created a set of enhanced accounting and auditing standards related to the financial reporting and auditing of all publicly traded companies in the United States as well as any affiliates of these companies. It mandates the evaluation and disclosure of the effectiveness of the internal controls implemented by a company. The chief executive officer and chief financial officer of the company are required to certify financial reports.

SOX necessitates that company executives act to ensure the security, accuracy, and reliability of all IT systems that provide for the reporting of financial information. The legislation holds company executives accountable for any failure to adequately protect this information. This accountability must be reflected in the internal controls used to manage the companies' information systems used for the processes of financial reporting.

Federal Sentencing Guidelines

In 1997, the United States extended its general sentencing guidelines to cover computer-related crimes as well as "old-fashioned" physical crimes. Under the guidelines, senior executives and corporate officers can be held personally liable – and subject to extensive fines – if the organizations that they lead fail to comply with laws. The guidelines make it clear that management has a serious obligation to protect its organization's informational assets, and those of others who have entrusted the organization with their data. A standard benchmark for whether that protection was delivered is the concept of due care, or the "Prudent Man Rule."

Children's Online Privacy Protection Act

The Children's Online Privacy Protection Act (COPPA) mandates protection for the personal information of children using the Internet. Children-focused websites are not the only sites that need to be aware of the law; general sites that collect personal information must obey the requirements of COPPA if they know that a user is under the age of 13.

Industry Specific Regulations

There are also numerous regulations issued by various regulatory agencies that impact security at the firms that they regulate. For example, the Federal Financial Institutions Examination Council (FFIEC), which regulates banks, has issued guidances related to online authentication, proper social media usage, etc. While technically not laws, these guidances strongly impact how banks address various aspects of information security.

Of course, there are many other relevant laws, and nations other than the United States have their own regulations as well; the aforementioned are just some primary examples.

Licensing

To license or grant license is to give permission or authorization. A license is the demonstration of that permission. In cases of software, for instance, the license is the right to use the software as long as the user agrees to the terms of the license. A party ("licensor") may grant license to another party ("licensee") as a constituent of an agreement between those parties. A simple explanation of a license is "a promise by the licensor not to sue the licensee."

In intellectual property law, a licensor grants the licensee the rights to do some action (such as install software, make use of a patented invention, or even watch a movie) without fear of retribution through an intellectual property infringement.

In legal terms, authorization is defined as the right to use a product or service within the agreed terms. Authorization may be implied (such as when using a public website for the purposes for which the site owner designed it) or explicit (such as occurs when using Internet banking after having authenticated using one's own valid credentials). In legal terms, the granting of permissions through authorization is in effect the granting of a license.

There are a number of Internet-related offer and acceptance issues that have not been completely resolved. For instance, the question of online software downloads generates its own difficulties; does the downloading of software constitute acceptance, installing the software, etc.? Many software vendor licenses state that the loading of the software onto a computer indicates your acceptance of the terms. The terms of the agreement are likely to be enforceable if the software company is able to demonstrate that the user had an opportunity to view the terms prior to installing the software.

The U.S. case of *Williams v. America Online, Inc.* demonstrates the difficulties that may occur. In this dispute, Mr. Williams initiated proceedings in Massachusetts stemming from a class action over the installation of AOL software. AOL asserted that the proceedings must commence in Virginia as the terms state that Virginia was the exclusive jurisdiction for any claim. Mr. Williams, however, argued that alterations to his computer came about before he agreed to the conditions. Mr. Williams described the complicated process by which he had to "agree" to the conditions after the configuration of his computer had already occurred.

Further, Mr. Williams demonstrated he was able to click "I agree" without seeing the terms of service. This meant that the actual language of AOL's terms of service failed to display on the computer screen unless the customer specifically requested it, overriding the default settings.

Case law (e.g., *Hyde v. Wrench*) has long demonstrated that a counteroffer amounts to a rejection of the original offer. In contracts formed by email, it is essential to ensure that the contract has been concluded and not that a counteroffer remains. Case law such as Stevenson v. McLean demonstrates that a counteroffer should be distinguished from a mere request for information as occurs commonly in email requests.

End-User License Agreements

An end-user license agreement (EULA) protects both the software author or copyright holder and the user from liability in the event that the software is not used as intended. Many EULAs are formed through a "shrink wrap" software agreement. This is offered to a user or purchaser either on the packaging or electronically at some point in the installation process. The EULA offers the option of accepting or rejecting a contract to license the software where the installation of the software is provisional on the acceptance of the agreement by the user who has to be in agreement to abide by the terms of the license.

It is common practice for a EULA to declare extensive limitations to any liability that may impact the vendor. Generally, most EULAs remove any liability from the software vendor if the occasion occurs that the software results in harm or loss to the end-user by crashing the computer or through any data loss.

EULAs can also be used in order to extend the applicable copyright provisions that are assigned through the law. A license can be far more restrictive than the general copyright provisions, e.g., as defined in sections 107-122 of the United States Copyright Act. A EULA may also increase the scope of control that the relevant copyright laws provide. EULAs are contractual controls, which are defined to extend the provisions that are precluded from copyright law.

Equipment-Specific and Site Licenses
Licensing can be assigned in a variety of ways, including the following:

■ Being restricted to use by a single user or individual
■ A site (real or virtual)
■ A combination of the client and the site

An instance of such a restriction would be a grant of license allowing the use of a product for a named company that can operate the software from a single named site. Some of the common inclusions that can be found in a licensing agreement include the following:

1. Definitions of the organization or the physical/logical site
2. Whether the license is for networked use and how many concurrent users can access the product at a single time
3. How long the license grant is valid

Using a license outside the terms of the agreement is in effect using an unlicensed product. This leaves the organization liable for any damages in the same manner as if it used pirated software.

One area that is frequently neglected in equipment-specific license agreements is that of replacement. It is vital to make certain that provisions are included in the license to allow for upgrades and system replacement on failure.

Open Source and GNU General Public Licenses
There are several types of open-source licenses. Merely altering the names may deploy Template Licenses (Apache, BSD, Linux, etc.). These are further divided into Academic versus Reciprocal Licenses. Academic Licenses began in universities and other institutions of higher learning (these were especially common at Berkeley and MIT) that wanted to deliver the widest circulation achievable. In the terms of an Academic License, there are no valid restrictions on "use, rewriting, and dissemination" (CCH). Reciprocal Licenses such as the GNU Public License (GPL) necessitate that any party involved in the distribution of the software proffer the source code for the complete work as disseminated. These licenses also require that all changes be distributed with the work.

In explaining the differences between the GPL (GNU Public License) and other open-source software licenses, we need to first look to property law and the common law concept of licensing. In the most basic terms, a license is a unilateral permission to use someone else's property. In this case, the property is not real property or a chattel but an intellectual property. Thus, the license is a right to make use of copyrighted material.

A license may be granted within a contract, but a license is not a contract in itself. We have to ask, "What is a contract?" Although simplified, a contract is a promise that is legally binding

(Contract law in Australia. Carter, J.W. and Harland, D.J. 2002. http://catalogue.nla.gov.au/Record/1607996). The three pillars of a contract in common law are:

1. Offer
2. Acceptance
3. Consideration

It is common for the legal novice to take the GPL as a contract; this is a fallacy. "Offer" was defined in the classic case of *Carlill v. Carbolic Smoke Ball Co [1893] 1 QB 256*. The court developed the terms of offer and acceptance in this case where the company had set aside funds and consideration was made for the goods. In a GPL arrangement, no offer can be said to be made and no consideration is supplied. Thus, the GPL is a pure or bare license and may not be attached to a contract.

A bare license can be revoked because it is not a contract and there has been no consideration. The court could recognize the user's dependence on the software to act as a substitution for consideration. This would prevent the license from being revoked.

As such, a GPL is not a contractual arrangement and may not be made into one. To see how this affects an issue of a license under property, it is necessary to look at the Copyright Act (CA). This statute defines four requirements for copyright protection:

1. *Created by a "qualified person": ss32(4), 84, 184 CA*
2. *Subject matter: "works" and "subject matter other than works": ss10, 32, 89-92 CA*
3. *Material form: ss10, 22 CA*
4. *Originality: s32 CA*

The GPL license states that redistribution of any "derived" works needs to be published under the terms of the GPL. Thus, any software created using a GPL base must remain under the GPL. This is the "traditional" format used in open-source licensing, the objective of which is to ensure that an open-source program will always stay open source.

A derivative work is a new production by an author created from a previously created work. A derivative work can be licensed and dispensed/disseminated by the author of the derivative work in the event that a license for the pre-existing work to create a derivative work already exists, allowing the creation of the new work from the former one. This license must also allow the author to distribute that derivative work.

The GPL can be distinguished from another of the "open-source" software license structures, the "FL – project-open 'Free License'." FL software is distributed openly without cost to use and modify. It is, however, classified as commercial software, but the license fee for use and modification is given without consideration. This is where the FL deviates from the GPL. Whereas the GPL provides the free distribution of any derived software, the FL requires consideration for this right.

Most open-source projects are joint works with no reason for the assigning of copyrights. In the case of a collective work, the collector is the author and can license and distribute the sole portion that has been created, but only with license to distribute from the authors of the constituent pieces themselves. In the GPL, this is an implied license attached to the chain of rights. Proprietary rights and assignments of the GPL come with an implied license of the GPL terms.

The GPL, condensed to its core, consists of an agreement, whether modified or unmodified, to unreservedly

- Copy the software.
- Modify the software.
- Redistribute the software.

"If you redistribute it, in modified or unmodified form, your permission extends only to distribution under the terms of this license. If you violate the terms of this license, all permission is withdrawn" (http://lwn.net/Articles/61292/).

Thus, the primary factors that distinguish open-source software licenses are basically no more than terms of legal art. In all cases, the moral rights are not assigned.

Piracy and Related Issues in Copyright Law

The Business Software Alliance or BSA (http://www.bsa.org) defines software piracy as follows:

> *Software piracy is the unauthorized copying or distribution of copyrighted software. This can be done by copying, downloading, sharing, selling, or installing multiple copies onto personal or work computers. What a lot of people don't realize or don't think about is that when you purchase software, you are actually purchasing a license to use it, not the actual software. That license is what tells you how many times you can install the software, so it's important to read it. If you make more copies of the software than the license permits, you are pirating.*

Access to copyrighted material without license is illegal in itself. It is analogous to receiving stolen property. Receiving stolen intellectual property is no different. A simple example is where a friend gives you a copy of a music album. This action is illegal for both parties (being caught is another issue).

You "may" have a defense if you can validly prove (and this is for you or your organization to prove itself beyond doubt) that you were under the belief that the file was for public distribution. In the IT security field, any such claim for credit card details, banking information, etc., has about a snowflake's chance in hell. The Recording Industry Association of America (RIAA) has determined that it is effective to charge the downloaders. You do not get access to all files on a P2P network. You have to select access, and as such you make the decision to access the file.

In a court case involving copyright infringement or media piracy, for the accused to be charged with an infringement on the copyright, the claimant needs to mutually:

- Show ownership of the copyright work.
- Demonstrate that the other party "violated at least one exclusive right granted to copyright holders under 17 U.S.C. § 106."

What an organization needs to know is that simply making files available for download is equivalent to distribution. The case *Elektra v. Perez (D. Or. 6:05-cv-00931-AA)* set this into U.S. law.

The United States has also introduced a detailed set of immunities as a part of the online copyright infringement liability limitation act, which is contained within the Digital Millennium Copyright Act, in order to ratify the provisions of the World Intellectual Property Organization (WIPO) Copyright Treaty. These provisions provide immunity from prosecution to Internet intermediaries involved in the mere transmission of packets, who maintain automated cache systems, who host third-party resources, and those who provide search tools. There are conditions associated with these immunities. It is required that the Internet intermediaries lack of knowledge of the transgression, they do not receive direct financial benefit from it, and that they respect and do not try to bypass copyright protection technologies.

General immunity provisions have also been introduced within the United States through the Communications Decency Act (1996). This act introduced the criminal offenses of intentionally creating, sending, transmitting, or displaying of obscene or indecent matter to minors. This act introduced a number of "Good Samaritan" provisions permitting Internet service providers (ISPs) to introduce blocking or filtering technology while not becoming classified by the courts as a publisher or editor. This allows an ISP to filter this material without assuming any responsibility for third-party content.

The EU E-Commerce Directive provides similar provisions, offering protection for both packet transmitters and cache operators. It is still possible, however, that an ISP could be required to either actively monitor content or at least to take down prescribed content following a notification or advice as to its existence. If, following being advised, the ISP does not remove the offending content, liability would still apply.

The U.S. Senate has approved S.B. 2248, a measure that grants immunity from prosecution to telecommunications companies such as ISPs that cooperate with intelligence-gathering requests from the government. This amendment to the Foreign Intelligence Surveillance Act (FISA) would, if passed, increase government powers to eavesdrop on communications in certain cases without a warrant. Though there is an increase of selected protections for Internet intermediaries, there are still issues. If, for instance, an ISP sees an action that violates the constitutional rights of its clients and does not immediately respond, it does not receive immunity if eventually forced to respond. Further, the immunity only applies selectively to government agencies and no other actions.

In the context of the Internet, the scope in which a party may be liable is wide indeed. A staff member or even a consultant (as an agent) who publishes prohibited or proscribed material on websites and blogs, changes systems or even data, or attacks the site of another party, and many other actions, could leave an organization liable. *Stevenson Jordan Harrison v. McDonnell Evans (1952)* provides an example of this category of action. This case hinged on whether the defendant (the employer) was able to be held liable under the principles of vicarious liability for the publication of assorted "trade secrets" by one of its employees, which was an infringement of copyright. The employee did not work solely for the employer. Consequently, the question arose as to sufficiency of the "master-servant" affiliation between the parties for the conditions of vicarious liability to be met. The issue in the conventional "control test" as to whether the employee was engaged under a "contract for services" against a "contract of service" was substituted in these circumstances with a test of whether the tortfeasor was executing functions that were an "integral part of the business" or "merely ancillary to the business." In the former circumstances, vicarious liability would extend to the employer. Similarly, a contract worker acting as Web master for an organization who loads trade-protected material onto his own blog without authority is likely to leave the organization he works for liable for his actions.

In the United Kingdom, copyright law is governed through the Copyright, Designs, and Patents Act 1988 (the "1988 Act"), with older materials originally governed by the Copyright Act of 1956, and the ensuing decisions of courts. (Some subsequent directives have also been made in order to implement European Union directives into United Kingdom law.) This is a common approach, with the Australian position, for instance, mirroring that of the United Kingdom, where protection of a work is free and automatic upon its creation and differs from the position in the United States, where work has to be registered to be actionable. While some divergences may be found, Australian copyright law largely replicates the frameworks in place within the United States and United Kingdom. The copyright term is shorter than these jurisdictions in Australia, being the creator's life plus 50 years, whereas the United Kingdom has a term of 70 years from the end of the calendar year in which the last remaining author of the work dies for literary works. As co-signatories to the Berne Convention, for the most part, foreign copyright holders are also sheltered in jurisdictions including the United Kingdom and Australia.

The 1988 Act catalogues the copyright holder's sole rights "to copy, issue copies of the work to the public, perform, show or play in public and to make adaptations." An ephemeral reproduction that is created within a host or router is a reproduction for the intention of copyright law. Though there appears to be no special right to broadcast a work over a network, a right is granted in Section 16(1)(d) to transmit the work or incorporate it into a cable program or offering. The notion of "broadcast" is limited to wireless telegraphy that may be received by the public. Interactive services are explicitly debarred from the designation of "cable program service" (S.7 (2)(a)). A proviso has been made for an individual as an infringer of the act in the event of remote copying. This is defined to encompass transmission or broadcasts of a copyrighted work using a telecommunications system where the individual should have reason to suppose that another party who views or otherwise receives the transmission will create an infringing copy.

The act includes provisions that inflict both criminal penalties and civil remedies for the creation, importation, or commercial dealing in items or services intended to thwart technological controls that protect or otherwise secure copyright works. Sanctions have also been included to cover any unauthorized interference with electronic rights management controls that are designed to secure a work against the unauthorized distribution of copyright works whose rights management controls have been interfered with or otherwise corrupted.

Liability is also possible for secondary infringement, including importing and distributing infringing copy prepared by a third party. The extent of the exclusive rights of the copyright holder is large enough to include an organization that utilizes or consciously allows another into its system in order to store and disseminate unauthorized reproductions of copyrighted works. This situation would create the risk of civil action. A contravention could constitute a criminal offense if a commercial motivation for copyright infringement could be demonstrated.

The Australian High Court decision in *Telstra Corporation Ltd. v. Australasian Performing Rights Association Limited* imposed primary liability for copyright infringement on Telstra in respect of music broadcast over a telephone "hold" system. A large part of the decision concentrated on the definition of the diffusion right in Australia. It follows from this decision that if an ISP broadcasts copyrighted works in the general course of disseminating other materials through the Internet, that diffusion is a "transmission to subscribers to a diffusion service" as defined by the Australian Copyright Act.

In the Australian case of *Moorhouse v. University of New South Wales*, a writer initiated a "test case" asserting copyright infringement against the University of New South Wales. The university had provided a photocopier for the function of allowing the photocopying of works held by the university's library. A chapter of the plaintiff's manuscript was copied by means of the photocopier. The library had taken rudimentary provisions to control the unauthorized copying. No monitoring of the use of the photocopier was made. Further, the sign located on the photocopier was unclear and was determined by the Court to not be "adequate." The Australian High Court held that, while the university had not directly infringed the plaintiff's copyright, the university had sanctioned infringements of copyright in that the library had provided a boundless incitement for its patrons to duplicate material in the library.

In a 2005 paper entitled "The Promise of Internet Intermediary Liability, "Ronald Mann and Seth Belzley, professors of law at Columbia University and the University of Texas at Austin, state that in their belief, the least cost intermediary liablity is likely to be upheld under existing United Kingdom, United States, and Australian law. The positions held by the court in *Telstra v. Apra* and *Moorhouse v. UNSW* define the necessary conditions to detail public dissemination and infringement through a sanctioned arrangement. The public dissemination of music clips on a website could be seen as being analogous to the copying of a manuscript with the ISP's disclaimer being held as an inadequate control. It is clear that the provision of technical controls, monitoring, and issuing of take down notices by the ISP would be far more effective at controlling copyright infringement than enforcing infringements against individuals.

Several cases have occurred in the United States involving ISPs or other service providers that hosted copyrighted material made available to those accessing the site. A significant decision was made in *Religious Technology Center v. Netcom On-Line Communication Services, Inc.* The case involved the posting of information online, which was disseminated across the Internet. The postings were cached by the hosting provider for several days and robotically stored by Netcom's system for 11 days. The court held that Netcom was not a direct infringer in summary judgment. It was held that the simple fact that Netcom's system mechanically created transitory duplicates of the works didn't constitute copying by Netcom. Arguments that Netcom was vicariously liable were furthermore discarded. The Electronic Commerce (EC Directive) Regulations 2002 warrants that the equivalent outcome would be expected in the United Kingdom.

The U.S. Congress has acted in response with a number of statutes that, among other things, are intended to protect the intermediary from the threat of liability. The Digital Millennium Copyright Act (DMCA) envelops the possibility of liability from copyright liability. The DMCA exempts intermediaries from liability for copyright infringement as long as the intermediaries adhere to the measures delineated in the statute; among the requirements in the statute, for example, is a mandate that intermediaries eliminate infringing material upon receipt appropriate notification from copyright holders.

In the United Kingdom, "fair dealing" exceptions are a great deal more restricted than those in the United States. Netcom, if tried in the United Kingdom, would have to deal with the explicit requirements of Section 17 of the 1988 Act, which entails a copy or replication to include an electronic storage of a copyrighted work. The act further covers the formation of transient or incidental copies. This increases the possibility that a court action in the United Kingdom would vary from the result obtained in the United States at least in the first instance. The inclusion of storage differentiates (ISPs) and Internet cache protocols (ICPs) from telephone providers, aligning them closer to publishers.

An ISP could attempt to argue a similarity to a librarian over that of a publisher, but this is unlikely to hold for most companies. Modern peer-to-peer networks have separated the network from software with a decentralized indexing process in an attempt to defend themselves from an exposure to vicarious liability as in Napster.

The success of modern peer-to-peer networks has resulted in the content industry targeting those individual copyright infringers who use peer-to-peer networks to disseminate or download copyrighted material. Existing peer-to-peer networks and software provide an investigator with a sufficient degree of information concerning individuals who attach to the network to identify the degree of infringement and possibly who is responsible. Recent advances to the P2P networking protocols have allowed users to screen their identity, removing the ability for copyright holders to bring their claims to court. As copyright infringement evolves, it will become more improbable to expect a solution through prosecuting individual users and organizations.

What Is an "Electronic Contract"?

A contract is any agreement where there is offer, acceptance, and consideration. Consideration may be money or anything of value.

The definition of e-commerce is the creation of a contract electronically. This definition has developed in the courts over 30 years of commercial transactions from the fax machine to email. It should come as a modest revelation that the law of contract is relevant to the study of e-commerce and hence relates to the analysis of computers.

In particular, email conversations and saved copies of contracts and associated documents may often be used to validate compliance and are discoverable. This means that the contracts, the associated files in their creation, and also any emails discussing the contract may be called as evidence in a court of law.

Technological developments and the advent of the Internet have led to new paradigms in international as well as local commercial activity. These developments have reduced the certainty of contractual negotiations, leaving a commonly held belief that the law of offer and acceptance does not readily apply to such transactions when conducted online.

Dealings and transactions that formulate or initiate contractual negotiations are not restricted to the written word. The law of offer and acceptance applies to new technology in the same way that it applies to technological advances of the past.

In the past, international commercial transactions were generally restricted to negotiations between commercial entities. The Internet has increased the scope of business to consumer dealings and even consumer-to-consumer transactions across jurisdictional borders. For this reason, the formation of a contract using the Internet creates segregation into two initial categories. These categories include those negotiations that:

- Occur strictly within a single jurisdiction.
- Involve multiple legal jurisdictions.

Another concern focuses on the relationship of parties. Many Web-based transaction engines act as third parties during the process of offer and acceptance. The interaction between the Web server and a third party, such as a payment clearinghouse, can complicate the formation of a contract. Because of the complications of third-party interactions in e-commerce, it is necessary to determine the legal standing of the third party. The third party could be a party to the contract, an agent, or one of the two contracting parties, or it may just be an ancillary facilitator or medium, across which and through whom the contractual bargaining occurs.

Without legislation detailing the legal position of electronic contracts, the process of offer, acceptance, and the terms of a contract using the Internet establishes itself by means of the general law of contract. Contractual dealings over the Internet will continue (for the most part) in the same manner as for the negotiation of terms of a contract in the physical world. Establishing offer, acceptance, and the terms of a contract remains the same whether the form is in writing, orally, or implied through the conduct of the parties in the same manner as existed prior to the rise of e-commerce over the Internet.

To establish the formation of an electronic contract using the Internet, one should refer to the general common law of contract and the doctrine of international law, which are legitimate. There is little fundamental difference between the process of offer and acceptance in the "real world" and the Internet. Whether conducted in writing, orally, or implied from the conduct of parties, contractual negotiations are formed in a similar manner whether completed by telephone, face to face, or over the Internet using methods such as email or the Web.

An electronic contract has a twofold structure. Thought of electronically, the contract is a sequence of numbers and code saved to some electronic or magnetic medium. Alternatively, the contract becomes perceptible through a transformation of the numeric code when broadcast to a computer output device such as a printer or screen. Legislation has satisfied this dichotomy, removing the uncertainty as to whether an electronic contract can be regarded as being a contract in writing. An electronic document is functionally equivalent to one on paper.

When one is contrasting contractual principles, it is clear that where a contract is not required to be in writing, little additional uncertainty could be created where the contract is completed electronically. In fact, it is clear that electronic evidence must hold greater weight than verbal evidence. What is not clear is the extent of the weight attached to the various forms of electronic evidence. The strength of a digital signature algorithm and the security surrounding the mechanisms used to sign an electronic document will respectively influence the weight associated with any piece of electronic evidence.

Computer Crime

There will always be those in the world who wish to gain some benefit without actually paying for it. As a result, electronic law will inevitably intersect with certain aspects of criminal law. Whether by an outsider or through the actions of disloyal employees, crime is something that is likely to remain with us for the foreseeable future. The Internet and digital networks create new vulnerabilities and methods that criminals can exploit for their own gain.

Many existing types of crimes can be replicated and transacted with the aid of an online environment. Further, novel new crimes designed to exploit the features and advantages of the Internet and other digital networks have emerged and are likely to continue to emerge in the future. Some examples of criminal activities that have benefited from the advances in digital technology include the following:

- Computer break-ins or trespass including the unauthorized admission to the whole or any element of a computer system without the right to do so
- Illegal interception without authority, created using technical methods of the nonpublic communication of computer data to, from, or within a computer system
- Interference with or the damaging, deletion, deterioration, alteration, or suppression of computer data without authorization
- Interfering with a system or the serious obstruction without authority of the execution of a computer system through the input, transmission, damage, deletion, deterioration, alteration, or suppression of any and all electronically maintained data
- Possession of obscenity or prohibited pornography, e.g., child pornography and bestiality
- Industrial espionage
- Harassment
- Electronic fraud, including email
- Webpage defacements (cyber vandalism)
- Theft of commercial documents

While none of these crimes is wholly new, the ease with which they may be committed and the difficulty in capturing the offender have added a new dimension to crime. For instance, it is unlikely that law enforcement officials will be able to take action against many cyber-criminals unless the majority of countries first enact laws that criminalize the behavior of the offenders.

Some of the primary issues that face law enforcement in cybercrime cases include:

- Increased investigative costs due to the need for high-priced specialists
- The difficulties of conducting "real time" investigations
- The ease of anonymity on the Internet
- Difficulties with jurisdictional issues
- The rate at which technology is evolving
- The irrelevance of geographic distance

Civil and Criminal Law

One of the key distinctions between all legal cases is whether a case is civil or criminal. Generally, a criminal case is one where the government punishes a person due to the person's undesired behavior. A civil case revolves around a person or company recovering damages or stopping some behavior, e.g., through injunction. Forensic practitioners are likely to encounter either type of case depending on whom they work for.

Criminal or penal law concerns those issues that are believed to affect the whole of the population. The fundamentals of criminal law are known as the *actus reus* (the guilty act) and the *mens rea* (the guilty mind) of the crime. The *actus reus* covers the actual act of having committed the crime. This is the physical element. In hacking, the physical act could be sitting at the offender's computer and starting an attack script.

The *mens rea* of an act is the mental element associated with the deed. This is more commonly known as intent. In some instances, recklessness may suffice to cover the element of intent. An example of intent could come from something like bragging. A hacker who announces over Internet relay chat (IRC) the intent to break into a site could be said to have intent. Conversely, a penetration tester who unknowingly attacks sites belonging to someone else under the honest belief that the site belonged to the tester's client would either be at worst reckless if the tester had not checked the address or could be shown to not have intent if the tester is acting in good faith.

There are a variety of civil actions. For the most part, these are either contract or tort actions. As an example of a tort, if you allow Bob to run his website on your server but do not give him any permission to do anything else and then he subsequently uses the server to send large volumes of unsolicited email, having your site blacklisted, you could recover damages. The rule is if you let somebody use your property and the person uses it in a way you did not anticipate or give authorization (license) for, you may recover for this tort of conversion. On the other hand, if you had offered the site to Bob for a monthly fee, which he accepted, the action would be for breach of contract.

At times, there will be occasions where the forensics professional will be involved in gathering information that is not strictly attached to a legal action. Some examples include cases where the material is:

- Highly offensive but not unlawful.
- Breach of procedure, policy, etc.
- Inappropriate only.

In "at will" employment situations, no legal wrong may have been committed. However, an employer may seek to minimize risk by removing the party who is the source of risk.

Intellectual Property

Intellectual property laws concern the protection of intellectual designs and works. It is important to understand that when using the Internet one may encounter many protected materials; images and memes shared on social media, for example, may legally belong to someone who has not authorized their distribution. . In addition, domain names themselves may be subject to copyright laws.

The law of intellectual property is aimed at the safeguarding of peoples' ideas. Intellectual property is an expanse of law that deals with the protection of intangible items such as ideas and creativity that exist in some tangible (or viewable or hearable) form, such as a movie, music file, name, or design. There are many separate subject areas in intellectual property law, including the following:

- Copyright
- Confidence
- Design rights
- Domain names
- Moral rights
- Performance rights
- Patents
- Passing off
- Trademarks

Copyright Laws

The United Sates Copyright Office site (www.copyright.gov) defines copyright as being "a form of protection provided by the laws of the United States" (title 17, U. S. Code) to the authors of "original works of authorship," including literary, dramatic, musical, artistic, and certain other intellectual works (*Figure 5.1*). This protection is available to both published and unpublished works. Section 106 of the 1976 Copyright Act normally proffers the copyright holder with the exclusive right to do and to authorize others to do the following:

- Reproduce the work in copies or phonorecords.
- Prepare derivative works based upon the work.
- Distribute copies or phonorecords of the work to the public by sale or other transfer of ownership, or by rental, lease, or lending.
- Perform the work publicly, in the case of literary, musical, dramatic, and choreographic works, pantomimes, and motion pictures and other audiovisual works.
- Display the work publicly, in the case of literary, musical, dramatic, and choreographic works, pantomimes, and pictorial, graphic, or sculptural works, including the individual images of a motion picture or other audiovisual work.
- In the case of sound recordings, to perform the work publicly by means of a digital audio transmission.

Figure 5.1 – **U.S. Copyright search**

Misuse of software in relation to copyrighting is a criminal offense with heavy fines imposed for anyone caught copying copyrighted software. If in doubt, do not copy. When implementing copyright policy within an organization, the following questions should be asked:

1. Are users in your department aware of the current copyright laws (i.e., copying software, unless specified, is unlawful)?
2. Is each software package only installed on one machine in your department?
3. Are warranty registration cards filed with the vendor?
4. Is each software package copyright documentation read before installation?

In the United Kingdom, copyright law is governed through the Copyright, Designs, and Patents Act 1988 (the "1988 Act") and the ensuing decisions of courts. The Australian position mirrors that of the United Kingdom where protection of a work is free and automatic upon its creation, and it differs from the position in the United States, where work has to be registered to be actionable.[1] While some divergences may be found, Australian copyright law largely replicates the frameworks in place within the United States and United Kingdom.

How Long Does a Copyright Last?

As with all things, copyright protection eventually ends; it is only a "limited monopoly." When copyrights expire, they fall into the public domain. With a number of exceptions, public domain works may be unreservedly copied or used in the production of derivative works without either the permission or authorization of the former copyright holder. In 1998, the contentious "Sonny Bono Copyright Term Extension Act" (CTEA) passed into law. This U.S. law added 20 years to most copyright terms and created a moratorium that in effect stops any new works from entering the public domain until 2019. CTEA was enacted to ensure protection for U.S. works in the foreign market and includes access restrictions over works published later than 1922. The U.S. Supreme Court rejected (*Eldred et al. v. Ashcroft, Attorney General* 537 U.S. 186) a popular challenge to the CTEA.

The copyright term is shorter than these jurisdictions in Australia, being the creator's life plus 50 years, whereas the U.K. has a term of 70 years from the end of the calendar year in which the last remaining author of the work dies for literary works.

Foreign copyright holders are generally protected in Western countries as a result of the Berne Convention for the Protection of Literary and Artistic Works, which mandates that signatories respect the copyrights of authors from other signatory countries the same way they recognize the copyrights of their own citizens Additionally, the Word Trade Organization's Agreement on Trade-Related Aspects of Intellectual Property Rights (TRIPS) requires WTO member states to respect the intellectual property of other WTO member states.

The Doctrine of "Fair Use"

Section 107 of the U.S. Copyright Act details the doctrine of "fair use." This doctrine has evolved through the decisions of a number of court cases over time. Reproduction of a selected work for criticism, news reporting, comment, teaching, scholarship, and research is included within the provisions of "fair use" as defined in Section 107 of the Act. The Copyright Office

---

1   The Australian Act is modeled on the 1956 U.K. Act.

does not provide the authorization to use copyrighted works. You need to seek permission from the owner of a particular copyrighted work.

Section 107 of the Act sets out four factors used in determining fair use:

1. The purpose and character of the use, as well as whether such use is of a commercial nature or is for nonprofit educational intentions
2. The nature of the copyrighted work
3. The degree and substantiality of the section used in relation to the copyrighted work as a whole
4. The effect of the use upon the potential market for or value of the copyrighted work

It is difficult to distinguish among use that is covered by "fair use" provisions and copyright infringement. There is no mention of the number of lines, words, and notes that may be taken from a copyrighted work before it constitutes an infringement.

Copyright and Fraud: Plagiarism

The *Webster New World Dictionary* describes plagiarism as taking ideas of another and passing them as "one's own." This section details the tools and detection factors involved when investigating plagiarism. A common misconception is that plagiarism hurts nobody. The reality is that it is a fraud and thus a criminal offense (see § 1341. Frauds and swindles). Plagiarism takes away from the effort of the author, and society suffers as a consequence.

Defining the Term "Trademark"

The United States Patent and Trademark Office (USPTO) defines a trademark as "a word, phrase, symbol or design, or a combination of words, phrases, symbols or designs, which identifies and distinguishes the source of the goods of one party from those of others." This definition includes brand names, symbols, slogans, a design of merchandise – even the packaging style, specific words, smell, specific color, or an amalgamation of any of the above that could aid the consumer in differentiating a particular product or service from others in an equivalent trade. Trademarks can fall into three primary categories: service marks, collective marks, and certification marks.

- **Service Mark –** The USPTO defines a service mark as "any word, name, symbol, device, or any combination, used, or intended to be used, in commerce, to identify and distinguish the services of one provider from services provided by others, and to indicate the source of the services." It is comparable to a trademark with the single distinction being that a service mark is designed to identify and differentiate the service of an organization from others in the equivalent field of trade.

- **Collective Mark –** The USPTO defines a collective mark as "a trademark or service mark used or intended to be used, in commerce, by the members of a cooperative, an association, or other collective group or organization, including a mark, which indicates membership in a union, an association, or other organization."

- **Certification Mark –** The USPTO defines a certification mark as "any word, name, symbol, device, or any combination, used, or intended to be used, in commerce with the owner's permission by someone other than its owner, to certify regional or other geographic origin, material, mode of manufacture, quality, accuracy, or other characteristics of someone's goods or services, or that the work or labor on the goods or services was performed by members of a union or other organization."

- **Service Mark and Trade Dress –** The difference between a trademark and a service mark is minor. Primarily, the differentiation occurs as one of product and service. A trademark (TM is used to represent an unregistered trademark) differentiates products of the same trade. A service mark (using the symbol SM for an unregistered service mark) differentiates services of the same trade. A trademark not only consists of a label, logo, or other identifying symbol; it may also cover the distinctive packaging belonging to a particular product (e.g., the shape of a Coke bottle).

  This is called trade dress. Color pattern, shape, design, arrangement of letters/words, packaging style, and graphical presentation form a part of trade dress. In early days, trade dress referred to the way a product was packaged to be launched in the market, but now even the product design is an inclusion element of trade dress. Elements of trade dress for a particular product do not affect the way in which the product is used. Federal law for trademarks applies to trade dress also. There is no distinction between trade dress and trademark, as the Lanham Act (also known as the "Trademark Act of 1946") does not provide any distinction between the two.

- **Trademark Eligibility and the Benefits of Registering –** Any individual or organization that wishes to use a unique identifier in order to categorize its goods or services can qualify for a trademark. The trademark needs to be unique and not misleading. To register a trademark, one needs to file the application form at the USPTO.

  Before the USPTO will accept an application to register a trademark, it must detail the following:

  - The applicant's name
  - A name and address required for correspondence
  - An apparent depiction of the mark
  - A list of the goods or services provided

  The applicant must also pay the application-filing fee for one or more sets of goods or services. The following points cover the benefits of registering a trademark:

  - It protects an organization's name/logo.
  - The registered owner attains exclusive rights of the mark and gains protection against trademark infringement.
  - The mark may be used to give more visibility to the product from other products in the same trade.
  - Following the trademark registration, it is updated in the trademark search database, which aids in the discouraging of other applicants from filing a comparable variety of trademark.
  - If a registered trademark is infringed, the title holder of the registered trademark can request that the infringing party pay damages.
  - It provides a foundation for filing the registration for the specific trademark in a foreign country.

- ***Trademark Infringement*** – A trademark infringement refers to the unauthorized use of a protected trademark or service mark, or the use of something very similar to a protected mark. The performance of any legal action to discontinue (or injunct) the infringement is directly related to whether the defendant's exercise of the mark has created a likelihood of confusion in the typical consumer. Where the court comes to a determination that a reasonable consumer would be confused, then the owner of the original mark can put a stop to the use of the infringing mark by the other party and may even receive damages. A party that holds the legal rights to a particular trademark can sue other parties for trademark infringement based on the standard "likelihood of confusion." In the United States, the Trademark Act of 1946, statutes § 1114 and § 1125, are specific to trademark infringement.

Patents and Patent Infringement

A patent is defined in common terms to be a right granted for any device, substance, method, or process that is new, inventive, and useful. It is essentially a monopoly right over a registered invention or discovery that is enforceable by law and provides the holder the exclusive right to commercially exploit the invention for the term of the patent. A patent is not automatic and it must be applied for and registered in each country in which it is to apply (there is no such thing as an international patent). Patents give useful protection in the event that an invented new technology will result in a product, composition, or process with considerable long-term commercial gain.

In the United States, the Patent and Trademark Office issues patents. Patents are effective up to 20 years from the date on which the submission is filed. In Australia and many other countries, there are two types of patents in operation.

Some countries support alternatives to the full patent process through means such as an innovation patent. These are designed to be a comparatively quick, inexpensive safeguard that only lasts to a maximum of 8 years. Patent laws allow for the granting of a patent on the new article not on the propositions that claim to put into practice those ideas to make the article. You cannot patent an idea.

Any article, process, or manufacturing technique that asserts a right to a patent is required to prove its utility. In 35 U.S.C. § 102, U.S. patent law states that an invention cannot be patented where:

- The invention was known or used by others in this country, or patented or described in a printed publication in this or a foreign country, before the invention thereof by the applicant for patent, or
- The invention was patented or described in a printed publication in this or a foreign country or in public use or on sale in this country more than one year prior to the application for patent in the United States, or
- The inventor has abandoned the invention, or
- The invention was first patented or caused to be patented, or was the subject of an inventor's certificate, by the applicant or the applicant's legal representatives or assigns property rights to another in a foreign country prior to the date of the application for patent in this country on an application for a patent or inventor's certificate filed more than twelve months before the filing of the application in the United States, or the invention was described in a patent that has already been granted in the United States.

The primary types of patents include the following:

- Utility patents, which are granted to an individual who ascertains or invents a new instrument, process, useful composition of matter, or manufacture. Some examples include the following:
  - ◻ A new process for the fraction distillation of petroleum
  - ◻ A novel manufacturing method for paper
  - ◻ A machine such as a motorbike or car
  - ◻ A previously undiscovered composition of matter including a drug
- Design patents are granted to an individual who creates a new, innovative design for an article of manufacture. It guards the look of an article, for example, the shape of the Apple iPod.
- Plant patents or breeders' rights are granted to an individual who conceives, discovers, or asexually reproduces a distinctive variety of plant.
- An innovation patent is a fast, inexpensive, but limited protection option.
- In 2014, the United States Supreme Court issued a ruling (*Alice Corp. v. CLS Bank*) that may bring into question the validity of various technical patents that are too abstract; merely adding that an abstract idea is run on a computer has been deemed not patentable. The full scope of the impact of this ruling is yet to be seen.

Document Management

It is an offense to destroy any document that is or may be used as evidence in an ongoing or potential judicial proceeding in most Western (at least the common law) jurisdictions. An organization must not destroy documents on the foundation that the evidence is unfavorable. The penalties for the destruction of documents that are suspected to possibly be subject to litigation may perhaps end in a charge of obstruction of justice (*Table 5.1*).

	Australia/NZ	United States	United Kingdom
Basic Commercial Contracts	6 years after discharge or completion	4 years after discharge or completion	6 years after discharge or completion
Deeds	12 years after discharge	A minimum of 6 years after discharge	12 years after discharge
Land Contracts	12 years after discharge	6 years after discharge	12 years after discharge
Product Liability	A minimum of 7 years	Permanent	A minimum of 10 years
Patent Deeds	20 years	25 years	20 years
Trademarks	Life of trademark plus 6 years	Life of trademark plus 25 years	Life of trademark plus 6 years
Copyright	75 years after author's death	120 years after author's death	50 years after author's death
Contracts and Agreements (government construction, partnership, employment, labor, etc.)	A minimum of 6 years	Permanent	A minimum of 7 years
Capital Stock and Bond Records	7 years after discharge	Permanent	12 years after discharge

Table 5.1 – **Minimum Document Retention Guidelines**

Electronic Espionage

The United Kingdom differs from the United States in its efforts at codification through the Restatement and Uniform Trade Secrets Act to introduce a legislative set of controls preventing electronic espionage. The English law as it relates to a breach of confidential information is exclusively derived from the common law as it has evolved through the cases. A duty of confidence is created when an individual obtains confidential information through a state of affairs where it would be inequitable for that knowledge to be divulged to another. This could be a result of the receiver of the information being on notice or having an agreement that the information was to be so handled. The contravention of the duty that can result is in a civil action for a breach of confidence. Actions for the breach of confidence occur in association with the leaking or other dissemination of data that has a commercial value. This includes any personal information regarding an individual such as credit cards, health information, etc.

Breach of confidence is complex. It enlarges to "reflect changes in society, technology and business practice." Furthermore, the right to privacy in the EU is incorporated in Article 8 of the European Convention on Human Rights. This expands the available actions connected with a breach of confidence to include safeguarding against the misuse of private information. Under the common law, it is generally required that the plaintiff prove three things in order to succeed in an action for a breach of confidence:

1. The information must be confidential without being seen as trivial.
2. The information was presented in a circumstance that required a commitment toward maintaining confidence.
3. An unauthorized use or exposure of the secret information must have occurred with a risk of damage occurring if action does not occur to stop the incident.

The jurisdictional basis in most common law countries of the action for breach of confidence is unclear. The foundation most regularly relied upon is contract. Frequently, the parties will have incorporated express terms relating to confidentiality, but the courts have also commonly acted on the basis of an implied confidentiality provision in an existing contractual relationship. The courts have also created an equitable obligation of confidentiality autonomous of any contractual relationship. This obligation applies to the initial beneficiary of the information and to third parties who receive unauthorized disclosures of confidential information. This has also been used in addition to a contractual obligation, and at times in substitution for a contractual obligation.

The duty that confidence need be conserved may be overshadowed through a variety of other civic causes. These call for disclosure in the public interest. Either the world at large or the appropriate authorities should be informed. It is generally necessary for a court to seek equilibrium for the protection of the public interest. This balance is judged in placing confidentiality against a use or disclosure that favors society and creates quantifiable gains. Protections over the disclosure of private data will not be reserved in the event that there is a just cause or excuse for disclosing it.

An ISP or company that hosts information on the Internet needs to consider the need to protect data against the needs of data protection and that of the public interest. A failure to safeguard the interests of clients places the intermediary in damage of civil actions. This issue is a particular concern for organizations that host data (who have some obligation unless explicitly excluded in contract) and particularly service providers specializing in the provision of security services. These providers are contracted to ensure that the security of their clients is maintained and are open to actions in both contract and negligence if they fail in their duties.

One of the greatest difficulties comes to pass as a consequence of the ISP or content hosting provider not having a contract with the owner of the confidential information to protect or monitor that data. The equitable doctrine, imposing a responsibility of confidentiality in respect of data that the recipient knows or should have known was confidential and further that was proffered under conditions that involve the confidentiality of data, may be appropriate in selected circumstances. Nevertheless, it is clear that there remains a substantial dilemma for the plaintiff in proving that such a responsibility exists. This would be predominantly true where an organization declares unawareness of what content was on the site.

Import/Export Laws

Import and export laws vary across jurisdictions. In the United States, a number of laws have come about to both protect and control interstate and international commerce as well as to control cryptographic functions. Cryptographic algorithms drive e-commerce as well as offer the ability to restrict access to data and protect communications. In the wrong hands, this capability can be used to stop the government from seeing the signals traffic of foreign nations and others involved in military or terrorist activities.

The Uniform Computer Information Transactions Act (UCITA) was introduced in the United States in order to provide a common legal framework to control the conduct of computer-related business transactions. UCITA contains stipulations that address import and export and media licensing as well as requiring that manufacturers present media users with the capacity to reject the terms of the license agreement prior to completing an installation process. It requires that the consumer also receive a complete refund of the purchase price paid.

It is not just cryptography that is controlled. U.S. companies can generally export high-performance computing systems to the majority of countries without needing an export license. Exceptions to this rule do exist, however. The Department of Commerce has designated Tier 3 and Tier 4 countries with severe limits on those technologies that may be deployed. Countries including India, Pakistan, Afghanistan, and several Middle East states are included in Tier 3. The Tier 4 list includes Cuba, Iran, Iraq, Libya, North Korea, Sudan, and Syria.

The Tier 3 countries are excluded from receiving computer systems or hardware with a capacity that could allow them to operate above 190,000 MTOPS (million theoretical operations per second) without a license that is issued from the U.S. Department of Commerce. Tier 4 countries are forbidden to receive any high-performance computers or hardware.

It was once virtually impossible to export encryption products outside of the United States. The impact on the security industry, software industry, and e-commerce led the government to change this policy in the late 1990s. These changes designated retail and mass-market security software classifications for the supply of cryptographic controls. A firm that is exporting cryptographic controls may submit its product for review by the Commerce Department (a review process that is generally complete in under 30 days) in order to export the software.

Upon a successful evaluation, the product or software evaluated may be freely exported (other than to restricted countries – such as those on the Tier 4 list).

Encryption

In information technology, encryption has been one of those contentious issues where the need to provide privacy and secure commerce is weighed against government controls, law, and order. While the majority of countries have come to recognize the benefits of encryption technology, this recognition is not universal.

Many aspects of encryption are double edged. Protecting the security authenticity and integrity of communications in electronic commerce and the general rights of free speech has to be considered against the potential risk that is posed by criminals and terrorists. Encryption provides the means both to secure commercial transactions, access, and authentication as well as to conceal illegal behavior. This has resulted in many governments classifying encryption technology as a munition. As a consequence, many governments strictly regulate the import/export and even use of encryption technology.

This is complicated because many governments do not publish their policies on encryption, which makes it difficult to find guidance. Compliance with international encryption regulations is a complex task with significant risk. This is particularly true when considering multinational corporations. For instance, an organization that has offices in both the United States and China will have difficulty in legally configuring a virtual private network (VPN) tunnel between their offices. In fact, violating these policies can be a significant risk due to monetary penalties but can also result in criminal sanctions. Some nations actually assigned the death penalty to the distribution of encryption products. It is important to investigate the local regulations and international controls concerning encryption any time you wish to implement encryption across international borders.

In recent years, most Western countries, such as the United States, United Kingdom, etc., have lifted the majority of restrictions concerning strong encryption. This means that encryption solutions may be exported or re-exported to most commercial and government end-users located in nearly all countries except the embargoed destinations and countries. These are usually the jurisdictions that have been designated as supporting terrorist activities. These countries are listed in Part 746 of the Export Administration Regulations (EAR) as embargoed destinations requiring a license for the export of encryption products. These countries include Cuba, Iran, North Korea, Sudan, and Syria.

When one is considering encryption products, it is important to remember that simply travelling to an embargoed destination with a laptop computer that has standard encryption products (such as IPSec) that come by default with many operating systems can be a crime.

Liability

Not acting to correct a vulnerability in a computer system may give rise to an action in negligence if another party suffers loss or damage as the result of a cyber-attack or employee fraud. Proximity is the initial phase of the assessment. The subsequent phase inquires as to whether policy considerations exist that could reduce or counteract the duty created under the initial stage. Given proximity, a conception first established in *Caparo Industries Plc.*

v. Dickman (1990) and reasonable foreseeability as established in *Anns v. Merton London Borough Council* (1978) A.C. 728, the question of whether there is a positive duty on a party to act so as to prevent criminals causing economic loss or harm to others will be likely found to exist in the cyber world. The test of reasonable foreseeability has, however, been rendered to a preliminary factual inquiry not to be incorporated into the legal test.

Many organizations argue that current standards of corporate governance for information systems pose a problem due to the large number of competing standards. While the number of standards may be daunting, it is also true that standardization is necessary. Standards create a minimum set of requirements – which may not be identical across standards but, in most cases, are similar at least in concept – that do offer significant security benefits. Without standards, more weaknesses and vulnerabilities would likely exist, and more mistakes would likely be made. PCI-DSS and COBIT are examples of standards.

Installation guidelines provided by organizations such as the Center for Internet Security (CIS) openly provide system benchmarks and scoring tools that contain the "consensus minimum due care security configuration recommendations" for the most widely deployed operating systems and applications in use. The baseline templates will not themselves stop a determined attacker but could be used to demonstrate minimum due care and diligence. Employers can be held to be either directly or vicariously liable for the criminal behavior of their employees.

Direct liability for organizations or companies refers to the class of liability that occurs when they permit the employee's action. Lord Reid in *Tesco Supermarkets Limited v. Nattrass* formulated that this transpires when someone is "not acting as a servant, representative, agent or delegate" of the company but as "an embodiment of the company." When a company is involved in an action, this principle is usually associated with the conduct of company officers when they are a surrogate for or "as the company." Being that company officers can assign their responsibilities, direct liability may encompass those employees who act under that delegated authority. The employer may be directly liable for a criminal action in cases where it can be demonstrated that an express act or oversight of the company caused or accepted the employee's perpetration of the crime.

Where the prosecution of the crime involves substantiation of *mens rea*, the company cannot be found to be vicariously liable for the act of an employee. The company may still be found vicariously liable for any criminal violation of an employee if the offense does not need *mens rea* for its prosecution or where either express or implied vicarious liability is produced as a consequence of statute. Strict liability offenses are such actions. In strict liability offenses and those that are established through statute to apply to companies, the conduct or mental state of an employee is ascribed to the company while it remains that the employee is performing within its authority.

The conduct of agents and employees can result in situations where liability is imposed vicariously on an organization through both the common law and by statute. The benchmark used to test for vicarious liability for an employee requires that the deed of the employee must have been committed during the course and capacity of his or her employment under the doctrine *respondeat superior*. Principals' liability will transpire when a "principal-agent" relationship exists. Dal Pont (Dal Pont, G.E., Law of Agency, Butterworths, 2001, [22.4]) recognizes three possible categories of agents:

1. Those that can create legal relations on behalf of a principal with a third party
2. Those that can affect legal relations on behalf of a principal with a third party
3. A person who has authority to act on behalf of a principal

Despite the fact that a party is in an agency relationship, the principal is liable directly as principal in contrast to vicariously: "This distinction has been treated as of little practical significance by the case law, being evident from judges' reference to principals as vicariously liable for their agents' acts." The consequence is that an agency arrangement will leave the principal directly liable rather than vicariously liable.

The requirement for employees "within the scope of employment" is a broad term without a definitive definition in the law, but whose principals have been set through case law and include:

- Where an employer authorizes an act, but it is performed using an inappropriate or unauthorized approach, the employer shall remain liable.
- The fact that an employee is not permitted to execute an action is not applicable or a defense.
- The mere reality that a deed is illegal does not exclude it from the scope of employment.

Unauthorized access violations or computer fraud by an employee or agent would be deemed remote from the employee's scope of employment or the agent's duty. This alone does not respectively absolve the employer or agent from the effects of vicarious liability. Similarly, it remains unnecessary to respond to a declaration made against an employer through asserting that the transgression was committed by the employee for his or her own advantage.

Social media has created a whole new collection of data leak liability issues. In June of 2014, a woman filed a lawsuit against the University of Cincinnati Medical Center alleging that an employee of the center posted a screenshot of her medical records onto Facebook within the context of a photo. While courts are yet to decide on this particular case, it is becoming increasingly clear that employers may be liable to the activities that their employees carry out on social media especially if the activities are in some way connected to their jobs, even if those activities occur outside of the office or office hours and even if they occur using personal social media accounts.

Upstream and Downstream Liability

The Internet has enabled many old crimes to be reborn. Many morally violating acts such as child pornography have become far more widespread and simpler due to the ease and reach of email. Many traditional crimes such as threats and harassment, blackmail, fraud, and criminal defamation have not changed in essence, but the ease of the Internet has made them more prevalent.

Organizations need to be aware that they can be held liable for the impact of actions that occur due to their inaction (downstream) as well as being impacted by others out of their control (upstream).

- **Spamming** – Spamming can be defined as sending unsolicited commercial emails (UCEs). The more common term for spam is *junk mail*. Spammers obtain email addresses by harvesting them from Usenet, bots, postings, DNS listings, or webpages.

- **Sexual Abuse of Children in Chat Rooms** – The increasing prevalence of instant messaging and Web forums has created a potential for sexual abuse to occur. It is common for pedophiles to use chat rooms for sexually abusing children by starting relationships with them online. This generally involves befriending the child, establishing a steady relationship, and then gradually introducing the child into pornography through images or videos that may contain sexually explicit material.

- **Child Pornography** – Images or videos that depict sexual behavior by children (with the definition of at what age one is no longer considered a child in this context varying between jurisdictions) are child pornography and illegal to possess (and, obviously, illegal to produce or distribute) in many jurisdictions, including throughout the United States. The anonymity and ease of transfer of child pornography provided by the Internet has created an international problem with which law enforcement continues to struggle

- **Prostitution and Human Trafficking** – The Internet has made the crimes of human trafficking and prostitution (which is also illegal in most jurisdictions) much easier to carry out than in the past.

- **Harassment** – Harassment may occur through all forms of media, and the Internet is no exception. Junk mail, sexually offensive emails, and threats delivered through online means (including both email and instant messaging) are all forms of harassment. The inappropriate accessing of sexually explicit, racist, or otherwise offensive material at the workplace is another form of harassment. This includes the sending of unwelcome messages that may contain offensive material to another coworker.

- **Identity Fraud** – Identity theft is becoming more widespread due to ease and profitability. This action involves the stealing of someone's identity for fraudulent financial gain. It is in effect a larceny. The sending of offers by email that are too good to be true, fake websites, and other forms of phishing are all used to capture an identity. Many groups specialize in the capture of information and make financial gains by selling this information to groups who will make illegitimate purchases or financial transactions.

Privacy Law

U.S. Justice Cooley defined privacy as a right to be left alone. Others see privacy as a right to be anonymous. These different definitions have different implications.

In legal terms, privacy is a two-sided coin. On one side there is the right to be free from government intrusion; on the other there is a right to be free from intrusions from private individuals. The nature of this right is a protection of our private lives.

The right of privacy comes from the common law. In particular, there are four pillars created as a result of tort. These are as follows:

1. The right to stop another from appropriating your name or likeness.
2. The right to be free from unreasonable intrusion through the intentional interference with another person's interests in solitude and seclusion.

3. Freedom from false light. This is freedom from publicity that presents a person to the public in a manner that damages their reputation (see section on defamation).
4. Freedom from public disclosure of private facts.

In addition, governments have imposed statutes aimed at further increasing the rights to privacy. In Europe, the right to privacy has been integrated into the European Treaty convention. The primary statutes enacted in the United States to protect privacy include the following in addition to laws mentioned earlier in this chapter:

- The Electronic Communications Privacy Act of 2000, which was designed to regulate the interception of electronic indications such as email.
- The Privacy Act of 1974, 5 U.S.C. § 552a, which has imposed limits on the amount of personal information that can be collected by federal agencies.
- The Fair Credit Reporting Act (FCRA), as amended October 13, 2006, regulates the collection and use of personal data by credit reporting agencies.
- The Federal Right to Privacy Act (1978) limits the amount of information from customer files that financial institutions may disclose to the U.S. federal government.
- The Video Privacy Protection Act of 1988 prohibits movie rental companies from disclosing customer names and addresses on the subject matter of their purchases for marketing use.
- The Cable Communications Policy Act of 1984 prohibits cable television companies from using their systems to collect personal data concerning their subscribers without their express consent.
- The Equal Credit Opportunity Act (ECOA) prohibits creditors from collecting data from applicants including gender, race, religion, birth control practices, national origin, and similar information.
- The Family Educational Rights and Privacy Act (FERPA) of 1974 allows students to examine and challenge their educational transcripts and other records.

The word *"privacy"* appears at no point in the U.S. Constitution. The result is that the right to privacy has developed as a separate body of law. In the United States, the Fourth Amendment to the Constitution, with its prohibition against "unreasonable searches and seizures," has built the foundation for many of these rights.

Privacy is a critical component of the European Union (EU) data protection regime with noncompliance being likely to lead to a variety of breaches both locally in the United

Kingdom and internationally.[2,3,4] The security principle of the U.K. Data Protection Act (1998) "requires that appropriate measures (technical and organizational) must be taken by data controllers against unauthorized or unlawful access to personal data and against accidental loss or destruction of personal data. It has significant application in a further education (FE) or higher education (HE) e-learning environment. Sinee an e-learning system may include data such as student details, a student's submitted work and academic results; this principle makes it vital that such data are securely maintained."

Likewise, the European High Court of Justice ruled in 2014 that people have a "Right to be Forgotten." That is, they have a right to be removed from search engine results that are "inadequate, irrelevant, or no longer relevant, or excessive in relation to the purposes for which they were processed." The arbiter of what meets that description is, as of now, the search engines themselves, but that may change in the future.

Consequently, an organization needs to ensure that practical measures are made to protect the personal information it stores from misuse and loss, unauthorized access, and modification or disclosure. Defending the confidentiality of personal information involves implementing practical steps to preserve the following:

- Physical security
- Computer and network security
- The security of the network infrastructure
- The proper training of employees

Data should be destroyed or de-identified when it is no longer needed for the function for which it was collected, or at least when any allowable derivative uses of the data or the intention of fulfilling a legal requirement to retain the data no longer exist. A security policy that incorporates the consideration of any privacy concerns that an organization may face is important. This document should establish the systems and controls that ensure personal information held or processed by the organization is not subject to unauthorized access or use. For instance, in an online environment, this policy could state that personal information would never be stored using a cleartext format on a database or other transaction server.

Organizations need to become conscious of the massive risks to their reputation that are related to a breach of security associated with the disclosure of personal information. For instance, Skeeve Stevens was convicted for illegally accessing computer systems controlled by AUSNet through the use of a user account and password related to one of AUSNet's

---

2   Official Directive 95/46/EC on the protection of individuals with regard to the processing of personal data and on the free movement of such data.

3   See Walden "Data Protection" in Reed and Angel (Eds.), *Computer Law (5th Ed. 2003, Chapter 11)*; *Oxford University Press; London, UK.*

4   The Privacy Amendment (Private Sector) Act 2000 ("Privacy Amendment Act") contains the provisions for ensuring privacy in Australia. Also see the Directive 95/46/EC (Data Protection Directive); the Irish Data Protection Acts 1998 and 2003; Article 8 of the European Convention on Human Rights; the UK Regulation of Investigatory Powers Act 2000; U.S. "Safe Harbor" Rules; Employers' Data Protection Code of Practice; Model Contracts for Data Exports; The UK Interception of Communications (Lawful Business Practice) Regulations 2000; Electronic Communications Directive; the UK Anti-Terrorism, Crime and Security Act 2001; Directive 2002/58/EC (the E-Privacy Directive); and the UK Privacy and Electronic Communications (EC Directive) Regulations 2003.

technical directors in 1995. He proceeded to alter the company's home page and displayed a communication that customer credit card information had been disseminated over the Internet. Next, he made the credit card data of selected individuals available over the Internet. Stevens was convicted and imprisoned for three years (an 18-month non-parole period was attached). The infringement resulted in only an inconsequential direct financial loss. AUSNet's reputation suffered a material loss, with the breach being alleged to have caused an extensive loss of consumer and business confidence. AUSNet estimated that the costs associated with this incident came to over $2 million through the loss of clients and contracts.

Organizations need to ensure that the data they maintain on their clients is secure, but additionally, in cases where organizations maintain some responsibility for the security and protection of client data, they also need to ensure that the data is adequately secured.

In December 2000, the Privacy Amendment (Private Sector) Act 2001 modified the Privacy Act in Australia, making it apply to various private sector organizations. This Australian legislation was updated to reflect the EU and is based on the Organization for Economic Cooperation and Development's (OECD's) Guidelines on the Protection of Privacy and Transborder Flows of Personal Data (1980). The National Privacy Principles (NPPs) in the Privacy Act detail the methods that the private sector should use to "collect, use, keep secure and disclose personal information."

These principles provide individuals with a statutory right to discern the extent of information held concerning them by an organization. They further introduce a right to correct information that is incorrect. The amended Privacy Act would cover an ISP or Internet content provider (ICP) in Australia. The state and territory privacy legislation also needs to be considered. Likewise, an organization in the United Kingdom would be covered under the principles laid out in European Union Directive 95/46/EC.

An organization that hosts sites for other parties could be held liable if it fails to maintain a reasonable level of system security and a breach of security leads to the compromise of an individual's private data.

Historically, the United Kingdom had no legislation that explicitly focused on the deceitful acquisition of pure information. In 1978 a UK court decided, for example, that data itself is not property, and, therefore, unable to be "stolen" (*Oxford v. Moss (1978)*). The case arose when a university student accessed the Examination Committee's premises without authorization, and then read and copied an exam paper. As the original exam paper was not taken, the student's actions were held not to be theft.

In the event that improperly obtained credit card numbers are published on a website, aiding the enactment of fraudulent transactions using those card numbers, if the site administrator knows or should have known of this action, liability may exist. It is possible that the ISP or ICH could also be a secondary participant in the crime. It is likely that a conspiracy charge could also exist in the event that the necessary agreement between the site owner and subscriber could be established (such as through a contract to not conduct standard checks).

Criminal liability may occur in instances where the subscriber of an ICP publishes passwords, allowing unauthorized access into a computer system. The United Kingdom's Computer Misuse Act (1990) may make an intermediary legally responsible for a breach achieved using stolen passwords;. Such provisions mirror many of the U.S. computer fraud laws that have been introduced at both the federal and state levels. The precise nature of any liability will be dependent on the facts of the case. In the event that the intermediary had advertised to a category of persons who were expected to execute an attack against a computer system using those passwords made available on the Web server, this could be seen as an incitement to commit an offense (such as through the U.K.'s Computer Misuse Act). To ascertain whether incitement has occurred, one must demonstrate that the defendant believed that the person so incited had the required *mens rea* to commit the offense. The *mens rea* for an offense under Section 1 of the Computer Misuse Act in the U.K., for instance, is defined simply as an intention by the defendant to gain entrance to a computer system where the defendant understands that such use of the system is not authorized. It is generally a simple fact to establish that authority was not given.

Alternatively, the organization could be charged with aiding, abetting, procuring, or counseling the commission of an offense. It remains that the prosecution needs to establish intention. This is knowledge of the acts that are known to be possible and have to be transferred in a manner that can assist or otherwise promote the commission of a criminal deed without actually requiring that a party to the action have an objective that such a criminal action be committed. A direct causal link that is associated with the procurement needs to exist. Aiding necessitates the support of the act without requiring consensus or causation. Abetting and counseling necessitate consensus without requiring causation.

In 2014 the United Kingdom began discussing enhancing the 1990 Computer Misuse Act. Among the proposed changes are a "Serious Crime Bill" that dramatically increases penalties for computer crime that can cause serious danger. Utilizing stolen information to blackmail people, and various other computer-related crimes, would also become more serious offenses.

Transborder Data Flow

There are a variety of fundamental challenges imposed through the borderless nature of the Internet and electronic networks. In everything from electronic commerce to cybercrime, domestic law has been fundamentally challenged. The issue of jurisdiction in electronic law concerns both the location of the parties to the matter and the location of the computers or other systems.

In the United States, the location where a case should be heard is further complicated by the requirement for the court to have two types of jurisdiction in order to hear a case. This is where the court needs both subject matter jurisdiction and personal jurisdiction.

Subject matter jurisdiction is the power of the court to hear the particular type of dispute being brought before the court. For example, criminal courts will hear matters concerning crimes; family court will address matters such as divorce; and a number of civil courts will hold a variety of tortuous and contractual matters.

Personal jurisdiction is related to the power to enforce a judgment over a defendant. This is often a question that is difficult to answer. A jurisdiction will define in statute how far the court believes it can reasonably assert personal jurisdiction over another. In some cases, this may only extend locally; in others, the perceived jurisdiction may encompass the entire globe. The difficulty arises when these jurisdictional boundaries conflict.

This matter can be complicated due to one party impacting a computer in another jurisdiction that is owned or controlled by a separate party in a third jurisdiction. In these cases, the difficulty of international law and treaty conventions becomes critical to the effect of handling of data.

Monitoring Employees

Monitoring employee actions is always a contentious issue. Whether it is legal is a matter of local regulations. Depending on the jurisdiction, there are many differences in what an employer can do to monitor its employees. Generally speaking, it is always best to notify employees and let them know that they are being monitored, if this is occurring. One of the key areas within an organization that addresses this issue is privacy policy. An organization's privacy policy typically needs to do the following:

- Evaluate the presumption of privacy, including phone and network monitoring.
- Evaluate and address the issues associated with the employees' reasonable expectations that the files on their computers and their phone and Internet communications are protected.
- Determine whether the organization's policy allows random physical searches, and decide if there is to be an active search program.

In any event, any monitoring needs to be conducted fairly. A process should be put in place to ensure that any monitoring is justified. Monitoring can be useful. In particular, it can provide evidence surrounding an attack or intrusion. Some of the various means that may be used to monitor employee activity include the following:

- Real time interception from monitoring the network and systems
- Keystroke recorders
- Email monitoring
- Court order
- Court-issued subpoena
- Review of log files
- Transactional data
- System usage history
- Intrusion detection systems and firewalls

In the United States, search and interceptions may be augmented with a "Reasonable and Articulable Facts Order" (18 U.S.C. 2703). Each country has its own set of regulations regarding the monitoring and privacy of employees. In places like the European Union, legislation generally favors the privacy of the individual. In the United States, legislation such as the following U.S. acts needs to be considered:

- Wiretap Act, 18 U.S.C. 2511
- Access to Stored Electronic Communications, 18 U.S.C. 2701
- Wire Fraud Act, 18 U.S.C. 1343
- Trafficking in Fraudulent Access Devices, 18 U.S.C. 1029
- Computer Fraud and Abuse Act, 18 U.S.C. 1030

This is always a balancing act, with the need to weigh individual privacy, the security of the organization, and local laws.

Some jurisdictions, for example, the state of New Jersey, have also banned employers from requesting personal social media account credentials from employees; employers wishing to monitor what their employees do on social media, or to prevent problems that could occur if employees make damaging posts without thinking, must find ways to work without violating such laws.

Litigation Support

E-discovery rules necessitate the keeping of electronic records created by an organization in the event that they are required for a lawsuit. In effect, what this means is that companies should archive email and other electronic records. In a 2006 survey conducted by *Computerworld*, 32% of respondents (IT managers) stated that their companies weren't at all prepared to meet the new e-discovery requirements. One of the trickiest issues pertaining to e-discovery involves the controls associated with the security of, and in particular the integrity of, the evidence an organization is required to maintain.

An organization is required to locate and produce any data or other electronic records that are requested in a lawsuit. Generally, an organization will be required to assure the court that its electronic documents and records are correct and that the integrity (both from inside the organization itself and from an external source) of the data has been maintained. However, discovery requests cannot merely be a fishing exercise, so it is essential that litigators ensure that they ask for the correct information the first time.

The Litigation Process of Discovery

Discovery is the progression of events that follow the initiation of legal proceedings. All parties in a legal proceeding are required to produce any requested and relevant documents or have presented testimony that they cannot provide these documents. The process of e-discovery involves electronic records such as emails or word processing documents. Rigidly enforced time limits make it vital for the parties to be able to retrieve documents and emails promptly.

E-discovery refers to finding and producing documents stored in electronic form in response to litigation or regulatory requirements. With more than 90% of all business documents being created digitally, it is becoming increasingly common to ask for copies of selected email communications or make broad requests for all electronic records. That trend will only intensify in the future.

Eric Rosenberg, former litigator with Merrill Lynch & Company, stated, "Basically what has happened in this country [the United States] is that discovery of documents which takes place as part of civil litigation and a part of criminal investigations has come to routinely include electronic documents." E-record and email retention is no longer simply about storing records. It is about managing risks. The risks of not properly managing email and other electronic documents are significant and increasing with time.

In December 2006, a number of amendments to the Federal Rules of Civil Procedure (FRCP) were introduced that simplified the process of managing electronic records associated with the litigation process. In order to allow a simplified process of accessing "electronically stored information," revisions and additions were introduced into Rules 16, 26, 33, 34, 37, 45, and Form 35. The U.S. Court's Federal Court website (http://www.uscourts.gov/rules/congress0406.html) contains additional information concerning these amendments. The amendments to the FRCP incorporate five aspects of the discovery:

1. The FRCP includes a definition of discoverable material.
2. The amendments incorporate processes concerning the timely consideration of issues relating to electronic discovery. This includes provisions for the format of the documents that are produced.
3. Provisions are made for instances where the discovery of electronically stored information would be difficult due to requirements to access sources that are not practically available.
4. The amendments have included a course of action that allows a party to assert a claim of privilege or work product protection subsequent to the production of the documents.
5. Protection of organizations that are attempting to act in good faith through a "safe harbor" limit on sanctions under Rule 37. The section protects an organization against the loss of electronically stored information that has occurred due to a routine process from computer systems.

Definition of Discoverable Material

The amendments to the FRCP introduce the terminology of "electronically stored information" into Rules 26(a)(1), 33, and 34. This definition reinforces the concept that electronically stored information (e-records including email) is discoverable. Electronically stored information includes any class of information or data generally that is or can be stored using an electronic or digital process. The definition is wide enough to incorporate any computer-based data. The definition also allows for the inclusion of new data types and systems.

Early Attention to Electronic Discovery Issues

The amendments to the FRCP require that the parties to a litigation process ensure that the discovery process is handled efficiently. The collection and provision of electronically stored information must follow strictly defined time constraints. This process is designed to avoid discovery disputes that may come about due to delay or error. Rule 26(a)(1)(B) of the FRCP introduces electronically stored information as an item to be included in a party's initial disclosures.

Rule 16(b)(5) of the FRCP allows the court scheduling order to include the disclosure or discovery of electronically stored information as appropriate. Rule 26(f) has expanded the catalog of topics that need to be argued in the "meet and confer process." This rule incorporates the requirement for a discovery plan designed to address any concerns associated with the discovery of electronically stored information. Concerns can include the format and even media on which that production will occur. This rule requires that both parties discuss any concerns related to the preservation of discoverable material as well as any claims of privilege or work product protection that may arise.

Format of Production

The format of production of an e-record is addressed through amendments to Rule 34(b) of the FRCP. This rule allows the requesting party to choose the form or forms in which it would prefer that the other party produces any electronically stored information. It is not required that the requesting party selects a form of production. This rule incorporates a process that allows for dispute resolution in the event that a party objects to the requested format(s).

The rule further affords that if the responding party does not agree to the stipulated form(s) or if no form of production is specified, the responding party is required to advise the requesting party of the form in which it is intended that the production of the electronically stored matter will be made. The rule incorporates an option that allows the party to produce the e-records either:

1.   In the form in which the information is normally held, processed, or stored
2.   In some other practical usable form

Electronically Stored Information from Sources That Are Not Reasonably Accessible

The changes to Rule 26(b)(2) have introduced a division that separates "reasonably accessible" electronically stored information from that which is not readily available. The changes to the rule signify that the responding party is not required to produce electronically stored information in the event that an unwarranted burden or cost would result and that the data is not reasonably available. The onus of proof lies with the responding party, who is required to demonstrate that the requested information is not reasonably available and that an undue burden or cost would ensue if the request was to be fulfilled. The court is able to issue a discovery order under the provisions of Rule 26(b)(2)(i), (ii), and (iii) only for good cause. The goal of these amendments is to develop an unbiased approach that favors the production of relevant information from more readily available sources.

The responding party is protected from undue cost or burden in the event that the information is not reasonably available in good faith. The requesting party gains the advantage of recognizing the sources of information that the responding party does not propose to investigate. The rule incorporates a process that can be used to acquire information that is difficult to uncover where this is reasonable based on the facts of the case.

Asserting Claim of Privilege or Work Product Protection after Production

Rule 26(b)(5) has been updated to incorporate a procedure that allows a party to declare a protective claim over materials that have been accidentally produced. This rule covers information that is asserted to be either trial preparation material or privileged information. The opposing parties are required to "return, sequester, or destroy" any information claimed as soon as the party seeking to ascertain the privilege or work product claim notifies the other party of the claim and the grounds being asserted.

The rule does not address whether the privilege or protection was waived by the accidental production. It does, however, disallow the receiving party from making any use or disclosure of the information. The rule also necessitates the producing party to preserve the information pending the resolution of the claim.

"Safe Harbor" Provisions

Rule 37(f) provides a safe harbor provision such that a court is not allowed to compel sanctions if a party to an action cannot present any electronically stored information that is unrecoverable due to a "routine, good-faith operation of an electronic information system" without exceptional circumstances having occurred. It provides for the routine modification, overwriting, and deletion of data that is associated with the standard operation of an information system.

The "routine operation of an electronic information system" provides for the standard design and programming of information systems such as the modification and overwriting of information that can occur as the normal operation of the system. This rule makes provisions for the functions of an information system that are "essential to the operation of electronic information systems" when there is "no direct counterpart in hard-copy documents."

Rule 37(f) is only applicable in cases where information has been made unrecoverable through the routine operation of an information system. This operation has to have occurred in good faith. The existence of a requirement to preserve (such as an order or existing litigation) can be used to aid in deciding if an operation was made in good faith. The rule explicitly states that "a party cannot exploit the routine operation of an information system to evade discovery obligations by failing to prevent destruction of stored information that it is required to preserve."

Evidence Preservation

Document everything! Maintain copious notes of everything you do. In digital investigations, the most critical thing to remember is documentation, or maintaining the chain of custody. Documentation must be maintained from the beginning to end of the engagement. Having an improper chain of evidence is worse than having no evidence at all!

Document the systems hardware configuration. After you have moved the system to a secure location where an appropriate chain of custody can be maintained, it is crucial to take the indispensable photographs from all sides. Take pictures as documentation of the system hardware components and how the connections and cables are arranged.

Document the system date and time. Documenting the system date and time is extremely important. An incorrect date and time stamp can allow the refuting of evidence and call into question the integrity of the findings. Even if everything else occurs perfectly, the mere fact that it got this point will impact the entire investigation.

Document file names, dates, and times on the system and create a timeline. The file name, creation date, and last modified date and time are of vital importance from an evidentiary standpoint when admitting digital evidence. The file name, size, content, and creation and modified dates have to be documented.

Document all of the findings. It is essential to document the results and evidence sequentially as the issues are recognized and evidence is discovered. A proper record of all the software employed in evaluation of the evidence should be prepared. Include the software license and the screen prints to show how software was used in the evidence collection process.

The admissibility of evidence in a court is determined by the relevance, reliability, and legal permissibility of the evidence.

Digital Forensics

Digital forensics, also known as computer forensics or cyber forensics, is a discipline that incorporates the collection and processing of digital data as evidence. This occurs through the systematic investigation and analysis of a computer system or other digital device. This process needs to follow an accepted set of standards that have been instituted for the collection of evidence in a manner that maintains its admissibility. Sensitivity analysis can also point to areas needing sound evidence. For example, if an important calculation, such as dealing with improvement in employee turnover, is highly sensitive to variations in its value, take the extra time to find support concerning why the specific quantity selected is trustworthy.

Digital forensics can be used to find the supporting evidence. A digital forensics professional needs to effectively and efficiently identify relevant electronic evidence associated with violations of specific laws as a part of a discovery order and per instructions.

- Identify and articulate probable cause necessary to obtain a search warrant and recognize the limits of warrants.
- Locate and recover relevant electronic evidence from computer systems using a variety of tools.
- Recognize and maintain a chain of custody.
- Follow a documented forensics investigation process.

The seven most crucial Do's and Don'ts that will apply to any forensic investigation are as follows:

1. **Ask Questions –** Inquire as to the nature of the request. The more knowledge you have regarding the investigation, the more effective you can be.
2. **Document Methodically –** No matter how simple the demand, write it down – even if you do not feel that you will perform that portion of work.
3. **Operate in Good Faith –** Generally, you should follow instructions from your superior or legal counsel in the course of an investigation. It may be possible that some investigative actions could be illegal. Bring this to the other parties' attention.
4. **Don't Get in Too Deep –** If any of the following conditions are true, you may need to make an important determination as to whether to continue yourself or call in other parties, such as law enforcement:
   - The investigation involves a crime.
   - The investigation is expected to result in serious discipline or termination of an employee.
   - The investigation requires that documents are prepared and maintained for court or a government investigative body and follow legal discovery rules.
   - Large-scale investigations over multiple jurisdictions should be conducted by experienced investigators.
5. **Decide to Investigate –** Involve people who are necessary to the investigation and don't make all the decisions yourself.
6. **Treat Everything as Confidential –** Regardless of who knows (or the rumors that surface), keep all information confidential and only disclose the information to those who need to know.
7. **File It –** Keep your documentation and store it safely. Always file it in a controlled manner, regardless.

Processes

The term "evidence location" refers to the process of investigating and gathering information of a forensic nature and particularly of legal importance. This evidence aids in the investigation of both criminal investigations and civil suits.

For instance, the Microsoft Windows operating system contains a number of locations that can act as a rich source of evidence. Information gathering through investigating hidden files can be extremely helpful to any investigation.

Even file attributes and time stamps are valuable. Often, perpetrators may attempt to change a file's attributes in order to either cover their tracks or hide important data that may be present in the system. Collating time stamps, for instance, can aid in reconstructing the actions taken by the suspect.

Some of the more important sources of electronic evidence on a Windows host include the following:

- Files
- Slack space
- Swap file
- Unallocated clusters
- Unused partitions
- Hidden partitions

Some of the most crucial areas to check for evidence within volatile data include registers, cache, physical and virtual memory, network connections, running processes, and disk, for instance, the page file (*Figure 5.2*). Any external device associated with the system should also be considered and checked for evidence: floppy, tape, CD/ROM, USB thumb drives, and printers. Captured data must then be gathered and saved in external devices so that it may be safely removed and kept offline at another location.

Figure 5.2 – **Digital evidence volatility requires that evidence is processed in order.**

RFC 3227 (Guidelines for Evidence Collection and Archiving) lists the order of volatility in a Microsoft Windows–based system as follows:

- Registers, cache
- Routing table, ARP cache, process table, kernel statistics
- Memory
- Temporary file systems
- Disk
- Remote logging and monitoring data that is relevant to the system in question
- Physical configuration, network topology
- Archival media

Documents, whether completed or still in draft, and working notes or scrap paper may be used as evidence in court. If working notes, etc., exist at the time of discovery, they are required to be included as sources of evidence and are subject to discovery.

- Computer-based information
- Photographs, maps, and charts
- Internal correspondence and email
- Legal and regulatory filings
- Company intranet access and publications
- Formal meeting minutes or transcripts
- Casual conservations
- Conversations at trade shows and events

A competitive organization may also be able to make use of and gain an advantage using the following:

- Marketing and product plans, especially prior to release
- Source code
- Corporate strategies and plans
- Marketing, advertising, and packaging expenditures
- Pricing issues, strategies, lists
- R&D, manufacturing processes, and technological operations
- Target markets and prospect information
- Plant closures and development
- Product designs, development, and costs
- Staffing, operations, organization charts, wage/salary
- Partner and contract arrangements including delivery, pricing, and terms
- Customer and supplier information
- Merger and acquisition plans
- Financials, revenues, P&L, R&D budgets

With the rise of identity fraud and other related offenses, the theft of proprietary company information and private personnel records is also increasing. The records sought include the following:

- Home addresses
- Home phone number
- Names of spouse and children
- Employee's salary
- Social security number
- Medical records
- Credit records or credit union account information
- Performance reviews

Rather than shutting the system down, there is a large amount of volatile evidence that may be collected on a live system. The section objectives include the following:

- Locating and gathering volatile evidence on a Windows host
- Investigating Windows file slack for evidence
- Interpreting the Windows registry and memory dump information
- Investigating the system state backups
- Analyzing Internet trace data and events

Documentation

A well-written investigative report tells a story in which one has to answer various questions such as who, when, where, why, and how. While one is answering these questions, supporting materials such as figures, tables, data, and equations are required if they help the story unfold in an effective form.

The supporting material can be referred to directly in the text and integrated in the writing to enhance the impact. It is advisable to number figures and tables in the same order as they are introduced in the report. For example, tables can be numbered as Table 1, Table 2, and so on. In the same way, figures can be labeled as Figure 1, Figure 2, and so on. Numbering the material avoids confusion and makes it easier to understand. To reduce narration and emphasize important facts, put tables and schedules in appendices.

Captions are preferred over simple titles, as the complete information adds to the conciseness of the presentation. If charts are used, they should be labeled, including axes and units. In a paragraph, if any table or figure is mentioned, then that figure or table should be inserted after the paragraph. One could also gather all supporting material after the reference section.

The following presents a possible layout of an investigative report. The presentation of accurate text is equivalent to being able to speak clearly. As such, always give your full attention to the layout and presentation of information in a report when you are writing. It is further advisable to consistently adhere to a single format throughout the report. This creates consistency. There are two main methodologies for creating a layout structure. There is decimal numbering and legal-sequential numbering. Decimal numbering is as follows:

1.0 Introduction
    1.1   The Nature of the Incident
    1.1.1   The Details of the Victim

2.0 First Incident
    2.1   The First Witness
    2.1.1   Witness Testimony – Witness No. 1

3.0 Location of Evidence
    3.1   Seizure of Evidence
    3.1.1   Transportation of Evidence

4.0 Analysis of Evidence
    4.1   Chain of Evidence
    4.1.1   Extraction of Data

5.0 Conclusion
    5.1   Results
    5.1.1   Expert Opinion

Legal-sequential numbering uses the following format:

I.   Introduction
    1.   Nature of the Incident
    2.   The Victim
    3.   Witness to the Event
    4.   Location of Evidence

II.   Examination
    5.   Chain of Evidence
    6.   Extraction of Evidence
    7.   The Analysis of Evidence

The legal-sequential numbering system is used in pleadings and is popular among lawyers. Roman numerals are used for the foremost aspect of the report, and Arabic numbering supports the information detail.

The most vital component of any investigative report is the use of effective language to communicate the information clearly. To do this, include signposts within the report. A signpost serves as a guide to the readers of the document that focuses their thought on a point or sequence of a process. Signposts highlight the main points that you wish to convey by creating a logical development of the information within the report. This makes it easier for the reader to view and comprehend the document.

For instance, the steps within the document could be introduced using a signpost such as "The first step in this section" or "The second step in the examination." These act as the signposts for the sequence of information.

Any good report will answer the five Ws: who, what, why, when, and where. Remember to document who was involved in the case and who requested it. Document what was done and why. When and where did it occur? A good report should explain the computer and network processes and document all salient aspects of the system.

A well-conducted investigation should also follow the SMART methodology:

- ***Specific:*** detail each component.
- ***Measurable:*** ensure that you record sizes, times, and other relevant material.
- ***Achievable:*** ensure that you have the resources to achieve your objectives.
- ***Realistic:*** report the facts; don't speculate.
- ***Time based:*** work within time constraints and deadlines and ensure that you recorded all the events as they occurred on the system.

Reports are critical to an investigation because they provide the means to provide the findings and other evidence to the necessary people. A report may be formal or informal, verbal or written, but it always needs to be grammatically sound: Ensure that you make use of the correct spelling and avoid any grammatical errors. When writing the report, avoid the use of jargon, slang, or colloquial terms, and ensure the clarity of writing because this is critical to the success of the report.

Writing a report is like thinking. The presentation of the report must flow logically to convey the information in a structured form. Discuss the results and conclusions. Remember that the final document is a combination of information generated during the investigation, the analysis, and the final conclusions.

When conducting the investigation, remember – document everything!

Security Incident Management Process

Despite the many numerous proactive measures taken by security-conscious organizations to prevent security incidents, situations, such as attempts to penetrate into systems or actual breaches, do arise. No entity is immune from cyberattacks or other attempts to gain inappropriate access to information and resources, so any security plan must account for the near certainty that security incidents are going to happen. It is important, therefore, that the ISSMP know how to establish and manage a security incident handling process.

Security incident management refers to the monitoring of security incidents and the execution of pre-planned responses to those situations, so as to ensure that the organizational responses to potential attacks are appropriate, adequate, organized, efficient, predictable, and auditable. Ultimately, the goal of incident management is not just to address the current incident but to enable the organization to properly identify, analyze, and rectify the issues that lead to the incident occurring – so as to improve the odds of preventing repeated, or similar, occurrences in the future.

Typically, incident response is managed by a group of people who together comprise a so-called "Incident Response Team," of which the ISSMP may be a member or a leader. In some organizations, the leader of the team is afforded the title "Information Security Incident Response Coordinator," "Information-Security Incident Response Leader," or something of the sort. This title is, of course, in addition to any other titles the leader may have as part of his or her job.

The need to properly plan for security incidents cannot be overstated. Criminals often exploit weaknesses caused by situations of which they are aware, so, while incidents can, and do, occur at any time, one set of times at which they are especially likely to occur is when other challenges are unfolding (e.g., after a natural disaster) and, as such, sticking to a pre-defined script dramatically improves the odds of warding off an attack, properly documenting what happened, and preventing future problems (i.e., of successfully handing the incident).

It is important to understand that while the terms "security incident" and "security event" are sometimes used interchangeably, they technically mean different things. A security incident is a detectable, human-caused deviation from the normal, expected behavior of information and the systems and people through which it flows and is stored. This is different than simple security events, which are similar deviations, but whose cause is unknown, and which may not be caused by human actions or have occurred based on the will of humans.

For example: If a computer system used for security fails because someone hacked it that is clearly a security incident. If a computer system used for security fails because the hard drive within it failed from normal wear and tear after many years of use, that is not truly a security incident, but it certainly may be a security event.

The aforementioned definitions notwithstanding, the ISSMP should understand how people within his or her organization use the terms "incident" and "event" and insure that any communications using such terms are not confusing or subject to misinterpretation.

The ISSMP should be prepared to be involved with the responses that security incidents demand. Furthermore, security events may require responses, and some may require full blown tracking like a security incident even though their root cause is not the desired actions of humans because they may put systems at risk of breach, threaten the security of information, or even put human beings at risk of physical danger.

Responses to events and incidents are not uniform across all situations; they are based on the severity of the threat potentially posed to the organization as understood from a particular incident or event. For that reason, the ISSMP should be able to classify different incidents and events. This is done by (ahead of time) establishing criteria for measuring them and applying such criteria as measuring sticks when an incident or possible incident, or even some events, occurs.

The process of indecent and event responses are often similar (at least at the start); in fact, at the start, they are typically identical because it is usually impossible to distinguish between the two upon the initial discovery that "something unexpected" has happened. Once an event has been determined not to have been of human origin, however, the process may be simpler: Methods of addressing the problem and preventing it in the future are normally created, implemented, and tested; and then, because no attack or signs of a future attack were involved, less consideration is given than had a true incident occurred.

The lifecycle of incident response, for which the ISSMP should help define procedures and execute them when necessary, includes:

- **Detection** – A technical employee may detect some anomaly, or external users may report something unusual to a helpdesk. Of course, anything reported to the helpdesk should be tracked with the helpdesk's standard helpdesk-ticket management system.

- **Determination of What Actually Happened** – It is likely that the ISSMP will be tasked to establish, and/or maintain, the process used for investigating security incidents. Typically, if a report is received via the helpdesk, the helpdesk team (or technical personnel) will attempt to ascertain that the reported situation is real. Attempts to replicate anomalies, or to check on the functioning of the system, should be done (only, however, if doing so in no way adversely impacts security). Some reports may be mistaken, based on user error by the person placing a call to, or emailing, the helpdesk, or reflect technical issues in the user's environment. Eliminating false reports is important because wasting resources investigating non-issues can cause frustration, and it can lead to security breaches if dedicating resources to non-issues causes inadequate resources to be available to address real problems. Remember, both insiders and external parties wishing to launch attacks may use such a method to distract security personnel.

- **Determination of Severity** – If the problem is determined to be real, appropriate parties must determine how severe the issue is; i.e., how much of a risk has been determined to exist?

- **Containment/Elimination of the Problem** – The ticket is assigned to the appropriate parties who are tasked with addressing the problem. They must apply their knowledge to fix it; this may involve technical activities, human activities, etc.

- **Determination of the Impact and Addressing the Impact** – Simply addressing an attack, or potential attack, is not sufficient. It is critical to understand what the full impact of the incident is. Did sensitive data leak that could undermine various projects? Did personal information leak that could put people at risk of identity theft? Was credit card information compromised, and should issuers and users be alerted to cancel cards? While these questions might seem simple to answer, in reality, they often are not. The process of determining what happened is complex, and, even after careful analysis, it is sometimes impossible to know for certain what the actual impact was. In such situations, it is normally best to err on the side of caution, for example, altering people to change their passwords if passwords might have been compromised but might not have been; however, sometimes such an approach is not taken, especially in situations in which a high cost is involved and the probability of the risk is relatively low or if doing so will lead to the weakening of security due to human factors (e.g., asking people to change a large number of passwords at one time is prone to lead to the reuse of weak passwords). Ultimately, the method for addressing the impact is a business decision. The ISSMP, however, should be prepared and able to help business folks, legal teams, compliance personnel, and others with their decisions by advising on the type of impacts that might exist and their relative likelihoods. Remember, some non-security personnel may be under the impression that if an attack has been successfully terminated, "things" can easily "return to normal" and that no lasting damage has been done, which is often not the case.

- **Determination of Lessons for the Future –** After analyzing the incident, the ISSMP should be able to help define steps to be taken to improve the situation going forward. A plan might include technological improvements such as the addition of additional security technology into an organization's infrastructure, new agreements with vendors, training for employees, terminating business relationships with various careless or harmful parties, and many other types of alterations intended to prevent a repeat of an incident and reduce the exposure should an incident occur.

- **Application of Lessons for the Future –** Implementing the lessons learned, and testing them. It is a very bad idea to define great procedures but not implement them or to implement them but not test them to make sure that they work. The ISSMP should make sure that theory is put into practice successfully.

Of course, proper documentation is necessary at all phases of the incident management process, as is management buy in.

As a result of security incidents, employees might be disciplined or fired, contracts terminated, or other significant actions taken based on proof of inappropriate actions on the part of the party being punished. It is important to realize, therefore, that the investigation of security incidents must properly preserve information and materials gathered. Furthermore, such items might be used as evidence in criminal or civil trials filed as a result of the incident. Law enforcement may ask for these items, and these items may also be subject to discovery requests by attorneys. Hence, a proper "chain of custody" must be utilized for any evidence gathered.

Likewise, throughout the entire process of investigating an incident, formal processes and procedures must be utilized, and proper documentation created and preserved. Controls must also be implemented governing who has the right to request an investigation and when they have such a right, who conducts the investigation, who collects evidence, who preserves it, and how, what documentation will be created, who creates it and when, and who preserves it and when, who creates and who preserves all records related to the investigation and when do they do so, who makes modifications to policies for the future and how such changes are made and when, etc. If in doubt, err on the side of documenting too much rather than too little; just keep the quality and organization of all materials up to par so that it can be read and easily understood later; remember, you may be called as a witness in court and asked to explain what you wrote and why you wrote it!

The procedures as to how and when to involve law enforcement as the investigation proceeds must be determined before an incident occurs. Just as law enforcement should initially be notified of any breach, it must be kept abreast of any relevant findings during the investigation. (Law enforcement need not be notified of some forms of incidents, and certainly not of events unless the event resulted in human physical or other injury or death, or various forms of property damage.)

Some jurisdictions may require that the public, or at least any people and organizations who may be impacted in some way by the security incident, be notified and kept abreast as the investigation unfolds. The ISSMP would likely work in conjunction with an official company spokesperson or the communications/marketing department to assist with such communications.

Because an organization may be impacted by the laws of multiple jurisdictions, it is best to consult the legal department in order to determine which laws do, and do not, apply in cases of security incidents.

Likewise, clear policies as to how to inform media of developments (including not only how and when but exactly whom within the organization is to be the spokesperson for the organization regarding such incidents) should be pre-defined. There should be one official spokesperson and one backup spokesperson in case the primary person is away; in general, it is a terrible idea to allow other members of the security department to comment on, or discuss, any security incidents with the public.

As noted earlier, not all incidents are identical in terms of risk level. For that reason, we tend to categorize incidents as soon as it is possible to do so with relative certainty of accuracy during the investigation process. The U.S. government uses the following seven categories and recommends the following timeframes for reporting. These are not necessarily appropriate for all organizations, but the model that they create together does serve as a good reference for establishing proper categories.

1. **Unauthorized Access** – Some party is believed to have gained unauthorized logical or physical access to a resource. Reporting of such an incident should occur within one hour of detection.

2. **Denial of Service** – Denial-of-service attacks are attacks that successfully impair normal system functions and operations by exhausting their necessary resources. The denial-of-service category includes two subcategories: An organization may be a victim of such an attack, or it may have its resources commandeered by others and used to launch, or participate in, a denial-of-service attack against others. In either case, if the attack is still ongoing and personnel are unable to successfully terminate it, the attack should be reported within two hours of detection.

3. **Malicious Code** – The successful infection of a system or network with malicious software that has not been removed or quarantined by security software. Reporting of such an incident should occur within one day of detection, unless the malware is still propagating and is, or is likely to become, widespread across the organization, in which case it should be reported within one hour of discovery.

4. **Improper Usage** – A human being has violated some computing use policy or policies, but such a violation has not resulted in another category of incident.

Reporting of such an incident should occur within one week of detection.

5. ***Scans, Probes, or Attempted Access*** – Evidence has been found that indicates that some party is seeking to scan, access, identify, or otherwise garner information about computers, networks, open ports, protocols in use, services available within the organization's infrastructure, etc. Since this type of reconnaissance is often done in preparation for an attack, such incidents must be reported even if no damage was done, or confidential information accessed, by the offending party. Reporting of such an incident should occur within one month of detection, unless the system being "attacked" is classified, in which case the incident should be reported within one hour of detection.

6. ***Investigation*** – Incidents in which there are unknowns and further analysis is necessary. Each group must define its own parameters for this type of situation.

7. ***Type of Incident*** – Exercise/Network defense testing, which is used for incidents detected during approved testing of the security program and its components.

Category 0 incidents are, of course, not real security incidents and do not need to be reported other than within the confines of the pertinent test program.

Of course, in mission critical, regulated, and other sensitive environments, some incidents may necessitate faster reporting times. On the other hand, unimportant systems may not mandate timeframes as strict as the government's general guidelines above. As such, reporting time requirements should be established by business system owners after meetings with legal, regulatory and compliance, security, and other pertinent departments.

During the investigation and mitigation process, it is important to track how many resources are utilized because it is important for management to understand the true cost of investigation and mitigation when they evaluate potential countermeasures to prevent reoccurrences. Furthermore, understanding the cost of the incident may be important for legal reasons (e.g., if a criminal is caught and the organization wishes to recoup damages from him or her via a lawsuit) or regulatory and compliance reasons.

Sometimes in house technical skills must be augmented with outside experts in order to best conduct a proper investigation of a security incident. It is, practically speaking, impossible for people to be experts in every area of technology, and, as such, scenarios may exist in which bringing in from the outside someone with a particular skill will produce a better chance of fully "getting to the bottom" of an incident and properly addressing it, in the most rapid and complete fashion, that utilizes internal resources. If the ISSMP determines that outside personnel are needed due to their possessing particular skills that would aid the organization in its mission of addressing the security incident, he or she should communicate as such to management. It is important to convey that the scenario does not imply that there is some sort of deficiency in the organization's security department and team, but, rather, that in order to operate at maximum fiscal efficiency the organization only employs people whose skillsets are normally needed on a regular basis and who have the ability to identity what resource/s to hire and leverage when other skills are necessary. By utilizing expert consultants, management should be informed, the business is actually saving money over the long term. These thoughts may sound simplistic, but, after a security incident, some people may be looking to find scapegoats. Don't let a security incident create unnecessary sensitive, political nightmares in which management unfairly blames technical resources for inadequate knowledge.

After an incident has been investigated and any risks curtailed, the ISSMP will likely be called upon to help lead the ultimate drive of the incident management process – to prevent repeated, or similar, occurrences in the future by applying knowledge learned throughout the security incident response process. It is critical that any lessons learned, or recommended improvements to security infrastructure and personnel counts/skills-bases, be detailed in writing and explained to senior management. There is a cost associated with everything; by explaining what problems the desired changes will prevent or reduce, and how they will do so, the security department is far more likely to get management buy-in and adequate funding.

Interviewing and Fact-Finding

Prior to starting any fact-finding exercise or investigation, it is essential to ensure that you have collected all the relevant background information and to create a plan. The fact-finding process works best when goals have been set in place and an interview plan has been created. The primary goals of any fact-finding exercise involve the following points:

- Establish rapport.
- Stress that the interview is seeking only the truth.
- Listen carefully.
- Evaluate the interviewee's responses to the questions with care.
- Take first-rate notes.
- Remain objective and composed.

When the interview begins, introduce yourself and explain the purpose of the interview. Always arrive on time or early for interviews and stick to the planned timetable. It is both good manners and sensible practice to ask the interviewees if they mind you taking notes or tape-recording an interview. If you do record an interview, also remember to take notes because the recorder can fail. Using a smartphone to make recordings is also not recommended as an incoming call could interfere with recording.

During the interview, make sure that you maintain an agenda and take responsibility for this. Ensure that you keep control of the interview and maintain its direction. You do not need to be insensitive in doing this, but it is important to keep the interviewee focused on the point of the interview. For instance, if you get sidetracked, make the comment that you will get back to that later and return to the agenda.

An interview plan list should be created with the following details:

- Interviewees – Who is to be interviewed?
- The order of the interviews.
- How much time has been allotted per interview?
- Classify the interviewees (such as by complainant, witness, subject).
- Research and list the allegations that pertain to each interviewee and the relevant facts for each of these.
- Write out the questions you intend to ask beforehand.
- The number of interviewers who will be present.
- A topic outline.

It is also recommended that you consider the type of interview and questioning techniques before starting the interview process. There are numerous physical and psychological factors involved with interviewing people that should be considered prior to the interview.

Preparing questions beforehand is important, but leave time for additional questions if needed. Open-ended questions are fine in moderation. Closed questions are far better. Closed questions could be worded as, "How many times did you enter the building on Saturday?" Open-ended questions allow the interviewee some freedom of response, such as, "How did you access the system?"

Where possible, maintain a positive focus and ensure that you have understood the answers proffered by the interviewee by summarizing them back. Always avoid allowing the interview to degenerate into a session in which the interviewee complains about everyone and everything. Avoid prejudging people and stick with gathering facts.

At the conclusion of the interview, thank interviewees for their time and make an appointment for another interview if necessary. It is also good practice to provide the interviewee with a copy of your notes of the interview. Interviewees should check your notes to ensure that you have accurately recorded what they told you. Transcribe your tape or write up your notes as soon as possible after the interview while the content is still fresh in your mind. In the event that you instructed the interviewee that you would provide a copy of your notes for validation, send a copy to the interviewee promptly and ensure that you revise your notes to incorporate any comments made by the interviewee.

It is important to find the truth about how systems are running and being maintained, as this allows management to specify "the decision rights and accountability framework to encourage desirable behavior in the use of IT" (Weill, P. and Ross, J.W. 2004. *IT Governance: How Top Performers Manage IT Decision Rights for Superior Results,* Harvard Business School Press, Boston).

In the interview and fact-finding process, it is important to maintain a high level of sensitivity and privacy. This involves inquiring discreetly when necessary. Ensure that you explain the privacy rights involved to the person being interviewed.

Interviews are divided into five Interview Phases, which are as follows:

- ***Phase 1*** – Introduction
- ***Phase 2*** – Build Rapport
- ***Phase 3*** – Questioning
- ***Phase 4*** – Summarize
- ***Phase 5*** – Close

In the introduction, explain the purpose of the interview, what will be expected during the interview, and the interviewee's privacy rights. In order to make the interview go smoother, attempt to build rapport with the interviewee. Always greet the interviewee with a handshake or other culturally accepted method. Use voice inflections, gestures, and facial expressions to set the tone of the interview. During the interview, use neutral terms with no editorial comments while expressing empathy or sympathy when appropriate. Imagine yourself in the position of the interviewees and hence treat them with dignity and respect. This includes using nonthreatening mannerisms and body language.

Summarize the interviewees' key points as they are made, but otherwise listen to their responses with minimal interruptions. In the event that an interviewee does not want to respond directly to a question, it is possible to use silence to force a response. Gestures and eye contact may also be used to encourage a response from the interviewee. Always ensure that you react to disclosures appropriately.

Do not take any responses that you receive at face value, and ensure that you test the accuracy of information that you received. Direct questions may be used to fill in the missing details from a vague or unfocused response. In the event that you do not receive the answer that you need, a re-interview may be necessary.

Some of the more common problems that occur during the interview fact-finding process include the following:

- Uncooperative interviewees
- Refusal to comply
- Intimidation from either party
- Requests for other attendees at an interview
- A loss of impartiality
- Reprisal
- Requests for advice from interviewees

Always record the answers that are given and include the method of the interview, name of the attendee, as well as the purpose, place, date, time, and other relevant information in your notes. When taking notes, ensure that they are detailed, factual, objective, clear and concise, and most importantly complete. Whenever you make notes that include direct comments from the interviewee, use quotation marks for the interviewee's comment and, if possible, ask the interviewee to initial the quote when the interview has concluded.

There are four generally accepted techniques that can be used to record an interview:

1. Sworn statement or declaration
2. Verbatim (such as a tape recording)
3. Results of interview (record of interview)
4. Video and teleconference interviews

At the conclusion of the interview, summarize the most important parts of it. Do this by reviewing your notes with the interviewee and allow the interviewee to clarify or add information as well as ensure that all the information is accurate. At this point, a second investigator may wish to ask further questions. Ask the interviewees if you should interview anyone else and why. Conclude by thanking the interviewees for cooperating with the process and advise them about whistleblower protections.

When closing an investigation, ask the complainant (if this is the situation) what he or she expects from the investigation. Always make sure that the interviewee understands that he has no inherent right to know the outcome of an investigation.

Searches (and the Fourth Amendment)

In much of the common law world (including the United States, United Kingdom, Canada, New Zealand, and Australia), law enforcement needs to obtain a legal authorization in order to search and seize evidence. Generally, this power is granted through a request for a search warrant, which states the grounds for the application including the law that has been broken. In the United States and the United Kingdom, the requirements further require that the application describe the specific premises to be searched as well as the items being sought.

In the United States, the Fourth Amendment and the Electronic Communications Privacy Act (ECPA) determine the lawfulness of a search. The Fourth Amendment only applies to government searches (such as those conducted by law enforcement officials). The ECPA applies to everyone (whether government or private) and prohibits the unlawful interception of or access to electronic communications.

In the physical world, there is a real limit on the length of time during which a search can be conducted. This rule does not impose much of a limit on electronic searches. As investigators are able to make a copy of the digital evidence (such as a hard drive), they are able to continue to search these files both for "strings" that are beyond the scope of the original warrant at their leisure.

Neither the Fourth Amendment nor the federal rules of criminal procedure require the investigator to promptly search the evidence. In fact, U.S. federal law provides little over the return of property seized pursuant to warrant. Suspects must file a motion in court, in which they either prove that the seizure was illegal or that the investigator no longer has any need to retain the evidence, to either have the digital evidence returned or destroyed.

As a result, law enforcement officials can keep a copy of any digital evidence they have seized under a warrant and continue to search it without any effective time limit. Fourth Amendment rules do not provide useful guidelines for investigators' conduct even in digital forensic labs. There are no limitations of the regions of a hard drive that a forensic computer analyst may examine for evidence, and the analyst may continue to look for evidence of other crimes.

The Fourth Amendment rule is that an investigator executing a warrant is able to look in any place listed on the warrant where evidence might conceivably be concealed. Traditionally, investigators were precluded from looking into any location where there is more evidence than the evidence they wish to seize. Electronic evidence, however, may be stored anywhere. The result is that an investigator can electronically look anywhere in search of digital evidence. *Katz v. United States* stated that "the fourth Amendment protects people, not places." The result is that the Fourth Amendment continues to be deeply tied to physical places.

Warrants

For something to be accepted as evidence in court, a warrant is generally required for law enforcement to search and seize evidence. There are exceptions to this need, including the following:

- When the evidence is in plain view all in sight.
- Where consent to search has been granted.
- Situations involving some exigency, such as an emergency threatening life or physical harm.

To obtain a search warrant, an investigator needs to convince the court of the following three points:

1. Some criminal act has been committed.
2. Evidence of a crime exists and is available.
3. It is probable that the evidence is likely to be found at the place being searched.

Anton Piller (Civil Search)

An Anton Piller order is a civil court order providing for the right to search premises and seize evidence without prior warning. In the United States, the Business Software Alliance has used these orders as a remedy when they are attempting to stop illegal software use (termed software piracy) and copyright infringement to achieve the recovery of property.

Ormrod LJ in *Anton Piller KG v. Manufacturing Processes Limited* in 1976 (U.K.) defined the three-step test for granting this order:

1. There is an extremely strong prima facie case against the respondent.
2. The damage, potential or actual, must be very serious for the applicant.
3. There must be clear evidence that the respondents have in their possession incriminating documents or things and that there is a real possibility that they may destroy such material before an *inter partes* application is able to be obtained in court.

In the United Kingdom, Anton Piller orders have been (for the most part) outmoded by the introduction of a statutory search order under the Civil Procedure Act 1997. These applications are still common in many places such as Canada and France.

Professional Ethics

Professional ethics defines a set of moral principles that determine conduct for professional work. Because professional work often requires specialized and unique knowledge, it carries the potential for misuse. Professional ethics provide guidance to avoid transgression or misconduct.

The cause-and-effect relationship that develops through the introduction of an ethical framework turns into practices and procedures that can cause professionals to "do the right thing" on the job. When professionals fail to maintain an ethical culture and standards, scandals such as those in the accounting profession that gave rise to the Sarbanes-Oxley Act leave the standing of such professions diminished in the public perspective.

When engaged in professional activities, you have an obligation to exercise honesty, objectivity, and diligence in the performance of your duties and responsibilities. Typical examples of principles include the following:

- Exhibit loyalty in all matters pertaining to the affairs of the organization or to whomever you may be rendering a service. However, you will not knowingly be a part of any illegal or improper activity.
- Refrain from entering into any activity that may be in conflict with the interest of the organization for whom you are performing work or that would prejudice your ability to objectively carry out your duties and responsibilities.

- Do not accept a fee or gift from an employee, a client, a customer, or a business associate of any sections of the organization in which you are working without the knowledge and consent of senior management.

- Be prudent in the use of information acquired in the course of your duties. Do not use confidential information for any personal gain or in a manner that would be detrimental to the welfare of the organization or its employees.

- When expressing an opinion, use all reasonable care to obtain sufficient factual evidence to warrant such expression. In your reporting, you shall reveal such material facts known to you, which, if not revealed, could either distort the report of the results of operations under review or conceal unlawful practice.

Mission, Vision, and Values Statements

Organizational strategy (Lane, 2004, http://www.wiley.com/WileyCDA/WileyTitle/product Cd-0631231935.html) needs to be organized along the limits of professional ethics. Such strategic plans generally consist of the following:

1. Vision is where we want to be.
2. Mission is our purpose or reason for existence.
3. Values are the principles that guide our behavior, give us a sense of direction, and also help us decide what is important and provide us with an ethical and moral foundation.

Just as the organization should have a mission or vision statement aligned to what its business goals are, it should also have such statements for IT and information security, and it should ensure that the statements promote an ethical culture within the organization and one's own role. Having a mission to comply with the laws, regulations, and organizational policy makes it more likely that this will occur and is essential if a culture of security is to be introduced. Vision and mission statements are very different documents. A vision statement sets the goals of the organization at a high level. The vision needs to state what the organization envisions in terms of growth, attitude to risk, cost, values, employees, etc. A component of the vision statement includes the development of a mission.

The Mission Statement

The mission statement is or at least should be a concise statement of the organization's strategy. It is developed from the perspective of a desired outcome, and it needs to be aligned to the vision statement. The mission statement answers three questions:

1. What do we do and why?
2. How do we do it?
3. For whom do we do it?

In assessing high-level policy, it is essential to test whether the policy is aligned to the mission of the organization. For instance, Google used to have a mission statement that said, "Do no evil." If Google were to introduce a policy that states, "We will track down and destroy any attacker who even pings our network," it is simple to see that the goal and the policy are not linked. Both organizational and personal mission statements are important and help in maintaining one's ethical values.

Information technology and security teams or departments should have their own mission statement. This should be a simple statement of purpose known by every member of the division because it:

- Provides a "reason for being."
- Provides clarity and focus to make choices.
- Is clear and concise.
- Should be accepted by the wider organization.
- Helps guide people toward doing the "right thing."

The Vision Statements

The vision statement outlines what the organization wants. This is what it wants to be and how it wants to be perceived by others. A vision statement is as follows:

- A plan for the future
- A source of inspiration
- The place to go when in need of clear decision-making criteria
- The source to ensure that policy aligns with the destination set by the organization

A vision statement expresses the destination of the organization in a manner that builds commitment:

1. It creates a sense of desire and builds commitment.
2. It paints the ideal future.
3. It is an expression made in terms of hope.
4. It is united with the values of the organization.

Again, vision statements can be produced both to align and to guide your own personal professional ethics and those of the organization of which you are a part.

A Statement of Values

Many organizations also develop a set of ethical principles that are designed to guide the organization. These principles are the statement of values. This document should be used as guidance when developing policy. This can also be called an organizational code of ethics when applied to an individual organization. All individuals certified by (ISC)² agree to abide by the following Code of Professional Ethics:

Code of Ethics Preamble

Safety of the commonwealth, duty to our principals, and to each other requires that we adhere, and be seen to adhere, to the highest ethical standards of behavior. Therefore, strict adherence to this Code is a condition of certification.

Code of Ethics Canons

- Protect society, the commonwealth, and the infrastructure.
- Act honorably, honestly, justly, responsibly, and legally.
- Provide diligent and competent service to principals.
- Advance and protect the profession.

These codes encourage the right professional behavior, such as

- Research
- Teaching
- Identifying, mentoring, and sponsoring candidates for the profession
- Valuing the certificate

And discourage such behavior as

- Raising unnecessary alarm, fear, uncertainty, or doubt
- Giving unwarranted comfort or reassurance
- Consenting to bad practice
- Attaching weak systems to the public network
- Professional recognition of, or association with, amateurs (other than in a mentoring scenario or some other appropriate situation)
- Associating or appearing to associate with criminals or criminal behavior

Protect Society, the Commonwealth, and the Infrastructure

- Promote and preserve public trust and confidence in information and systems.
- Promote the understanding and acceptance of prudent information security measures
- Preserve and strengthen the integrity of the public infrastructure.
- Discourage unsafe practice.

Act Honorably, Honestly, Justly, Responsibly, and Legally

- Tell the truth; make all stakeholders aware of your actions on a timely basis.
- Observe all contracts and agreements, express or implied.
- Treat all constituents fairly. In resolving conflicts, consider public safety and duties to principals, individuals, and the profession in that order.
- Give prudent advice; avoid raising unnecessary alarm or giving unwarranted comfort. Take care to be truthful, objective, cautious, and within your competence.
- When resolving differing laws in different jurisdictions, give preference to the laws of the jurisdiction in which you render your service.

Provide Diligent and Competent Service to Principals

- Preserve the value of their systems, applications, and information.
- Respect their trust and the privileges that they grant you.
- Avoid conflicts of interest or the appearance thereof.
- Render only those services for which you are fully competent and qualified.

Advance and Protect the Profession

- Sponsor for professional advancement those best qualified. All other things equal, prefer those who are certified and who adhere to these canons. Avoid professional association with those whose practices or reputation might diminish the profession.
- Take care not to injure the reputation of other professionals through malice or indifference.
- Maintain your competence; keep your skills and knowledge current. Give generously of your time and knowledge in training others.

Interpreting Policy as a Security Professional – Ethics

Assessing policy can often require the evaluation of ethical principles. Policies dictate how the organization will operate. This covers operational aspects such as awareness, employee monitoring, and how issues such as software piracy will be handled. These all require the development of an ethical organizational culture.

The security posture or the aspects of corporate culture that cover security are, for the most part, significant when attempting to develop, implement, or enforce security policy. Corporate culture always exists, whether it is intentionally cultivated or it develops organically. Senior management can attempt to shape corporate culture by imposing corporate values and standards of behavior that specifically reflect the objectives of the organization; however, the extant internal culture within the workforce can subvert this process.

A conscious effort to establish a culture that embraces security should be based on a process of communicating the message through the following:

- Vision statements
- Mission statements
- Doctrine or core values
- Frequent internal writings on related topics
- Awareness sessions

The key to establishing values is frequent, consistent, and repeated communications.

No organization is homogeneous. Within an organization, divisions will also have their own cultures and hence different security postures. To be successful at developing, implementing, and enforcing security policy, a leader needs to be sensitive to the character of the departments as well as the overall organization.

Assessing the security posture and implementation of a culture of security requires looking for evidence of senior management's involvement in the cultural engineering exercise. Does the organization even have a security mission statement?

The 10 Commandments of IT Security Ethics

The following is an example of a code of ethics suggested by the Computer Ethics Institute (Washington, DC, USA).

1. Thou shalt not use a computer to harm other people.
2. Thou shalt not interfere with other people's computer work.
3. Thou shalt not snoop around in other people's computer files.
4. Thou shalt not use a computer to steal.
5. Thou shalt not use a computer to bear false witness.
6. Thou shalt not copy or use proprietary software for which you have not paid.
7. Thou shalt not use other people's computer resources without authorization or proper compensation.
8. Thou shalt not appropriate other people's intellectual output.
9. Thou shalt think about the social consequences of the program you are writing or the system you are designing.
10. Thou shalt always use a computer in ways that insure consideration and respect for your fellow human beings.

Hacker Code of Ethics

Statements are made by many who like to call themselves hackers, saying how they will limit damage, not create loss, and generally that they make systems better by exploring. Ethical hacking without authorization is still illegal, and social engineering is considered to be an act of fraud.

Former Attorney General Janet Reno started a public-private alliance to restrain Internet crime through teaching children "that hacking is the same as breaking and entering."

Human Resource Issues

Human resource (HR) departments have a crucial role to play in regard to the security of an organization. The human resources department needs to be involved with the organization's security to decrease the risks associated with the following:

- Human error, theft, fraud, or misuse of facilities
- Users who are unaware of information security threats and concerns, and are not equipped to support the corporate security policy in the course of their normal work
- Minimizing the damage from security incidents and malfunctions and learning from such incidents

Some of the key areas needed within an organization that should be fulfilled by HR are as follows:

- Ensuring that "Terms and Conditions of Employment – Employment Letters/Contracts" have been issued and cover the security requirements of an organization.
- Ensuring that rmployee confidential information undertaking documents have been completed.
- Creating and issuing policies on intellectual property rights and ensure that an employee undertaking document has been signed.
- Creating and enforcing policies on privacy issues such as sharing employee information.
- Creating and conducting induction training.
- Suggesting disciplinary process for management.
- Ensuring that a grievance procedure exists.
- Conducting exit interviews for staff leaving the organization.
- Checking information security clearance levels where needed.

All of these issues help to reduce risk and increase the levels of professional standards and ethics that are applied within an organization.

Compliance with Legal Requirements

To avoid breaches of any statutory, criminal, or civil obligations and of any security requirements, the design, operation, and use of IT systems may be subject to statutory and contractual security requirements. Legal compliance is a detailed topic and is specific to both locality and industry. It has become a major driver for information technology investments. "Compliance" in the true sense of the word entails a legal requirement or a standard for context.

It is important that the organization's security administrator is familiar with the pertinent legal standards and requirements for his or her location and industry. Compliance issues demand that organizations look beyond the hype of current laws and regulations to address topics such as corporate governance, privacy, encryption laws, signature laws, and critical infrastructure requirements simultaneously.

International organizations must understand the legal requirements of various jurisdictions, including the similarities and conflicts among them. They also need to address the ethical concerns that are commonly different across cultures.

A failure to understand the broader context of applicable legal and ethical requirements could result in multiple problems. Conflicts among the ethical and legal issues that apply in different countries may become apparent from a lack of understanding regarding the differences in various jurisdictions. This is likely to result in compliance failures or in over compliance as well as a number of ethical breaches. Any of these issues is likely to cost an organization in the end.

FAQs

Q: *What do I need to do if I want to commence legal action for corporate espionage?*

A: To successfully prosecute corporate espionage, it is necessary to prove that the information has value. This can be a monetary value, a hidden value, or an economic advantage to an adversary/competitor. You also need to demonstrate that the information was protected and properly marked for protection, that policies and procedures were in place, and that awareness training was instituted.

Q: *Why shouldn't I use passive voice when writing my reports?*

A: "The author wrote the words in his diary" employs active voice. "The words in the diary were written by the author" illustrates passive voice. When writing a report, avoid any form of the verb *to be*, such as *is*, *are*, *was*, and *were*. Read your writing aloud; you'll find that passive voice can lead you to lapse into a sing-song schoolchild reading his "what I did last summer" essay out loud. It is much more difficult to take passive voice seriously.

Q: *What is considered public domain?*

A: Like all things, copyright protection eventually ends; it is only a "limited monopoly." When copyrights expire, they fall into the public domain. With a number of exceptions, public domain works may be unreservedly copied or used in the production of derivative works without either the permission or the authorization of the former copyright holder. At some stage in the Clinton administration, the contentious Sonny Bono Copyright Term Extension Act (CTEA) passed into law. This Act added 20 years to most copyright terms. It also created a moratorium that, in effect, stops any new works from entering the public domain until 2019. The bill was enacted to ensure protection for U.S. works in the foreign market.

5

Law, Ethics, and
Incident Management

Q: *What is wrong with using acronyms in my reports?*

A: Three-letter acronyms (TLAs) are the bane of all good reports. Acronyms often conflict within similar spheres. However, when you take a range of different occupations and knowledge fields, people start to read different meaning into this technical jargon. The result is that the report is less clear to the average reader.

Q: *I work for an ISP in the United States and have discovered child pornography on a website we host. What should I do?*

A: Under the Protection of Children from Sexual Predators Act of 1998 (Sexual Predators Act), ISPs are required to notify law enforcement of websites containing child pornography on their server(s). Failing to report it could mean that the ISP will be fined.

Summary

In this chapter, we have discussed the impact that domestic and international laws and regulations have on information security. The ISSMP candidate should understand legal issues and concepts in relevant areas such as privacy, import/export, computer crime, intellectual property, and civil and criminal liability. We also discussed incident management; the ISSMP candidate should have a deep understanding of the incident handling process – and be able not only to develop procedures for incident response, but also to oversee the execution of the full gamut of incident response. This includes not only understanding how to manage the actual technical and procedural aspects, but also thorough knowledge of investigations and reporting. Understanding how these must be conducted in order for their results to have credibility, and how evidence must be gathered and preserved in order to be deemed trustworthy and admissible, are important elements of this domain as well.

5

Law, Ethics, and Incident Management

References

http://csrc.nist.gov/publications/nistpubs/800-61rev2/SP800-61rev2.pdf

http://oag.ca.gov/ecrime/databreach/reporting

http://www.bakerlaw.com/files/Uploads/Documents/Data%20Breach%20documents/Data_Breach_Charts.pdf

https://www.us-cert.gov/government-users/reporting-requirements

Domain 5: Review Questions

1. Under the Electronic Communications Privacy Act, the expression "electronic communications" does NOT incorporate which of the following?

    I. Tone only paging devices
   II. Electronic funds transfer information
  III. Tracking devices
  IV. Wire or oral communications

    A. I, II, III, and IV
    B. I
    C. I and II
    D. I and III

2. The Digital Millennium Copyright Act (DMCA) has specific provisions designed to legislate against and thus aid in preventing what type of action?

    A. Circumvention of technologies used to protect copyrighted work
    B. Creation of malicious code
    C. Digital manipulation or alteration of copyrighted computer code
    D. Digital reproduction of copyrighted documents and artwork

3. What questions are asked when deciding the outcome of a U.S. federal trade mark dilution case? (Chose all that are correct)

    A. When was the mark created?
    B. How distinctive is the mark?
    C. Who owns the mark?
    D. How unique and recognized is the mark?

4. To sue for copyright infringement in the United States, what is the first step that a copyright holder must take?

    A. No action is necessary, as copyright attaches as a right of the author as soon as the work is created.
    B. Register a copyright application with the Copyright Office of the Library of Congress.
    C. Formally publish the work.
    D. Put the alleged infringer on notice that you intend to bring an action.

5

Law, Ethics, and Incident Management

5. The judge in a civil court case can issue an order allowing for a civil search of another party's goods and to seize specific evidence. This order is known as a(n)

    A. Subpoena

    B. Doctrine of Exigent Circumstances

    C. Anton Piller Order

    D. Search warrant

6. Your company has a policy prohibiting pornography on company equipment, and an employee has become aware of a network user who has an image of a nude child on his computer. When you investigate the matter, you find that the person has several photos of children on a nude beach, but none of them involves sex or focuses on the child's genitalia. Which of the following is true?

    A. It is child pornography, and the computer user can be charged with possession of child pornography.

    B. It is child pornography, and the computer user can be charged or disciplined.

    C. It is not child pornography, and the computer user can be disciplined.

    D. It is not child pornography, and the computer user cannot be charged or disciplined.

7. Your team has detected that an outside party attempted to do a port scan on a highly sensitive system. According to the U.S. government model, what is the maximum amount of time that should elapse before the relevant information is reported?

    A. One hour

    B. One day

    C. One week

    D. One month

8. Tracing violations or attempted violations of system security to the user responsible is a function of what?

    A. Authentication

    B. Access management

    C. Integrity checking

    D. Accountability

9. Why is a conflict of interest considered troubling from the standpoint of fraud prevention?

    A. A conflict of interest violates canons of professional responsibility.

    B. A conflict of interest is obviously unethical and causes waste.

    C. A conflict of interest can be a sign of fraud, if not a source of it.

    D. A conflict of interest violates federal law and is therefore illegal.

10. The penalties that can be sanctioned to the losing party in a civil case can include

    A. Probation

    B. Community service

    C. Fines

    D. Imprisonment

11. Evidence needs to be one of the following in order to be deemed as admissible in a court of law:

    A. Conclusive

    B. Incontrovertible

    C. Irrefutable

    D. Relevant

12. RFC 1087 sets the IAB "Ethics and the Internet" categorization of unethical actions. Which of the following is NOT considered as unethical under the IAB?

    A. Downloading pornography

    B. Compromising user privacy without authorization

    C. Taking resources such as stationary and using equipment for personal uses

    D. Seeking to gain unauthorized access to resources

13. What is an evidence gathering technique that occurs when a law enforcement officer entices a party into enacting a criminal offense they may not have otherwise committed with the aim of capturing the person in a "sting" operation; is this considered legal or illegal?

    A. Enticement/legal

    B. Coercion/legal

    C. Entrapment/illegal

    D. Enticement/illegal

14. Which expression is used to describe the process where a party is provided with sufficient temptation such that they may hand over evidence of a crime that the individual has committed?

    A. Enticement

    B. Coercion

    C. Entrapment

    D. Encouragement

15. What penalties does the CFAA hold for people who create and release malware?

    A. The CFAA has both civil and criminal sanctions.

    B. The CFAA has criminal sanctions.

    C. The CFAA has civil sanctions.

    D. The CFAA does not incorporate malware and is targeted at fraud such as phishing and financial fraud.

16. Which of the following is not considered to be intellectual property?

    A. Patents, servicemarks, and trademarks

    B. Plant grower's rights

    C. Computer hardware

    D. Trade secrets

17. Which term best describes the situation where an individual attacks (hacks) a computer system with the motive of curiosity or the thrill of seeing what is there?

    A. Scoping attack

    B. Digital thrill seeking

    C. Recon attacks

    D. Phishing

18. The Fourth Amendment to the U.S. Constitution sets the standard for what action?

    A. Free speech

    B. Commercial transactions and interstate commerce

    C. Individual privacy

    D. Government searches or seizure

19. Why is prevention alone NOT sufficient to protect a system from attackers?

    A. Even the finest preventive measures experience failures.

    B. The maintenance of preventive measures is labor intensive.

    C. It is hard to put preventive measures into operation.

    D. Prevention by itself is an expensive alternative.

20. A set of principles that is derived from a cultural or religious authority and standards is known as:

    A. Policy

    B. Law

    C. Guidelines

    D. A moral code

5

Law, Ethics, and Incident Management

Appendix A
Answers to Domain Review Questions

Domain 1 – Security Leadership and Management

1. Organization mission statements

    A.   Are nontechnical in nature, so ISSMPs do not have to understand them

    B.   Are quickly put together by senior management

    C.   Provide everyone in the organization overall direction and focus for their activities

    D.   Are very specific and provide specific goals and objectives

The correct answer is **C**. ISSMPs must base justifications for security on the organization's mission. It takes management months to agree on a mission statement. The mission statement provides an overall focus and direction from which specific goals and objectives are developed.

2. Which types of organizations need to have a formally documented mission statement?

    A.   Commercial enterprises

    B.   Nonprofit organizations

    C.   Government agencies

    D.   All the above

The correct answer is **D**. All organizations need to have a formally documented mission statement if they want to be successful.

3. Deploying Internet security solutions that are acceptable by clients requires knowing the client's

   A. Expectations and location
   B. Location and technical knowledge
   C. System capabilities and expectations
   D. Expectation and technical knowledge

   The correct answer is **C**. On the Internet, solutions do not depend upon location or technical knowledge, because you need to assume that the solution must be readily available to the client within a normal commercial PC configuration. Forcing a client to install, wait for, or buy additional technology on its system will result in the client going to a competitor. See the smartcard example in the External Influences section.

4. All organizations' security solutions are influenced by the following:

   A. Laws, employee culture, profit, and competition
   B. Goals, client expectations, regulations, and profit
   C. Group and client expectations and competition capabilities
   D. Profit, organization objectives, client capabilities, and senior management

   The correct answer is **C**. Government is not influenced by profit. All the rest of the answers are incorrect.

5. A system's security solutions must be

   A. Cost effective, risk based, and acceptable
   B. Risk based and within division budget restraints
   C. Practical and 95% effective
   D. Acceptable by senior management and provide an ROI

   The correct answer is **A**. Senior management accepts the risk so division bud get is not a restraint. There is a standard measure of acceptable effectiveness. ROI is not the only reason management selects a security solution. Sometimes management makes decisions based on requirements: regulatory, end-user acceptability, public relations, etc.

6. A specific piece of information's level of classification is dependent on

   A. Need to know
   B. Cost of producing the information
   C. Impact if compromised
   D. Affordability of required security

   The correct answer is **C**. Classification is dependent on the impact if the information were to be compromised. The rest of the answers are determined after the information is classified.

7. System security boundary must be determined early based on all but the following.

    A.   Understanding the mission, goals, and objectives

    B.   Coordinating the review with the end users

    C.   Identify the system components that support each of the business functions

    D.   Determining who is operationally and fiscally responsible for the system

The correct answer is **B**. The review must be coordinated with the system manager, program manager, or system owner, not the end user.

8. Security boundary is important to establishing

    A.   Who will be doing the certification effort

    B.   Scoping the security effort

    C.   Determining which regulations and laws apply

    D.   If the system will need an Internet connection or not

The correct answer is **B**. What regulations and laws apply is determined by what the mission and function of the system are. Whether the system needs an Internet connection is dependent on the operations. Who does the certification is dependent on what is in the boundary, but it is more of a management decision. Answer b is the best answer.

9. The implementation phase of the System Development Life Cycle includes

    A.   Conducting an initial security test

    B.   Identifying security solutions

    C.   Determining if the security is acceptable to operate

    D.   Defining the system security requirements

The correct answer is **C**. Identifying security solutions and initial testing are conducted in the Development Phase and defining requirements is done in the Initiation Phase.

10. The ISSMP's job is to provide security support at the end of which phase in the System Development Life Cycle?

    A.   Disposition and Disposal

    B.   Operation and Maintenance

    C.   Implementation

    D.   Initiation

The correct answer is **A**. ISSMP supports a system's security throughout the entire system life cycle.

11. Risk assessments are done in which phases of the System Development Life Cycle?

    A. Initiation

    B. Initiation and Implementation

    C. Implementation and Disposition and Disposal

    D. Initiation, Implementation, and Operations and Maintenance

    The correct answer is **D**. This is the best answer because risk assessments are done throughout all the phases of the SDLC.

12. Who sets the information security standards for the public sector?

    A. National Security Agency (NSA)

    B. International Organization for Standardization (ISO)

    C. National Institute of Standards and Technology (NIST)

    D. International Electrotechnical Commission (IEC)

    The correct answer is **C**. NIST is assigned to provide IT security standards for all U.S. government agencies and the public sector.

13. Families of controls are identified in which of the following documents?

    A. NIST Special Publication 80053

    B. ISO 27002

    C. DODI8500.2

    D. All the above

    The correct answer is **D**. All three identify the public, private, and defense sectors, respectively.

14. The ISSMP decides between using quantitative and qualitative risk assessment based on

    A. The budget process

    B. Threats

    C. Vulnerabilities

    D. Management decision processes

    The correct answer is **D**. Risk assessments are used to make decisions on how much security is enough. If management decision processes are based on numerical assessments, it is best to use a quantitative assessment. If they make decisions on conceptual evaluations, use qualitative assessments.

15. Assurances are those activities that provide management with what about security solutions?

    A.   Due diligence

    B.   Protection

    C.   Cost effectiveness

    D.   ROI

The correct answer is **A**. Assurances like review, audit, evaluation, and certification provide management with confidence that the security solutions will be effective.

16. Which of the following provides a measurement of how well an organization's process includes the capability of continuously improving its processes?

    A.   Common Criteria Evaluation and Validation Scheme

    B.   OCTAVE

    C.   Software Engineering Institute's Capability Maturity Model

    D.   Commonly Accepted Security Practices and Regulations

The correct answer is **C**. SEI/CMM is about the evaluation of the maturity of organizational processes. The others are about the processes for creating and evaluating security programs and products.

17. Interconnections with other systems outside the system security boundary can have the following effects on a system:

    A.   Increased dependencies to support the other system's security requirements

    B.   Requirement to notify when a security event occurs on your system

    C.   Obligation to inform the other system when outages are going to occur

    D.   All the above

The correct answer is **D**. Connecting to another system that will support your system's communication or storage/processing capabilities, or accepts or provides data from and to your system can add new requirements on your operations.

18. Annual Loss Expectancy and ROI are expressed in the following units:

    A.   Currency and percentage

    B.   Percentage and level of risk

    C.   Cost of security and percentage

    D.   Percentage and cost savings

The correct answer is **A**. ALE is potential loss measured in financial terms, and ROI is percentage return on what was invested.

19. Plan of Actions and Milestones (POA&M) is

    A. A security plan

    B. A management tool

    C. A list of all the systems security solutions

    D. A checklist of actions for monitoring security during the Implementation Phase

The correct answer is **B**. The POA&M is a list of actions and resources that have to be taken to secure known vulnerabilities in systems used by management to track the status and needs for a system's security.

20. The ideal presentation to senior managers should follow which of the following rules?

    A. 20page justification

    B. Five slides

    C. Answer all the questions that the audience could ask

    D. Be presented in 5 minutes

The correct answer is **D**. Management has limited time to listen and read, so the justification should be one page and the presentation should be four pages. You want the audience to ask questions so they can become engaged with the problem and solution. A good presentation should be close to 5 minutes in length. Selling senior management on approving a solution for a security issue is one of the hardest jobs that an ISSMP will have to do. For many people selling is not easy for many reasons: they are asking for money; they have to give a presentation; they find it difficult to write a justification or determine the ROI; the audience will ask questions; and many more.

Domain 2 – Security Lifecycle Management

1. How does the need for security compare between systems developed for sale or external use and systems developed for in-house use?

    A. Systems for sale or external use always have more security concerns.

    B. Systems developed for in-house use always have more security concerns.

    C. Systems developed in house require security efforts on the part of the internal security team, while those developed for external use can have security outsourced.

    D. Both systems have security concerns that must be carefully addressed.

The correct answer is **D**. Both systems have security concerns that must be carefully addressed.

2. When should a project's security measures be addressed?

    A. As close to the start of the project as possible

    B. Only after security issues are exploited

    C. After the initial project design is done

    D. When the functional specifications are being written

The correct answer is **A**. As close to the start of the project as possible. Security measures can require significant changes in design, and this is least problematic and least expensive the earlier in the project it is done.

3. Which of the following pose the greatest risk of perpetrating a catastrophic theft of an organization's valuable data without expending great resources to do so?

    A. Foreign governments and their sponsored hackers

    B. Employees

    C. Activists from hacktivist groups such as Anonymous

    D. Customers

The correct answer is **B**. Employees often have access to a treasure trove of sensitive information, and they don't need to pay hackers, or otherwise expend resources, to steal it.

4. How does the use of Rapid Application Development (RAD) affect security planning?

    A. The compressed time between releases means security planning and concerns must be brought up early and stressed often.

    B. The process of iterative development means security is built in automatically.

    C. Security issues are more common in RAD projects.

    D. Security issues are less common in RAD projects.

The correct answer is **A**. The compressed time between releases means security planning and concerns must be brought up early and stressed often. This means the concerns are kept at the forefront of the project team's awareness and addressed as early as possible in RAD's short cycles.

5. What security risks are associated with the use of prototyping and prototyping tools?

    A. Prototypes always allow hackers to understand what a business plans to do for security in its finished products.

    B. Prototyping helps ensure secure code.

    C. Prototyping tools write code with an eye toward that code's security.

    D. Prototypes and prototyping tools tend to generate basic and insecure code that must be carefully reviewed before use in the finished product.

The correct answer is **D**. Prototypes and prototyping tools tend to generate basic and insecure code that must be carefully reviewed before use in the finished product. Prototyping is intended to get basic functionality up fast and tends to have no concession toward security. No prototype code, no matter how it is generated, should make its way into the finished product without a full security review.

6. Risk analysis is a method to do what?

    A. Find all possible security issues and how to exploit them.

    B. Gather data on the cost to mitigate security threats and the possibility of the threat being exploited.

    C. Decide how much money to spend on security.

    D. Compare risks and rewards of having a security program

The correct answer is **B**. Gather data on the cost to mitigate security threats and the possibility of the threat being exploited. Risk analysis is the process of obtaining the data necessary to decide what security threats to mitigate, but does not make the decisions.

7. What mitigations should be listed in a risk analysis?

    A. Only those of the project itself

    B. Only mitigations that are software or network related

    C. . Only those that can be mitigated with security technology

    D. All mitigations that apply to a risk the project has or inherits

The correct answer is **D**. All mitigations that apply to a risk the project has or inherits. Mitigations can include physical mitigations, policy mitigations, as well as other types of mitigations.

8. How many levels of risk and mitigation must be taken into account during a risk analysis?

   A. Only the first level of identifying the risk and its immediate mitigation

   B. As many levels as needed to reach a level of mitigation that is no longer feasible

   C. Two levels—the risk and its mitigation and then the mitigation if that first mitigation fails

   D. The same number of levels as listed for maximum response times in the security plan

The correct answer is **B**. As many levels as needed to reach a level of mitigation that is no longer feasible. Defense-in-Depth is a fundamental concept of security, and exploring and documenting all reasonable levels of mitigation and risk may uncover previously hidden security considerations.

9. Security cost is defined as what when writing a risk analysis?

   A. The monetary costs of developing and implementing security measures, including consulting, hardware, additional software, and development process costs

   B. The productivity losses associated with time lost to implement and abide by security measures

   C. Both of the above

   D. None of the above

The correct answer is **C**. Both of the above. Both costs that are directly monetary and indirect costs must be taken into account when deciding what security mitigations to implement.

10. Who should review and sign off on security plans?

   A. Key players as well as anyone mandated by the enterprise itself

   B. Only those people required by the enterprise's policies

   C. Outside consultants only

   D. A third-party auditor

The correct answer is **A**. Key players as well as anyone mandated by the enterprise itself. The more variety in roles and in people both inside and outside the actual development team that review the Security Plan, the greater the chance of flushing and addressing potential risks early.

11. When are security reviews necessary?

    A. When legally mandated or required by company policy

    B. It depends on the project

    C. When any changes are made

    D. When a breach occurs

The correct answer is **B**. It depends on the project. There must be a balance between legal and company requirements and the sensitivity and importance of the project itself.

12. What impact can access to a project's source code have on security?

    A. It improves security because more people can look for issues.

    B. It has no real effect. There isn't much interest in enterprise in-house projects.

    C. It can compromise security and access should be limited.

    D. The source code cannot impact security. Only executable code that actually runs can impact security.

The correct answer is **C**. It can compromise security and access should be limited. Not only can security be compromised by someone with direct access, but it can also lead to source code being leaked publicly and further compromise occurring.

13. Who should have access to a project's bug or defect database?

    A. Everyone at the company.

    B. Only those who require access to do their jobs.

    C. It should be public.

    D. The IT support team

The correct answer is **B**. Only those who require access to do their jobs. Because the defect database is the repository of security defects, only those who require access to do their jobs should be able to read or write to this database.

14. Web 2.0 projects often have more security needs in what area?

    A. Data encryption, transmission, and storage

    B. Server hardening and updating

    C. Both of the above

    D. None of the above

The correct answer is **C**. Web 2.0 has more emphasis on data being passed back and forth between a client and the cloud, data is more easily captured. The heavy reliance on servers also makes the servers more likely to be attacked.

15. What impact does virtualization have on security?

    A.   Unique risks must be taken into account.

    B.   No impact. Security is treated exactly as if virtualization is not in use.

    C.   Virtualization reduces security risks.

    D.   The same issues as those relevant to all of the systems being run on the virtual machines combined.

The correct answer is **A**. Unique risks must be taken into account. Not only does virtualization include risks present in non-virtualized environments, but it also has a set of special security risks of its own that must be addressed. Answer A is better than answer D because there are also additional risks caused by the virtualization, some of which might be present, for example, even if no systems run on the instantiated virtual machines.

16. What is the role of security in the maintenance phase of a project?

    A.   Security must be maintained by regular code and security reviews by patching and updating software and hardware.

    B.   Security must be maintained by patching and updating software and hardware, and by security reviews, but code reviews are no longer necessary.

    C.   Security must be maintained by regular code and security reviews, but patching is irrelevant to this issue.

    D.   Security is no longer needed during the maintenance phase.

The correct answer is **A**. The maintenance phase requires involvement of security and the security plan with a goal of keeping security high and even improving mitigations.

17. What is the difference between a public cloud system and a community cloud system?

    A.   A public cloud involves a third party providing services to an organization via the Internet; a community cloud is a private cloud that is shared between several parties.

    B.   A public cloud involves a third party providing services to an organization via the Internet; a community cloud infrastructure means the organization manages some resources available in house and has other resources provided to it by an external third party.

    C.   A public cloud involves a third party providing services to an organization via the Internet; a community cloud is another word for a private cloud.

    D.   They are the same.

The correct answer is **A**.

18. What types of security testing should be done on the system to ensure that it meets its security bar?

    A. Component level security testing is more than able to validate the system's security.

    B. Component level, end-to-end, and penetration testing should all be used to validate the system's security.

    C. End-to-end security testing is the best way to validate that the system meets its security bar.

    D. Penetration testing is the best way to validate that the system meets its security bar.

The correct answer is **B**. Component level, end-to-end, and penetration testing should all be used to validate the system's security. Each type of security testing has blind spots that can be offset by the strength of one or more of the other types of security testing.

19. What kind of data should be used in security testing?

    A. Mock data that follows real patterns

    B. Live data with sensitive information stripped out

    C. Live data in its entirety

    D. Live data with sensitive information stripped out

The correct answer is **A**. Mock data that follows real patterns. It's relatively trivial to generate this data, and using any kind of real data presents an additional security risk to that data, as test data, test systems, and test networks are often open to access by someone who could compromise that data, and having it brings no real benefit.

20. What benefit does using components or software that is certified or accredited bring to a system's security?

    A. Neither certification nor accreditation never has an effect on the system's security.

    B. In some cases, it can help increase the system's security level.

    C. It negatively affects the system's security.

    D. Certification can help improve security, but accreditation has no impact on security.

The correct answer is **B**. It can help increase the system's security level. The certification process produces components or software that is known to meet a set of standards, and this means the testing or mitigations the system must implement can be limited to issues not on those standards.

Domain 3 – **Security Compliance Management**

1. Cyber vulnerability testing consists of which of the following activities?

    A. War driving and war dialing

    B. Network probing and network scanning

    C. Penetration testing

    D. All of the above

The correct answer is **D**. Vulnerability testing consists of a variety of activities including war dialing, war driving, network scanning, network probing, and penetration testing.

2. Which of the following statements is true?

    A. The main benefit of using an MSSP is to turn over all responsibilities and wash your hands of the entire enterprise security burden.

    B. MSSP relationships can be more casual because most MSSPs are willing and capable to take on the enterprise security responsibilities.

    C. Operations, monitoring, detection, notification, and resolution may be outsourced, but the security responsibility is only shared, not abdicated.

    D. When using an MSSP, in-house security efforts are no longer necessary.

The correct answer is **C**. Operations, monitoring, detection, notification, and resolution may be outsourced, but the security responsibility is only shared, not abdicated.

3. What is the intent of metrics?

    A. Objective measurement of the enterprise risk posture

    B. Objective evaluation of value to the organization in terms of business need

    C. Determine if operations are performing within SLAs

    D. Objective measurement of the enterprise security posture

The correct answer is **B**. The intent of metrics is objective evaluation of value to the organization in terms of business need.

4. An emerging formal practice to identify key people, process, technology, and environment that fulfill the mission and then to align security operations with these key resources is known as what?

    A. Enterprise risk management

    B. Enterprise security management

    C. Risk management

    D. Mission assurance

The correct answer is **D**. Mission assurance is an emerging formal practice to identify key people, process, technology, and environment that fulfill the mission and then to align security operations with these key resources.

5. Given the existence of enterprise security guidance, and that enterprise employees, business partners, vendors, and other covered entities are aware and under stand the policies, standards, procedures, and guidelines, there is a need to enforce compliance in daily operations. Enforcement requires which of the following?

    A. Monitoring for noncompliance

    B. Detecting and responding to noncompliance

    C. Both a and b

    D. None of the above

The correct answer is **C**. Now that the security guidance is out there, and there is reasonable proof that the enterprise employees, business partners, vendors, and other covered entities are aware and understand the policies, standards, procedures, and guidelines, there is a need to enforce compliance in daily operations. Enforcement requires monitoring, detecting, and responding to areas of noncompliance.

6. Which of the following statements is false about the Enterprise Security Standard (ESS)?

    A. You can develop an ESS from an industry security standard or from security legislation or both.

    B. The structure of the ESS becomes the foundation for the enterprise security framework (ESF).

    C. To save money, and since the ESS is unique to each organization anyway, developing the ESS from staff experience, though somewhat arbitrary, is an acceptable practice.

    D. The enterprise security standard (ESS) is a list of all applicable security controls grouped by families.

The correct answer is **C**. The enterprise security standard (ESS) is a list of all applicable security controls grouped by families. There are many standards from which to derive an ESS, including National Institute of Technology (NIST) Special Publication (SP) 80053 Recommended Security Controls for Federal Information Systems, International Standards Organization (ISO) 27002 The Code of Practice for Information

Security Management, and many others. You can use the standard as is or customize the ESS from other compliance requirements included in security legislation (e.g., Healthcare Insurance Portability and Accountability Act [HIPAA], Sarbanes-Oxley, and European Union Directive on Data Protection). The structure of the ESS becomes the foundation for the enterprise security framework (ESF).

Why NIST SP 80053? My company is not a United States Civilian Federal organization, so why do I care about NIST standards? First, it is an industry standard, which is a lot better than being arbitrary in your approach to enterprise security planning. Second, it is free and easily obtainable.

7. Which of the following statements is true about incident response?

    A.   Some potential members of an incident response team are senior management, legal, corporate communications, and operations.

    B.   Incident response team (IRT) and cyber incident response team (CIRT) are similar phrases for the same organizational function.

    C.   The news media will print what they want anyway, so it is okay for anyone on the security team to speak to them about security incident details.

    D.   All cyber incidents are unique and upon detection are immediately escalated to subject matter experts (SMEs).

The correct answer is **A**. Who should be on the incident response team? What enterprise roles and departments should be represented on the team? CIRT team members should include senior management, security, legal, help desk, corporate communications, information technology, and business unit/ operations.

8. Which of the following statements is false?

    A.   In a given environment, people perform processes using technology to produce results.

    B.   Security is a support structure of safeguards for cost management and never contributes to revenue generation.

    C.   A key differentiating characteristic of the cyber domain from the other domains is physical proximity.

    D.   The complement to legislative compliance is good business practice.

The correct answer is **B**. In a given environment, people perform processes using technology to produce results.

Security may contribute directly to revenue generation by offering security services or mechanisms for a fee. A key differentiating characteristic of the cyber domain from the other domains is physical proximity. Additionally, this chapter material addresses the complement to legislative compliance, which is good business practice, to optimize the interests of stakeholders.

9. What is the purpose of a service level agreement (SLA)?

    A. The SLA is only used as a formal agreement between the enterprise and external service providers to establish services, performance parameters, and financial penalties for performance outside of specified parameters.

    B. The SLA records common understanding about the services provided and the performance parameters within which to provide the services.

    C. The SLA specifies performance measurements in terms of thresholds, e.g., number of transactions per hour, available bandwidth, and downtime tolerances.

    D. The SLA is a formal agreement that specifies pay for performance within operations departments.

The correct answer is **B**. The SLA records common understanding about the services provided and the performance parameters within which to provide the services.

10. What is the enterprise risk posture?

    A. Intentionally assumed position of safeguards throughout the entire organization

    B. The probability of specific eventualities throughout the entire organization

    C. The aggregation of all the safeguards and precautions that mitigate risk

    D. The formal articulation of an intentionally assumed position on dealing with potential negative impact

The correct answer is **D**. The enterprise risk posture is the formal articulation of an intentionally assumed position on dealing with potential negative impact.

11. What is data exfiltration?

    A. The unauthorized use of USB devices

    B. The unauthorized transmission of data between departments

    C. The unauthorized transmission of data into the organization from a service provider

    D. The unauthorized transmission of data out of the organization

The correct answer is **D**. Data exfiltration is the unauthorized transmission of data out of the organization.

12. Which of the following groups is not representative of the nine core security principles?

    A. Nonrepudiation, possession, utility

    B. Authorized use, privacy, authorized access

    C. Confidentiality, integrity, authenticity

    D. Availability, privacy, utility

The correct answer is **B**. Nine security core principles provide a foundational framework to implement and run security operations: confidentiality, integrity, availability, possession, utility, authenticity, nonrepudiation, authorized use, and privacy.

13. Which of the following is true about a Security Compliance Management Program (SCMP)?

    A. Governance identifies and enumerates all relevant security compliance requirements. These may include legislation, regulation, directives, instructions, contractual obligations, and good business practice.

    B. The planning function determines the appropriate steps to take to establish and maintain compliance. The results of planning will include a list of necessary security technologies to insert in IT operations.

    C. Implementation takes the policies, standards, procedures, and guide lines and inserts them into information technology systems. Deployment makes compliance part of daily operations throughout the enterprise.

    D. The role of adjudication is to resolve conflicts in the best interest of enterprise senior management and executives.

The correct answer is **A**. Governance identifies and enumerates all relevant security compliance requirements. These may include legislation, regulation, directives, instructions, contractual obligations, and good business practice.

The planning function determines the appropriate steps to take to establish and maintain compliance. The results of planning will include a list of necessary policies, standards, procedures, and guidelines that convey expected behavior within the organization to establish and maintain compliance.

Implementation takes the policies, standards, procedures, and guidelines and inserts them into enterprise daily activities. Deployment makes compliance part of daily operations throughout the enterprise.

The role of adjudication is to resolve these conflicts in the best interest of the stakeholders and the enterprise.

14. Which of the following is false about system hardening?

    A. System hardening is the elimination of known vulnerabilities, exploits, and generally turning off or uninstalling unnecessary functions.

    B. Each operating system, each version of the same operating system, and each patch release of the same operating system may have a different procedure for hardening the system.

    C. Disabling unused services will require OS parameter changes at the kernel or registry level, or modifications to services that initiate or run at startup.

    D. None of the above.

The correct answer is **D**. System hardening is the elimination of known vulnerabilities, exploits, and generally turning off or uninstalling unnecessary functions. Each operating system, each version of the same operating system, and each patch release of the same operating system may have a different procedure for hardening the system. Disabling unused services will require OS parameter changes at the kernel or registry level, or modifications to services that initiate or run at startup.

15. What is the difference between legislative management and litigation management?

    A. Litigation management is the use of lobby groups by senior management to establish working relationships with the local judiciary, and legislation management is the use of lobby groups with Congress to influence the content of security laws.

    B. Legislative management attempts to avoid litigation, and litigation management intends to minimize the negative effects on an organization in the event of an incident.

    C. Litigation management involves establishing working relationships between senior management, security personnel, and the enterprise legal department, and legislative management is the result of this working relationship.

    D. Litigation management comes before legislative management.

The correct answer is **B**. Legislative management addresses compliance with legislation and attempts to avoid litigation through safeguarding against the occurrence of incidents. The complement to legislative management is litigation management, where the intent of litigation management is to minimize the negative effects on the organization in the event of an incident that leads to litigation.

16. Which of the following is a true statement about digital policy management (DPM)?

    A. A digital policy infrastructure is the collection of policy managers, policy clients, PDPs, and PEPs.

    B. DPM is the process of creating and disseminating information technology (IT) policies.

    C. DPM is the automated enforcement of policy on the network.

    D. None of the above.

The correct answer is **C**. Digital policy management (DPM) is the automated enforcement of policy on the network. A digital policy infrastructure is the collection of policy managers, policy clients, PDPs, and PEPs. Note: While the latter sentence is true, this speaks to digital policy infrastructure, not DPM.

17. The most dangerous type of malware is

    A. A spear phishing attack because it targets a specific weakness in people.

    B. A zero day exploit because it tries to exploit unknown or undisclosed vulnerabilities.

    C. A physical breach because it is the hardest to see coming.

    D. An insider threat using a USB thumb sucker attack because of unique knowledge of the enterprise.

The correct answer is **B**. The detection safeguards assist in detecting known threats (e.g., malware with known signatures); however, the most dangerous malware is a zero day exploit. A zero day threat or attack tries to exploit unknown or undisclosed vulnerabilities.

18. Which of the following statements about bots is false?

    A. A bot is a type of malware that performs a specific function as directed by the bot herder.

    B. A bot is a term for software robot.

    C. Successful penetration of a PC by a bot makes that PC part of a botnet.

    D. A bot has a limited lifetime, typically less than 60 days, and must perform its nefarious activities before it removes itself from the infected system.

The correct answer is **D**. A bot is a term for a software robot; exposure to bots is one type of vulnerability. Successful penetration of a PC by a bot makes that PC part of a botnet, or a network of software robots. That bot may then transmit to other computers on the Internet according to the direction of the master program (bot controller, also known as a bot herder) directing the bots. The bot may lay dormant until invoked by the controller.

19. What is the purpose of security policies?

    A. To provide a description of acceptable behavior within the enterprise

    B. To clearly convey the uses for security services and mechanisms within the enterprise

    C. To exert control over the organization by the security department

    D. To provide a description of acceptable behavior with the intent of minimizing risk to the organization

The correct answer is **D**. Security policies provide a description of acceptable behavior with the intent of minimizing risk to the organization: risk that may occur in the form of legislative and regulatory compliance, technical risk, environmental risk (e.g., clean and safe work environment), and the execution of processes and tasks.

20. A privately held restaurant chain in New Jersey, USA is likely thinking about its compliance needs. Which is likely to apply?

    A. HIPAA

    B. GLB

    C. PCI-DSS

    D. SEC rules

The correct answer is **C**. PCI DSS is a related to payment card data security, which is relevant to restaurants. HIPAA is related to healthcare information, GLB is related to financial institutions, and SEC rules pertain to publicly-traded companies..

Domain 4 – **Contingency Management**

1. Which one of the following is not a benefit of developing a disaster recovery plan?

    A. Reducing disruptions to operations

    B. Training personnel to perform alternate roles

    C. Minimizing decision making during a disastrous event

    D. Minimizing legal liability and insurance premiums

The correct answer is **B**. Answers a, c, and d are all benefits of developing a DRP.

2. A business continuity policy should be reviewed and reevaluated

    A.   Annually in light of management's strategic vision

    B.   Biannually in preparation for an audit review

    C.   Whenever critical systems are outsourced

    D.   During implementation of system upgrades

The correct answer is **A**. Each year, a policy should be reviewed and reevaluated in light of the strategic vision management sets for the organization and the business continuity program.

3. Which of the following is a key phase of BC and DR plans?

    A.   Damage assessment

    B.   Personnel evacuation

    C.   Emergency transportation

    D.   Emergency response

The correct answer is **D**. The four key phases of BC and DR plans are pre-disaster, emergency response, recovery, and post-recovery.

4. The vitally important issue for emergency response is

    A.   Calling emergency services

    B.   Protecting the corporate image

    C.   Accounting for employees

    D.   Employee evacuation

The correct answer is **C**. Accounting for employees is vitally important.

5. The third stage in the development of business continuity plans is

    A.   Define Business Continuity Management strategy.

    B.   Exercise, review, and maintain the policy.

    C.   Understand the organization.

    D.   Develop and implement the BCM policy.

The correct answer is **D**. The third of four distinct stages in the development of BC plans is develop and implement the BCM policy.

6. Which one of the following is not required for understanding the organization? Understanding the organization's

    A. Organization chart

    B. Risk appetite

    C. Information technology infrastructure

    D. Core business functions

The correct answer is **A**. Answers b, c, and d are required to understand the organization.

7. Key milestones in developing the project plan and governance include all of the below except

    A. Risk analysis

    B. Data gathering

    C. Audit approval

    D. Training, education, and awareness

The correct answer is **C**. Audit approval is not a key milestone.

8. The output of a business impact analysis is

    A. A prioritized list of critical data

    B. A prioritized list of sensitive systems

    C. The recommendation for alternate processing

    D. The scope of the business continuity plan

The correct answer is **A**. The output of the BIA step is a prioritized list of critical data, roles, and IT resources that support your organization's business processes.

9. When a critical system cannot function at an acceptable level without input from a system on which it is dependent, which of the following statements is incorrect?

    A. The system on which it is dependent is at a higher priority.

    B. The system on which it is dependent is at a lower priority.

    C. The system on which it is dependent is at the same priority.

    D. The critical system feeds a lower priority system.

The correct answer is **B**. It will not work for one system to have a higher priority than another system on which it critically depends, unless it can continue to function without the dependency at an acceptable level.

10. People based threats include

    A. Theft, whitelisting, industrial action

    B. Industrial action, blacklisting, pandemics

    C. Pandemics, theft, industrial action

    D. Pandemics, call forwarding, theft

The correct answer is **C**. People based threats include pandemics, theft, and industrial action.

11. Risk acceptance is usually most appropriate when

    A. Impact is high and probability is low.

    B. Probability is high and impact is low.

    C. Impact is high and probability is high.

    D. Impact is low and probability is low.

The correct answer is **D**. Where the probability of a threat occurring is low and the impact to the security of the information system is low, then generally, the cost to implement security features will outweigh the value of the assets to be protected and the risk will be acceptable.

12. Heat maps reflect the level of risk an activity poses and include all of the below except

    A. A suggested risk appetite boundary

    B. Proposed risk countermeasures

    C. Risk zones

    D. Color coding

The correct answer is **B**. Countermeasures are not included in the heat map.

13. A System Information Form contains all of the following information except

    A. Recovery priority

    B. Maximum outage time

    C. Dependencies on other systems

    D. Recovery point objective

The correct answer is **D**. The recovery point objective is not included in the System Information Form.

14. The Notification Activation Phase of the BCP/DRP includes

    A. A sequence of recovery goals

    B. Activities to notify recovery personnel

    C. The basis for declaring an emergency

    D. The assessment of system damage

The correct answer is **A**. The sequence of recovery goals is included in the Recovery Phase.

15. Documenting recovery procedures is for

    A. Implementing recovery strategy

    B. Highlighting points requiring coordination between teams

    C. Outsourcing disaster recovery system development

    D. Providing instructions for the least knowledgeable recovery personnel

The correct answer is **C**. Outsourcing the preparation of procedure documentation to a professional services organization specializing in disaster recovery system development is an option.

16. The primary purposes of testing are to

    A. Satisfy audit requirements.

    B. Check that sources of data are adequate.

    C. Raise staff awareness of recovery plans.

    D. Prove the ability to recover from disruption.

The correct answer is **A**. Answers b, c, and d are all purposes of testing.

17. Plan maintenance should be scheduled

    A. After testing to account for hardware or personnel changes

    B. In anticipation of audit activity

    C. When changes are made to protected systems

    D. When changes are made to supported business processes

The correct answer is **B**. If a, c, and d are accomplished there is no need to prepare for auditors.

18. Communications is a critical activity during the response and recovery phases of an incident. The communications plan must provide

    A. Alternative types of communications media

    B. A list of contacts reachable through a communications tree

    C. Alternative communications service providers

    D. Immediate access to mobile devices for key communicators

The correct answer is **C**. Answers a, b, and d are specifically listed as requirements to be included in the Communications Plan.

19. An Emergency Operations Center must be provided to centrally manage the incident. It should include

    A. A provision for secure and confidential discussions

    B. Office space for recovery team leaders

    C. Access to all BC and DR plans

    D. Forms of refreshment for EOC personnel

The correct answer is **B**. Recovery teams would be located at the recovery site, not the EOC.

20. Thorough training in plan activities helps ensure

    A. All team members understand their responsibilities.

    B. All team members understand the roles of others.

    C. Team cooperation.

    D. Plans are current.

The correct answer is **D**. Thorough team training helps ensure that all members understand their responsibilities, the roles of others, and team cooperation when it is needed most.

Domain 5 – **Law, Ethics, and Incident Management**

1. Under the Electronic Communications Privacy Act, the expression "electronic communications" does NOT incorporate which of the following?

    I. Tone only paging devices
    II. Electronic funds transfer information
    III. Tracking devices
    IV. Wire or oral communications

    A. I, II, III, and IV
    B. I
    C. I and II
    D. I and III

The correct answer is **A**. The U.S. Wiretap Act defines "electronic communication" as any transfer of signs, signals, writing, images, sounds, data, or intelligence of any nature transmitted in whole or in part by a wire, radio, electromagnetic, photo-electronic, or photo-optical system that affects inter state or foreign commerce, but does not include the following:

- Any wire or oral communication (defined as aural communications in the statute);
- Any communication made through a tone only paging device;
- Any communication from a tracking device (as defined); or
- Electronic funds transfer information stored by a financial institution in a communications system used for the electronic storage and transfer of funds. 18 U.S.C. §2510 (12).

None of the other answers is correct. As listed above, the act specifically excludes all of the above. As such, any of the other selections would be only partially correct.

2. The Digital Millennium Copyright Act (DMCA) has specific provisions designed to legislate against and thus aid in preventing what type of action?

    A. Circumvention of technologies used to protect copyrighted work
    B. Creation of malicious code
    C. Digital manipulation or alteration of copyrighted computer code
    D. Digital reproduction of copyrighted documents and artwork

The correct answer is **A**. The Digital Millennium Copyright Act imposes liability on those who circumvent technological measures that are designed to control access to copyright protected works.

Answer b, the creation of malicious code, is not covered in the DMCA. Malicious code would be covered under the Computer Misuse Act. Although copyright provisions cover the situations mentioned in answers c and d, the specific provisions detailed within the Digital Millennium Copyright Act cover the circumvention of protective technologies and not the manipulation or reproduction of copyrighted works.

3. What questions are asked when deciding the outcome of a U.S. federal trade mark dilution case? (Chose all that are correct)

    A.   When was the mark created?

    B.   How distinctive is the mark?

    C.   Who owns the mark?

    D.   How unique and recognized is the mark?

The correct answers are **C** and **D**. Under the Trademark Act of 1946 ("Lanham Act"), as amended, the three questions used to determine the "fame" of a mark in federal trademark cases include asking who owns the mark, how unique a mark is, and how recognized a mark is. Answer a is not correct as the date that a mark was created is not relevant when deciding on a trademark dilution case. Trademarks do not expire as long as they are maintained. As a result, the date that they were initially registered is irrelevant. Answer b is not correct. Although a distinctive mark may aid in recognition, there are many marks that are easily recognized and not significantly different from other registered trademarks.

4. To sue for copyright infringement in the United States, what is the first step that a copyright holder must take?

    A.   No action is necessary, as copyright attaches as a right of the author as soon as the work is created.

    B.   Register a copyright application with the Copyright Office of the Library of Congress.

    C.   Formally publish the work.

    D.   Put the alleged infringer on notice that you intend to bring an action.

The correct answer is **B**. Although copyright is attached to all works as soon as it is created, it needs to first be registered before a party can sue for copyright infringement. Registration is with the Library of Congress, and the U.S. fed eral courts have exclusive jurisdiction over copyright infringement cases.

Answers a, c, and d are incorrect. Although copyright attaches to all works when they are created, in order to take action within the courts the copyright needs to be registered. In the United States, copyright registration needs to be filed at the Copyright Office of the Library of Congress.

5. The judge in a civil court case can issue an order allowing for a civil search of another party's goods and to seize specific evidence. This order is known as a(n)

    A. Subpoena

    B. Doctrine of Exigent Circumstances

    C. Anton Piller Order

    D. Search warrant

The correct answer is **C**. Anton Piller Order. A subpoena requires the party served to deliver the items listed in the order to the court. The doctrine of exigent circumstances presents exclusion to the search and seizure rules for law enforcement when they are involved in an emergency or otherwise dangerous situation. Search warrants are only issued in criminal cases. An Anton Piller Order is a civil order that is used in many countries to allow the court to obtain information that may otherwise be lost in a civil case.

6. Your company has a policy prohibiting pornography on company equipment, and an employee has become aware of a network user who has an image of a nude child on his computer. When you investigate the matter, you find that the person has several photos of children on a nude beach, but none of them involves sex or focuses on the child's genitalia. Which of the following is true?

    A. It is child pornography, and the computer user can be charged with possession of child pornography.

    B. It is child pornography, and the computer user can be charged or disciplined.

    C. It is not child pornography, and the computer user can be disciplined.

    D. It is not child pornography, and the computer user cannot be charged or disciplined.

The correct answer is **C**. It is not child pornography, and the computer user can be disciplined. The images do depict naked minors, but none of the images focus on the child's genitalia. In the 1996 case United States v. Dost, a federal judge suggested a six step method of evaluating images to deter mine whether the nude image of a child could be considered legal or illegal.

Part of these criteria was whether the focal point was the child's genitalia or pubic area. Despite it not being illegal, the company does have a policy to deal with pornography stored on company computers, so the user can be punished through this policy. Even if the photographs are not classified as pornography (which is a decision that only a court can generally make), they remain as inappropriate material and violate company policy. Answers a and b are incorrect because these images are not considered to be child pornography. Answer d is incorrect because although the image isn't illegal, the person can still be disciplined under the corporate policy.

7. Your team has detected that an outside party attempted to do a port scan on a highly sensitive system. According to the U.S. government model, what is the maximum amount of time that should elapse before the relevant information is reported?

    A. One hour

    B. One day

    C. One week

    D. One month

The correct answer is **A**. One Hour. Reports of port scans on highly sensitive systems (such as classified systems in a government setting) should be made within one hour – or, if possible, immediately upon detection.

8. Tracing violations or attempted violations of system security to the user responsible is a function of what?

    A. Authentication

    B. Access management

    C. Integrity checking

    D. Accountability

The correct answer is **D**. Auditing capabilities make sure that users are account able for their actions, verify that the security policies are enforced, act as a deterrent against improper actions, and may be used as investigation tools.

9. Why is a conflict of interest considered troubling from the standpoint of fraud prevention?

    A. A conflict of interest violates canons of professional responsibility.

    B. A conflict of interest is obviously unethical and causes waste.

    C. A conflict of interest can be a sign of fraud, if not a source of it.

    D. A conflict of interest violates federal law and is therefore illegal.

The correct answer is **C**. A conflict of interest is an avenue for a fraud to occur, but this does not mean that it has to always occur.

10. The penalties that can be sanctioned to the losing party in a civil case can include

   A.   Probation

   B.   Community service

   C.   Fines

   D.   Imprisonment

The correct answer is **C**. Fines. In a civil trial, the only penalty that can be awarded is a fine. The fine is issued with the purpose of proffering restitution to the victim.

11. Evidence needs to be one of the following in order to be deemed as admissible in a court of law:

   A.   Conclusive

   B.   Incontrovertible

   C.   Irrefutable

   D.   Relevant

The correct answer is **D**. Relevant. The standard tests that are associated with checking the admissibility of evidence include the relevance, reliability, and legal permissibility.

12. RFC 1087 sets the IAB "Ethics and the Internet" categorization of unethical actions. Which of the following is NOT considered as unethical under the IAB?

   A.   Downloading pornography

   B.   Compromising user privacy without authorization

   C.   Taking resources such as stationary and using equipment for personal uses

   D.   Seeking to gain unauthorized access to resources

The correct answer is **A**. Downloading pornography. Although pornography is considered to be unethical (and it can even be illegal in some countries), pornography is not unanimously unethical in all societies, communities, organizations, and situations. On the other hand, b, c, and d are generally considered as being not acceptable. Review "Internet Architecture Board (IAB)—'Ethics and the Internet' (RFC 1087)."

13. What is an evidence gathering technique that occurs when a law enforcement officer entices a party into enacting a criminal offense they may not have otherwise committed with the aim of capturing the person in a "sting" operation; is this considered legal or illegal?

    A. Enticement/legal

    B. Coercion/legal

    C. Entrapment/illegal

    D. Enticement/illegal

The correct answer is **C**. Entrapment/illegal. Entrapment is the act of encouraging an individual to become involved in a crime that the individual may have had no intention of committing by a law enforcement officer or other official. Coercion involves forcing or intimidating an individual to testify or confess. Although there are ethical arguments against enticement, it is generally considered to be legal.

14. Which expression is used to describe the process where a party is provided with sufficient temptation such that they may hand over evidence of a crime that the individual has committed?

    A. Enticement

    B. Coercion

    C. Entrapment

    D. Encouragement

The correct answer is **A**. Enticement. Entrapment is the act of encouraging an individual to become involved in a crime that the individual may have had no intention of committing by a law enforcement officer or other official. Coercion involves forcing or intimidating an individual to testify or confess. Enticement involves tempting an individual into providing evidence or to leading another party to it.

15. What penalties does the CFAA hold for people who create and release malware?

    A. The CFAA has both civil and criminal sanctions.

    B. The CFAA has criminal sanctions.

    C. The CFAA has civil sanctions.

    D. The CFAA does not incorporate malware and is targeted at fraud such as phishing and financial fraud.

The correct answer is **A**. The Computer Fraud and Abuse Act (CFAA) presents a combination of criminal and civil penalties that may be used to punish an individual who is convicted for manufacturing or distributing malware such as viruses, worms, Trojan horses, and other malicious code.

16. Which of the following is not considered to be intellectual property?

    A.   Patents, servicemarks, and trademarks

    B.   Plant grower's rights

    C.   Computer hardware

    D.   Trade secrets

The correct answer is **C**. Patents, servicemarks and trademarks, trade secrets, plant grower's rights, and copyrights are incorporated into the realm of intellectual property. Computer hardware is considered physical property or chattel property.

17. Which term best describes the situation where an individual attacks (hacks) a computer system with the motive of curiosity or the thrill of seeing what is there?

    A.   Scoping attack

    B.   Digital thrill seeking

    C.   Recon attacks

    D.   Phishing

The correct answer is **B**. "Digital Thrill Seeking" is an attack resultant of a naive belief in the individual's right to access information no matter the con sequences. These individuals must be made conscious of the fact that even seemingly harmless computer intrusions can trigger criminal sanctions and result in damage. Scoping attack is made up. Recon attacks involve collecting information concerning a prospective target. Phishing involves the criminally fraudulent process of misleading an individual through electronic communication under the pretense of a trustworthy establishment, to reveal personal or confidential information (i.e., banking information, credit card numbers, and passwords).

18. The Fourth Amendment to the U.S. Constitution sets the standard for what action?

    A.   Free speech

    B.   Commercial transactions and interstate commerce

    C.   Individual privacy

    D.   Government searches or seizure

The correct answer is **D**. The Fourth Amendment to the U.S. Constitution sets the standard by which "probable cause" is judged. When a law enforcement officer conducts a search or seizure involving private property, the officer needs to ensure that it adheres to these standards. The courts have interpreted this amendment to mean that an authorized representative of the U.S. government (i.e., law enforcement) must obtain a valid warrant prior to attempting to obtain involuntary admittance or access to the property of another individual. Free speech is enshrined within the first amendment to the U.S. Constitution.

19. Why is prevention alone NOT sufficient to protect a system from attackers?

    A. Even the finest preventive measures experience failures.

    B. The maintenance of preventive measures is labor intensive.

    C. It is hard to put preventive measures into operation.

    D. Prevention by itself is an expensive alternative.

The correct answer is **A**. No system is perfect. As such, even the best and most secure system can experience a failure and security breach. When develop ing a security system, it is necessary to ensure that controls (such as incident handling) are in place to recover from a breach or other failure.

20. A set of principles that is derived from a cultural or religious authority and standards is known as

    A. Policy

    B. Law

    C. Guidelines

    D. A moral code

The correct answer is **D**. Morals are an ethical code derived from a religious or cultural standard.

Printed in the United States
by Baker & Taylor Publisher Services